▶ THE COMPLETE BIKE OWNER'S MANUAL
Introduction

Bikes can take you far and wide and to get the best out of every ride you need to keep your bike in the best possible condition. Bikes do not run on your muscles alone; the interplay of pedals, chain, wheels, steering, and gear and brake systems gives power and control to your bike. In this book, we show you how to fit, adjust, and maintain each part of your bike.

Whether you are a skilled mechanic or a beginner, learning how to fix and maintain your bike at home will save you time, energy, and money. It's also great to know that you can be miles from home and fix a problem in the unlikely event of mechanical failure.

This book uses high-quality CGI illustrations to detail every component of your bike. With no hands in the way to obscure detail and vivid imagery, the step-by-step instructions offer unprecedented clarity and get you close to every part of your bike.

Starting with the essentials
To lay the groundwork, this guide first explains the design and components of many different types of bike. Advice on suitable clothing, rider accessories, and setting your riding position will give you the information you need to get the best use out of your bike in everyday riding.

The "Getting Started" chapter shows you how to set up a workshop and use bicycle maintenance tools. Setting up your own workshop is easy, and there are just a handful of essential and low-cost tools that you will need. As you decide to replace or repair certain parts of your bike, your collection of tools will slowly build. The chapter also shows you how to carry out routine jobs, such as cleaning your bike and lubricating moving parts, and provides information on dealing with emergency repairs.

Maintenance and repairs
Whether you ride your bike on the road, on a track, or over mountains, it will benefit from a good maintenance routine. Each chapter shows you how to care for a specific system on your bike. Chapters include advice on choosing the best components for your type of bike; an in-depth look at the key parts, with unique terms and names explained;

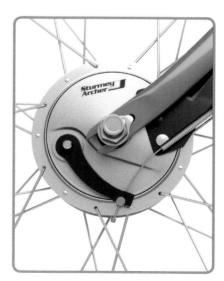

Regular care will keep your bike running smoothly and safely.

CLAIRE BEAUMONT – CO-AUTHOR

and information on how to set, adjust, and service particular parts. Annotated images and workshop tips cover a variety of models. There is advice on how to spot signs of trouble before costs spiral; detailed exploded diagrams and cutaways show you how each part of your bicycle works together, and how to make on-the-go adjustments without the risk of getting stranded on a ride.

Replacing and upgrading parts

Regular maintenance helps to stave off wear and tear. However, poor weather, grit, road salt, and general use will degrade most components over time, and these parts will need to be replaced.

Removing worn parts and replacing with new is tackled chapter by chapter with the step-by-step guides. While the general principles of braking, gear change, wheel construction, and suspension have not changed, major brands often have their own proprietary systems – for example, for the size of bearings, the size of the chain or cables, or the way some parts fit onto the bike. Each chapter

covers the variations between the three major brands (Shimano, SRAM, and Campagnolo) and what to look out for when purchasing replacement parts.

If you want to improve your cycling performance, upgrading specific parts of your bicycle will help to make it lighter, make the ride smoother, and enable you to change gear faster and more precisely. Changing the handlebar, stem, and saddle are fairly straightforward tasks. More complex jobs such as replacing the drivetrain (the engine) of the bike or fitting new suspension forks are expensive upgrades but will have a beneficial effect on performance. The step-by-step sequences show every stage of these procedures so you can tackle them with ease.

All of this information, together with a maintenance planner plus diagnostic and troubleshooting tips at the end of the book, will help you to enjoy efficient, safe riding for the full lifespan of your bicycle.

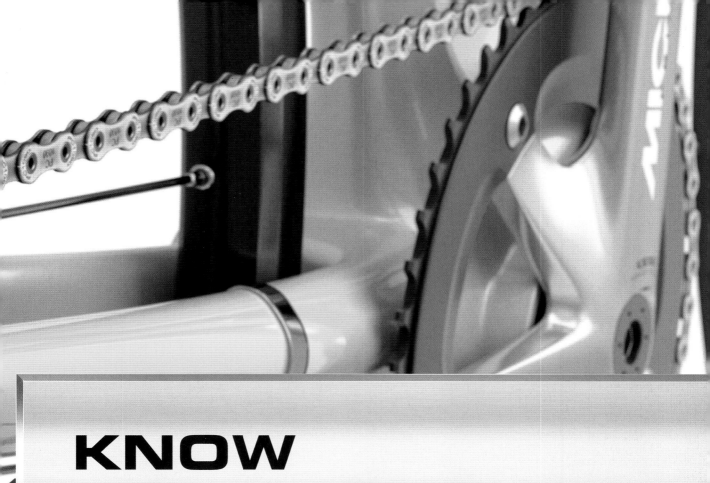

KNOW YOUR BIKE

Road bikes

Road bikes are sleek and lightweight, and intended for use on smooth tarmac. Their narrow wheels and thin tyres mean they are able to roll quickly over smooth surfaces, enabling them to cover long distances at a fast pace. Drop handlebars allow the rider to sit in a more aerodynamic, forward-leaning position, thus transferring more power to the pedals. Racing bikes, hybrids, single speed, and e-bikes all use components known as the drivetrain to power the bike, while gears make cycling easier. Frames are light and rigid, with steel and aluminium popular with the consumer market, and carbon fibre and titanium used more widely at competition level.

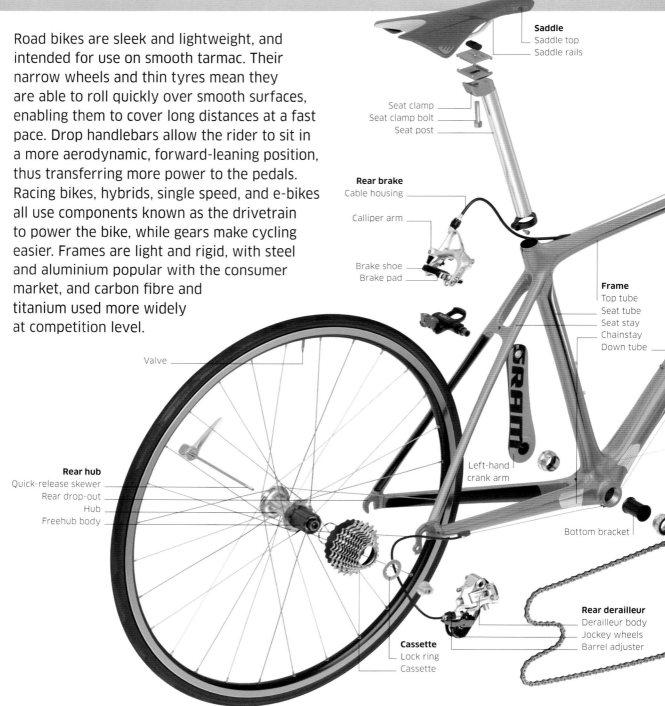

Saddle
Saddle top
Saddle rails

Seat clamp
Seat clamp bolt
Seat post

Rear brake
Cable housing

Calliper arm

Brake shoe
Brake pad

Frame
Top tube
Seat tube
Seat stay
Chainstay
Down tube

Valve

Left-hand
crank arm

Rear hub
Quick-release skewer
Rear drop-out
Hub
Freehub body

Bottom bracket

Rear derailleur
Derailleur body
Jockey wheels
Barrel adjuster

Cassette
Lock ring
Cassette

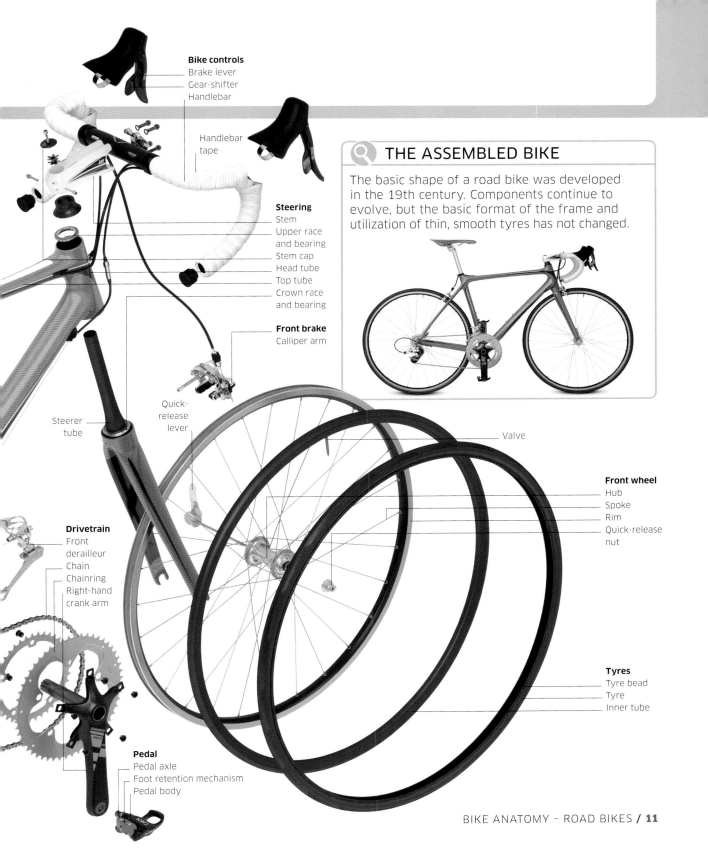

Bike controls
Brake lever
Gear-shifter
Handlebar

Handlebar tape

Steering
Stem
Upper race and bearing
Stem cap
Head tube
Top tube
Crown race and bearing

Front brake
Calliper arm

Quick-release lever

Steerer tube

THE ASSEMBLED BIKE

The basic shape of a road bike was developed in the 19th century. Components continue to evolve, but the basic format of the frame and utilization of thin, smooth tyres has not changed.

Valve

Front wheel
Hub
Spoke
Rim
Quick-release nut

Drivetrain
Front derailleur
Chain
Chainring
Right-hand crank arm

Tyres
Tyre bead
Tyre
Inner tube

Pedal
Pedal axle
Foot retention mechanism
Pedal body

Off-road bikes

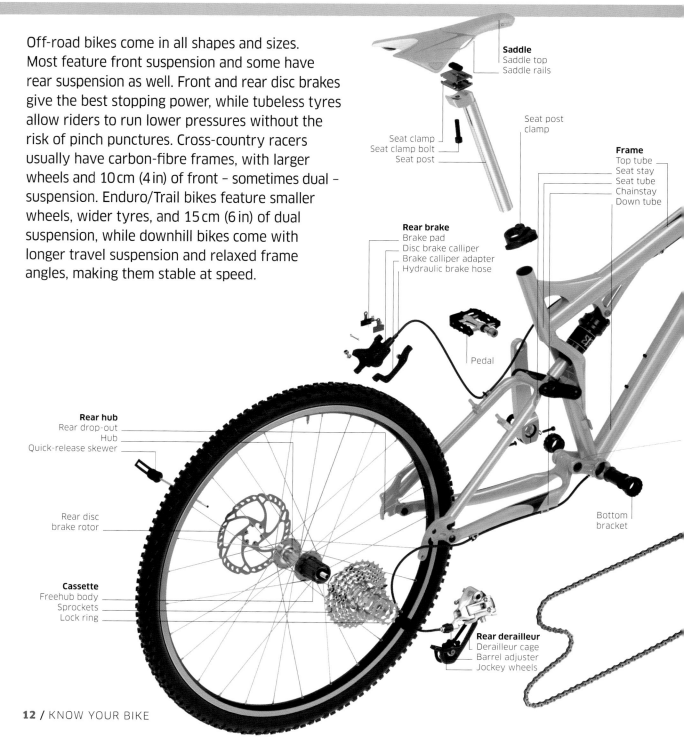

Off-road bikes come in all shapes and sizes. Most feature front suspension and some have rear suspension as well. Front and rear disc brakes give the best stopping power, while tubeless tyres allow riders to run lower pressures without the risk of pinch punctures. Cross-country racers usually have carbon-fibre frames, with larger wheels and 10 cm (4 in) of front – sometimes dual – suspension. Enduro/Trail bikes feature smaller wheels, wider tyres, and 15 cm (6 in) of dual suspension, while downhill bikes come with longer travel suspension and relaxed frame angles, making them stable at speed.

Saddle
Saddle top
Saddle rails

Seat post clamp

Seat clamp
Seat clamp bolt
Seat post

Frame
Top tube
Seat stay
Seat tube
Chainstay
Down tube

Rear brake
Brake pad
Disc brake calliper
Brake calliper adapter
Hydraulic brake hose

Pedal

Rear hub
Rear drop-out
Hub
Quick-release skewer

Rear disc brake rotor

Bottom bracket

Cassette
Freehub body
Sprockets
Lock ring

Rear derailleur
Derailleur cage
Barrel adjuster
Jockey wheels

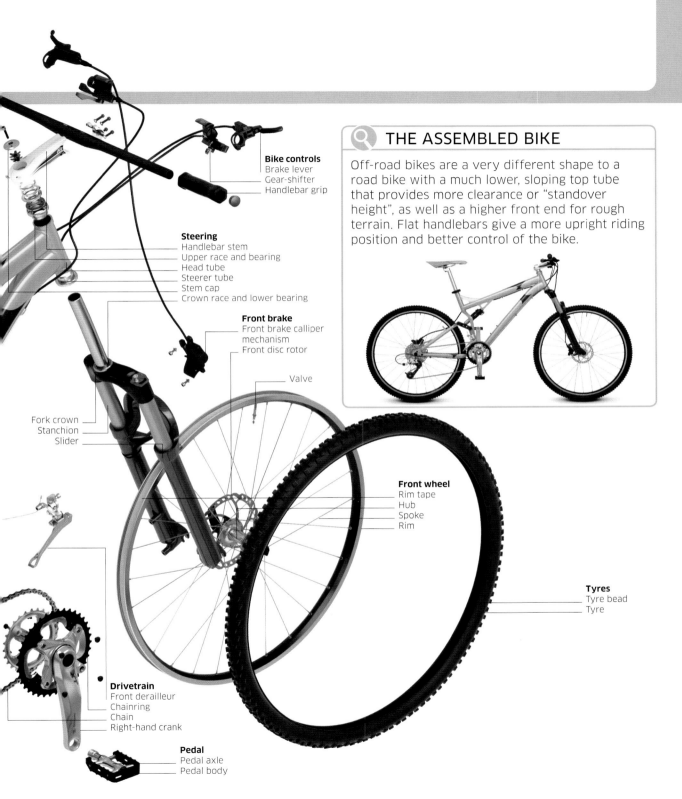

Bike controls
Brake lever
Gear-shifter
Handlebar grip

Steering
Handlebar stem
Upper race and bearing
Head tube
Steerer tube
Stem cap
Crown race and lower bearing

Front brake
Front brake calliper mechanism
Front disc rotor

Valve

Fork crown
Stanchion
Slider

THE ASSEMBLED BIKE

Off-road bikes are a very different shape to a road bike with a much lower, sloping top tube that provides more clearance or "standover height", as well as a higher front end for rough terrain. Flat handlebars give a more upright riding position and better control of the bike.

Front wheel
Rim tape
Hub
Spoke
Rim

Tyres
Tyre bead
Tyre

Drivetrain
Front derailleur
Chainring
Chain
Right-hand crank

Pedal
Pedal axle
Pedal body

▶ COMPONENTS
Utility bikes

Being designed for reliable everyday use, rather than for sporting pursuits, utility bikes offer an ideal combination of comfort, reliability, and durability. They are heavier than sports bikes, but nevertheless easy to ride. Utility bikes often utilize simple, robust components and older technology, but are maintained in a similar way to newer designs.

◉ COMMON COMPONENTS LOCATOR

With padded seats, flat handlebars, durable transmissions, and sometimes luggage panniers, utility bikes are built for comfort and convenience. Some models feature front suspension to smooth over bumps.

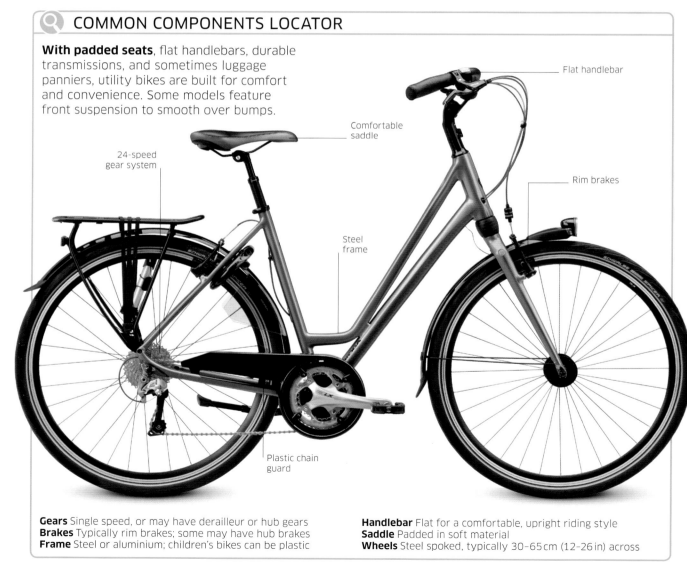

Flat handlebar

Comfortable saddle

24-speed gear system

Rim brakes

Steel frame

Plastic chain guard

Gears Single speed, or may have derailleur or hub gears
Brakes Typically rim brakes; some may have hub brakes
Frame Steel or aluminium; children's bikes can be plastic

Handlebar Flat for a comfortable, upright riding style
Saddle Padded in soft material
Wheels Steel spoked, typically 30–65 cm (12–26 in) across

Buyer's tip: Utility bikes often feature basic parts, although these can be upgraded or replaced to suit your needs. Many bike components feature standard fittings, so can be easily swapped.

SHOPPER BIKES

Brakes Rim (pp.98–117)
Gears Derailleur (pp.140–149); Hub (pp.150–155)
Suspension None

HYBRID BIKES

Brakes Rim (pp.98–117); Hub (pp.122–125); Disc (pp.118–121)
Gears Derailleur (pp.140–149); Hub (pp.150–155)
Suspension None

FOLDING BIKES

Brakes Rim (pp.98–117); Hub (pp.122–125)
Gears Derailleur (pp.140–149); Hub (pp.150–155)
Suspension None

FIXED/SINGLE-SPEED BIKES

Brakes Rim (pp.98–117)
Gears Single speed
Suspension None

E-BIKES

Brakes Rim (pp.98–117); Hub (pp.122–125)
Gears Derailleur (pp.140–149); Hub (pp.150–155)
Suspension None

CARGO BIKES

Brakes Rim (pp.98–117); Hub (pp.122–125)
Gears Derailleur (pp.140–149); Hub (pp.150–155)
Suspension None

▶ COMPONENTS
Road bikes

Whether intended for touring, racing, or even an intense commute, road bikes are designed with speed in mind, prioritizing performance over comfort. The most advanced bikes feature cutting-edge technology with computer-designed, wind-cheating, carbon frames and razor sharp, instant electronic gear-shifting.

◉ COMMON COMPONENTS LOCATOR

Road bikes sacrifice both durability and comfort in the pursuit of speed. Slim tyres and lightweight wheels are aerodynamic but provide little insulation from bumps in the road, while narrow sadddles offer minimal padding.

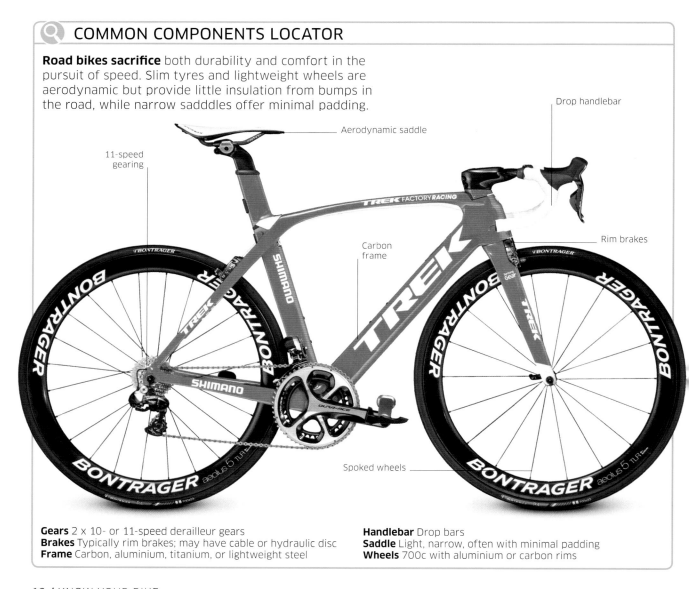

Drop handlebar

Aerodynamic saddle

11-speed gearing

Carbon frame

Rim brakes

Spoked wheels

Gears 2 x 10- or 11-speed derailleur gears
Brakes Typically rim brakes; may have cable or hydraulic disc
Frame Carbon, aluminium, titanium, or lightweight steel

Handlebar Drop bars
Saddle Light, narrow, often with minimal padding
Wheels 700c with aluminium or carbon rims

TOURING BIKES

Brakes Rim (pp.98–117); Disc (pp.118–121)
Gears Derailleur (pp.140–149); Hub (pp.150–155)
Suspension None

GRAVEL BIKES

Brakes Rim (pp.98–117); Disc (pp.118–121)
Gears Derailleur (pp.140–149); Hub (pp.150–155)
Suspension None

TRACK BIKES

Brakes None
Gears Single speed
Suspension None

TIME TRIAL/TRIATHLON BIKES

Brakes Rim (pp.98–117)
Gears Derailleur (pp.140–149)
Suspension None

CYCLO-CROSS BIKES

Brakes Rim (pp.98–117); Disc (pp.118–121)
Gears Derailleur (pp.140–149); Hub (pp.150–155)
Suspension None

COMFORT/SPORTIVE BIKES

Brakes Rim (pp.98–117); Disc (pp.118–121)
Gears Derailleur (pp.140–149); Hub (pp.150–155)
Suspension None

COMPONENTS
Off-road bikes

Off-road or mountain bikes come in a range of designs, from entry-level models best suited to gravel trails to bikes designed for steep and rocky mountain descents.

Being equipped with wide, knobbly tyres that may be tubed or tubeless, mountain bike tyres offer excellent grip and traction while the bike's suspension system limits shocks.

COMMON COMPONENTS LOCATOR

Good suspension and wide, tough tyres are essential when trail riding on a mountain bike. Many models also feature disc brakes, which may even be hydraulically powered for precise braking control.

Saddle on dropper seat post

Flat handlebar

30-speed gear system

Hydraulic disc brakes

Carbon frame

Spoked wheels

Brakes Typically disc, cable, or hydraulic
Gears 1 x 10, 1 x 11, or 3 x 9 are common variants
Frame Aluminium, carbon, or steel

Handlebar Flat and wide for maximum control
Saddle Robust and often fitted to a dropper seat post
Wheels Often 66cm (26in), 70cm (27.5in) and 73.5cm (29in)

HARDTAIL BIKES

Brakes Rim (pp.98–117); Disc (pp.118–121)
Gears Derailleur (pp.140–149)
Suspension Front (pp.192–199)

CROSS-COUNTRY BIKES

Brakes Rim (pp.98–117); Disc (pp.118–121)
Gears Derailleur (pp.140–149)
Suspension Full (pp.192–203)

DOWNHILL BIKES

Brakes Disc (pp.118–121)
Gears Derailleur (pp.140–149)
Suspension Full (pp.192–203)

FAT BIKES

Brakes Disc (pp.118–121)
Gears Derailleur (pp.140–149)
Suspension None

TRIALS/DIRT BIKES

Brakes Rim (pp.98–117); Disc (pp.118–121)
Gears Single speed
Suspension Front (pp.192–199); none

E-MOUNTAIN BIKES

Brakes Disc (pp.118–121)
Gears Derailleur (pp.140–149)
Suspension Front or full (pp.192–203)

Road bikes

Road bike riding is all about riding your bike efficiently, so you can get as far and as fast as you choose. A good riding position that suits your desired combination of comfort, power output, and aerodynamics can help. First, you should choose a bike with the correct-sized frame (see box, opposite), and then adjust the contact points – saddle, handlebar, and pedals – to fit your requirements and find a neutral position for safe, efficient riding.

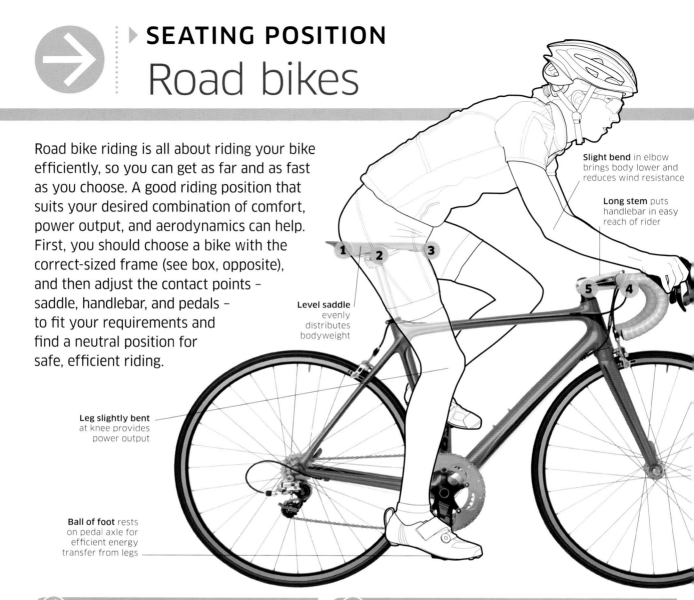

Slight bend in elbow brings body lower and reduces wind resistance

Long stem puts handlebar in easy reach of rider

Level saddle evenly distributes bodyweight

Leg slightly bent at knee provides power output

Ball of foot rests on pedal axle for efficient energy transfer from legs

BEFORE YOU START

- Collect a tape measure, spirit level, metre ruler, and Allen keys.
- Set your cleat position (see pp.186–187).
- Set your bike on a level surface, ideally with the rear wheel mounted on an indoor trainer so you can sit on the saddle and pedal while stationary.
- Pump up the tyres to the correct pressure.
- Put on your normal riding gear and cycling shoes.
- Record your existing set-up by measuring from the centre of the bottom-bracket (BB) to the top of the saddle; horizontally from the saddle nose to the BB centre; and from the saddle nose to the centre of the handlebar.

1 SADDLE HEIGHT

Find an efficient pedalling position by ensuring you have a slight bend in your knee when your leg is extended. To check this, adjust the seatpost until your leg is straight and the heel of your cycling shoe barely touches the pedal when you are sitting in the saddle with the lower crank in the 6 o'clock position.

Straight leg with slight bend in the knee

Heel of shoe just grazing pedal

Workshop tip: Make any adjustments gradually, and try them out by riding to judge the effect on your position and comfort. Bear in mind that your ideal position may alter over time as your fitness, flexibility, and aspirations change.

5 STEM LENGTH

Your stem length needs to be the long enough that you can grip the hoods comfortably without feeling stretched. A good technique to ensure you have the right length is to hold the drops and look down at the wheel hub. The handlebar should obscure the hub. If the hub is visible in front, you need a longer stem; if you can see it behind the handlebar, swap the stem for a shorter one.

Clear line to hub

4 HANDLEBAR HEIGHT

Adjust the height of your handlebar for your needs by moving it in relation to the mid-point of your saddle. For recreational riding, set the bar level with, or 1–2cm (0.4–0.8in) below, the saddle. For a more aerodynamic road bike riding position, set the bar 8–10cm (3.14–3.93in) below the saddle. To alter height of the handlebars, you can remove the stem and reposition the spacers, flip the stem, or fit a high- or low-rise stem.

Spacers

3 SADDLE FORE/AFT

Move the saddle along its rails to adjust your centre of gravity and ensure that you are well balanced when riding. Position the saddle so that your forward knee is over the pedal axle when you sit with the cranks horizontal. To check, sit on the saddle in your normal riding position hold a metre ruler against your kneecap; the end of the ruler should pass over the pedal axle.

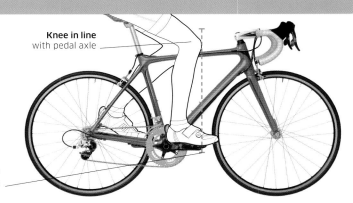

Knee in line
with pedal axle

End of ruler
passes pedal axle

2 SADDLE ANGLE

Ensure your weight is evenly distributed through the sit bones of your pelvis by setting your saddle at a neutral angle, with the front two-thirds of the saddle horizontal. You can alter this angle by up to 2 degrees for comfort, but any more than this may cause painful pressure on your groin and perineum and excess transfer of body weight onto your arms and hands.

ROAD BIKE SIZING

- **Road bikes are sized according** to the length of the seat tube, and are described in cm – from 48–60cm – or as S/M/L/XL.
- **Check you have sufficient** "standover clearance" when standing with your legs either side of the top tube. 2–5cm (1–2in) between your groin and the frame is ideal.
- **Consider a bike's "stack" and "reach"** – the distances vertically and horizontally from the centre of the bottom-bracket to the top of the top tube – when buying a bike, since you cannot alter these later.

Off-road bikes

Mountain biking is a more fluid form of cycling than road riding. Riders shift between different positions for climbing, descending, jumping, or absorbing bumps, and to respond rapidly to twisting trails, rough terrain, and changes in gradient. Finding the right position involves setting the contact points – saddle, handlebar, and pedal cleats – to suit your riding style.

Relaxed wrists provide grip and control

Slightly angled saddle improves climbing position

Bodyweight evenly distributed for effective suspension and traction

BEFORE YOU START

- Gather tools – tape measure, metre ruler, spirit level, Allen keys.
- Set your cleat position (see pp.186–187).
- Adjust suspension to normal riding settings (see pp.194–195; 202–203); set dropper seat post to normal (see pp.70–71).

1 SADDLE HEIGHT

Adjust the seat post to set the saddle at a comfortable position. For trail riding, a good benchmark is to set the saddle at hip height. For efficient pedalling when climbing, use the road-bike saddle-height method (see step 1, p.21). Downhill, technical riding is easier with the saddle 2.5–5 cm (1–2 in) below the hip.

2 SADDLE ANGLE

Changing the angle of the saddle help you adapt your bike and riding position for the ride you are on. For trail riding, angle the saddle slightly nose-down for a better seating position on climbs. For downhill riding, angle the saddle slightly nose-up so you can grip it between your thighs on fast descents and corners.

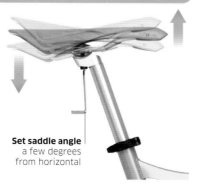

Set saddle angle a few degrees from horizontal

3 SADDLE FORE/AFT

Slide the saddle along the rails until its centre aligns with the mid-point between the rear axle and bottom bracket. This puts your body in a position that gives balanced handling, even tyre traction, and efficient suspension performance.

Set saddle to avoid cramped or stretched position

7 GEAR/BRAKE LEVER ANGLE

Angle your gear- and brake levers at a slant of 45 degrees from horizontal for a neutral, relaxed wrist position with good access to the controls. For a personal fit, adopt your normal riding position – seated or standing on the pedals – and angle the levers so your wrist is relaxed and straight.

Forearm aligned with brake- and gear-levers

6 GEAR/BRAKE LEVER POSITION

For optimum braking power and steering control, place the brake and gear-shift levers where you can easily reach them. Holding the grip in your usual riding position, slide the brake lever along the bar until you can pull it with just your index and/or middle finger. Next, with your hand still in its normal grip position, set the gear-shift lever where you can easily reach it (you might need to slot it in between the grip and brake lever to achieve this).

Brake with one finger for best power and grip

5 STEM POSITION

Choose a stem that suits your style of riding but make sure you are not cramped or overreaching as this can cause lower back pain. Shorter stems (50–70mm (2–2.75 in)) are best for rapid steering; longer ones (80–100mm (3–4 in)) are best for climbing. Stem angle also affects handling – a high-rise stem gives a stable position, but steering will be less precise. Use a low-rise stem or place the spacers above the stem for a more agile position.

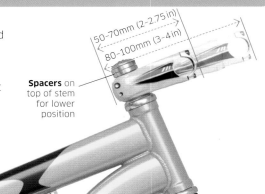

50–70mm (2–2.75 in)
80–100mm (3–4 in)

Spacers on top of stem for lower position

4 RISER-BAR ANGLE

Most mountain bikes are fitted with riser bars – the ends rise up and sweep back from the middle of the handlebar. Release the clamp and twist the bar so that when viewed from the side the rise is angled parallel with the front fork. Angling the bar further back will place pressure on the wrists and back; further forward puts excess weight over the front wheel and impairs handling.

Low-rise stem for precise steering

⊙ MOUNTAIN BIKE SIZING

■ **Mountain bikes** are sized by seat-tube length, usually in inches – from 13 to 24 in – or as XS/S/M/L/XL.

■ **If choosing a new bike**, check for sufficient "standover clearance". You should be 5–8cm (2–3 in) above the top tube when standing astride it.

■ **"Stack" and "reach"** – measured vertically and horizontally from BB centre to top of top tube – are the key dimensions for working out if a bike is long and high enough for you.

▶ ACCESSORIES
Essential kit

There are some pieces of equipment that you will use on almost every ride. Some are necessary for personal safety, and others make cycling more convenient or comfortable. All are essential tools for a cyclist, so it is worth taking the time to find the best pieces of kit for your needs.

⚙ INNER TUBES

Inner tubes vary according to the diameter of a bike's wheel and the width of its tyre. Their valves vary so ensure you have the right pump.

Schrader valve tube   Long presta valve tube   Presta valve tube

⚙ SADDLEBAGS

Clip a small, discreet saddlebag to the rails of your saddle so as not to restrict movement when riding. It will generally have space for a spare tube, a puncture repair kit, tyre levers, and a small multi-tool. Larger versions also allow you to carry spare clothing.

Tool bag

Traditional   Waterproof

⚙ PUMPS

Pumps with broad, long barrels are easy to use when inflating wide tyres but may take longer to reach the high pressures required on a road bike.

Screw top

Valve head

Rubber grip

Mini-pump   CO₂ inflator   CO₂ canister   Frame pump

⚙ ON-ROAD TOOLKIT

Consisting of a multi-tool, tyre levers, and puncture repair kit, a basic toolkit is useful for all basic repairs. Ensure that the multi-tool you take on a ride is equipped with tools to suit the fittings on your bike.

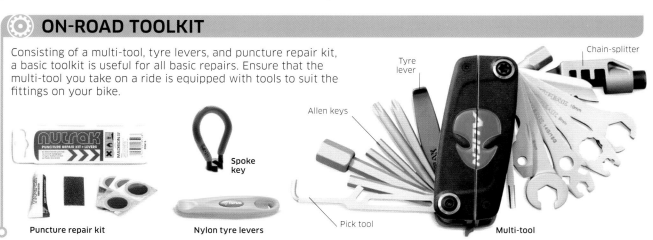

Chain-splitter

Tyre lever

Allen keys

Spoke key

Pick tool

Puncture repair kit   Nylon tyre levers   Multi-tool

WATER BOTTLES AND STORAGE

Hydration is essential when riding, not just in the summer months. Road bikes often have bottle cages, while off-road cyclists frequently use hydration packs.

Bottle cage

Bottle

Triathlon bottle

Mouthpiece

Hydration pack

Rucksack and hydration pack

LOCKS AND STORAGE

Many types of lock are available, with multiple security devices required in some cases to padlock the various parts of your bike.

D-lock

Chain lock

Cable lock

MUDGUARDS

Mudguards keep your clothes and bike clean in the rain. Off-road guards need regular cleaning to prevent them from clogging up.

Bolt

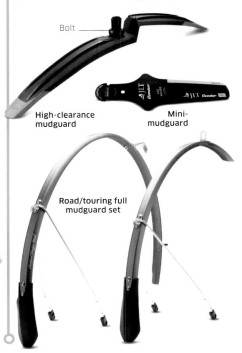

High-clearance mudguard

Mini-mudguard

Road/touring full mudguard set

LIGHTS

Modern LED bike lamps can rival car headlights. Flashing lights alert traffic to your presence, while high-powered beams are great for off-road riding.

LED with rubber clip

Clip-on light

Emergency front and rear LEDs

Battery pack

Night-riding lights

Bike technology

Bike and accessory manufacturers are quick to develop and adapt cutting-edge technology. In particular GPS has transformed bike navigation, largely eliminating the need for you to carry maps. Heart-rate monitors and power meters make tracking your performance much easier.

COMPUTERS

Even the simplest bike computer will calculate your speed and the distance you have travelled. Wireless devices are more expensive but look neater.

Wired digital bike computer

Large-screen computer

GPS

Super-accurate, smaller GPS devices are increasingly common. Higher-end versions can be uploaded with detailed maps and offer turn-by-turn navigation.

GPS phone

Compact model

GPS watch

Mini GPS

Full-colour GPS

HEART-RATE MONITORS

Heart-rate monitors are an affordable way to ensure that your training is both targeted and effective. Modern versions can be linked to your smartphone and any training apps you may have.

Heart rate watch

Built-in heart rate monitor

Strap monitor

Velcro monitor

Monitor helmet

POWER METERS

A sophisticated training tool, power meters track the amount of effort you are putting into your cycle to give you an instant measurement of how much you are exerting yourself. In addition to recording your training progress, you can use them to keep yourself cycling at the correct intensity for the duration of your bike ride.

Heel clip

Hub attachment

Power meter sensor

Pedal power meter

Hub meter

Crank power meter

CAMERAS

Mounted on a helmet or directly on a bike, a lightweight camera is a helpful piece of equipment that can be used to relive downhill exploits or record evidence of any accidents.

Smash-proof lens

Helmet-mounted camera

Cycle camera

Camera light

MISCELLANEOUS

New devices use GPS technology to make it possible for you to navigate or keep track of your training progress with a single glance, while the latest powerful mini-speakers can now fit in a bottle cage.

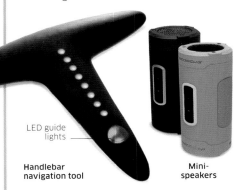

LED guide lights

Handlebar navigation tool

Mini-speakers

DYNAMOS/POWER GENERATORS

Modern dynamos are a convenient way of running lights and are more environmentally friendly than battery-powered LEDs. Some versions can even simultaneously charge your smartphone.

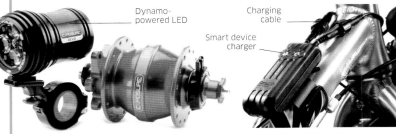

Dynamo-powered LED

Charging cable

Smart device charger

Dynamo and light

Smartphone charger

Optical touchpad

Smart eyewear with heads-up performance display

SAFETY AND SECURITY

Radar sensors warn you about nearby traffic, while light-up helmets ensure that you will remain visible in all weathers, and smart locks eliminate the need to carry keys.

Radar device

Crash sensor

Rear light camera

Smart bike lock

Front headlights

Helmet with integrated lights

▶ ACCESSORIES
Utility equipment

For both touring and commuting it is inevitable that you will need to carry things with you. Over long distances transporting kit on the bike is more comfortable. For shorter journeys a backpack or messenger bag can often be more convenient and easier to use.

BACKPACKS/MESSENGER BAGS

Backpacks can cope with bigger, heavier loads more comfortably than messenger bags, which offer easier access to their contents.

Commuter
bag

Roll-top
rucksack

Mountain
bike bag

RACKS AND PANNIERS

Pannier racks carry big loads but cannot be fitted to all bikes. Longer chainstays are necessary to accommodate large rear panniers and lightweight forks will not be able to cope with front racks.

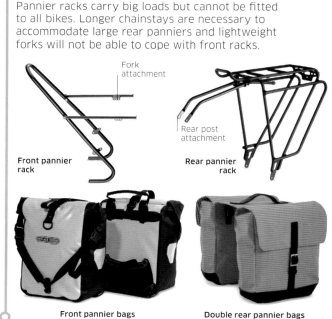

Fork
attachment

Front pannier
rack

Rear post
attachment

Rear pannier
rack

Front pannier bags

Double rear pannier bags

FRAME BAGS

By distributing weight within your bike's frame, these bags affect handling less than traditional panniers, making them particularly suited to off-road riding. They are often lighter and provide a more balanced ride.

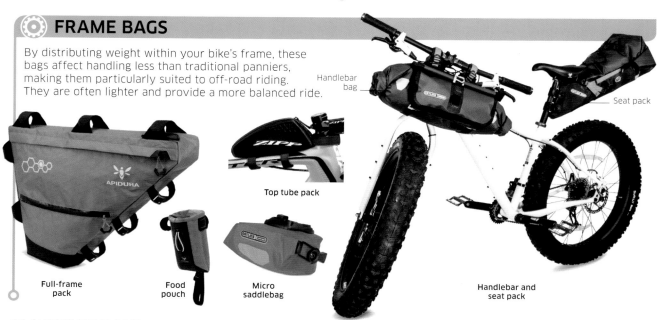

Full-frame
pack

Food
pouch

Micro
saddlebag

Top tube pack

Handlebar
bag

Seat pack

Handlebar and
seat pack

Tailfin pannier bags
fitted to rack

OTHER RACK SYSTEMS

A front or rear basket is convenient for carrying shopping. Top-mounted bags often have a quick-release mechanism.

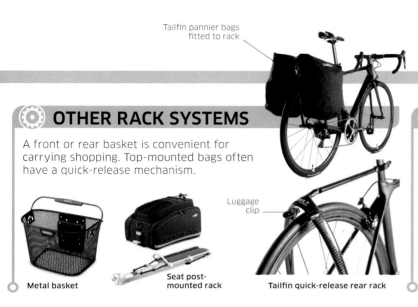

Luggage
clip

Metal basket

**Seat post-
mounted rack**

Tailfin quick-release rear rack

HANDLEBAR BAGS

Handlebar bags provide easy access to important items, while bar-mounted map pockets are useful for navigation.

Map
pocket

**Clear
map case**

Handlebar bag

CHILD SEATS AND TRAILERS

A small child can be carried in a child seat. As they get bigger a trailer or trailerbike may be more appropriate.

Seat
tube
attachment

Quick
release

Converts to
buggy

**Seat tube-mounted
child seat**

**Top tube-mounted
child seat**

**Pannier-mounted
child seat**

**Two-seat
child trailer**

LUGGAGE TRAILERS

Useful on shopping trips or for carrying extra gear, double-wheel trailers offer good stability. Single-wheel versions are better for off-road.

Waterproof
cover

Trekking
trailer

Smaller
wheels

Flag for
visibility

Frame
bars

**Flatbed
standing trailer**

**Standing
trailer**

**Journey
trailer**

Road riding

Everyday clothes are fine for short trips, but for longer rides or if the weather is bad you will be a lot more comfortable in the correct kit. Wearing clothing cut for the specific movements your body makes while pedaling will make a huge difference to your ride experience. Fabrics are lightweight and breathable, which enables your sweat to evaporate, extra padding absorbs shock, and water and wind-proof layers protect you from the elements.

ESSENTIAL LAYERS

Being too hot or too cold is uncomfortable, so adding and removing layers is a useful way to keep your core body temperature consistent. Layers trap heat, and should be easily removed or added to. An all-weather layered outfit might consist of:

- A breathable base layer worn next to your skin. This wicks away moisture on hot days and retains heat on cold ones.
- A middle layer of stretchable jersey that protects from the sun and helps to regulate your body temperature.
- A removable weatherproof or windproof shell layer that protects you from the rain and offers your skin ventilation when you sweat.

ROAD CLOTHING

Cycling clothes are designed to fit close to your body, with longer sleeves and backs cut to accommodate a forward-leaning riding position. Breathable fabrics "wick" sweat away from your skin, while bib shorts have comfortable straps in place of restrictive waistbands.

1. **Wicking base layer** keeps you dry and warm.

2. **Short-sleeved shirt** with high neck to shield you from the sun.

3. **Sleeveless gilet** outer layer for warmth and wind protection.

4. **Bib shorts** are padded for extra comfort in saddle.

5. **Thin wicking socks** draw perspiration away from your feet.

6. **Fingerless mitts** are padded, while absorbant patches can be used to wipe away your sweat.

7. **Road helmet** is lightweight and aerodynamic with good ventilation.

8. **Cycling shoes** have rigid soles, ensuring your feet a stable platform.

9. **Glasses** protect eyes from sun, as well as insects and stones.

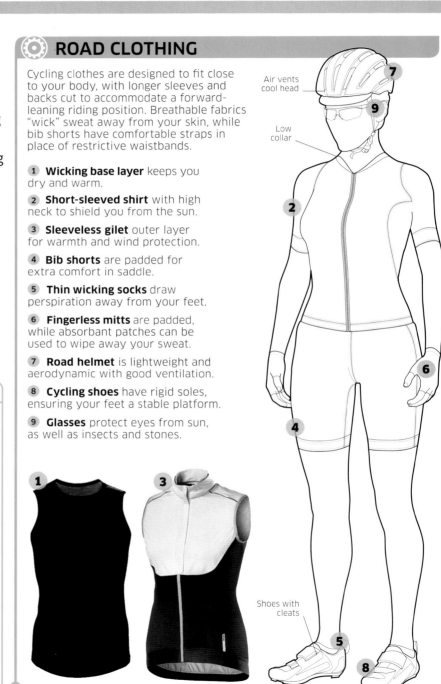

Air vents cool head

Low collar

Shoes with cleats

EXTRAS

From protective glasses and cleat covers to lightweight caps, gloves, and warmers, bike accessories fulfil a range of functions and offer you added comfort.

Cleat covers

Mirrored glasses

Cycling cap

Full-finger gloves

Arm warmers

HI-VIS GEAR

High-visibility clothing is essential if you cycle at night or on dull days. Some garments have added reflective areas, and you can customize your gear with stick-on patches.

Helmet

Gloves

Jacket

FOR WET WEATHER

While riding in the rain may be unavoidable, it is still possible for you to stay dry with the right kit. Key items include waterproof jackets and packable capes.

Fleece-lined for warmth

Hood shields face

Overshoes

Helmet rain cover

Waterproof rain jacket

Lightweight, showerproof jacket

Waterproof cape

FOR COLD WEATHER

Warm clothing is a must if you want to keep riding through the winter. Gloves, thermal vests, and bib tights all help to regulate body temperature.

High-visibility strip

Straps lined with fleece

Insulated gloves

Micro-wool socks

Thermal vest

Windproof, full-sleeve jacket

Full-length bib tights

Off-road riding

Looser and less form-fitting than road-bike clothing, off-road clothes prioritize freedom of movement. Baggy mountain bike shorts are hard-wearing, with practical pockets, and padded liners for extra comfort on rough, rocky terrain. The loose clothing gives you a greater range of movement. Waterproof options can help you withstand splashes of mud and water on the trail, while full-face helmets and body armour help protect you on more extreme rides.

⊛ MOUNTAIN BIKE CLOTHING

Off-road clothing is designed to allow you as broad a range of movements as possible. Baggy shorts accommodate protective knee pads and are designed to be worn over padded lycra shorts, or feature an integrated liner, so you do not need underwear. Breathable fabrics keep you insulated as well as dry, and shoes have durable soles with ample tread.

1 **Wicking underlayer** moves your sweat away from your skin.

2 **Baggy jersey** offers you a full range of movements.

3 **Softshell mountain bike jacket** protects against wind and showers.

4 **Baggy shorts** with a padded liner give you a more comfortable ride.

5 **Merino socks** provide warmth.

6 **Full-finger, padded gloves** with extra grip protect your hands.

7 **Lightweight, vented helmet** fully covers your head.

8 **Ankle-height** shoes with off-road cleats allow you to pedal efficiently.

9 **Glasses** with orange or yellow interchangable lenses.

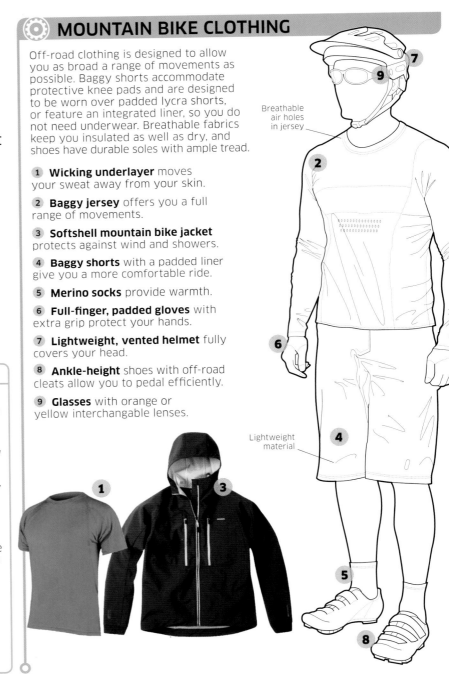

Breathable air holes in jersey

Lightweight material

⊛ BEFORE YOU BUY

Comfort and flexibility are crucial to off-road gear so be sure to shop around and try clothes on before you buy.

- Ensure shorts and trousers allow you to move your legs freely.

- When trying on tops and jackets, make sure they allow you room to stretch upwards, and that they do not ride up to expose your back.

- Choose clear glasses that can be worn all year round. Some have interchangeable lenses – yellow ones are good for overcast or dull light conditions.

- Helmets should fit properly. Always buy the right size headgear; check that it comes with the correct certification.

⚙ EXTRAS

Good-quality accessories will reduce the risk of broken bones and bruises. Full-face helmets are vital for extreme mountain biking, while goggles protect eyes from debris. Knee and elbow pads give you maximum flexibility without compromising your safety.

Lightweight polycarbonate shell

Full-face helmet

Anti-fogging lenses

Flexible joints

Goggles

Elbow protectors

Knee protectors

🔍 CLOTHING CARE

Off-road clothes can be expensive so always check the manufacturer's instructions before washing them in case you inadvertently damage them. Avoid household fabric softeners as they can damage a material's wicking properties.

- ■ Wash any mud off in the shower before putting your clothes in the washing machine.
- ■ Clean your shorts after every ride to avoid bacterial build-up.
- ■ Wash your cycling clothes separately – they need a cool, gentle setting with a low spin speed. Use a detergent that works at low temperatures.
- ■ Zip up your jacket before putting it in the machine to prevent the zip tearing other clothes.
- ■ Air-dry Lycra-based or other stretchy clothing. Hot tumble driers can wreck expensive kit.

⚙ FOR WET WEATHER

Taking to the trails in wet weather is a lot more comfortable if you are wearing the right clothing. Overtrousers protect your legs from wheel spray, and socks may come with waterproof liners.

Elasticated waistband

Nonslip soles

Waterproof shoes

Lined socks

Water-resistant overtrousers

Waterproof hardshell jacket

Wide straps for comfort

⚙ FOR COLD WEATHER

Jackets with dropped backs and high necks keep the cold out and the heat in. You can wear your neck warmers like scarves, or folded upwards to keep ears warm. Full-length bib tights form an insulating layer against your skin.

Windproof layer

Neck warmer (aka buff)

Insulated winter gloves

Thermal underlayer

Full-sleeve, waterproof thermal jacket

Full-length bib tights

GETTING STARTED

Workshop tools

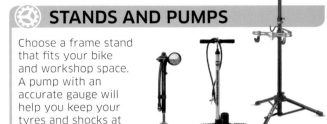

Bike tools are a low-cost investment that could save you large amounts of money in the long run. Having a proper tool set to hand will allow you to carry out most maintenance tasks and keep your bike at peak performance. Start by purchasing the basics, adding more specialist tools as needed.

STANDS AND PUMPS

Choose a frame stand that fits your bike and workshop space. A pump with an accurate gauge will help you keep your tyres and shocks at the right pressure.

Shock pump   Floor pump   Frame stand

ESSENTIAL TOOLKIT

There are some basic tools that you cannot do without. These will allow you to perform a range of common tasks in order to keep your bike on the road.

Mechanic tools
- Multi-tool
- Adjustable spanner
- Set of spanners
- Pliers
- Screwdrivers – flat- and cross-head

Other equipment
- Puncture-repair kit
- Tyre levers
- Oil
- Grease
- Degreaser

PLIERS AND SCREWDRIVERS

A small set of screwdrivers incorporating varying sizes of flat- and cross-heads is useful for making small adjustments. Needle-nose pliers are suitable for tight areas.

Razor-sharp edge

Needle-nose pliers   Pliers   Cable cutters   Cross- and flat-head screwdrivers

SPANNERS AND KEYS

The number and variety of available spanners and keys can be intimidating, so start by buying an adjustable spanner that you can use on a range of tasks. Supplement this with a good set of Allen keys and then, as you grow in confidence, start buying tools that are designed for specific tasks.

Headset spanners

Adjustable spanner

Cone spanners

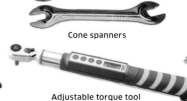

Pedal wrench

Adjustable torque tool

Set of spanners

Ring end

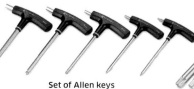

Set of Allen keys

Torx keys

CLEANING TOOLS AND SPARE PARTS

- Bike-specific brushes
- Bucket and sponges
- Chain keeper
- Alcohol-based cleaner
- Bike polish
- Cable housing (brake/gear)
- Inner tubes (correct size/ valve type for your bike)
- Inner cables (brake/gear)
- Brake pads
- Cable end caps

 # CHAIN AND CASSETTE

Different brands and types of cassette require different tools so check that the one you buy is compatible with your bike. Chain whips enable cassette removal, and some come in combination with a lock ring tool.

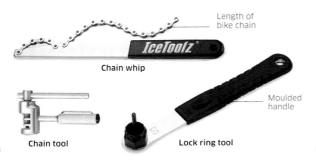

Length of bike chain

Chain whip

Moulded handle

Chain tool

Lock ring tool

 # CRANKS AND BBS

The bottom bracket (BB) requires specific servicing tools that may be worth buying if you want to remove or tighten the BB, for example. Crank pullers are useful to ensure you can evenly and efficiently remove the crank.

BB ring spanner with preload cap tool

Chainring peg spanner

Splined BB remover tool

Crank puller tool

 # SPECIALIST EQUIPMENT

In addition to the essential workshop tools, there are many other bits of kit that will make maintenance tasks easier. You may not use them very often, but they could save you time and money in the long run. For example, a chain wear indicator could prevent expensive cassette repairs later.

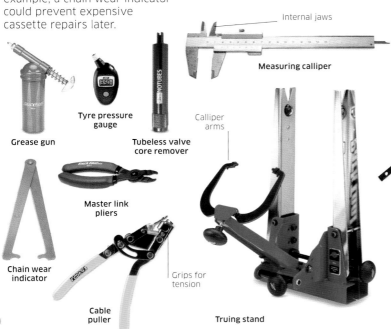

Internal jaws

Measuring calliper

Tyre pressure gauge

Tubeless valve core remover

Grease gun

Calliper arms

Master link pliers

Chain wear indicator

Grips for tension

Cable puller

Truing stand

BLEED KIT

Hydraulic disc brakes will eventually need bleeding in order to keep them performing at their peak. Kits make it easier and quicker to do a thorough bleed but make sure you get the appropriate kit for your brakes.

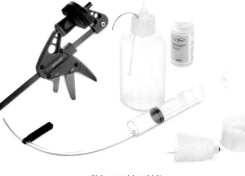

Shimano bleed kit

Bleed blocks and keys

▶ TOOLS AND TECHNIQUES
Workshop techniques

From vintage models to cutting-edge superbikes, all bicycles employ the same basic technology of nuts and bolts. Nevertheless, there are a few basic principles – as well as some less obvious workshop hints and tips – that will help to make maintenance more straightforward and precise, and that, if followed correctly, should save you time and money.

PREPPING PARTS

Threaded components should be "prepped" – prepared – prior to assembly. Clean them with degreaser or alcohol-based cleaner, then apply the appropriate agent to them, as outlined below.

- **Grease** Use for most parts, especially: crank bolts, pedal axles, cable-clamp bolts (on mechs and brakes).

- **Threadlock** Use for parts that are prone to rattling loose, such as: jockey-wheel bolts, brake-calliper or disc-rotor bolts, stem face-plate bolts, and cleat bolts.

- **Antiseize** Use for parts that are prone to binding up, especially those that are made of aluminium or titanium.

- **Carbon-assembly paste** Use when either or both parts are carbon (except for stem/steerer-tube contact, which should be left dry).

DIRECTION OF TIGHTENING

Nearly all parts tighten clockwise (to the right) and loosen anti-clockwise (to the left). The exceptions are pedals and some bottom brackets. To check, inspect the threads – they slope upwards towards the direction of tightening.

Clockwise (standard) thread   Anti-clockwise (less common) thread

MECHANICAL ADVANTAGE

When working on parts that require significant force to loosen, such as a cassette lock ring, place tools at 90 degrees to each other, the part, or your bracing hand, to increase the mechanical advantage – the amount by which the tool amplifies the force you are applying.

Chain whip

PUSH DOWN

Tighening or loosening parts is easier if you position the tool so that you can push downwards. Be aware that this reduces the effort required, so be careful you do not overtighten the part.

DANGER AREAS

When working near potentially dangerous areas, position tools so that if your hands slip they move away from sharp parts, such as chainrings, sprockets, and disc-brake rotors.

Position tools away from danger area

CROSS-THREADING

Occurring when two threaded parts are screwed together without properly aligning the threads, cross-threading can lead to stripped threads. To avoid it, screw the part in by hand so that you can feel when the two threads are "seated" and can tell immediately if the force required to turn the part increases; if it does, then loosen the part and start again. Try screwing the part the other way until you feel a slight click – this is the feel of the threads engaging. Tighten carefully by hand.

Pedal and crank cross-threading is common

CARING FOR TOOLS

Look after your tools with the same level of care as you would your bike. Keep everything clean – grit, grease, and water can cause your tools to rust or wear out. Keep an eye on the condition of your tools, and throw away any that show signs of wear – rounded Allen keys or spanners with worn jaws can damage the bicycle parts you use them on. Store your tools in the dry, out of sunlight, ideally hanging them up on a tool board or similar.

HEXAGONAL HEADS

When working on bikes fitted with hexagonal-head nuts and bolts (rather than the Allen bolts found on most modern bikes), use the ring end of a combination spanner, or a socket spanner. These grip the head on all six faces, rather than just two faces (as an open-ended spanner does).

Ring spanner on a hexagonal-headed bolt

RECESSED BOLTS

If you are working on a recessed Allen bolt, you might need to use the long axis of your Allen key to reach it. If the bolt is tight, you can increase the leverage by sliding a close-fitting length of tubing over the Allen key's shorter axis.

Insert key at right angle to bolt head surface

EXPOSED BOLTS

Allen and Torx bolts have a recessed head that can fill with mud or other dirt, especially on pedal cleats. Take care to clean out any dirt or debris before trying to loosen or tighten these bolts, so that the key can fit in easily.

Dig out dirt before inserting Allen key

LOOSENING BLOW

Pedal threads, crank bolts, and bottom-bracket cups can get very tight. Often a short, sharp blow on the spanner with the heel of your hand or a rubber mallet will loosen them. If not, place a length of tubing or a spare seat post over the handle of the tool to increase leverage.

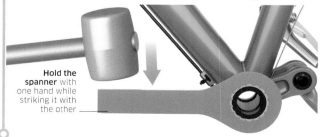

Hold the spanner with one hand while striking it with the other

The M-checks

The M-checks are a series of tests you can use to ensure your bike is functioning safely. You have a duty to pedestrians, motorists, and other cyclists – not to mention yourself – to ensure your bike is safe, so perform the M-checks regularly.

Named after the M-shaped path of the checks, the M-checks are a thorough series of inspections of a bicycle's frame and components for wear and tear, damage, and poor adjustment. Start at the front wheel, then work up the fork to the handlebar and controls, over the frame and saddle, and finally on to the gears.

PRE-RIDE CHECKS

In addition to the periodic M-checks, you should make a series of pre-ride safety checks every time you ride your bike.

(1) **Pull brake levers** to check adjustment of pads and that wheels can be locked.

(2) **Inspect brake pads** for wear and alignment with rim.

(3) **Twist stem, handlebar, saddle, seat post** in turn to check that all clamp bolts are tight. (For carbon parts, do not twist or push – instead, check bolts with a torque wrench).

(4) **Squeeze tyres** to check pressure.

(5) **Grip wheels** to check quick-releases/wheel nuts are secure in drop-outs.

A WHEEL AND FRONT HUB

The first area to check is the front of the bike. Start by slowly spinning the wheel, then move on to the hub, fork, and brake.

While spinning the wheel, check that:

(1) **Tyre tread/sidewalls** are not worn, and pressure is correct.

(2) **Rim brakes** do not rub.

(3) **Disc brake rotor** is straight.

(4) **Rim** is true, with no cracks, or wear in the braking surface, or bulges at the spoke holes.

(5) **Tyre bead** is seated in the rim, with no inner tube visible.

(6) **Spoke** tension is even.

Push the top of the wheel sideways to check that:

(7) **Wheel nut/quick-release** is secured tight in the drop-out.

(8) **Hub bearings** are tight.

Visually inspect:

(9) **Fork** for dents or cracks.

Apply brake to check that:

(10) **Brake** functions correctly.

(11) **Suspension bushings** are not worn by pushing forward with the brake applied.

B HEADSET AND HANDLEBAR

Next, check the "cockpit" – the bar, stem, headset, and controls.

(1) **Apply front brake,** turn handlebar 90 degrees, hold steerer, and push forward. Any play indicates loose headset bearings.

(2) **Inspect bar** for dents/straightness.

(3) **Check end-plugs** are inserted.

(4) **Grip brake and gear** levers to check they are securely fastened.

(5) **Check bar** is at 90 degrees to wheel with your legs either side of front wheel.

(6) **Grip bar** to check all stem bolts are tight.

C BOTTOM BRACKET

Move down to the BB area to begin the drivetrain checks.

① **Wobble cranks** side-to-side by hand. Movement indicates a loose BB.

② **Spin pedals** to check axles turn.

③ **Twist pedals** on their axles to check bearings are tight and threads are securely tightened on cranks.

④ **Shift gears** so the chain is in the smallest chainring and middle of cassette then backpedal to check chainrings are straight, bolts are tight, and chain is free of stiff links.

⑤ **Check front derailleur** is tight, parallel to chainrings, and not worn.

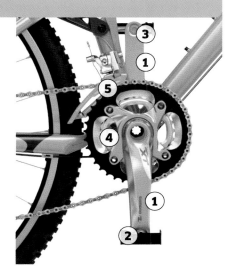

D FRAME, CABLES, SADDLE AND SUSPENSION

Travelling back up the bike, check the frame, cables, saddle, and suspension.

① **Check each frame tube** for dents/cracks by running your fingers over it. (Clean the bike before doing this.)

② **Inspect cable** outers/hydraulic hoses for wear, especially where they rub on frame.

③ **Check seat post** is tight in clamp.

④ **Check saddle** is securely clamped on the seat post, and look down on it to check its alignment with top tube.

⑤ **Check rear suspension's** shock by holding the saddle and pushing on the tyre. Check for play in the linkage bushings/bearings.

Ensure shock absorber is moving correctly

E REAR WHEEL

Finish the M-checks by inspecting the rear wheel, brakes, and gears.

① **Stand behind wheel** to check rear derailleur and hanger are not bent. Look for loose pivots and worn jockey wheels.

② **Spin the rear wheel** to check for tyre or rim wear, spoke tension, and brake alignment.

③ **Check the rear brake** functions.

④ **Check for hub play** by pushing the wheel's top then secure axles.

⑤ **Run through gears** to ensure derailleurs are correctly adjusted. Inspect sprockets for worn teeth.

⑥ **Use a chain measurer** to check for chain wear.

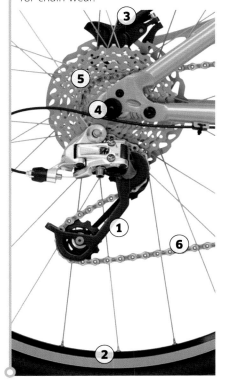

Cleaning your bike

The first line of defence in maintaining your bike is regular cleaning to prevent a build-up of dirt that can wear out parts. Work over your bike, cleaning the dirtiest areas first. Follow every step listed here for a complete wash, or clean each area as it gets dirty.

CLEANING TIP

Never turn your bike upside down when cleaning it – dirty water can seep inside the frame and damage the saddle and handlebar. If you do not have a frame stand, lean the frame against the wall vertically.

Rest rear drop-out against wall

Fork drop-outs and handlebar on ground

MUD AND ROAD MUCK

Before cleaning your bike, remove any accessories. Depending on the riding conditions and the type of cycling you do – off-road riding is notorious for spreading mud – it may require washing all over. Begin by spraying or brushing the dirt away, paying special attention to these areas:

① **Tyres**

② **Wheels**

③ **Frame**

④ **Under saddle**

⑤ **Under the down tube**

⑥ **Fork legs**

⑦ **Brace**, crown, inside steerer (mountain bikes)

⑧ **Brake callipers** (road bikes)

Spray your bike all over with a cycling-specific detergent that will not damage the paintwork and brakes, and then rinse with water.

DRIVETRAIN

For the best results when cleaning the drivetrain, remove the wheel and loop the chain around a chain-keeper clamped to the rear drop-out.

① **Begin turning the pedals** backwards, then brush or spray degreaser onto the chain. Scrape dirt off the jockey wheels with the plastic bristles of a brush as you backpedal.

② **Apply degreaser** to chainrings. Scrub using a sponge on both sides of the chain and chainrings.

③ **Degrease** the front and rear derailleurs with a small bottlebrush.

④ **Hold a sponge**, brush, or chain bath against the chain while backpedalling to dislodge dirty lubricant.

⑤ **Rinse off degreaser** thoroughly – any left will repel future lubricant.

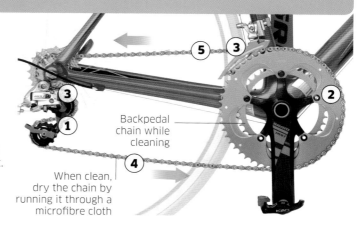

Backpedal chain while cleaning

When clean, dry the chain by running it through a microfibre cloth

---

TOOLS AND EQUIPMENT

- Brushes and sponge
- Degreaser
- Rag and microfibre cloth
- Bike detergent
- Chain-keeper (optional)
- PTFE-based bike polish

Workshop tip: Do not clean your bike with hot water, which can melt the grease that coats threads and bearings. If using a hose, keep the pressure low and do not aim the water at the bearings. Detergents should be specially formulated for cleaning bicycles.

CASSETTE, WHEELS, ROTORS

The most effective way to clean the wheels is by removing them from your bicycle.

(1) **Scrub the cassette** with a brush and degreaser to remove any dirty lubricant and grime, scrubbing the rear of the cassette (coming at it from the hub side). Use a rag to "floss" back and forth between cogs to remove hard-to-reach grime.

(2) **Wash the tyres**, spokes, and hub body with bike detergent.

(3) **Wipe the rim** with a rag soaked in bike detergent, checking the braking surface for wear as you do so. Repeat the process with the front wheel.

(4) **Clean the disc rotors** with disc-cleaning spray, which removes dirt without leaving a residue that can contaminate pads.

FRAME AND FORK

For best results use bike detergent to sponge-wash the frame, fork, and any other dirty areas, such as the brakes, pedals, and inside faces of the cranks.

(1) **Clean under the saddle**, down tube, bottom bracket, and inside the stays.

(2) **Remove any grit** from the brake callipers and pads.

(3) **Replace the wheels** and leave to drip-dry. Disperse moisture by spraying with a PTFE-based bike polish, then apply lubricant as necessary (see pp.44–45).

Clean dirty bar tape or grips with rag soaked in penetrating oil

Rear stays are prone to dirt build-up

ELECTRONIC GEARS

Although electronic gears and drive systems are designed to work in wet conditions, be careful when cleaning them with water and detergents. To be safe, use a bike detergent or a specialist electronic shifter cleaning spray, which will clean and dry without needing to be wiped or rinsed off.

- Avoid using alcohol-based cleaner, soaking electronic parts in degreaser, or using sprays or brushes that can damage seals.

- If the junction box is dirty, remove it from the bike and cables, and clean it with bike detergent. Carefully wipe any charge ports or battery stations.

- Fit a rubber boot over crank-mounted power-meters before cleaning them in order to protect them from water.

Lubricating your bike

Lubricating your bike is as important as cleaning it and should be done immediately after every single bike wash. Lubricant and grease reduce friction on moving parts so it is especially important to keep your chain lubricated. Lubricants also form a seal to protect bike components against water and corrosion, and they create a protective barrier between different materials – such as a steel frame with an aluminium seat post inside – that prevents parts from seizing up.

CHAIN AND REAR DERAILLEUR

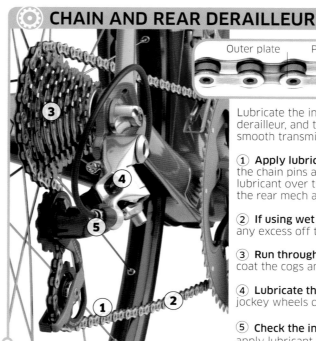

Outer plate   Pin   Roller

Lubricate the inside of the chain, rear derailleur, and the cables to ensure a smooth transmission.

① **Apply lubricant** to the inside of the chain pins and rollers. Hold the lubricant over the chain in front of the rear mech as you turn the pedals.

② **If using wet lubricant**, wipe any excess off the outer plates.

③ **Run through the gears** to coat the cogs and chainrings.

④ **Lubricate the pivots**, springs, and jockey wheels of the rear derailleur.

⑤ **Check the inner cables**, then apply lubricant to them.

CRANKS AND WHEELS

Lubricate the front derailleur and pedals at the same time as the spokes.

① **Lubricate** the front mech pivots and the springs.

② **On the wheels**, drip a small drop of lubricant where each spoke enters the nipple, to prevent any corrosion.

③ **Lubricate** the retention spring of clipless pedals.

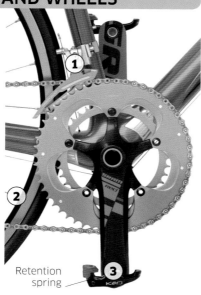

Retention spring

RIM BRAKES

Lubricate the brake pivots and cables to ensure powerful, effective braking.

① **Lubricate the pivots** of the brake callipers.

② **Dribble lubricant** into the cable housing; open the brake quick-release lever and shift the gears to expose the inner cables.

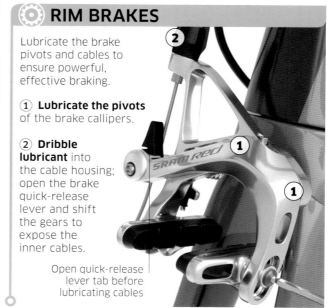

Open quick-release lever tab before lubricating cables

Workshop tip: When applying lubricant, use the smallest amount possible, and wipe away any excess. This is because lubricants will become contaminated with dirt over time, eventually forming a grinding paste that wears out components.

SUSPENSION PIVOTS, SEAT POST

Grease the suspension to ensure it moves freely and also lubricate the seat post as it is the part most likely to seize inside the frame.

① **Apply grease** or carbon-assembly paste to the base of the seat post and inside the top of the seat tube, to prevent seizing.

② **Check the full-suspension pivots** on mountain bikes then apply grease to the pivot bearings or lubricant to the bushings.

③ **Dribble specialist suspension lubricant** into the rear shock, then push downwards on the saddle to distribute it.

Lubricate bushings or bearings

SUSPENSION FORK

Lubricate the front fork to keep it responsive.

① **Dribble suspension lubricant** down the stanchion.

② **Use a cable tie** to prise back the seal, allowing the lubricant to penetrate inside the fork sliders. Pump the fork to distribute the lubricant.

Apply lubricant to fork stanchion

TYPES OF LUBRICANT AND GREASE

You should always use bike-specific lubricants; household oils are too thick, and penetrating oil is suitable only for cleaning away lubricant and grease you have applied.

- **Wet lubricants** use a heavy, oil-based formula. They are ideal for wet, muddy conditions as they are less likely to be washed off. However, they can trap dust and grime.

- **Dry lubricants** use a light formulation with the lubricant suspended in a solvent. The solvent evaporates after application, leaving the lubricant as a dry, waxy film on the chain. These lubricants pick up less dirt than wet lubricants, but must be reapplied more often. They are most useful in dry conditions and sandy, dusty terrain.

- **Basic grease** reduces friction on static parts such as bearings and threads. Some types of grease are waterproof; others are designed specifically to protect high-temperature areas such as disc brake pistons.

- **Anti-seize grease** contains particles of copper or aluminium to prevent two surfaces seizing together due to corrosion.

- **Carbon-assembly paste** contains microparticles that improve friction. It is ideal for components that must be tightened to low torque values, such as carbon-fibre parts.

► MAINTENANCE AND REPAIR
Protecting your frame

Bikes are designed to cope with intensive use. However, you can extend your bike's lifespan by protecting the frame from damage caused by debris, parts rubbing each other, or even wear from your own legs and feet. Protective items for specific areas are shown here.

3 CABLE DONUTS/SPIRALS

Fitting rings or spirals of rubber or plastic around the cable outers will help to stop them slapping against your frame.

Donuts | Spirals |

Rider's knees may rub top tube

Chain may "slap" against chainstay

2 DOWN-TUBE PROTECTORS

Fit a down-tube protector, or a section of old tyre fixed on with cable ties, to your bike to protect it from impact from stones and debris.

Cover base of down tube

Some down- tube protectors cover bottom bracket

1 TUBE PROTECTORS

Apply tube protectors or tape such as "helicopter tape" (see Workshop tip) to areas vulnerable to scratches, chips, or strikes from debris.

Strips may be shaped to fit curved areas

7 CHAINSTAY GUARD

Fit a chainstay guard to protect the frame from chain slap, which occurs when the chain bounces repeatedly against the frame. You could buy a neoprene or plastic chainstay protector. Alternatively, you can use "helicopter tape" or even an old inner tyre (see box, right).

4 FRAME PATCHES

Apply small stickers or pieces of tape to the frame wherever the cable outers rub.

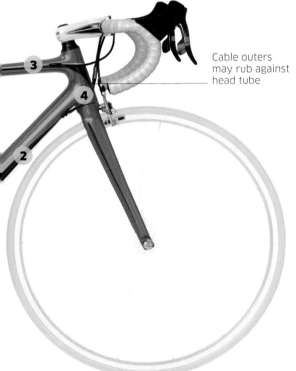

Cable outers may rub against head tube

PROTECTION IN TRANSIT

Before transporting your bike, pad the frame and secure the handlebar.

- Fix foam lagging around the frame with tape.
- Pad the delicate front forks and rear derailleur area.

Turn handlebars to lie parallel to frame

5 DOWNHILL BIKE CHAIN GUARD

A chain guard will help to stop the chain falling off the chainrings when you ride over rough terrain. In addition, fit a bash guard to protect the chainrings against debris strikes from beneath the bike.

Bash guard

6 ROAD BIKE CHAIN CATCHER

This simple bolt-on device will stop the chain from slipping off the inner (small) chainring and possibly damaging the frame.

End of chain catcher lies beside inner chainring

DIY CHAINSTAY PROTECTION

Cut a section of old inner tube and wrap it around the chainstay to protect the frame against chain slap.

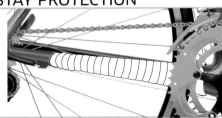

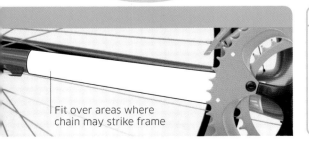

Fit over areas where chain may strike frame

Emergency repairs

It is inevitable that at some point you will need to make road- or trail-side repairs of some kind. Carry basic supplies such as food, water, a phone, and money, and put together a repair kit (see box, right). A pre-ride safety check (see p.40) will reduce the chance of a mechanical problem, and if you learn basic repair skills such as how to fix a puncture and how to use quick fixes (see box, opposite) you should have the knowledge you need to get home safely.

🔍 REPAIR KIT

In addition to the kit you normally carry in a saddlebag (see pp.24–25), take a few extras to help fix problems that could otherwise end your ride. Equipment will depend on your bike set-up, but examples include:

- Chain masterlink
- Cable ties
- Tyre boot (5 cm /2 in) square of old tyre)
- Duct tape
- Derailleur hanger

- Presta–Schrader valve converter (for using petrol station tyre inflators on road bikes)
- Valve extender (for screwing over the valve if a Presta tip breaks)

⚙ PUNCTURE REPAIR

Punctures are the most common problem that cyclists encounter. A puncture may result from a sharp object piercing a tyre, or may occur in a sudden impact, if the inner tube gets pinched between the tyre and the wheel rim. This damage produces two parallel, slit-like holes, sometimes called a "snakebite" puncture. Always carry tyre levers and a puncture repair kit; these kits contain patches to repair an inner tube, plus items such as sandpaper, glue, and chalk.

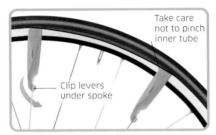

Clip levers under spoke

Take care not to pinch inner tube

1 **Remove the wheel** and check the tyre for the cause of the puncture. Push the lever under the tyre bead and lift it off the rim. Do the same with the second lever, and slide it around the rim.

2 **Once you have taken off** one side of the tyre you can remove the inner tube by sliding it out. Check over the tube to try and find the cause of the puncture.

6 **Roughen the hole site** with sandpaper to prepare the surface of the rubber for the glue. The roughened area should be slightly larger than the repair patch you will be using.

Ensure glue area is larger than patch

7 **Apply glue** to the whole of the roughened area, centred over the puncture. Leave the glue for about 30–60 seconds until it becomes tacky. Ensure that it is not runny in consistency.

Press for 30–60 seconds

8 **Apply the patch** in the middle of the tacky area, making sure you have covered all of the hole. Press it from the centre outwards to push out any air bubbles. Leave the patch to dry.

Repair tip: If you lose an essential part while on a ride, see if you can borrow a part from elsewhere on your bike as a quick fix. For example, you could replace a cleat bolt with a bottle-cage bolt, or use a wheel or seat post quick-release lever as a tyre lever.

⚙ QUICK FIXES

Even if you keep your bike well-maintained and carry out regular safety checks (see pp.40–41), mechanical failures can still occur. In such cases, or if you lack spare parts or tools, try these roadside fixes.

Broken spoke	■ Remove the spoke, or if that is not possible wrap it around its neighbour for stability. Open up the brake calliper.
Bent wheel	■ If the wheel is seriously bent, place the bent part of the rim over the front of your knee, then pull the wheel from the side to straighten the rim. As a last resort, hit the rim on the ground to get rid of the bend. Replace the rim when you get home.
Split rim	■ Use zipties to bind the split together. Ensure that you take great care riding home.
Broken rear derailleur	■ Remove the derailleur then use a chain tool to shorten the chain. Reconnect it with a masterlink, then ride home single speed.

Check for air escaping

3 **If you cannot find** the cause, pump air into the tube and listen for the hiss as air escapes. To find a tiny hole, lift the tube to your lips (where your skin is sensitive) to feel for escaping air.

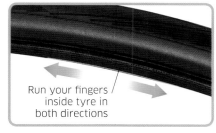

Run your fingers inside tyre in both directions

4 **If you still have not discovered** the cause of the puncture, run your fingers carefully around the inside of the tyre to feel for any sharp objects. Once found, check the corresponding area of the tube.

Mark centre of hole

5 **Mark the hole area** with a Biro or a crayon, with the hole at the centre. Check the other side of the tube again in case the puncture is a "snakebite" type, with a second hole on the other side.

Dust chalk to cover glue beyond the patch edge

9 **Grate chalk dust** against the repair-kit box and spread the dust over the glued area. This chalky dust will help to prevent the inner tube from sticking to the inside of the tyre.

Run fingers under inside tyre to check for dirt

10 **Check the inside** of the tyre and the rim again. Remove whatever caused the puncture, and any other bits of grit, dirt, or debris that could puncture your newly repaired inner tube.

11 **Fit one side** of the tyre into the rim. Part-inflate the tube so that it is soft but holds its shape. Insert the tube under the tyre and fit the valve through the rim. Re-seat the tyre in the rim.

STEERING
AND SADDLE

Headsets

A headset enables the forks to rotate within the head tube as you turn the handlebar. Older, threaded-types (see pp.54–55) are fastened to a thread on the fork's steerer tube, which is connected to the handlebar with a quill stem. On modern threadless headsets (see pp.56–57), the stem clamps directly onto the steerer tube of the forks. There are two types of threadless headset – integrated (shown right) and external cup. Integrated headsets have cartridge bearings that sit inside the head tube of the frame. To replace a cartridge bearing, simply pull it out and put a new one into place. The external cup system has cups that are pressed into the frame. These need to be fitted with a headset press tool.

Stem bolts secure stem to steerer tube

Top tube joins head tube and seat tube

Bearing cover protects bearing

Upper race contains upper bearings

Down tube is joined to head tube

⚙ PARTS FOCUS

The headset contains two sets of bearings, contained within races, which enable the handlebar and front wheel to turn.

① The **star nut** is located inside the steerer tube, and pulls the stem and fork together inside the head tube.

② On a modern threadless headset the **spacers** (as shown here) enable you to adjust the height of the stem and handlebar.

③ **Bearings** ensure that your handlebar and forks can turn smoothly. You need to keep them well maintained (see pp.54–57).

④ The **crown race** is the lowest bearing race on the headset. It sits below the lower head tube race, on the crown at the top of the forks.

Top cap bolt threads into the star nut inside steerer tube

Stem connects handlebar to steerer tube

①

②

③

Upper bearing contains individual ball bearings

Compression ring holds bearing in place

Ball bearings reduce friction, allowing forks to move smoothly

Bearing spacer holds loose bearings in place

Steerer tube connects forks to stem and handlebar

Head tube houses steerer tube

Stem clamp secures handlebar to stem

Handlebar can be turned freely due to bearings in headset

Fork crown joins forks to steerer tube

③

④

Lower race sits at base of head tube

Lower bearing sits inside lower race

Forks turn as handlebar is moved

Threaded headsets

Threaded headsets secure the forks using adjustable and locking nuts that screw onto the threaded steerer tube. They feature either ball or cartridge bearings. Notchy or rough steering is a sign that your headset needs servicing.

BEFORE YOU START

- Secure your bike in a frame stand
- Prepare a clear space where you can lay out the parts
- Remove the handlebar and stem (see pp.58–59)
- Remove the front wheel (see pp.78–79)

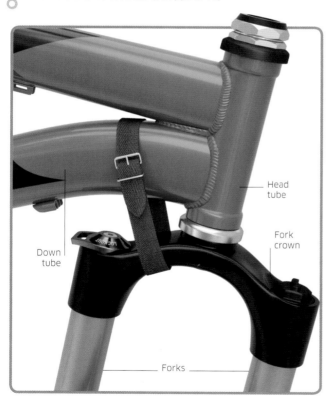

Head tube

Fork crown

Down tube

Forks

1 **Secure the forks** to the down tube of the frame with an adjustable strap. This will stop them dropping out of the frame as you loosen the adjustable race and the locknut.

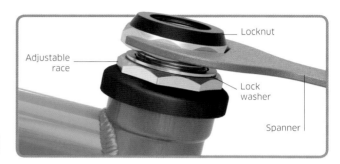

Locknut

Adjustable race

Lock washer

Spanner

2 **With the forks secured** to the down tube, unscrew the locknut with a spanner. Remove the lock washer, any spacers, and the adjustable race, so that you can access the bearings in the headset.

Gently lift out bearing clip with screwdriver or tweezers

Bearings may be loose or in clip, as shown

3 **Remove the bearings** from the top race, and check that the races are smooth and undamaged. Replace any worn bearings. If the races are worn, you will need to source a replacement headset.

Remove strap to release forks

Crown race

4 **Remove the adjustable strap** and lower the forks from the head tube so that you can access the bearings in the crown race. Remove, check, and clean the bearings. Replace them if they are worn.

Workshop tip: Make a note of the order and position of any seals, washers, and spacers removed. If the races contain loose bearings, count how many there are before removing them, and use a magnet to stop them from falling on the floor or rolling away.

Grease crown race

5 **Apply a liberal amount** of grease to the crown race, and reinstall the bearings, or insert new ones if required.

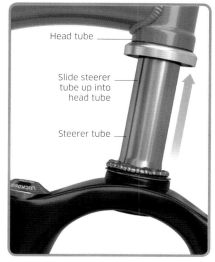

Head tube

Slide steerer tube up into head tube

Steerer tube

6 **Slide the steerer tube** into the head tube. Secure the forks using the strap until the locknut is flush against the down tube.

PARTS FOCUS

A typical threaded headset consists of cups, bearings, and a pair of threaded nuts that secure the forks and adjust the movement.

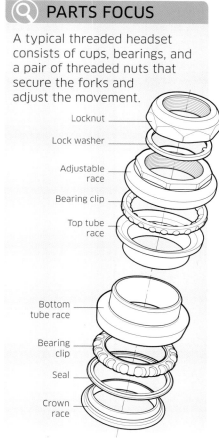

Locknut

Lock washer

Adjustable race

Bearing clip

Top tube race

Bottom tube race

Bearing clip

Seal

Crown race

Adjustable race

Bearings

Grease

Top tube race

7 **Grease the inside** of the top tube race and insert the bearings. Screw the adjustable top tube race onto the steerer tube.

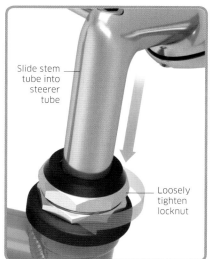

Slide stem tube into steerer tube

Loosely tighten locknut

8 **Fit the lock washer** and nut, then insert the handlebar stem into the steerer tube, tightening the locknut with your fingers.

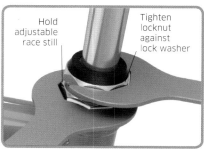

Hold adjustable race still

Tighten locknut against lock washer

9 **Using two spanners**, fully tighten the locknut against the lock washer. Position the handlebar, then tighten securely.

Threadless headsets

Threadless headsets secure the forks by allowing the handlebar stem to clamp around the steerer tube. A top cap compresses everything together. As with threaded headsets, a rough or notchy feeling when steering is usually an indication that the bearings need servicing or replacing.

 BEFORE YOU START

- Secure your bike in a frame stand
- Remove the front wheel (see pp.78–79)
- Release the brake and gear cables, if required
- Support the forks with an adjustable strap (see pp.54–55)

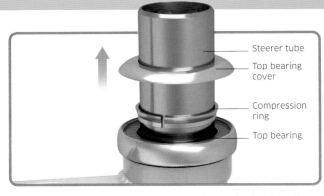

Steerer tube

Top bearing cover

Compression ring

Top bearing

2 **Push the steerer tube** down through the head tube. If it sticks, tap the top of it with a rubber mallet to free the compression ring. Remove the top bearing cover and the compression ring.

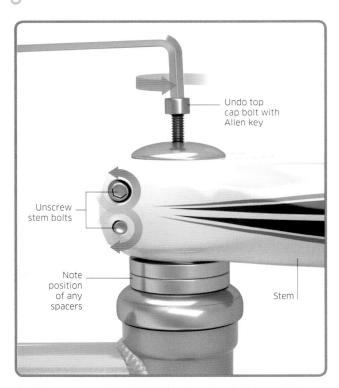

Undo top cap bolt with Allen key

Unscrew stem bolts

Note position of any spacers

Stem

1 **Unscrew and remove the top cap bolt**. Loosen the stem bolts and pull the stem off the steerer tube, along with any spacers. Place the stem down carefully, so as not to damage gear or brake cables.

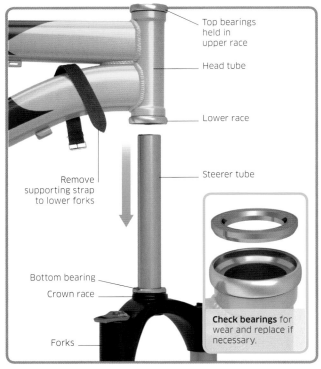

Top bearings held in upper race

Head tube

Lower race

Remove supporting strap to lower forks

Steerer tube

Bottom bearing

Crown race

Forks

Check bearings for wear and replace if necessary.

3 **Lower the forks** out of the head tube. Remove the top bearing from the upper race, and the bottom bearing from the crown race. Clean the bearings, inside the head tube, and the races.

Workshop tip: Use an adjustable strap to prevent the fork from dropping out of the headset when the compression ring is removed. Otherwise, support it with your hand.

Top bearing

Apply fresh grease inside upper race

4 **Liberally grease the inside** of the bearing races, as well as the bearings, even if new. Fit the top bearing into the upper race.

Maintain upwards pressure on forks once inserted.

5 **Slide the bottom bearing** down the steerer tube, then insert the steerer tube up through the head tube – hold it in place.

Compression ring presses onto top bearing

6 **Slide the compression ring** down on to the steerer tube, and push it into the upper race, ensuring it is the right way up.

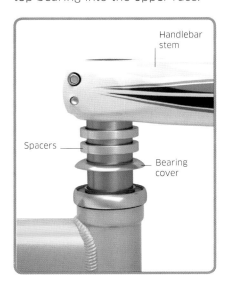

Handlebar stem

Spacers

Bearing cover

7 **Replace the bearing cover** over the bearings, install any spacers required, and loosely reattach the handlebar stem.

Take care not to overtighten bolt

Top cap

8 **Refit the top cap** and bolt, and tighten to remove any slack in the headset. Avoid overtightening, as this will make the steering stiff.

Check for play before tightening stem bolts

9 **Refit the front wheel**, ensuring that the handlebar and stem are straight, before securing the bolts on the side of the stem.

Handlebars and stems

Top cap bolt
secures stem to
steerer tube

A handlebar is essential for steering your bike. As you turn the bar, the stem turns the fork, adjusting the direction of the front wheel. The bar also holds the brake levers and gear-shifters. There are two forms of handlebar: "drop" types for road bikes and straight for mountain bikes. Handlebars and stems also come in a range of sizes. Wider bars will suit you best if you have broad shoulders, while longer stems enable you to adopt an aerodynamic position for racing. When replacing your handlebar, you should note the diameter of the exisiting one, as the replacement will have fit your stem clamp.

Stem bolts are loosened
to adjust alignment
of handlebar

Headset
allows handlebars
and forks to
turn smoothly

Electrical tape
holds gear and brake
cables to handlebar

Brake and gear
cables are routed
from handlebar
to frame mounts

Bar end plugs
push into ends
of drop handlebar

⚙ PARTS FOCUS

The handlebar is a relatively simple component on a bike but it has a crucial role, so ensure that it is secure and fitted correctly.

① The **stem** joins the handlebar and steerer tube.

② The **stem clamp** has a face plate that bolts over the handlebar, holding it to the stem. The diameter of the stem clamp must match that of the bar.

③ The **handlebar** holds the brake levers and shifters. Most handlebars are made of aluminium; top-end versions may be carbon.

④ **Handlebar tape and grips** improve grip and comfort for the rider. Handlebar tapes are used to cover gear and brake cables.

⑤ **Bar end plugs** cover each end of a drop handlebar and secure the bar tape.

⑤

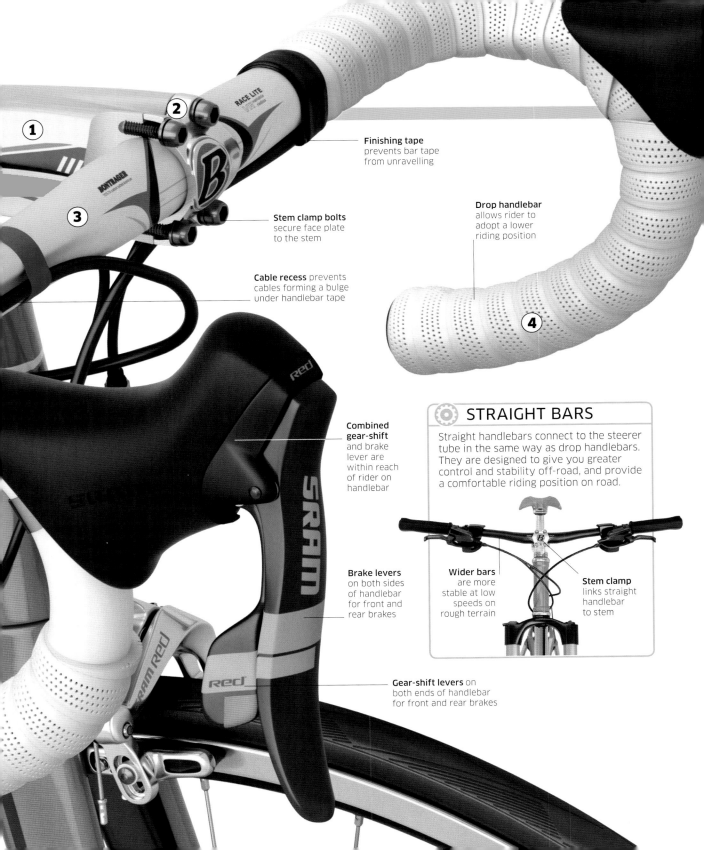

①

②

③

Finishing tape
prevents bar tape
from unravelling

Drop handlebar
allows rider to
adopt a lower
riding position

Stem clamp bolts
secure face plate
to the stem

Cable recess prevents
cables forming a bulge
under handlebar tape

④

**Combined
gear-shift**
and brake
lever are
within reach
of rider on
handlebar

⚙ STRAIGHT BARS

Straight handlebars connect to the steerer
tube in the same way as drop handlebars.
They are designed to give you greater
control and stability off-road, and provide
a comfortable riding position on road.

Brake levers
on both sides
of handlebar
for front and
rear brakes

Wider bars
are more
stable at low
speeds on
rough terrain

Stem clamp
links straight
handlebar
to stem

Gear-shift levers on
both ends of handlebar
for front and rear brakes

Drop and straight handlebars

A handlebar does not need to be replaced routinely, but it is something you may need to do after an accident, or if you want to upgrade it, or improve the look or comfort of your bike. It is a simple task, and the steps are similar for straight and drop handlebars (shown here).

BEFORE YOU START

- Ensure that your stem and new handlebar are compatible with your bike
- Take note of the angle and position of the old handlebar
- Measure the existing position of the brake and gear levers
- Secure your bike in a frame stand

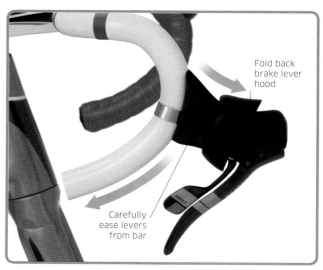

Fold back brake lever hood

Carefully ease levers from bar

2 **Expose the clamp bolts** on the gear and brake levers. Using an Allen key or spanner, loosen the first lever clip and slide the lever from the bar. Repeat for the second lever. Let the levers hang by the cables.

Unwrap bar tape

Cables remain attached

If existing grips on flat handlebars are stuck, carefully cut through them with craft knife to access brake or gear levers.

1 **Remove the bar tape** or grips (see pp.62–65). If required, fold back the brake-lever hoods to give you better access to the handlebar, and cut away any tape holding the brake and gear cables in place.

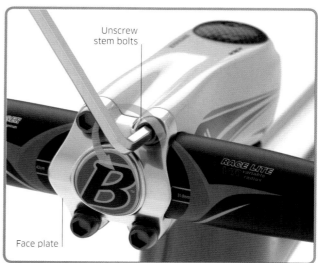

Unscrew stem bolts

Face plate

3 **Undo the stem bolts** on the face plate and remove the plate. If you are replacing like for like, note the bar angle. Lift out and clean the bar with cleaning fluid, checking the stem for damage.

TOOLS AND EQUIPMENT

- Tape measure
- Frame stand
- Craft knife
- Set of Allen keys or spanners
- Cleaning fluid
- Cloth
- Grease or fibre grip

Workshop tip: Adjust the position and angle of your brake and gear levers until they are comfortable for your riding style. Readjust as necessary.

Secure handlebar, leaving bolts just loose enough for small adjustments to be made later.

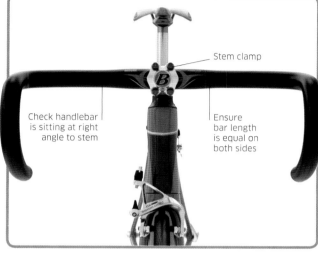

Stem clamp

Check handlebar is sitting at right angle to stem

Ensure bar length is equal on both sides

4 **Apply a little grease** to the new bar, face plate and stem bolts. If you are fitting carbon fibre bars apply "fibre grip" to increase friction. Tighten the bolts just enough to hold the new bar in place.

5 **Centre the handlebar** to ensure that it sits straight in the stem clamp – most bars have markings to help you do this. Adjust the angle to your preference, then tighten the bolts fully, working diagonally.

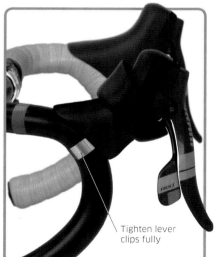

Tighten lever clips fully

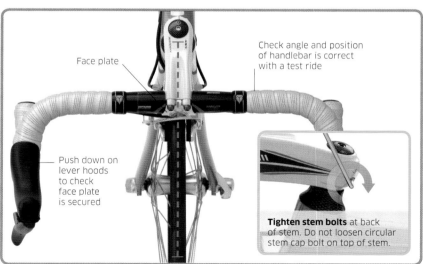

Face plate

Push down on lever hoods to check face plate is secured

Check angle and position of handlebar is correct with a test ride

Tighten stem bolts at back of stem. Do not loosen circular stem cap bolt on top of stem.

6 **Reinstall the levers**, adjusting the angle. Tighten the bolts and tape up the cables. Replace the bar tape or grips (see pp.62–65).

7 **Ensure the stem is aligned** with the front wheel, then loosen the two stem bolts by a quarter of a turn. Holding the front wheel between your knees, twist the handlebar to align the stem. Tighten the bolts incrementally, alternating between the left and right bolt.

Replacing handlebar tape

Handlebar tape provides comfort and grip for your hands, as well as protection for your cables. Sweat, poor weather, and regular use can all dirty the tape, or cause it to loosen, wear thin, and tear. Worn tape is easy to change.

BEFORE YOU START

- Source a handlebar tape suitable for your handlebar
- Wash your hands so you do not soil the new handlebar tape
- Unravel the handlebar tape and lay it out
- Cut 20cm (8in) strips of electrical tape with scissors

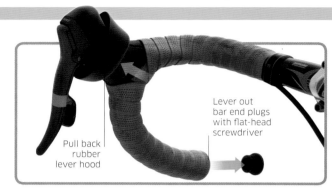

Pull back rubber lever hood

Lever out bar end plugs with flat-head screwdriver

1 **Pull back each rubber lever hood** from the body of the brake levers to expose the handlebar tape beneath. Lever out the bar end plugs from both ends of the handlebar with a flat-head screwdriver.

Cut away old electrical tape with craft knife

2 **Beginning at the stem**, carefully unwind the old handlebar tape. If your bike has concealed brake or gear cables, remove any electrical tape holding them in place, as it is likely to be worn or loose.

Secure cables with electrical tape

3 **Clean the handlebar**, using an alcohol-based cleaner to remove any dirt or leftover glue residue. Replace the electrical tape, ensuring that the cables follow their original routes along the bar.

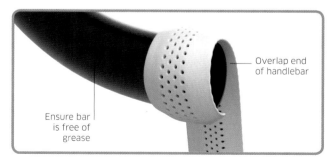

Overlap end of handlebar

Ensure bar is free of grease

4 **Attach the end** of the handlebar tape to the bottom of the handlebar, overlapping the end of the bar by half of the width of the tape. Wind the tape around the bar in a clockwise direction.

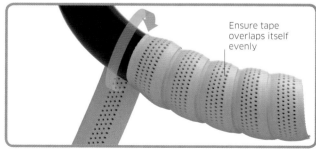

Ensure tape overlaps itself evenly

5 **Maintain an even tension** on the tape as you apply it. The tape should evenly overlap up to half the width of the previous turn. If present, ensure the glue strip sticks to the handlebar only.

Workshop tip: Always wrap replacement handlebar tape in a clockwise direction – from the inside of the bar outwards. The tape will tighten as your hands naturally twist outwards when cycling, keeping it in position.

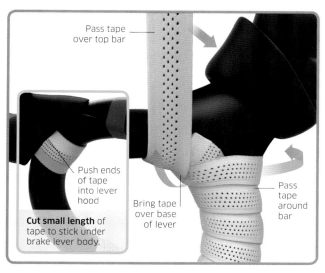

Pass tape over top bar

Push ends of tape into lever hood

Cut small length of tape to stick under brake lever body.

Bring tape over base of lever

Pass tape around bar

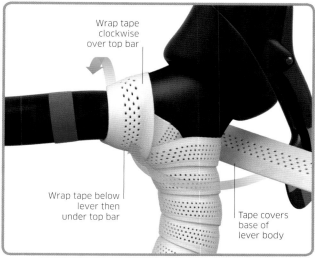

Wrap tape clockwise over top bar

Wrap tape below lever then under top bar

Tape covers base of lever body

6 **At the brake levers** pass the tape around the bar and below the base of the lever body. Bring it under and over the bar on the other side of the lever. Be sure to maintain an even tension.

7 **Wrap the tape** back over the bar and beneath the lever body in the opposite direction as before then pass it back over the top bar. Continue covering the top bar in a clockwise direction.

Stick electrical tape half on handlebar tape and half on bar, securing the ends.

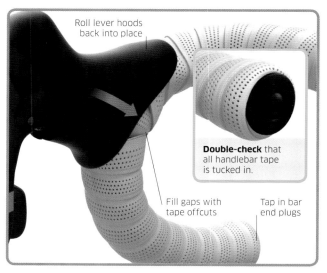

Roll lever hoods back into place

Double-check that all handlebar tape is tucked in.

Fill gaps with tape offcuts

Tap in bar end plugs

8 **When the tape reaches t**he handlebar stem, cut the last 8–10 cm (3–4 in) at a shallow angle towards the bar. Wrap the remaining tape around the bar, then secure it in place using electrical tape.

9 **Roll the lever hoods** back into place and check there are no gaps. Push the ends of the tape into the ends of the handlebar, and secure them by tapping in the bar end plugs with a rubber mallet.

Replacing handlebar grips

Grips have a big influence on bike handling and will need replacing when they fade, rip, or twist out of position. You may also want to upgrade your grips to improve your bike's performance. Standard grips are held in place by friction, while lock-on grips are secured to the bar with small bolts. Replacing both types is a simple task.

BEFORE YOU START

- Secure your bike in a frame stand
- If you are using lock-on grips, assemble them in advance
- Loosen the brake and gear levers, and slide them into the middle of the handlebar to give you better access

Gently break up any sticky residue with screwdriver

2 Insert a small, flat-head screwdriver under the grip, pushing it inwards about 2.5 cm (1 in) to loosen and break the seal. If the grip is sealed shut, push the screwdriver in from the opposite end.

Plastic bar end plug

Remove lock-on grip from handlebar, by unscrewing retaining bolt using Allen key, then slide grip off bar.

1 Pull the bar end plugs out of the bar with your fingertips. If they are tight and hard to remove, use a small, flat-head screwdriver to lever out the plug. Avoid damaging the plugs if you are reusing them.

Straw

Spray degreaser under grip in several places to help loosen it

Repeatedly turn grip from side to side to work degreaser between bar and grip along its length, which will aid removal.

3 Lift up the grip with the screwdriver to create a gap. Insert the degreaser straw into the cavity and spray degreaser on all sides. The grip should now be loose enough to pull from the bar. Twist it off.

Workshop tip: If the grips are hard to fit, thread 2–3 cable ties inside them. Slide each grip onto the handlebar, and when it is in place pull out the ties.

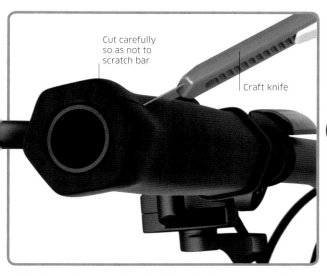

Cut carefully so as not to scratch bar

Craft knife

4 **If the grip remains stuck** to the bar, run a sharp craft knife along its length, taking care not to cut or scratch the metal underneath. Carefully peel the grip away from the bar and discard it.

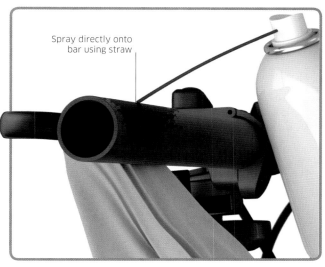

Spray directly onto bar using straw

5 **Clean the handlebar thoroughly** with degreaser to remove any oil, dirt, or residue left by the old grip. Wipe away any remaining fluid and rub dry. If the bar is open, check that the inside of it is dry too.

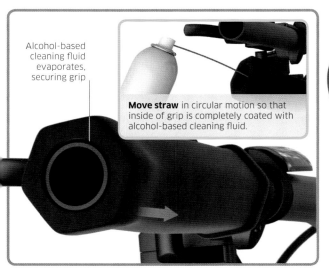

Alcohol-based cleaning fluid evaporates, securing grip

Move straw in circular motion so that inside of grip is completely coated with alcohol-based cleaning fluid.

6 **Spray the bar** and the inside of the grip with an alcohol-based cleaning fluid. Slide the grip onto the bar and twist it into position, making sure that the edge is flush. Leave the grip to set for 10 minutes.

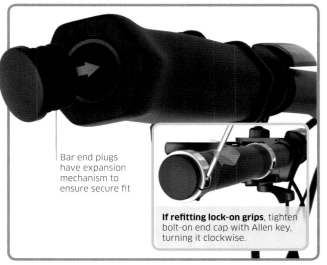

Bar end plugs have expansion mechanism to ensure secure fit

If refitting lock-on grips, tighten bolt-on end cap with Allen key, turning it clockwise.

7 **Push in the bar end plug** so that it is aligned with the end of the grip and it does not stick out from the end of the bar. If the bar end plugs are tight, tap them in gently with a rubber mallet.

Seat posts and saddles

Choosing a saddle is a personal decision, as you need to be comfortable. Saddles are available in a range of widths and shapes, with padding and cut-outs for comfort. Road bike saddles are longer and narrower than mountain bike ones, while those for touring bikes are wider to provide a greater contact area for longer rides. The saddle has rails on the underside to fix it to the seat post. The rails allow you to adjust the saddle position and angle, and they connect to the seat post. Seat posts are available in different lengths and diameters, and their height can be adjusted (see pp.68–69). They are commonly made from aluminium or carbon fibre.

Saddle skin may be synthetic fibre or leather

Nose may be reinforced with Kevlar to protect against damage

Saddle flexes on rails to provide cushioning for rider

Brake cable port

Top tube forms top of bike frame

⚙ PARTS FOCUS

The **saddle** is secured to the seat post by a pair of rails, and the seat post slides into the seat tube on the frame.

(1) Steel, titanium, or carbon **rails** under the saddle allow you to fit the saddle to the seat post and to adjust its position forwards or backwards.

(2) The **saddle rail clamp** attaches the saddle to the seat post by clamping over the rails. Most designs allow the angle of the saddle to be adjusted.

(3) The **seat post** connects the saddle to the seat tube. You adjust the saddle height by raising or lowering the seat post – ensure the minimum insertion mark is inside the frame (see pp.68–69).

(4) The **seat-post clamp** secures the seat post inside the seat tube.

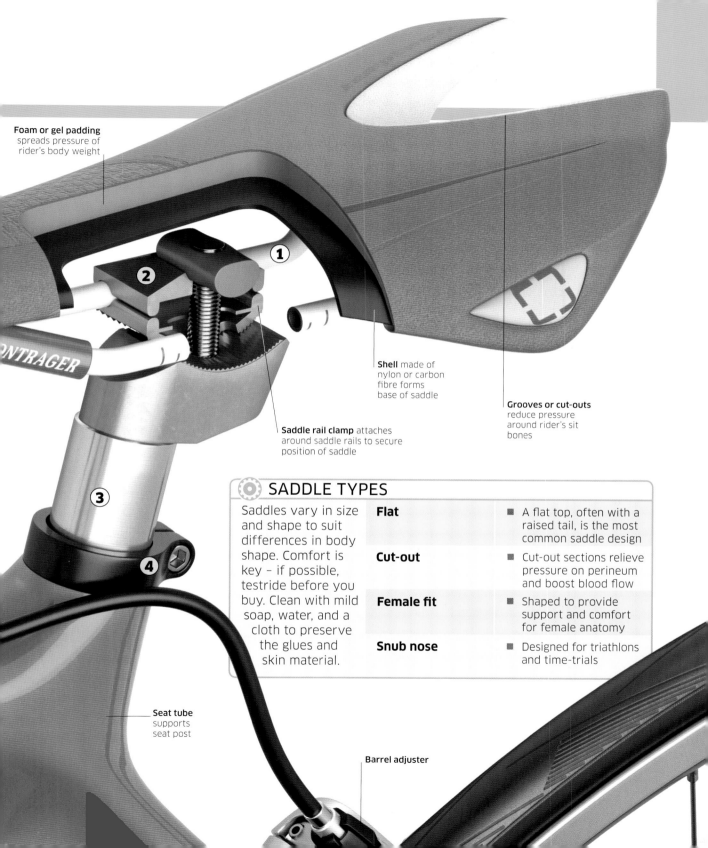

Foam or gel padding spreads pressure of rider's body weight

①

②

Shell made of nylon or carbon fibre forms base of saddle

Grooves or cut-outs reduce pressure around rider's sit bones

Saddle rail clamp attaches around saddle rails to secure position of saddle

③

④

SADDLE TYPES

Saddles vary in size and shape to suit differences in body shape. Comfort is key – if possible, testride before you buy. Clean with mild soap, water, and a cloth to preserve the glues and skin material.

Flat	■ A flat top, often with a raised tail, is the most common saddle design
Cut-out	■ Cut-out sections relieve pressure on perineum and boost blood flow
Female fit	■ Shaped to provide support and comfort for female anatomy
Snub nose	■ Designed for triathlons and time-trials

Seat tube supports seat post

Barrel adjuster

▶ ADJUSTING A SEAT POST
Seat post maintenance

Ensuring that your saddle is at the right height is essential for riding efficiency and comfort, and helps you to prevent knee and hip injuries. Adjusting the height is a simple task, although your seat post can become stuck over time.

🔧 BEFORE YOU START

- Secure your bike in a frame stand
- Clean the seat post and clamp using a cloth and cleaning fluid
- Ensure that the saddle is firmly fitted

ADJUSTING THE SEAT POST HEIGHT

Loosen clamp bolt with Allen key or spanner

Seat post

Hold saddle and pull upwards to lift seat post out of frame.

1 **Loosen the seat post clamp bolt** or quick-release lever just enough for you to pull the post out easily. Do not force it. If there is resistance, twist the saddle in both directions as you pull.

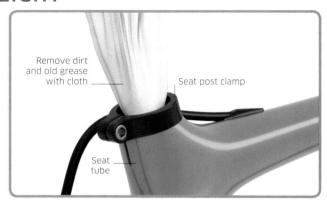

Remove dirt and old grease with cloth

Seat post clamp

Seat tube

2 **Clean the seat post**, seat post clamp, and the top of the seat tube with a cloth to wipe away dirt and surface corrosion. If the clamp bolt is rusty or the clamp shows signs of damage, replace the clamp.

Apply grease with soft brush

Prevent seizure and corrosion with grease

Clamp bolt

Carefully insert seat post back into seat tube.

3 **Grease the upper part** of the seat tube, the area just inside the frame, and the clamp bolt thread. Apply anti-slip compound to carbon frames and seat posts instead of grease, so the seat post will not slip.

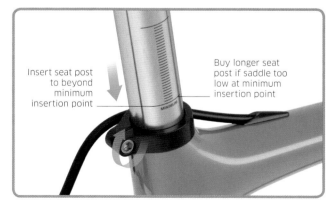

Insert seat post to beyond minimum insertion point

Buy longer seat post if saddle too low at minimum insertion point

4 **Set the saddle** to your preferred ride height (see pp.20–23), and check that it is straight. Tighten the seat post clamp bolt or quick-release lever. Ensure you do not overtighten the bolt or lever.

FREEING A STUCK METAL SEAT POST

Wipe any penetrating oil from paintwork

Distribute oil by moving saddle

Loosen and slide clamp up seat post. Spray penetrating oil where seat post enters seat tube.

LOOSE SEAT POSTS

If your seat post is slipping or squeaks, check that the clamp is properly tightened, and that you have the correct post for your frame.

- If your seat post is still slipping the likely causes are dirt or rust on the seat post and clamp.

- Remove and clean the seat post and clamp, wiping off any dirt or rust. Re-grease the seat post and clamp, and refit to bike.

- If the seat post still slips or squeaks, it may be worn and in need of replacing.

1 **Loosen the seat post clamp bolt** or quick-release lever. If the bolt is difficult to move, spray it with penetrating oil and leave to soak in. Slide the clamp up the seat post and spray penetrating oil onto the seat post where it enters the seat tube. Twist the saddle to distribute the oil.

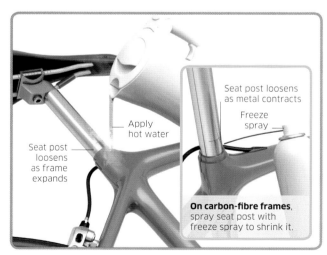

Apply hot water

Seat post loosens as frame expands

Seat post loosens as metal contracts

Freeze spray

On carbon-fibre frames, spray seat post with freeze spray to shrink it.

Prevent seat post sticking by applying grease

Seat tube

2 **If your frame is made** of metal and the seat post remains stuck, pour hot water around the top of the seat tube. This will cause the metal to expand, loosening it against the seat post. Repeat as required.

3 **After removing the seat post**, clean inside the seat tube with a cloth to get rid of any dirt, then apply plenty of grease. Clean and re-grease the seat post and clamp to prevent them seizing again.

Dropper seat posts

Dropper seat posts enable you to lower the height of your saddle while you are riding, either by pressing a remote lever on the handlebar or by pulling a lever under the saddle. They are a popular upgrade for mountain bikes, and can be mechanical (as shown here) or hydraulic.

BEFORE YOU START

- Remove the existing seat post (see pp.68–69)
- Secure your bike in a frame stand
- Clean the inside of the seat tube with cleaning fluid
- Plan how the cable will be routed – internally or externally

Ensure lever is easy to reach

1 **Attach the remote lever** to your handlebar, following the manufacturer's instructions. Position it within easy reach.

Route cable internally or externally

2 **Depending on your frame**, feed the cable housing from the top of the seat tube, to the exit point near the head tube.

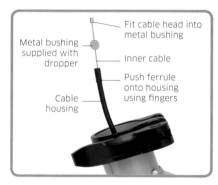

Fit cable head into metal bushing

Metal bushing supplied with dropper

Inner cable

Push ferrule onto housing using fingers

Cable housing

3 **Slot the metal bushing** onto the cable and slide the cable head into it. Fit a ferrule to the housing, and thread the cable along it.

Dropper trigger

Cable stop and ferrule

Cable head and bushing in trigger

4 **Fit the bushing** and cable head into the trigger mechanism. Insert the ferrule on the housing into the cable stop on the trigger.

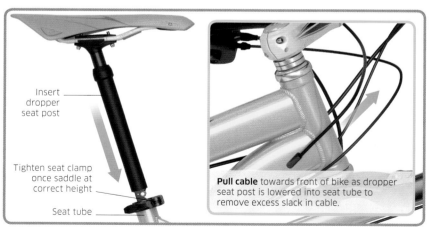

Insert dropper seat post

Tighten seat clamp once saddle at correct height

Seat tube

Pull cable towards front of bike as dropper seat post is lowered into seat tube to remove excess slack in cable.

5 **Insert the dropper seat post** into the seat tube, while pulling the control cable and housing through from the front of the frame towards the handlebar. Set the saddle to the correct ride height, with the dropper post fully extended.

Workshop tip: If your dropper post and frame have internal routing, you may need to remove the bottom bracket (BB) so that the cable can travel around the base of the seat tube (see pp.176–181).

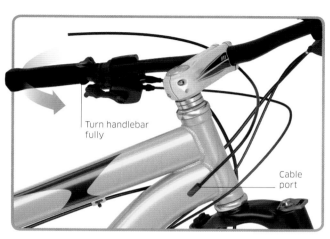

Turn handlebar fully

Cable port

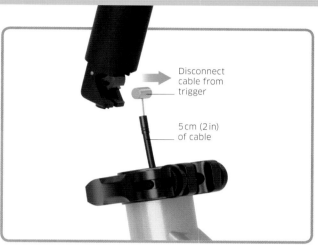

Disconnect cable from trigger

5 cm (2 in) of cable

6 **Ensure you have enough cable** and housing for the handlebar to turn fully. Turn the handlebar as far as possible from the cable port, and use a tape measure to see how much cable you need.

7 **Remove the dropper seat post** and disconnect the cable from the mechanism. Pull both the cable and housing up through the seat post until about 5 cm (2 in) protrudes from the top.

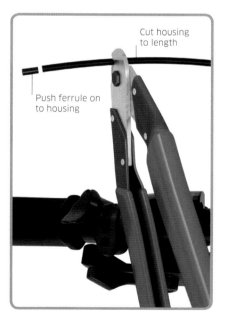

Cut housing to length

Push ferrule on to housing

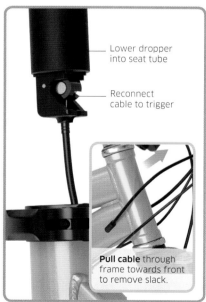

Lower dropper into seat tube

Reconnect cable to trigger

Pull cable through frame towards front to remove slack.

Adjust position of lever if required

Tension cable by pressing lever 10–12 times to bed it in, and remove slack and movement.

8 **Pull enough cable** through the housing at the seat post end, so the empty housing at the remote lever can be cut to length.

9 **Reconnect the cable** to the dropper mechanism and refit the dropper seat post to the seat tube. Set the saddle height.

10 **Fasten the cable** to the remote lever according to the manufacturer's instructions, and adjust the cable accordingly.

WHEELS

Wheels

There are multiple types of bicycle wheel available, each with different capabilities and advantages. You may want just one type of wheel, or several to use at different times, depending on the kind of riding you are doing. Take care when upgrading your wheels as they are front- and rear-specific and some are only compatible with 11-speed drivetrains.

TYPE	SUITABILITY	SPOKES
UTILITY/TOURING For everyday riding and adventure cycling, wheels need to be strong and built of durable materials. Low weight and "pro bike" looks are of secondary importance.	■ **Commuting**, or long-distance riding with luggage. ■ **Light off-road riding** on a road or hybrid bike.	■ **Stainless steel**, plain gauge, attached with hooks through flange holes and with nipples through rim eyelets. ■ **Up to 36 spokes**, with more on trekking or touring bikes.
FAST ROAD These wheels, often made with aero parts, are fitted to high-end road and race bikes. Made of carbon or aluminium alloy, they blend lightness, stiffness, and strength to enable fast, smooth road riding.	■ **Road racing,** sportives, and cyclo-cross bikes, or to complement a light bike. ■ **Hill riding,** where having lighter, faster wheels offers a serious performance advantage.	■ **Usually stainless steel**, but can be aluminium or even composite. They are aero or bladed on some models. ■ **Typically** 20–32 spokes. Radial lacing is popular on front wheels.
TRAINING ROAD Fitted as standard to many mid-price road bikes, training wheels are suitable for all types of road riding apart from racing and can be used for winter training.	■ **General road riding** and training. ■ **Regular, longer**, non-competitive, rides, as the wheels are sturdy enough for heavy usage.	■ **Stainless steel**, plain gauge, attached with hooks through flange holes and with nipples through rim eyelets. ■ **More spokes** than a lightweight wheel: usually 28–36.
MOUNTAIN BIKE These wheels are designed for tough, off-road riding conditions but some wheel types provide lightness and stiffness as well, especially when used on MTBs with suspension.	■ **Off-road cross-country** and downhill racing on mountain bikes with suspension on forks and/or the back end. ■ **Muddy** and slippery off-road conditions.	■ **Stainless steel** or aluminium, depending on quality and lightness of the build. ■ **Typically 28–32 spokes** on a standard MTB wheel, but can be as few as 24 on a lightweight type.

In addition, the axle attachments (skewer or quick-release) need to be compatible with the bike frame. Be aware that the various components of a bicycle wheel are measured in several different ways, with rim width, tyre width, and wheel diameter all affecting a tyre's performance. For simplicity, measurements here are given in the most common denomination.

RIMS

- **Aluminium,** with braking track for use with calliper brakes.
- **Mostly clincher design,** with internal reinforcement on heavy-duty versions.
- **Wider variants** will take heavy-duty and MTB tyres.

- **Alloy or carbon fibre** with eyelets for spokes.
- **Hardened brake surface** (for calliper brakes only).
- **Sections vary** from box to V.
- **Rim bed** must match the tyre: clincher, tubular, or tubeless.

- **Heavier and stronger** than lightweight versions, often with a box or shallow V section.
- **Lighter rim** with no braking track on disc-enabled wheels.
- **Mostly designed** for use with clincher tyres, but can also be used with tubeless tyres.

- **Commonly aluminium,** with no braking track on disc-braked bikes.
- **Can be carbon** on high-performance versions.
- **All MTB rims** are designed for use with either clincher or tubeless tyres.

HUBS

- **Usually** made of alloy.
- **The flange is small** with sealed or cup-and-cone bearings and a quick-release or through-axle fixing.
- **There is often a heavy-duty axle** on load-carrying bikes, especially on the rear wheel.

- **These are normally small flange** with annular bearings and a spindle with quick release.
- **Disc-enabled designs** have a threaded disc carrier or boss, and a through-axle closure of the wheel.

- **Usually made of alloy** with a spindle and quick-release skewer or a through-axle fixing to bike.
- **These may have cup-and-cone** bearings, which require greasing and correct adjustment.

- **Usually** made of alloy, with competition wheels built in carbon.
- **The flange is small** with holes or straight pull slots for spokes.
- **The axle** has a closure to fix the wheels in the bike.
- **Sealed bearings** protect against dirt.

VARIATIONS

- **Popular** in standard 700c size.
- **Also popular** in smaller 26 in size, which can take larger-volume tyres with heavier tread patterns. These wheels are more suitable for rough tracks and paths.

- **Industry standard is 700c,** with rim widths of 13–25mm (the most popular being 18/19mm).
- **Wider rims are suitable** for tyres with larger volumes ranging from 25–40mm.

- **Industry standard is 700c,** with rim widths from 13–25mm (the most popular being 18/19mm).
- **Wider rims can be used** for tyres with larger volumes ranging from 25–40mm.

- **The three most common sizes** are 29in, 26in, and 27.5in (also termed 650b).
- **The latest types** include the slightly smaller 584mm+ and 622mm+ options, some of which are interchangeable on the same bike.

Wire-spoke wheels

Wheels are your bike's contact point with the ground. When you ride over rough terrain or bumps, the tyre and rim absorb impacts and transmit these to the spokes, which flex to cushion the shock at the rim. Spokes brace the rim in relation to the hub. Some performance racing wheels feature bonded composite spokes, but most bikes have wire ones. Most spokes are made of stainless steel; the latest aero, flat, or bladed profiles can streamline and improve a bike's performance. Spokes are attached to the rim by nipples. Turning the nipple alters the spoke tension and the alignment of the rim.

⚙ PARTS FOCUS

A wheel comprises a hub, spokes, a rim, and a tyre. Rear wheels have more spokes than front wheels, as they power the drivetrain.

① The **wheel hub** supports the spokes. It transmits motion through the spokes to the rim, so is under significant load when moving.

② **Wheel rims** are made of alloy or carbon, and have a recess to hold the tyre. There are several depths and designs for different riding styles.

③ The side edge of the rim provides a **braking surface** for bikes with rim brakes. If it is worn, you should replace the wheel (see pp.78–83).

④ The **spokes** may be "laced" in various patterns, such as radial, crossed, or mixed, for strength and to absorb braking and acceleration forces.

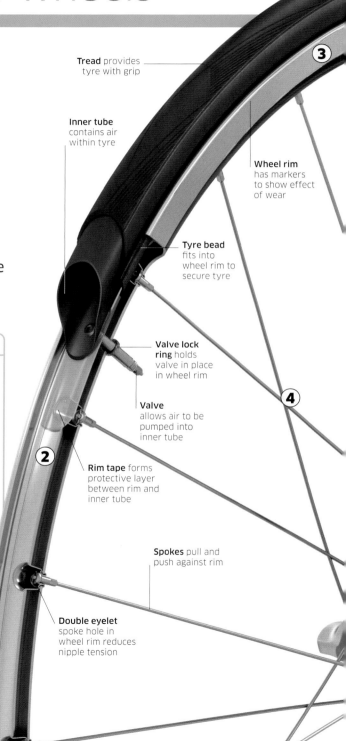

Tread provides tyre with grip

③

Inner tube contains air within tyre

Wheel rim has markers to show effect of wear

Tyre bead fits into wheel rim to secure tyre

Valve lock ring holds valve in place in wheel rim

④

Valve allows air to be pumped into inner tube

②

Rim tape forms protective layer between rim and inner tube

Spokes pull and push against rim

Double eyelet spoke hole in wheel rim reduces nipple tension

Spoke nipple
connects spoke to rim and allows spoke tension to be adjusted

SPOKE EYELETS

Steel eyelets are used on aluminium rims to reinforce the spoke hole and prevent the spoke pulling through.

Steel eyelet

Spoke

Spoke nipple
held in eyelet

Front forks
connect wheel to frame

Tyre provides contact point between wheel and road or track

Quick-release lever enables wheel to be removed without tools

Flange is point where spokes attach to hub

①

Quick-release front wheels

It is often necessary to detach a front wheel to transport a bike, or repair a puncture. Most modern bikes have quick-release wheels, which can be removed without tools. Wheels on older bikes sometimes have conventional bolts, which can be undone using a spanner.

BEFORE YOU START

- Secure your bike in a frame stand
- Check whether there is any rust or corrosion on the quick-release lever; if so, spray around the area with oil

Brake calliper

1 **Loosen the front brake** using the quick-release tab on the brake calliper. This widens the gap between the pads, so the tyre can pass through. (Campagnolo callipers are released via a button on the gear-shifter.)

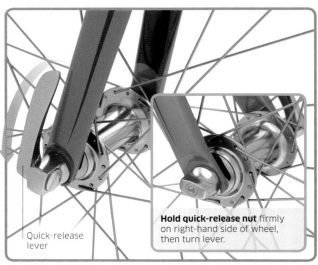

Quick-release lever

Hold quick-release nut firmly on right-hand side of wheel, then turn lever.

2 **Locate the quick-release lever** on the wheel hub, if fitted. Open the lever and gradually unscrew it, but do not remove the nut fully. If bolts are fitted, unscrew on both sides using a spanner.

Front forks

3 **Lift up the frame** and push the wheel out and away from the front forks. If the wheel does not drop out, undo the quick-release lever or bolts a little more without fully loosening.

Workshop tip: If you need to detach both wheels from your bike, take off the front one first. This will help you to avoid dragging the chain or bashing the rear derailleur on the ground.

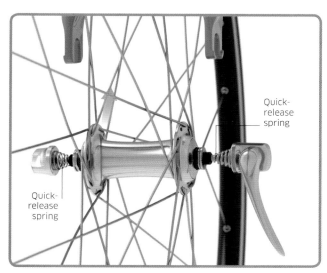

Quick-release spring

Quick-release spring

Press firmly to close lever tightly

4 **To refit your front wheel**, check that the springs are in place on both sides of the quick-release mechanism, and that the lever is on the left-hand side of the bike. Lower the forks onto the wheel.

5 **Place the wheel** on the floor, using the weight of the bike to keep it straight. Hold the nut, and tighten the quick-release mechanism. For older bikes, tighten both wheel bolts.

Return brake pads to original position

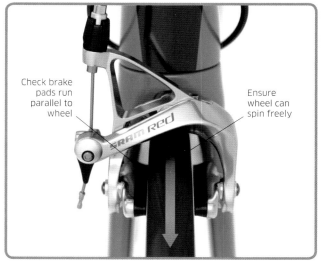

Check brake pads run parallel to wheel

Ensure wheel can spin freely

6 **Close the quick-release tab** (or press the button on the lever if you have Campagnolo brakes). Ensure that the brake pads are correctly positioned on the rim.

7 **Stand in front of your bike** with the front wheel between your knees and check that it is centred between the brake pads. If it is not, undo the quick-release and repeat steps 3–7 to refit the wheel.

▶ REMOVING AND REFITTING A WHEEL
Wheels with a cassette

Removing and refitting a rear wheel involves releasing and reattaching the chain from the rear hub. This task requires more care on bikes with a cassette and rear derailleur (mech), as these are vital components of the drivetrain. It is a simple process, only taking a few minutes, especially if the wheel has a quick-release mechanism.

BEFORE YOU START

- Spray the lever with oil if there is rust or corrosion
- Shift the chain into the largest chainring at the front
- Shift the chain onto the smallest rear cog
- Secure your bike in a frame stand

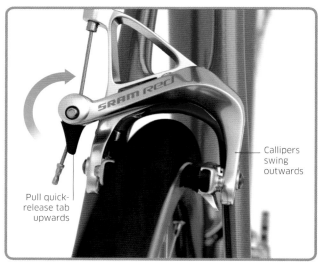

Callipers swing outwards

Pull quick-release tab upwards

2 **Locate the quick-release tab** on the rear brake calliper or on the lever hood, and pull it upwards to open it. Once released, the callipers will widen, letting the wheel pass easily between the brake pads.

Push quick-release lever downwards

1 **Loosen the rear wheel**, holding the quick-release nut on the non-drive (left) side with one hand. With your other hand, rotate the quick-release lever 180°, opening the mechanism.

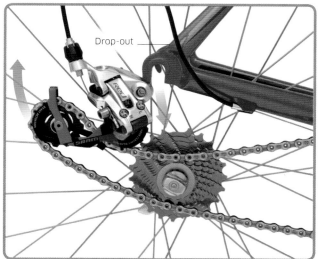

Drop-out

3 **Hold the rear derailleur** in your hand, and pull it backwards and upwards. The wheel should come free from the drop-outs. If not, turn the quick-release lever one more turn and repeat until it does.

Workshop tip: Some quick-release systems have a locking mechanism for security reasons. Both sides tighten together and connect through a hollow axle. Always keep the appropriate keys packed with your puncture repair kit in case of a puncture.

Free chain from cassette

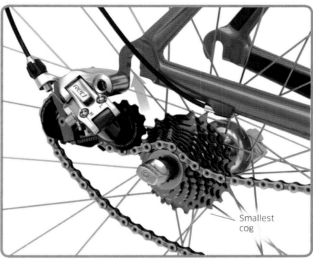

Smallest cog

4 **Lift the frame** up by the saddle or the top tube, allowing the rear wheel to move forward slightly. Carefully guide the cassette away from the chain. If the chain sticks to the cassette, lift it away by hand.

5 **To refit the rear wheel**, ensure the rear derailleur is shifted into the highest gear. Guide the wheel into position, allowing the chain to sit on top of the smallest cog, and lower the frame.

Rotate quick-release lever upwards

Close quick-release tab

Wheel should spin freely

6 **Pull the wheel** upwards and backwards, slotting it into the drop-outs. Make sure the wheel is centred in the frame.

7 **Close the quick-release lever** to secure the rear wheel. The tension should be the same as before – firm but not too tight.

8 **Close up the brake pads** using the tab on the calliper or the button on the lever hood. Spin the wheel to check the pads are aligned.

Wheels with a hub gear

Hub gears mainly feature on commuting and utility bikes, and also on some mountain bikes. In order to remove the rear wheel with the hub gear from the frame, you will first need to disconnect the hub from the brake cable.

BEFORE YOU START

- Clean any dirt from around the hub gear
- Make a note of any washers
- Ensure that the gear cable is in good condition
- Secure your bike in a frame stand

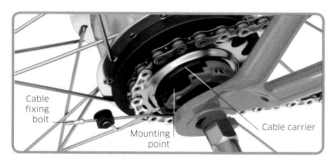

Cable fixing bolt

Mounting point

Cable carrier

2 **Holding the cable carrier** in position with the Allen key, use your free hand to remove the cable fixing bolt from the mounting point on the cable carrier. If it is tight, ease it out using pliers.

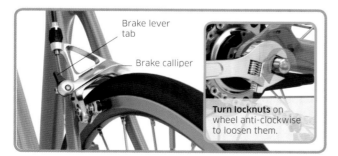

Brake lever tab

Brake calliper

Turn locknuts on wheel anti-clockwise to loosen them.

4 **Open the rear brake callipers** according to the type fitted on your bike (see pp.112–117). Loosen the locknuts on the wheel using a spanner, but do not remove them from the wheel entirely.

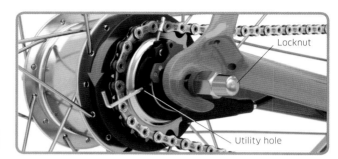

Locknut

Utility hole

1 **Using the gear-shifter**, set the hub into first gear. Locate the "utility hole" on the cable carrier on the hub and insert an Allen key. Use the Allen key to rotate the carrier, so that the gear cable becomes slack.

Hub gear

Housing stop

Cable housing

3 **Pull the cable** around to the front of the hub, then free the end of the cable housing from the housing stop on the hub gear. Move the cable away from the rear wheel.

Rear drop-out

Rear hub

Locknut

5 **Ease the wheel** out of the rear drop-outs, and lift the chain from the rear hub. Rest the chain on the frame. Holding the wheel with one hand, lift the frame away from it.

Workshop tip: When retightening the wheel locknuts, use a tool that you can take with you out on the road. You will then be able to adjust the wheel if necessary when cycling.

Rear drop-out

Tighten locknut with spanner

Coloured washer

6 **Refit the wheel** by guiding the axle back into the rear drop-outs, ensuring that the coloured washers sit outside the frame. Lift the chain back onto the hub, then half tighten the wheel locknuts.

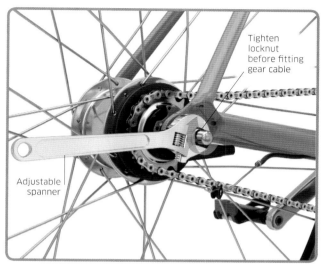

Tighten locknut before fitting gear cable

Adjustable spanner

7 **Align the wheel** so that it rotates centrally within the frame, and position it so that the chain is fully engaged on the hub. Secure the locknuts using a spanner, making them as tight as possible.

Rotate cable carrier with Allen key

8 **Refit the gear cable** by securing the housing into the housing stop. Rotate the cable carrier towards the housing stop, then insert the cable fixing bolt into the mounting point (reversing steps 1–3).

Engage brake callipers once wheel is in place

9 **Ensure the wheel spins** evenly and re-engage the brake callipers according to the type you have. Test the gears to check they shift cleanly. If they do not, you will need to adjust them (see pp.152–153).

Clincher tyres

Flat tyres are caused by air leaking from the inner tube, either because of "pinch flat" – the tube being pinched – or because a sharp object has pierced the tube. You should also replace your tyres if the top section is worn or if threads appear on the side wall.

BEFORE YOU START

- Remove the wheel from your bike, (see pp.78–83)
- Remove the old tyre (see pp. 48–49)
- Unfold the new tyre and push it into shape
- Check that the inner tube is in good condition and the valve is not bent
- Check that the rim tape is in good condition; replace it if not
- Ensure that the tyre is the right width and size for the wheel

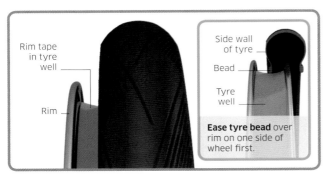

Rim tape in tyre well

Rim

Side wall of tyre

Bead

Tyre well

Ease tyre bead over rim on one side of wheel first.

1 **Fit the first side** of the tyre onto the wheel, pushing the bead over the rim on one side, and working it round the wheel with your hands. If it feels tight use a tyre lever to hook the bead onto the rim.

Ensure tyre is fitted all way around

Rim

Bead against rim

Fitting one side of tyre creates void for inner tube.

2 **Ease the tyre** across the well, pushing the bead to the far edge of the rim, thereby creating space for the inner tube. Rotate the tyre, pushing the tyre across fully around the wheel.

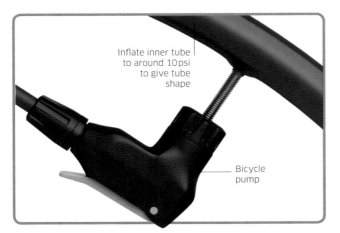

Inflate inner tube to around 10 psi to give tube shape

Bicycle pump

3 **Remove the valve cap** and retaining nut from the inner tube, and partially inflate it just enough so that it takes its shape. Do not over-inflate the tube, as you will struggle to feed it into the tyre.

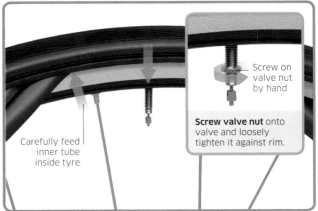

Carefully feed inner tube inside tyre

Screw on valve nut by hand

Screw valve nut onto valve and loosely tighten it against rim.

4 **Insert the inner-tube valve** through the valve hole in the rim, so that it sits straight. Working away from the valve on both sides, ease a small section of tube into the tyre, then fit the valve nut.

TOOLS AND EQUIPMENT

- Rim tape
- Tyre lever
- Bicycle pump

Workshop tip: Try to finish fitting the tyre opposite the valve, as this provides more tyre material to help lever the bead over the wheel rim edge.

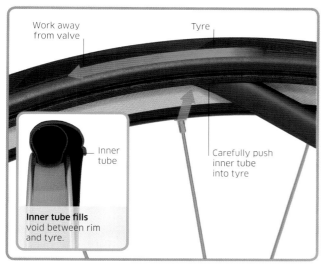

Work away from valve

Tyre

Inner tube

Inner tube fills void between rim and tyre.

Carefully push inner tube into tyre

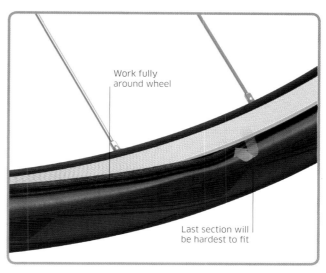

Work fully around wheel

Last section will be hardest to fit

5 **Keep working from the valve**, in both directions, tucking the inner tube inside the tyre, so that it sits in the well between the tyre and the rim. Ensure the inner tube is not twisted or kinked at any point.

6 **Roll the second bead** of the tyre over the rim, making sure it does not pinch or twist the inner tube. If the tyre is too tight to fit by hand, carefully use tyre levers. Deflate the inner tube.

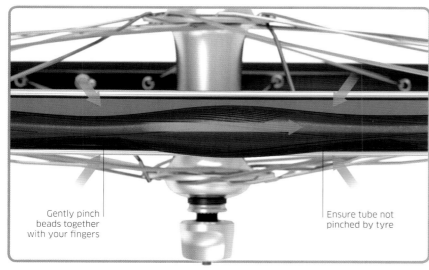

Gently pinch beads together with your fingers

Ensure tube not pinched by tyre

7 **Once the tyre is fitted**, squeeze the tyre beads together to expose the rim tape, and check that the inner tube is not pinched between the rim and the bead – which could cause a "pinch flat". If the tube is pinched anywhere, carefully wiggle the tyre to release the trapped tube.

8 **Inflate the tyre** to the correct pressure – which is usually printed on the tyre – and refit the wheel to the bike (see pp.78–83).

Tubeless tyres

Tubeless tyres, often fitted to mountain bikes, fit firmly against the wheel rim without an inner tube, reducing the risk of punctures. If the tyre is cut, sealant in the tyre instantly dries around the hole, which prevents the tyre from deflating.

 BEFORE YOU START

- Ensure that the wheel and tyres are tubeless-compatible
- Unfold the new tyre and push it into shape
- Remove the wheel from the bike (see pp.78–83)
- Remove the tyre from the wheel (see pp.48–49)

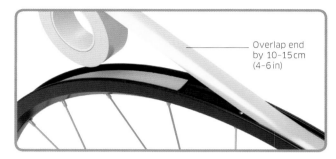

Overlap end by 10–15 cm (4–6 in)

2 **Apply tubeless rim tape** to the well of the wheel, covering the spoke holes and the valve hole. Apply even tension to the tape, ensuring that it comes up to the edges, and is free of wrinkles.

Locate position of valve hole

Valve hole

3 **Locate the valve hole** and carefully pierce the tape with a craft knife, or similar sharp object, so that the valve can be pushed through. Make sure that you do not make the hole too large.

Clean thoroughly with alcohol-based cleaner

1 **If the wheel is tubeless-compatible**, move directly onto step 5. If not, remove any existing rim tape, and clean away any sticky residue and grease on the rim using an alcohol-based cleaner.

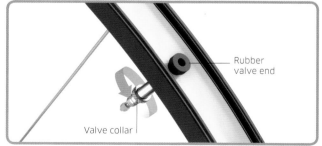

Rubber valve end

Valve collar

4 **Remove the valve collar**, push the valve through the hole, and secure the rubber end to the rim tape. Refit and tighten the valve collar on the inside of the wheel until it is secure against the rim.

Workshop tip: After adding sealant and inflating the tyre, cover the wheel and valve stem area in soapy water. Wait for 10–20 seconds, then check the tyre for any places where the soapy water bubbles. Bubbling means that the tyre is leaking.

Squeeze tyre onto rim with fingers

Tyre bead

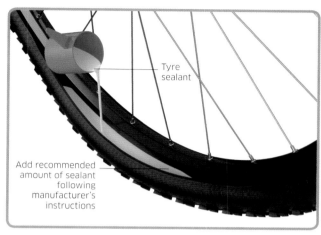

Tyre sealant

Add recommended amount of sealant following manufacturer's instructions

5 **Mount the tubeless tyre** to the rim by hand – using tyre levers may damage the tape. Once fitted, inflate the tyre to 100 psi, and soak the rim with warm, soapy water to help identify any leaks.

6 **To seal the tyre**, first deflate it fully by releasing the air valve. Then, using your fingers, prise a small section of the tyre from the rim on one side. Pour tyre sealant into the gap.

Rotate tyre once closed

Squeeze tyre closed

Inflate tyre with pump or air-compressor

Tyre will snap into rim as it inflates

7 **Close the tyre** up again using your fingers, then rotate the wheel several times to spread the sealant inside.

8 **Inflate the tyre** to 90 psi using a pump or compressor, then hang up the wheel with the valve in the eight o'clock position to set.

🔍 VARIATIONS

Certain brands of sealant can be injected directly into the tyre via the valve using a syringe.

- Follow steps 1–5 to fit the tyre, then deflate it fully.

- Following the instructions provided, fill the syringe with the recommended amount of sealant.

- Attach the end of the syringe to the opened tyre valve and inject the sealant into the tyre. Rotate the tyre to spread the sealant.

- Detach the syringe and inflate the tyre (see step 8).

Tightening loose spokes

Over time, the spokes on your bike's wheels can become slack, causing the wheels to lose shape. "Truing", or straightening wheels, is achieved by adjusting the tension of the spokes on either side of the rim. Even spoke tension is key to the strength and integrity of a wheel. You can adjust spoke tension by tightening or loosening the spoke nipples adjacent to the wheel rim.

BEFORE YOU START

- Secure your bike in a frame stand so that you can spin the wheel freely
- Ensure that you have the correct size spoke key

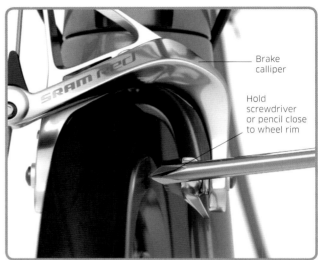

Brake calliper

Hold screwdriver or pencil close to wheel rim

2 **Rest a screwdriver** or pencil against the brake calliper and spin the wheel. Note the areas where the rim touches the tool and mark the rim using a piece of chalk. Repeat on the other side of the rim.

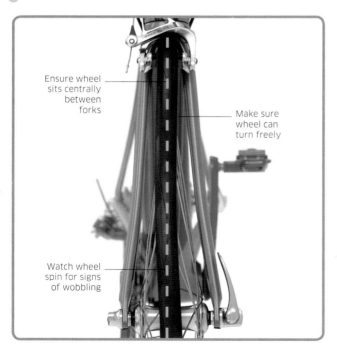

Ensure wheel sits centrally between forks

Make sure wheel can turn freely

Watch wheel spin for signs of wobbling

1 **Stand in front** of the wheel and check that it is centred between the forks. Adjust it if necessary (see pp.78–79). Spin the wheel and, watching from the front, check if it wobbles from side to side.

Loose spokes flex easily

3 **Press the spokes** nearest to the chalk marks to identify any that feel more slack than the others. Spokes on opposing sides of the rim counter the pull of each other, so you will need to adjust both sides.

Workshop tip: If you find some of the nipples on the spokes are hard to turn, do not force them, as the spoke could snap. Spray them with penetrating oil, wait for a few minutes, then try again. Repeat if necessary.

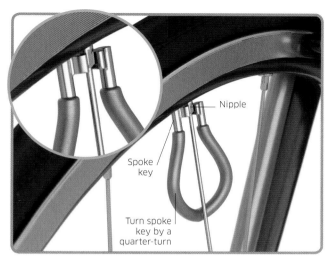

Nipple

Spoke key

Turn spoke key by a quarter-turn

Spin wheel

4 **If the wheel wobbles** to one side when spun, loosen the spoke nipple on that side by turning it clockwise, and tighten the loose spoke on the opposite side of the rim by turning the nipple anti-clockwise.

5 **Using the screwdriver** or pencil, spin the wheel to check for any further wobble. Adjust 2–3 spokes at a time to avoid uneven tension. Work around the wheel, loosening and tightening.

Turn nipple with spoke key

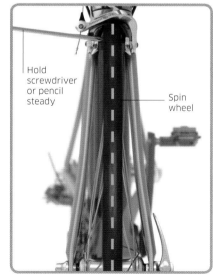

Hold screwdriver or pencil steady

Spin wheel

CHECK THE WHEEL

It is important that you hold the screwdriver or pencil still when checking the trueness of a wheel. If it moves while the wheel is turning, you will not be able to assess where it deviates from true. If you cannot hold it steady, try the following:

- Securely attach the screwdriver or pencil to the brake calliper using a rubber band. You will have to reattach it each time you retest the wheel.

- Attach a wire tie to the calliper, pulling it tight. Cut the end so it just avoids the rim. This, too, will need refitting later.

6 **Turn the spoke key** in very small increments. Any adjustment, however slight, will affect the rest of the wheel.

7 **With your screwdriver** or pencil in place, check to ensure that the wheel is running straight. Readjust as required.

Wheel hubs

The hub, at the centre of your bike's wheel, consists of an axle, shell, and flange. The axle is secured to the frame at the drop-outs. The hub shell contains bearings, which allow it to rotate around the axle. The flange at each end of the axle has holes drilled to hold the spokes. The number of spoke holes on the hub corresponds with the number of them on the wheel rim. Hubs traditionally have 28, 32, or 36 spoke holes. The higher the number of spokes, the stronger the wheel is, although it will also be heavier. Hubs may be made from steel, machined alloy, or carbon fibre. High-quality hubs use cartridge bearings and additional seals, to keep them running more smoothly for longer.

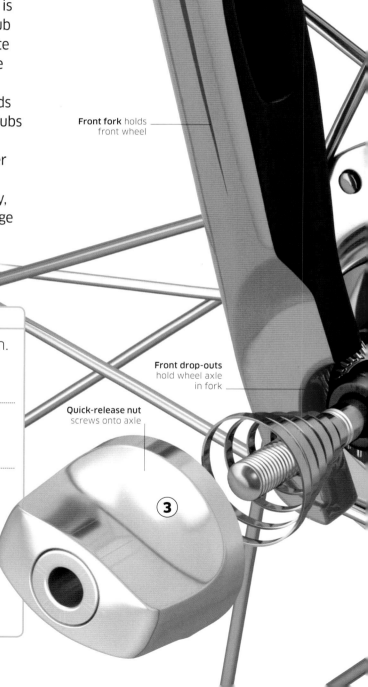

Front fork holds
front wheel

Front drop-outs
hold wheel axle
in fork

Quick-release nut
screws onto axle

③

PARTS FOCUS

The wheel hub enables the wheel to turn. It is fixed to the frame at the axle, and connects to the rim via the spokes.

① The **axle** passes through the wheel hub. It has threaded ends onto which the cone nut and locknuts are screwed to hold it in place.

② The **bearings** inside the hub shell allow the wheel to rotate freely. They may sit inside a sealed cartridge or be loose within the bearing races. You should service hub bearings regularly (see pp.92–95).

③ The **quick-release mechanism**, passing through the centre of the axle, allows you to remove the wheel quickly without tools.

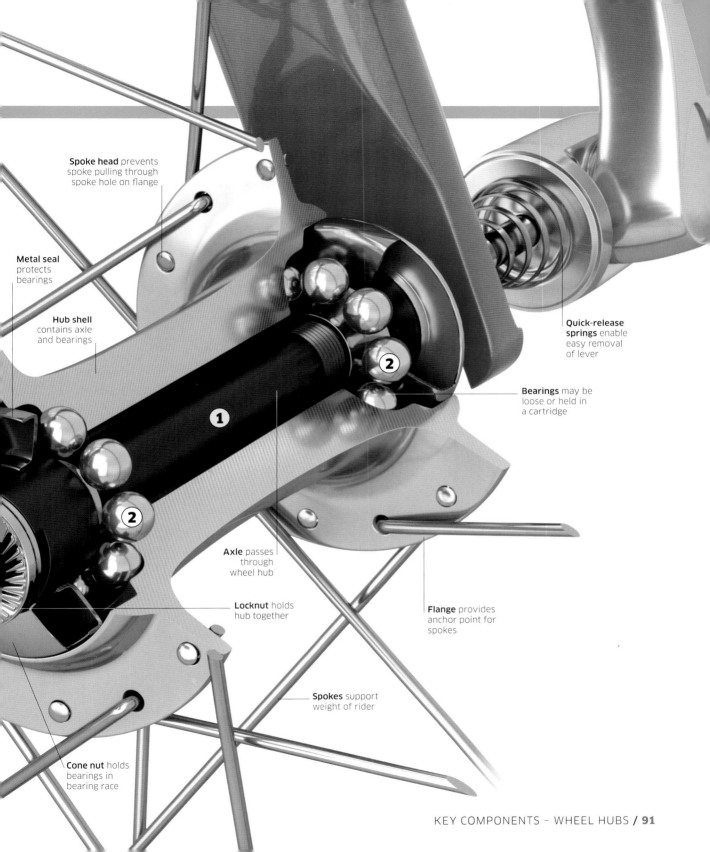

Spoke head prevents spoke pulling through spoke hole on flange

Metal seal protects bearings

Hub shell contains axle and bearings

Quick-release springs enable easy removal of lever

Bearings may be loose or held in a cartridge

Axle passes through wheel hub

Locknut holds hub together

Flange provides anchor point for spokes

Spokes support weight of rider

Cone nut holds bearings in bearing race

▶ **SERVICING A WHEEL BEARING**
Press-fit cartridge-types

The wheel bearings are often contained within cartridges that need specialist tools to replace. The bearings can be serviced, however, and you should do this regularly to prevent wear, and to prolong their life. Servicing a hub cartridge involves cleaning and re-greasing the bearings. A press-fit hub is simply held closed by the forks, and should pop open when removed. The telltale sign that your bearings need attention is when your bike's wheels feel rough when cycling, or make a rumbling or grinding noise.

Quick-release mechanism

 BEFORE YOU START

- Prepare a clear space where you can lay out the parts
- Secure your bike in a frame stand

1 **Remove the wheel** from your bike (see pp.78–83) by opening the quick-release lever or loosening the retaining bolts. Relax the brake callipers and ease the wheel from the frame.

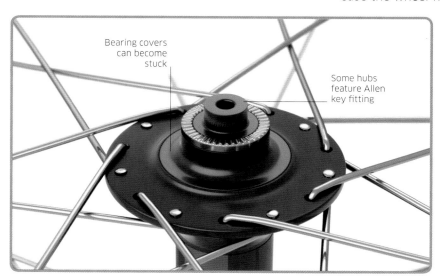

Bearing covers can become stuck

Some hubs feature Allen key fitting

2 **When the wheel is clear of the forks**, pop off the press-fit bearing cover. If it is stuck, carefully prise it away with a flat-head screwdriver. (Some bearing covers have an Allen key fitting – for these, use an Allen key to twist the covers off, rather than unscrew them.)

3 **Lift off the bearing cover** to reveal the protective dust seal over the cartridge bearing. Clean the cover before replacing it later.

Workshop tip: If you are unsure whether the bearings in your wheel hubs need servicing, spin each wheel while resting your ear on the saddle, as any noise from the wheel hub will be amplified through the bike frame.

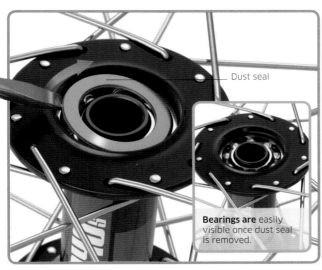

Dust seal

Bearings are easily visible once dust seal is removed.

4 **Use a thin-bladed tool**, such as a screwdriver, to pry off the seal to expose the bearings. Take care not to damage the edge of the seal, as this could make it less effective when refitted.

PARTS FOCUS

A typical press-fit hub with cartridge bearings has a bearing cover at each end, held in place by compression.

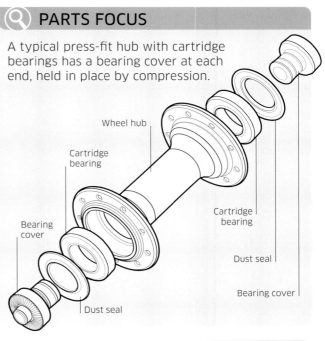

Wheel hub

Cartridge bearing

Bearing cover

Dust seal

Cartridge bearing

Dust seal

Bearing cover

Straw of degreaser can

5 **Flush the bearings** with degreaser, rotating them as you do so. Clean away any old grease and dirt with a cloth.

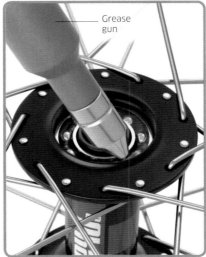

Grease gun

6 **Once the cartridge is** dry, lightly coat the bearings, with fresh grease. Replace the protective dust seal.

7 **Replace the bearing cover**, and repeat steps 2–6 on the other side of the hub. Refit the wheel, checking that it spins freely.

▶ SERVICING A WHEEL BEARING
Cup-and-cone types

A rumbling or slow spinning wheel, and play at the axle, are signs that the bearings are worn. Replacing your hub bearings once a year will ensure a longer life for your hub and wheel. There are many brands of bearing, all of which are fitted in similar ways.

BEFORE YOU START

- Refer to your owner's manual to check which type of hub your bike has
- Select the correct size of cone spanner for the hub
- Source the right size of replacement bearings
- Release the front brake callipers (see pp.112–117)

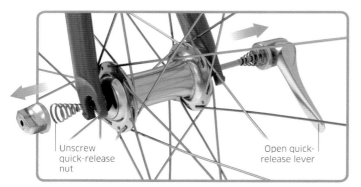

Unscrew quick-release nut

Open quick-release lever

1 **Remove the front wheel** from the bike by either opening the quick-release mechanism (see pp.78–79) or loosening the retaining nuts with a spanner. Lay the wheel on a flat surface.

Locknut

Cone nut

2 **Holding the cone nut** in place with one cone spanner, unscrew the locknut with a second. Remove the locknut, and any washers and spacers, noting the order in which they were removed.

Seal protects bearings

3 **With the locknut removed,** fully unscrew the cone nut to expose the bearing seal that protects the bearings inside.

Remove axle to access bearings

4 **Leaving the cone** on the other end of the axle in place, draw the axle through the hub and remove it completely.

Remove bearing seal

5 **Check if the bearing seal** can be prised out to access the bearings. If so, carefully ease it out with a flat-head screwdriver.

TOOLS AND EQUIPMENT

- Cone spanners
- Flat-head screwdriver
- Magnet
- Degreaser
- Cleaning cloth
- Grease
- Tweezers

PARTS FOCUS

Wheel bearings consist of similar components, regardless of brand.

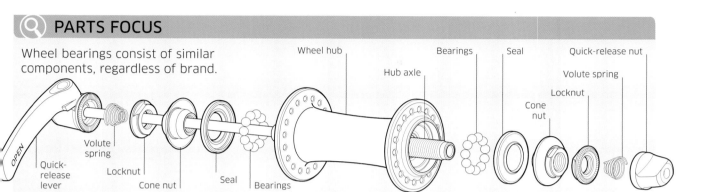

Wheel hub · Bearings · Seal · Quick-release nut · Hub axle · Volute spring · Locknut · Cone nut · Quick-release lever · Volute spring · Locknut · Cone nut · Seal · Bearings

Clean inside hub with a cloth and degreaser. Check for wear and damage.

6 **If the bearing seal cannot be removed**, lift out the bearings using a magnet. Count how many there are and place them in a container. Repeat this for the bearings on the other side of the hub axle.

Bearings · Grease

7 **Grease one of the bearing surfaces**, then replace the bearings using tweezers – fitting the same number as you removed. Turn the wheel over and repeat the process on the other end of the axle.

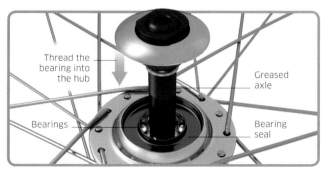

Thread the bearing into the hub · Greased axle · Bearings · Bearing seal

8 **Rethread the axle** through the hub and refit any spacers or washers in the correct order – take care not to dislodge any of the bearings. Refit the cone nut, tightening it with your fingers.

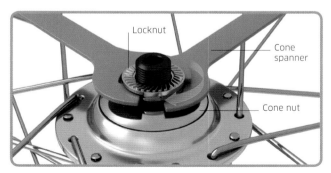

Locknut · Cone spanner · Cone nut

9 **Using two spanners**, reverse the process in step 2, tightening the locknut against the cone nut. Do not tighten the cone nut itself again – this will prevent the wheel from turning freely and can crush the bearings.

BRAKES

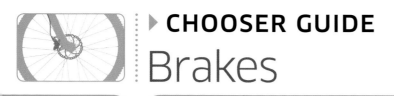

Brakes

All brake systems work in broadly the same way: when activated, brake pads push against part of the wheel surface to create friction and slow the bike. The pressure is applied either at the rim of the wheel (dual-pivot, cantilever, centre-pull, V-brake) or at the hub (disc brake). Although their basic function is the same, the various brake systems have different strengths

TYPE	SUITABILITY	OPERATION
DUAL-PIVOT The most popular cable-operated brake, dual-pivot brakes have been in use for over 45 years. Dual-pivot systems are reliable and lightweight; in particular, they are lighter than disc brakes.	■ **Road cycling**, from racing to sportives and training. ■ **Lightweight** road bikes. ■ **Use in warm, dry** conditions. ■ **Limited tyre clearance** rules out use on off-road bikes.	■ **The cable pulls up** on the arm of the calliper to bring the brake pads into contact with the rim of the wheel. ■ **Modern dual-pivot brakes** exert more pressure than traditional single-pivot designs.
DISC Universally adopted for mountain biking, disc brakes are increasingly popular on road bikes. High-quality systems often have hydraulically operated brakes, while budget disc brakes use simpler cable operation.	■ **Both off-road and road bikes**, especially in wet or muddy conditions or for use in carrying loads. ■ **Cyclo-cross** or gravel riding. ■ **Use in winter** or poor weather.	■ **At the wheel hub**, pistons on one or both sides of the wheel push the brake pads onto a disc. ■ **Activation is either** by cable (mechanical systems) or by hydraulic pressure from fluid in a hose connected to the brake lever.
V-BRAKE Often fitted to hybrids, utility bikes, tandems, and older mountain bikes, V- or linear-pull brakes give lots of power. Specialist versions are also used on road and TT bikes.	■ **A wide range of uses**, including on commuter and utility bikes, mountain bikes, and tandems, as the long calliper arms produce considerable leverage and stopping power, and good feel. ■ **Off-road riding** as the long arms allow fitting of fat tyres.	■ **The two long, spring-loaded** calliper arms are mounted on the metal bosses on the fork, and act on the rim. ■ **When the brake is applied**, the cable housing pushes one arm while the inner cable, running above the tyre, pulls the other.
CANTILEVER/CENTRE-PULL Cantilever systems are derived from a brake design that has been in use for nearly 100 years. They are popular with cyclo-cross riders due to their simplicity and low weight, and because they allow large tyre clearances.	■ **Cyclo-cross race bikes**, where they remain popular despite the increasing availability and effectiveness of disc brakes. ■ **Touring bikes**, as they allow for the use of large tyres.	■ **Cantilever and centre-pull brakes** operate on the same principle: of a transverse "straddle" wire pulling upwards on a pair of calliper arms. ■ **Both types operate via cables** running to brake levers on the handlebar.

and weaknesses. A disc brake provides almost immediate stopping power, but will weight your bike down more than a dual-pivot. Similarly, V-brakes can be very powerful, but there is a risk you might flip the bike if used too suddenly when riding at very high speed. Also consider that some systems, like hydraulic disc brakes, may require maintenance more regularly.

KEY COMPONENTS

- **Dual-pivots consist of** callipers, brake blocks, barrel adjusters, and a quick-release lever.
- **Cables connect to** brake levers attached to the handlebar.

- **Discs or rotors** that attach to the wheel hubs.
- **Callipers**, which operate the discs.
- **Cables or hydraulic hoses** that run back to the brake levers.

- **Calliper arms that are** fixed to the upper forks at the front and to the rear stays at the back.
- **Cables,** which are activated by flat bar levers.
- **A quick-release lever** for the "noodle" over the arms.

- **Cantilever brakes that** have arms fixed to bosses on the fork, and a "yoke" or link wire.
- **Centre-pull brakes** that have crossed arms connecting to a central mount above the wheel.

POSITION

- **The front brake** is normally attached to the fork crown and the rear to a brake bridge in the rear stays.
- **A threaded stud** in the back of the brake is secured with a flush-fit Allen bolt.

- **Discs are located** in the centre of one side of the wheel.
- **The callipers are fixed** to the lower end of one fork leg on the front wheel, and to the rear triangle of the seat and chainstays on the rear wheel.

- **V-brakes are normally** sited at the top of the forks in front, and high on the seat stays at the rear.
- **"Aero" types** lie flush with the fork legs at the front. On rear brakes, they lie behind the bottom bracket.

- **Cantilever brakes** can only be fitted to bikes with permanently-attached threaded bosses on the top of the front fork legs and high up on the rear stays.
- **Centre-pull brakes** are attached using a centre bolt on the fork crown and seat stay bridge.

ADJUSTMENTS

- **Brake blocks can be moved in or out** with the barrel adjuster.
- **Dual-pivot brakes** can be centred using a recessed screw in the calliper.
- **The angle of the blocks** can be adjusted on a dished washer.

- **Hydraulic disc brakes** do not normally need adjusting; the pistons in the calliper will automatically keep the pads close to the disc.
- **Mechanical disc brake pads** may need to be moved closer to the rotor as they wear.

- **The lever arms** can be moved in and out using a small adjustment screw on the spring where the lever arm is attached to the boss.
- **The quick-release lever** on top of the cable disengages one lever arm completely.

- **The brakes are adjusted** either at the bolts holding the arms or (on centre-pull brakes) at the stirrup linking the brake cable to the straddle wire.
- **Fine tuning** is offered on some cantilevers via a grub screw on the arm itself.

Rim brakes

Rim brakes engage rubber pads against the sides of the wheel rim to create friction and slow your bike. When you pull the brake lever, the brake cable comes under tension, pulling the brake arms into position, while a powerful spring returns the brake arms to the open position when you release the brake lever. Most modern road bikes use dual-pivot callipers, which exert higher pressure than single-pivot callipers. Cantilever and V-brake callipers have pairs of independent arms. You will see them on mountain, cyclo-cross, and touring bikes, as they offer greater stopping power and tyre clearance.

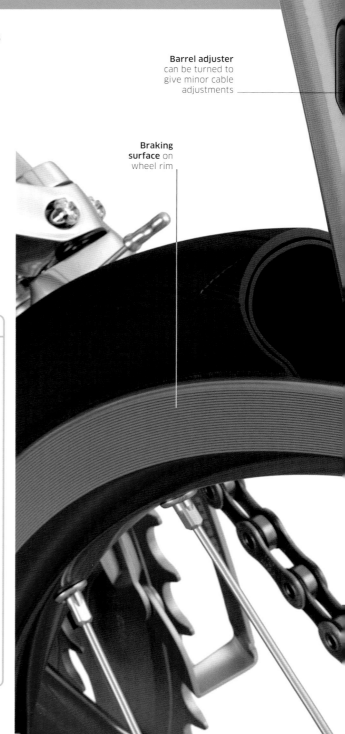

Barrel adjuster can be turned to give minor cable adjustments

Braking surface on wheel rim

PARTS FOCUS

Rim brakes may be twin-armed callipers that rotate around a dual or single pivot, or may have brake arms mounted on the fork legs.

(1) The **brake pads** press onto the rim to slow the wheel. They are made of rubber-based compounds; specific types are used for carbon or ceramic rims.

(2) Brake callipers are mounted on **pivot points** that allow the arms to move and provide leverage. Modern systems feature two pivots.

(3) The **brake arms** press the brake pads onto the braking surface. There are different types of mechanism to suit road and off-road bikes.

(4) Single- and dual-pivot brakes have a single calliper **mounting bolt** on the frame. Cantilever and V-brakes have one bolt for each calliper arm.

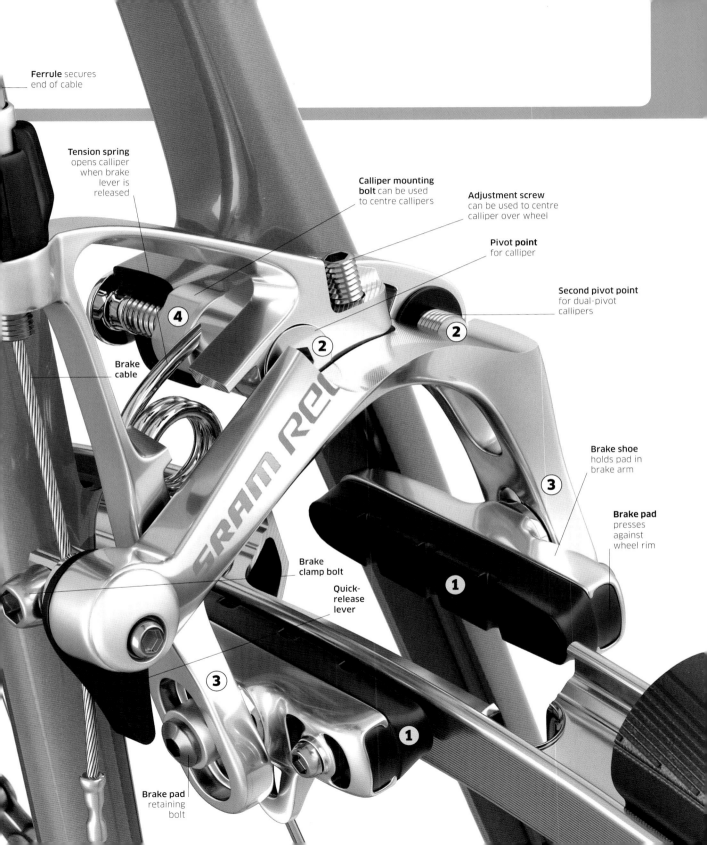

Ferrule secures end of cable

Tension spring opens calliper when brake lever is released

Calliper mounting bolt can be used to centre callipers

Adjustment screw can be used to centre calliper over wheel

Pivot point for calliper

Second pivot point for dual-pivot callipers

4

Brake cable

2

2

Brake shoe holds pad in brake arm

3

Brake pad presses against wheel rim

SRAM RE

1

Brake clamp bolt

Quick-release lever

3

1

Brake pad retaining bolt

Drop handlebars

Brake cables wear and stretch over time, reducing the power of your brakes. When correctly fitted, the cables should allow you to turn your handlebar fully in each direction, and to brake firmly with no looseness or judder as you pull the lever.

🔧 BEFORE YOU START

- Refer to your owner's manual to check the correct torque settings of your bike's cable clamp bolts
- Check the existing cable routing for incorrectly sized sections
- Make a note of the existing cable routing
- Source the correct cables for your bike

Cable clamp bolt

Cable end cap

1 **Using cable cutters** cleanly snip the end cap off the existing cable, so the cut end pulls through the cable clamp easily.

2 **Undo the quick-release** lever and unscrew the cable clamp on the brake calliper with an Allen key. Pull the cable free.

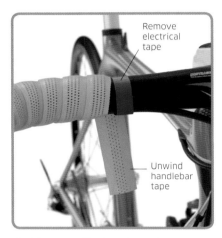

Remove electrical tape

Unwind handlebar tape

3 **Unwrap the bar tape** to expose the cable housing. Release the cables from the bar by cutting the cable tape with a craft knife.

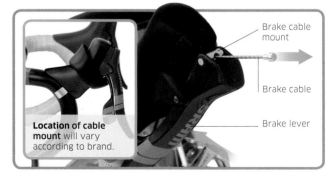

Brake cable mount

Brake cable

Brake lever

Location of cable mount will vary according to brand.

4 **Squeeze the brake lever** to expose the cable mount, and pull the end of the cable out using pliers. You may need to fold the rear hood of the brake levers forward to access the cable.

Free housing from frame mounts

5 **Pull the cable** completely free from the bike, working towards the levers. Remove each length of housing, making a note of where each piece came from, and where each end was located.

Workshop tip: Lubricating cable inners during installation protects them from water and rust, and keeps them running smoothly for longer. Dab some dry lube between your finger and thumb, and gently pull the cable through your fingers to coat it.

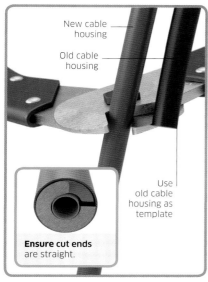

New cable housing

Old cable housing

Use old cable housing as template

Ensure cut ends are straight.

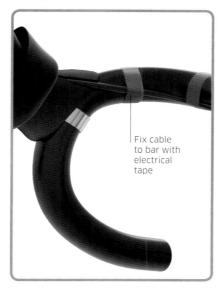

Fix cable to bar with electrical tape

Cable mount

Squeeze lever to reveal cable mount

6 **Cut new lengths** of cable housing, using the existing sections as a template. To ensure a clean cut, do not cut at an angle.

7 **Attach the new housing** to the bar with tape, following the original route, then fit handlebar tape over it (see pp.62–63).

8 **Thread a new cable** through the brake cable mount in the lever mechanism, then feed it inside and along the new housing.

Cable end caps fit into mounting points

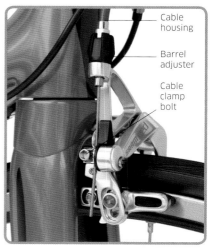

Cable housing

Barrel adjuster

Cable clamp bolt

9 **Continue to feed the cable** along the bike, towards the brake, threading it through the housing. Fit ferrules where required. If the cable gets jammed, do not force it. Ensure there is sufficient slack in the cable to allow the handlebar to turn freely.

10 **Secure the end** of the cable to the brakes, according to the type you have, then adjust them (see pp.112–117).

Straight handlebars

It is simpler to fit new brake cables to bikes with a straight handlebar than it is to fit them to bikes with a drop bar (see pp.102–103), as the cables are easier to access. Wear and damage to cables are more frequent on mountain bikes, so you will need to replace them more often.

🔧 BEFORE YOU START

- Source new cables that are suitable for your bike
- Secure your bike in a frame stand
- Prepare a space where you can lay out the new cables, so they are tension-free and unwound when you need them
- Check that the brake pads are in good condition

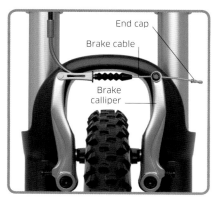

End cap
Brake cable
Brake calliper

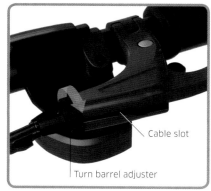

Cable slot
Turn barrel adjuster

Nipple
Cable mount
Ferrule

1 **Detach the brake cable** from the calliper, according to the type you have (see pp.112–117). Cut the end cap off the cable.

2 **Loosen the barrel adjuster** on the brake lever. Align the cable slots in the adjuster and the lever body to release the cable.

3 **Squeeze the lever** to expose the cable mount. Ease the cable out of the cable slots and free the nipple from the mount.

Remove cable ties and clips from frame
Remove cable and housing

Cable cutters
New cable housing

Open out cut ends of new housing with the pointed tool.

4 **Make a note of the original routing** before removing the cable. Working from the brake levers, pull the cable through the housing, and unclip each section of housing from the frame mounts in turn. Remove any cable ties, and keep any clips that you want to reuse.

5 **Cut the new cable housing,** using the old pieces as a template. Push ferrules onto the ends of each new piece of housing.

Workshop tip: Before buying a new brake cable, check which type is recommended for your bike. Make sure the cable has the correct nipple at the end that fits into the brake lever – in general, barrel nipples are used on mountain bikes and pear nipples on road bikes.

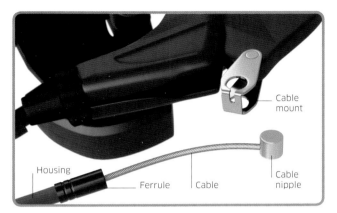

Housing
Ferrule
Cable
Cable mount
Cable nipple

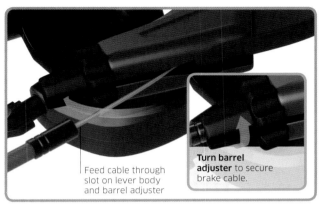

Feed cable through slot on lever body and barrel adjuster

Turn barrel adjuster to secure brake cable.

6 **Squeeze the brake lever**, and hook the nipple of the new cable into the cable mount. Reversing step 3, release the lever to secure the nipple; feed the free end of the new cable into the cable housing.

7 **Feed the cable** into the cable slot in the brake lever body and barrel adjuster. Push the ferrule on the cable housing into the barrel adjuster, then rotate the barrel adjuster to lock the cable in place.

Ensure housing curves smoothly, with no sharp bends

Fit housing into cable frame mounts

Noodle

Trim excess cable with cable cutters

Tighten cable clamp with Allen key

Crimp end cap over cut end of brake cable using pair of pinchers.

8 **Working towards the brakes**, thread the new cable along the frame, following the original route, and threading it through lengths of housing where required. Refit any clips and cable ties.

9 **At the brake calliper**, thread the cable through the noodle and rubber cover, reversing step 1. Feed the cable into the cable clamp, and tighten the bolt. To adjust the brake see pp.112–117.

Replacing hoses

Hydraulic brake systems usually come correctly fitted and ready for use. In some cases, however, it may be necessary to change or shorten one of the hoses. Brake hoses also need to be replaced if they are damaged or start to leak, which will cause the brakes to fail.

BEFORE YOU START

- Secure your bike in a frame stand
- Clean the brake callipers and levers thoroughly
- Source the correct hoses, brake fluid, and brake bleed kit for your system
- Lay out the fittings supplied with the hose kit (see steps 4-6)
- Lay down a plastic sheet, and put on goggles and gloves

Rear brake calliper

Brake lever

Front brake calliper

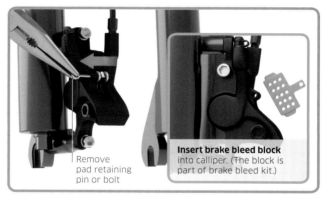

Remove pad retaining pin or bolt

Insert brake bleed block into calliper. (The block is part of brake bleed kit.)

1 **Following the route** of the existing hose, measure the amount of new hose you need by running it along the frame from the brake lever to the calliper. Use a hose cutter to cut the new hose to length.

2 **Remove the brake pads** (see pp.120–121) to prevent them being contaminated with brake fluid. Insert a brake bleed block between the pistons to stop them closing when the system is refilled with fluid.

Compression nut

Rubber cover

Brake lever

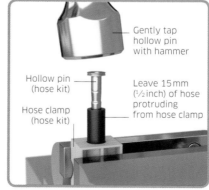

Gently tap hollow pin with hammer

Hollow pin (hose kit)

Hose clamp (hose kit)

Leave 15mm (½inch) of hose protruding from hose clamp

Ensure head of hollow pin is flush with hose

Rubber cover

Olive

Compression nut

3 **Remove the existing hose** by sliding back the rubber cover at both ends, and unscrewing the compression nuts with a spanner.

4 **Fit each end** of the new hose into the hose clamp, and hold it in a bench vice. Tap a hollow pin into the ends with a hammer.

5 **Prepare the lever end** of the hose by threading the rubber cover, compression nut, and olive onto the hose, in that order.

CAUTION! Some brake systems use "DOT" fluid, which is corrosive. When applying it, always wear safety gloves and goggles, protect your frame with plastic sheets, and wipe up spills.

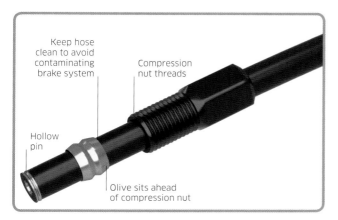

Keep hose clean to avoid contaminating brake system

Compression nut threads

Hollow pin

Olive sits ahead of compression nut

Compression nut

Olive

Mounting point

Tighten compression nut firmly, squashing olive to form seal.

6 **Prepare the calliper end** of the new hose in the same way as for the lever end (see step 5). Place the hose down carefully on a clean surface until you need it to prevent losing any of the fittings.

7 **Insert the new hose** into the mounting point on the calliper and push it in firmly. Slide the olive and compression nut down the hose. Using a spanner, screw the compression nut into the calliper.

Refit hose clips where required

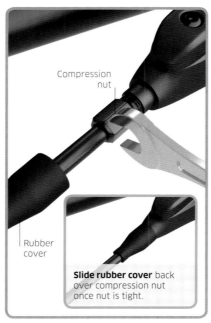

Compression nut

Rubber cover

Slide rubber cover back over compression nut once nut is tight.

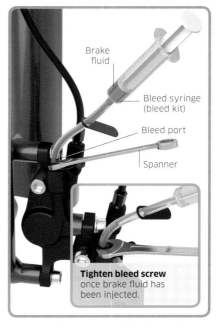

Brake fluid

Bleed syringe (bleed kit)

Bleed port

Spanner

Tighten bleed screw once brake fluid has been injected.

8 **Fix the new hose** along the frame. Make sure that the handlebar can turn fully each way without the hose kinking.

9 **Firmly insert the end** of the hose into the brake lever. Tighten the compression nut using a spanner, as shown in step 7.

10 **Inject brake fluid** into the bleed port of the calliper until the system is full, and then bleed the brakes (see pp.108–109).

Bleeding the system

Hydraulic brake systems require bleeding to eliminate any air in the system, normally as a result of servicing, fitting, or refitting a brake hose, or because of moisture seeping in. Air in your brakes will make them feel spongy and they will function less effectively.

BEFORE YOU START

- Source the recommended brake fluid and brake bleed kit for your bike (see pp.36–37)
- Secure your bike in a frame stand and cover the floor
- Remove the wheels (see pp.78–81)
- Remove the brake pads; fit a bleed block (see pp.120–121)
- Put on safety goggles and gloves, and keep a cloth handy

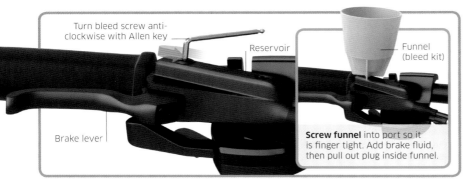

Turn bleed screw anti-clockwise with Allen key

Reservoir

Funnel (bleed kit)

Brake lever

Screw funnel into port so it is finger tight. Add brake fluid, then pull out plug inside funnel.

Unscrew mounting bolts with Allen key

Brake bleed block (bleed kit)

Brake calliper

1 **Loosen and rotate the brake lever**, so the reservoir is horizontal. Remove the bleed screw from the bleed port on the reservoir. Screw the bleed funnel into the port. Wearing safety gloves and goggles if using "DOT" brake fluid, add a little fluid to the funnel.

2 **Remove the brake calliper** from the fork by unscrewing the mounting bolts. Allow the calliper to hang freely.

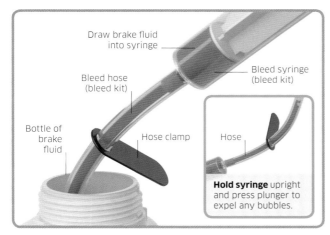

Draw brake fluid into syringe

Bleed syringe (bleed kit)

Bleed hose (bleed kit)

Bottle of brake fluid

Hose clamp

Hose

Hold syringe upright and press plunger to expel any bubbles.

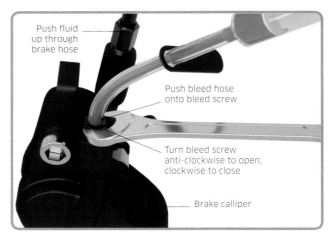

Push fluid up through brake hose

Push bleed hose onto bleed screw

Turn bleed screw anti-clockwise to open; clockwise to close

Brake calliper

3 **Push the bleed hose** onto the syringe, then draw brake fluid into the syringe by pulling on the plunger. Once filled, hold the syringe upright to allow any bubbles to float towards the end of the hose.

4 **On the brake calliper**, push the bleed hose onto the bleed screw. Open the screw with a spanner, then inject brake fluid into the calliper, and up to the bleed funnel on the lever. Retighten the bleed screw.

TOOLS AND EQUIPMENT

- Brake fluid
- Brake bleed kit
- Frame stand
- Plastic sheets
- Goggles and gloves
- Cloth
- Set of Allen keys
- Set of spanners
- Adjustable strap or tape

CAUTION! Some brake systems need "DOT" fluid, which is corrosive. When using it, always wear safety gloves and goggles, protect your frame with plastic sheets, and wipe up spills.

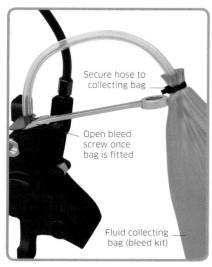

Secure hose to collecting bag

Open bleed screw once bag is fitted

Fluid collecting bag (bleed kit)

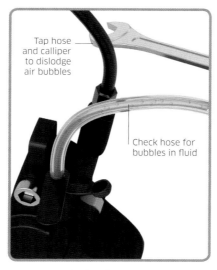

Tap hose and calliper to dislodge air bubbles

Check hose for bubbles in fluid

Surplus brake fluid collects in funnel

Squeeze lever carefully to avoid spilling brake fluid

5 **Leave the hose** attached to the bleed screw and replace the syringe with a fluid collecting bag. Half-fill the funnel with brake fluid.

6 **Press the brake lever** to drive fluid through the system to the bag. Once the fluid in the hose is bubble-free, close the bleed screw.

7 **Carefully squeeze** the brake lever a few times. If the action feels firm, you have successfully bled all of the air from the system.

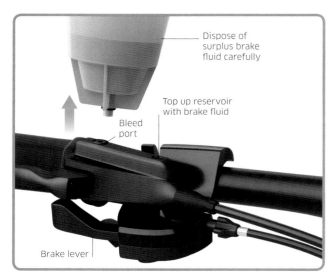

Dispose of surplus brake fluid carefully

Top up reservoir with brake fluid

Bleed port

Brake lever

Secure brake lever with strap

8 **Fit the plug** inside the bleed funnel and unscrew it from the port. Fill the reservoir to the top with fluid, then refit the bleed screw. Reattach the brake calliper, and return the lever to its original position.

9 **If the brakes seem** spongy, squeeze the lever and secure it to the grip. Stand the bike upright and leave overnight, to encourage any air to rise to the top of the system, then repeat steps 1–8.

Replacing brake pads

Cold and wet weather can be hard on brake pads. When grit and water mix they form a paste which gradually wears the rubber down. Brake pads worn down to the shoe can cause brake failure and damage to the rim. A scratching sound when you brake indicates that your pads are worn.

 BEFORE YOU START

- Secure your bike in a frame stand
- Remove the wheel (see pp.78–83)
- Replace the wheel if the "wear dots" have worn off the rim
- Loosen the brake pad bolt with penetrating oil

DUAL-PIVOT BRAKES

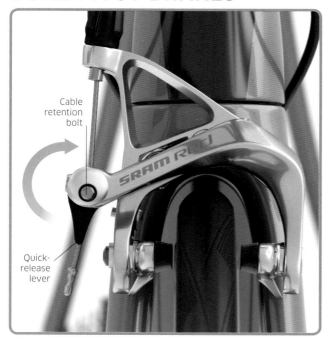

Cable retention bolt

Quick-release lever

1 **Open the quick-release lever** on the brake calliper, if fitted. If the brake calliper does not have a quick-release lever, undo the cable retention bolt with a spanner or an Allen key.

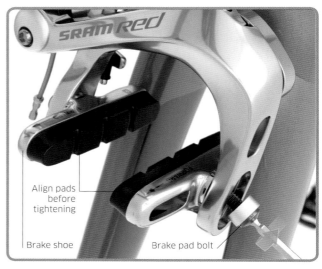

Align pads before tightening

Brake shoe

Brake pad bolt

2 **Undo the brake pad bolts** on the calliper arms with an Allen key, and remove the old pads. Put the new pads in place (they will be marked "left" and "right"). Replace the bolts, and tighten.

Close quick-release lever

Tighten brake pad bolt with Allen key

3 **Refit the wheel** (see pp.78–83). Raise or lower the pads until they strike the rim at its outermost edge. Holding them in place, tighten the brake pad bolts, then adjust the calliper (see pp.112–117).

Workshop tip: Brake pads are left- and right-specific, and each brake Shoe is marked with an "L" or "R" to help identify it. Look for the word "TOP" on the pad or shoe to ensure you do not fit it upside down. Wipe the pads down after riding in the wet to reduce wear.

V-BRAKES AND CANTILEVER BRAKES

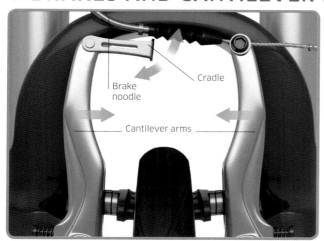

Brake noodle

Cradle

Cantilever arms

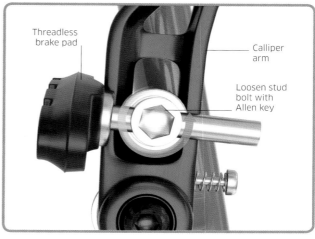

Threadless brake pad

Calliper arm

Loosen stud bolt with Allen key

1 **Squeeze the arms** of the V-brake calliper and release the brake noodle from the cradle. Cantilever brakes have a straddle wire that unhitches from the left cantilever arm (see pp.114–115).

2 **If you are replacing** a threadless brake pad, loosen the stud bolt on the calliper, slide out the pad, and replace it with the new one. Align the brake pad and loosely tighten the stud bolt.

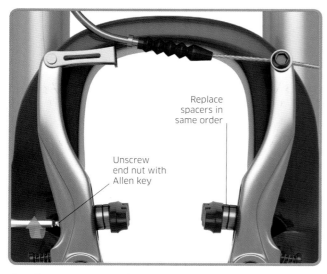

Replace spacers in same order

Unscrew end nut with Allen key

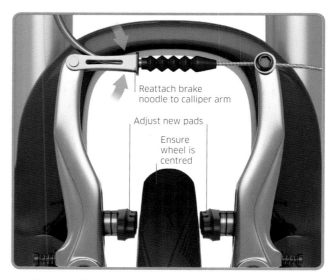

Reattach brake noodle to calliper arm

Adjust new pads

Ensure wheel is centred

3 **If you are replacing** threaded pads, loosen the end nut on the stud bolt. Remove the brake pad and spacers. Fit the new pad by inserting the stud through the calliper arm. Retighten the end nut.

4 **Replace the wheel** and reattach the brake noodle to the calliper arm. Adjust the position of the brake pads so that they are aligned, ensuring that they do not touch the tyre. Tighten the end nut.

V-brakes

V-brakes are common on both mountain and hybrid bikes, and are designed to accommodate fatter off-road tyres. Like all brake systems, the pads gradually become poorly aligned as they wear down, meaning that your brakes feel spongy, and become or less powerful. Due to their quick-release mechanism and simple design, V-brakes are considered to be one of the easiest of all brakes systems to install and to adjust. Using just simple tools, the pads can be realigned correctly in a matter of minutes.

BEFORE YOU START

- Check the wear indicator on your brake pads
- Source suitable replacement pads if required
- Secure your bike in a frame stand, so that you can spin the wheel freely

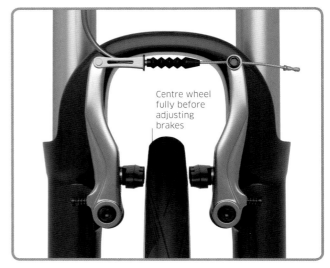

Centre wheel fully before adjusting brakes

1 **Check your wheel** to ensure that it is centred (turning freely and at equal distance from each fork arm). Make sure the quick-release is not overtightened on one side.

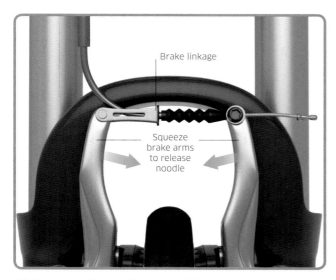

Brake linkage

Squeeze brake arms to release noodle

2 **Squeeze the spring-loaded brake arms** together with one hand, so that the pads touch the wheel rim. This will release the tension in the brake linkage, allowing it to be disconnected.

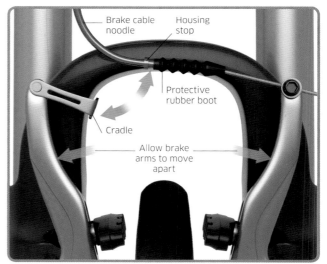

Brake cable noodle

Housing stop

Protective rubber boot

Cradle

Allow brake arms to move apart

3 **Unclip the housing stop** on the brake cable noodle from the cradle, to separate the brake linkage. Release the brake arms, allowing them to open away from the wheel, giving you access to the pads.

TOOLS AND EQUIPMENT

- Frame stand
- Set of Allen keys
- Cross-head screwdriver

Workshop tip: When adjusting the spring tensioner screws, any changes you make to the tension on one side will also affect the other. Avoid tightening the springs as a means to balance the pads too often, as it can increase cable stretch. Adjust them fully as shown.

Leave cable in arm

Allen key

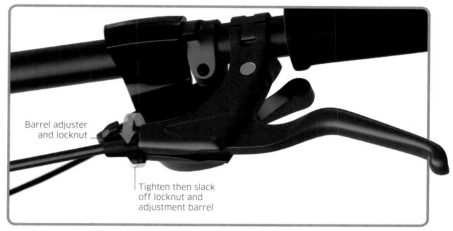

Barrel adjuster and locknut

Tighten then slack off locknut and adjustment barrel

4 **Loosen the cable** retention bolt with an Allen key, to allow the cable to slide freely within the bolt.

5 **On the brake lever**, wind out the barrel adjuster 2–3 full turns to provide slack in the cable. At the brake arm, take up this slack by pulling up to 5 mm of cable through the retention bolt, and hold the cable in place with your fingers.

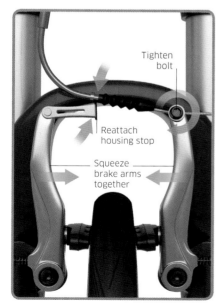

Tighten bolt

Reattach housing stop

Squeeze brake arms together

Check brake pads do not rub wheel

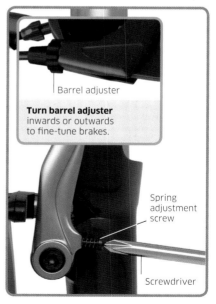

Barrel adjuster

Turn barrel adjuster inwards or outwards to fine-tune brakes.

Spring adjustment screw

Screwdriver

6 **Reattach the brake** linkage and hold the pads close to the rim. Pull the brake cable taut, and tighten the retaining bolt.

7 **Squeeze the brake lever** 10–12 times to bed in the cable. Rotate the wheel several times to ensure brake pads are not rubbing.

8 **Check the brake pads** sit evenly, around 1.5 mm from the wheel rim. Adjust the spring tensioner screws on both arms.

Cantilever brakes

Developed for mountain bikes, cantilever brakes feature outward-facing lever arms to provide adequate space for wide or knobbly tyres. The pads swing in an arc when the lever is pulled, and move down- and inwards. Pad alignment to the rim is critical to braking performance.

BEFORE YOU START

- Remove the tyre if you need to get a better view (see pp.78–83)
- Check that the wheel is centred in the forks
- Wipe away any dirt or rubber build-up around the pad
- Source replacement pads if the existing ones are worn

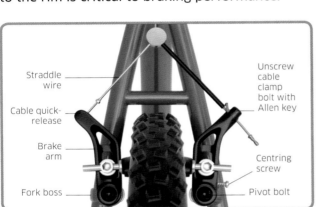

Straddle wire

Cable quick-release

Brake arm

Fork boss

Unscrew cable clamp bolt with Allen key

Centring screw

Pivot bolt

1 **Squeeze the lever arms inwards** and disconnect the straddle wire from the quick-release on the left lever arm. Unscrew the clamp bolt on the right arm, and release the cable. The arms will hang loose.

Pivot bolt

Clean fork bosses to remove dirt and old grease, then re-grease.

2 **Using an Allen key**, undo the pivot bolts and ease the arms off the fork bosses. Check the spring-tension pins on the back of the arms. Note which hole on the bosses the springs are inserted into.

3 **Slide the brake arms** back onto the fork bosses, ensuring that you return the spring-tension pins on each one to their original hole on the bosses. Tighten the pivot bolts. Check the arms move freely.

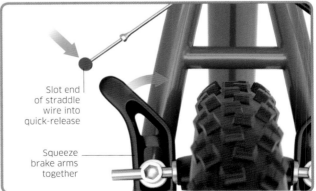

Slot end of straddle wire into quick-release

Squeeze brake arms together

4 **Squeeze the brake arms** together with one hand, and use your other to reinsert the straddle wire into the quick-release slot on the left-hand brake arm. Push it in fully so it is secure.

Workshop tip: Before adjusting your brakes, ensure the wheels are correctly seated in the drop-outs, with all of the nuts or quick-release levers tight. Check the pads are not set too low on the rim as a lip will form on the lowest edge making alignment impossible.

Brake cable

Cable clamp bolt

Insert cable through clamp bolt to its original position.

Ensure brake arms are parallel

Centring screw

5 **Still squeezing the brake arms** together, use your free hand to feed the brake cable into the cable clamp bolt on the right-hand brake arm. Once in place, secure the cable by tightening the bolt.

6 **To ensure both lever arms are** at an equal distance from the wheel rim, providing even stopping power, turn the centring screw on each lever arm. The arms should be parallel to the rim.

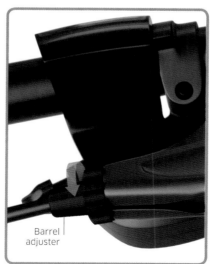

Barrel adjuster

Ensure pads are evenly spaced

7 **Loosen and adjust** the brake pads, so they are horizontal to the rim and strike it squarely. Retighten the bolts fully.

8 **Turn the barrel adjuster** on the brake lever, anti-clockwise, by up to three turns until the pads sit 2–3 mm from the rim.

9 **Make final fine adjustments** to the position of the brake pads and arms. Ensure the pads are aligned, and the arms centred.

Dual-pivot brakes

On a dual-pivot brake, the calliper has two arms that push the pads into the wheel rim at slightly different angles. Over time, the brake pads wear and move with use, and will need to be adjusted so that they remain effective. You may also need to recentre the calliper and adjust the tension on the brake cable to relieve any slack.

 BEFORE YOU START

- Secure your bicycle in a frame stand
- Brush off any corrosion from the calliper bolt heads
- Wipe any dirt or residue build-up from the brake pads
- Source new brake pads if yours are worn

Quick-release lever tab

Brake cable

2 **Release the brake cable** by opening the quick-release lever, if fitted, or by undoing the cable-clamp bolt. The brake calliper arms will move outwards, well clear of the wheel rim.

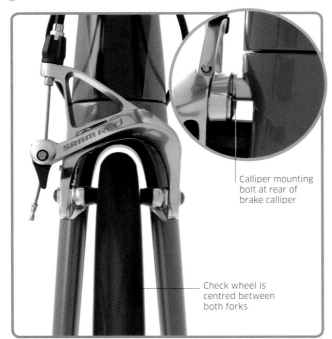

Calliper mounting bolt at rear of brake calliper

Check wheel is centred between both forks

1 **Spin the wheel** to check that it is fully centred between the forks. The centre of the tyre should also be directly aligned with the calliper mounting bolt. Adjust the wheel if required (see pp.78–83).

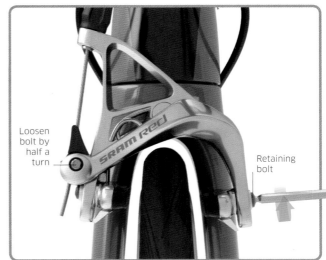

Loosen bolt by half a turn

Retaining bolt

3 **Loosen the retaining bolt** on each brake pad. Move the left pad so that the top of it aligns with the top of the rim. Align the base of the right pad with the base of the rim. Tighten both pad bolts.

Workshop tip: Squealing brakes are caused by vibrations between the pads and rim. To stop this, "toe-in" each brake pad towards the rim. Loosen the brake-pad-retaining bolt, and rotate the washer behind the pad until the pad surface is parallel to the rim.

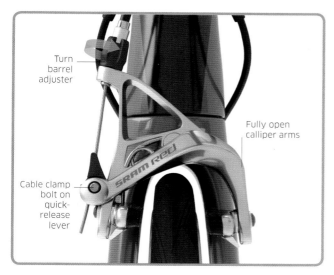

Turn barrel adjuster

Fully open calliper arms

Cable clamp bolt on quick-release lever

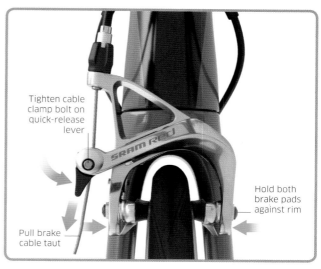

Tighten cable clamp bolt on quick-release lever

Hold both brake pads against rim

Pull brake cable taut

4 Open the barrel adjuster by 3–4 clockwise turns with your hand. Loosen the cable clamp bolt on the back of the quick-release lever with an Allen key. This will allow the brake cable to move freely.

5 Squeeze the pads against the rim with one hand. Pull the cable taut with the other. Retighten the cable clamp bolt on the quick-release lever. Squeeze the brake lever several times to bed in the cable.

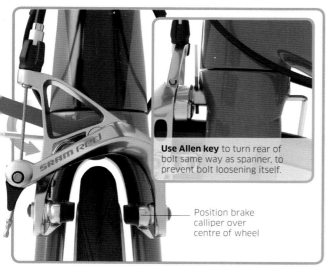

Use Allen key to turn rear of bolt same way as spanner, to prevent bolt loosening itself.

Position brake calliper over centre of wheel

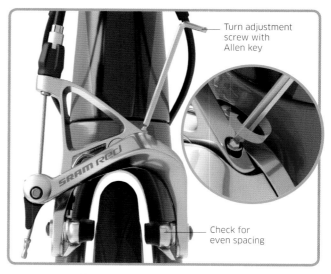

Turn adjustment screw with Allen key

Check for even spacing

6 Check that the brake calliper is centred. To adjust it, loosen the mounting bolt (see step 1) with a cone spanner. Insert an Allen key behind the bolt, then adjust the calliper. Retighten the mounting bolt.

7 Some callipers have an adjustment screw used for centring. In these cases, turn the adjustment screw in the direction required until the callipers are centred and the pads evenly spaced from the rim.

Hydraulic disc brakes

In a disc brake system, a pair of brake pads mounted on a calliper act on a metal disc rotor at the wheel hub. Disc brakes are activated by cable or hydraulically. In a hydraulic system, mineral oil or DOT fluid contained in sealed hoses provides the pressure. The brake lever houses a "master cylinder" at the handlebar. When you pull the lever, the master cylinder pushes the fluid to pistons at the calliper, which press the brake pads against the disc rotor. On a cable-operated system, the brake lever pulls the brake cable, which acts on the pistons at the calliper to close the pads. The disc rotor mounts to a hub within the wheel.

PARTS FOCUS

Disc brakes are mounted on the wheel hubs. Both hydraulic and mechanical systems use pads fixed to callipers fixed to the frame.

① Each **piston** in the brake calliper is forced by hydraulic fluid or mechanical tension onto the brake pads as the brake lever is pressed.

② The **brake pads** in the calliper are held clear of the disc rotor by a spring when not in use. They are pressed against the rotor by pistons.

③ The **disc rotor** is fixed to the wheel hub. It turns with the wheel, between the calliper arms, until the brake lever is pressed.

④ The **calliper body** contains the pistons and brake pads. In a hydraulic system it is sealed to maintain the fluid pressure.

Quick-release lever
allows wheel to be removed without using tools

Front fork
supports brake calliper

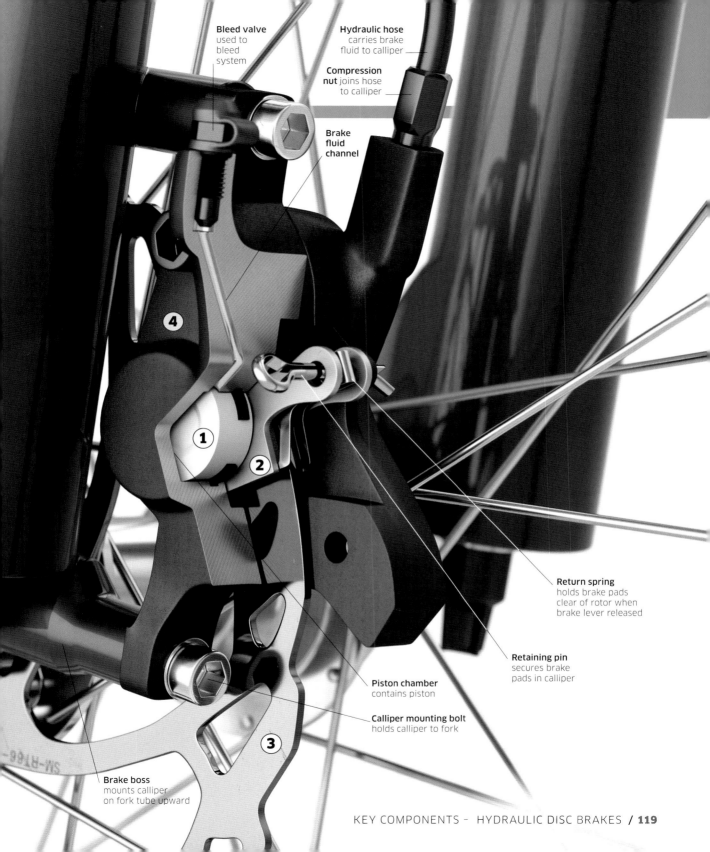

Bleed valve used to bleed system

Hydraulic hose carries brake fluid to calliper

Compression nut joins hose to calliper

Brake fluid channel

④

①

②

Return spring holds brake pads clear of rotor when brake lever released

Retaining pin secures brake pads in calliper

Piston chamber contains piston

Calliper mounting bolt holds calliper to fork

③

SM-RT66

Brake boss mounts calliper on fork tube upward

Disc brakes

Disc-brake pads wear down over time, especially during the winter months, when they pick up more grit from wet roads and muddy trails. A harsh grinding noise when braking indicates that they need urgent replacement to avoid damaging the disc rotor. Pads should be replaced when there is 1.5 mm of material remaining.

 BEFORE YOU START

- Secure your bike in a frame stand
- Remove the wheel (see pp.78–83)
- Remove old disc rotor
- Put on clean gloves before handling the new brake surface
- Wipe away any dust or dirt from the new disc rotor

Screw in bolts with Allen key

2 Screw in the rotor mounting bolts, fastening each in place loosely, before tightening them fully to the recommended torque settings. Work in a star formation (from 1–6) to avoid distorting the disc.

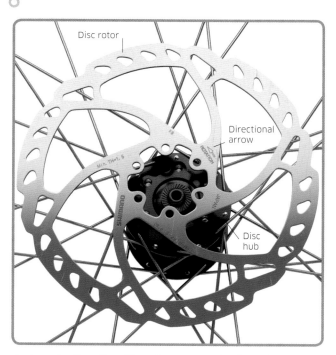

Disc rotor

Directional arrow

Disc hub

1 Locate the directional arrow etched on the surface of the new disc rotor, then align the disc rotor with the hub, fitting it in accordance with the manufacturer's instructions.

Push pads apart gently, to prevent damaging piston and calliper.

Front fork

3 Using a large, flat-head screwdriver, tyre lever, or pad pusher, ease the pads apart and reset the pistons. Then remove the old pads to allow sufficient space for the new, thicker pads.

TOOLS AND EQUIPMENT

- Frame stand
- Cloth and gloves
- Set of Allen keys
- Flat-head screwdriver, tyre lever, or pad pusher
- Needle-nose pliers
- Degreaser or brake cleaner and cloth

Pads retained by a split pin or bolt

Carefully extract brake pads to avoid damaging calliper.

Spray empty gap and clean cavity with rag

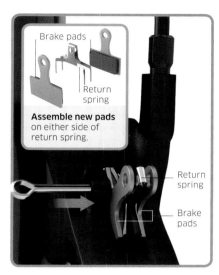

Brake pads

Return spring

Assemble new pads on either side of return spring.

Return spring

Brake pads

4 **Remove the pad-retainer** – either a bolt or split pin (as above) – and ease the brake pads and spring from the calliper.

5 **Clean inside the brake calliper** by spraying it with degreaser or brake cleaner. Remove any dirt, grease, or brake dust with a cloth.

6 **Assemble the pads** and spring (inset), then insert them into the calliper. Fit the replacement pad retaining pin or bolt.

Disc rotor

Calliper bolt

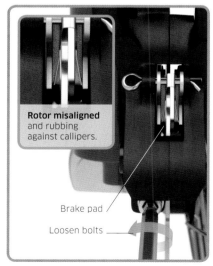

Rotor misaligned and rubbing against callipers.

Brake pad

Loosen bolts

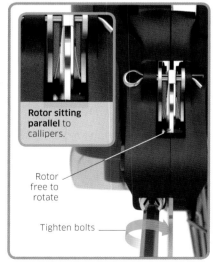

Rotor sitting parallel to callipers.

Rotor free to rotate

Tighten bolts

7 **Refit the wheel** and check that the rotor is centred between the pads, and that it spins freely without rubbing.

8 **If the wheel does rub**, loosen the calliper bolts and adjust the position of the calliper so that the rotor can spin freely.

9 **Retighten the bolts** once the calliper is aligned. Squeeze the brake lever several times to bed in the new pads.

Drum brakes

Commonly used on utility bikes, where their extra weight is offset by extreme longevity, drum brakes are housed inside a specialist hub. Pulling the brake lever activates a brake arm on the outside of the hub, which pushes the internal brake pads against the brake liner on the inside of the hub, slowing the wheel. Since the braking assembly is sealed inside the hub, drum brakes deliver the same braking power in dry, wet, icy, or muddy conditions, and the parts wear slowly. Most drum brakes, such as the Sturmey Archer XL-FD (shown here), are simple in construction but cannot be easily serviced at home. However, cable tension can be adjusted (see pp.124–125).

⚙ BRAKE ACTION

The brake cable pulls the brake hub arm, pushing the internal pads against the brake liner until the lever is released.

Brake pads　　　　Brake hub lever

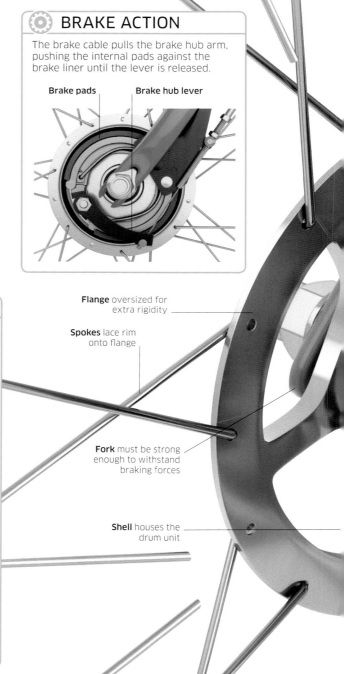

⚙ PARTS FOCUS

Drum brakes require a specialist hub and a fork or frame that can accept the torque arm, so retro-fitting is possible only on some bikes.

① The **brake pads** are made from a durable metal composite and wear very slowly. Once worn, they cannot be replaced – a new drum unit is required.

② The **brake liner** is the surface within the drum that the brake pads come into contact with. It wears slowly and cannot be replaced.

③ The **hub brake arm** is pulled by the cable and activates the brake pads. Press the arm inwards when adjusting the cable.

④ The **barrel adjuster** allows you to make minor adjustments to the brake cable, which will stretch over time (see pp.124–125).

Flange oversized for extra rigidity

Spokes lace rim onto flange

Fork must be strong enough to withstand braking forces

Shell houses the drum unit

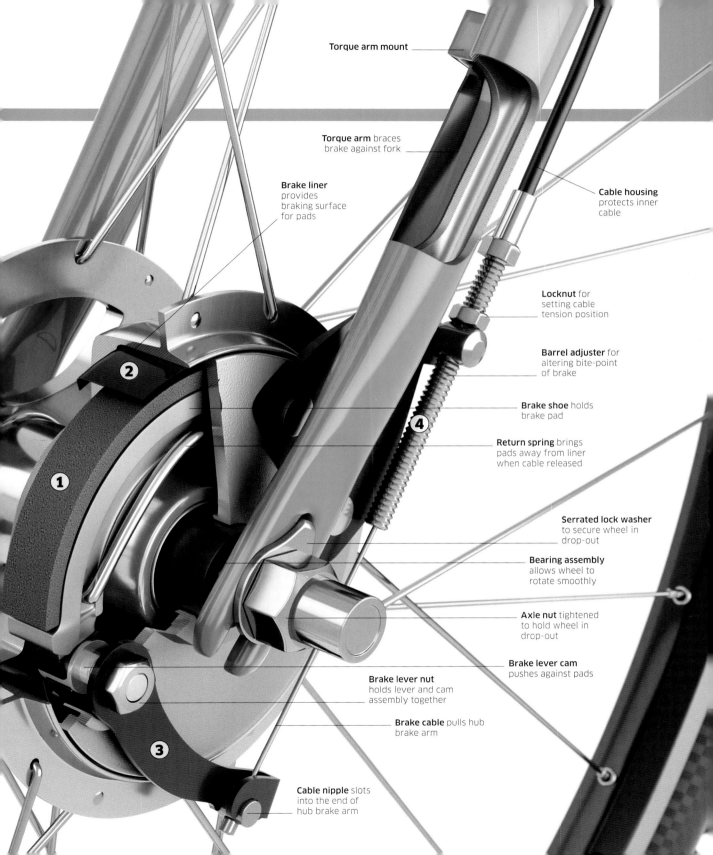

Torque arm mount

Torque arm braces
brake against fork

Brake liner
provides
braking surface
for pads

Cable housing
protects inner
cable

Locknut for
setting cable
tension position

Barrel adjuster for
altering bite-point
of brake

Brake shoe holds
brake pad

Return spring brings
pads away from liner
when cable released

Serrated lock washer
to secure wheel in
drop-out

Bearing assembly
allows wheel to
rotate smoothly

Axle nut tightened
to hold wheel in
drop-out

Brake lever cam
pushes against pads

Brake lever nut
holds lever and cam
assembly together

Brake cable pulls hub
brake arm

Cable nipple slots
into the end of
hub brake arm

▶ **INSTALLING AND ADJUSTING BRAKE CABLES**

Drum brake cables

Drum brakes are fitted mainly on commuter and utility bikes, and are largely maintenance-free. If the internal brake pads are worn, you must replace the entire unit. If the brake cables need to be adjusted or replaced, however, this is a fairly straightforward task.

⊙ BEFORE YOU START

- Secure your bike in a frame stand
- Make a note of the existing cable routing
- Remove the old cable by following steps 1-5, shown below, in reverse

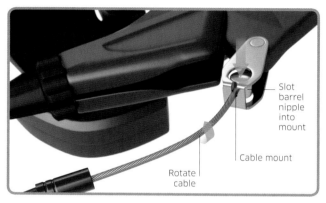

Slot barrel nipple into mount

Cable mount

Rotate cable

1 **To fit a new cable**, pull the brake lever to expose the cable mount. Push the barrel nipple of the cable into the mount, and rotate the cable anti-clockwise so that the nipple locks into it.

Ferrule

Rotate adjuster to hold cable secure once it has slotted into place.

2 **Align the slots** in the brake lever and the barrel adjuster, and thread the cable through the slots. Seat the ferrule of the cable housing into the barrel adjuster. Turn the adjuster to fix the cable in place.

Check you can turn handlebar fully

3 **Route the cable** along the frame from the brake lever to the hub, following the original routing. Secure the cable to the frame, ensuring that you leave sufficient slack so the handlebar turns fully.

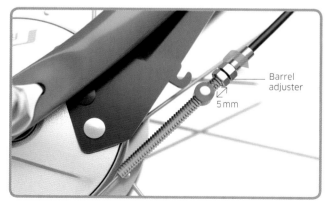

Barrel adjuster

5 mm

4 **At the drum end** of the cable, rotate the barrel adjuster so that there is around 5 mm of thread showing below the locknut (this will allow for fine adjustments later).

Workshop tip: Some drum brakes need a brake cable with a factory-fitted nipple on each end: a barrel nipple for the brake lever and a pear nipple for the hub brake arm. To remove this type of cable you will have to cut off one of the nipples.

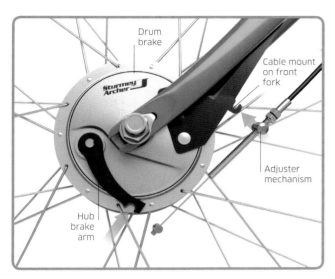

Drum brake

Cable mount on front fork

Adjuster mechanism

Hub brake arm

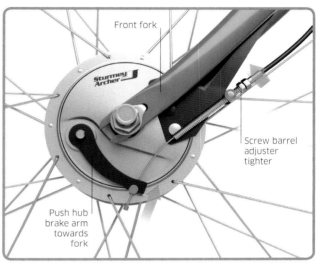

Front fork

Screw barrel adjuster tighter

Push hub brake arm towards fork

5 **Secure the adjuster mechanism** onto the hooked cable mount on the fork (for a front brake) or the chainstay (for a rear brake). Push the hub brake arm towards the fork. Fit the cable nipple into the end.

6 **Push the hub brake arm** towards the fork again, then tighten the barrel adjuster to take up the slack in the cable. Tighten it until the brake engages when the wheel is turned.

Barrel adjuster

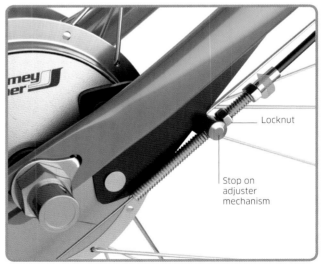

Locknut

Stop on adjuster mechanism

7 **Release the brake arm**, and slacken the barrel adjuster off until the brake disengages when you turn the wheel by hand. Pull the brake lever to ensure the brake engages, stopping the wheel.

8 **Pull the brake lever** 10–12 times to remove any slack. Once you are happy with the bite-point of the brake, tighten the locknut against the stop on the adjuster mechanism to set the cable tension.

TRANSMISSION

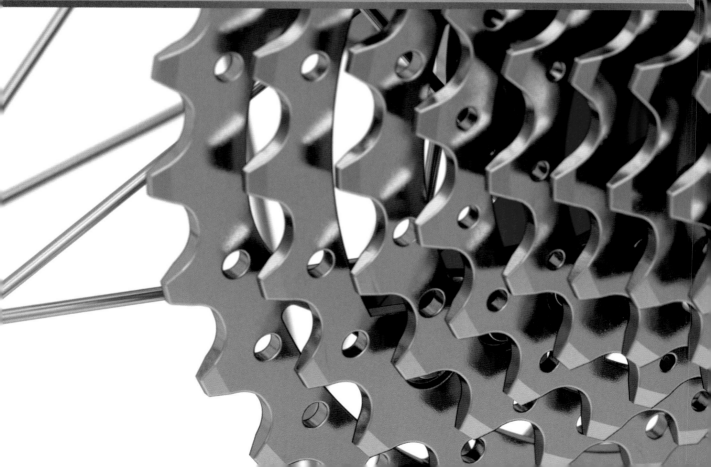

Transmission systems

Gears make slow cycling uphill and fast downhill easier if you push harder. There are multiple transmission systems that make changing gear possible. The fragile-looking but surprisingly effective and generally reliable derailleur is most popular and still the device of choice on road bikes and utility bikes. Changing gears on a derailleur has undergone significant evolution

TYPE	SUITABILITY	OPERATION
HUB GEARS In a hub gear system, the gears are enclosed within the rear wheel hub. As the gears are shielded from the road, they are less vulnerable to the general wear and tear of riding.	■ **Low-maintenance** utility bikes, trekking bikes, folding bikes, and city bikes (such as those used in bike-sharing schemes).	■ **Hub gears** are operated with a single gear-shifter on the handlebar that moves cables around the central "sun gear".
DERAILLEURS In a derailleur system, a lever on the handlebar is connected by a cable to the derailleur, which moves the chain between cogs (on a rear derailleur) or chainrings (on a front derailleur).	■ **All types of road riding**, from racing to touring and utility bikes.	■ **On a rear derailleur**, the cable from the brake lever pulls the mechanism to move the chain to a cog. Two jockey wheels maintain tension in the chain. ■ **A front derailleurs** has a cage to guide the chain as it is moved.
FIXED GEARS Fixed wheel is the original single-gear system. There is no freewheel; the pedals will keep turning even if you stop pedalling.	■ **Track cycling**, basic city bikes, and training rides to hone pedalling skills.	■ **The cog** is fixed to the rear hub, and turns with the wheel. Some types have a "flip-flop" hub, with a fixed gear on one side and a freewheel on the other.
E-GEARS In an electronic gear system, the gears are changed with switches rather than mechanical levers. A switch on the handlebar is connected by a wire to a battery pack and a small electric motor that drives the derailleur.	■ **Racing** and competitive road events such as sportives (though e-gears are becoming available to a wide range of cyclists). ■ **Not advisable** for touring or trekking as use is limited by the need to charge the batteries.	■ **Buttons** and paddle-operated switches fitted to the brake levers, or sited remotely on the bar, operate small motors in the front and rear derailleurs. ■ **Battery power is supplied** by a single cell for wired units or by individual cells on wireless types.

with combined brake and gear-shift levers now being overtaken by buttons operating electronic gear mechanisms. Hub gears provide a reliable alternative to derailleurs, requiring minimal, if any, servicing. Fixed-gear or single-speed bikes are simple to ride and need little maintenance but offer no assistance on steep climbs or extra speed on downhill straights.

KEY COMPONENTS

- **The set of small gears** that turns around a "sun gear" fixed to the axle, all within a larger "ring gear".

- **Rear derailleurs** are made up of a body, screws to limit the range of movement, a barrel adjuster to fine tune cable tension, and a gear hanger.
- **A front derailleurs** has a body, with no extra parts.

- **The cog that sits** on the rear hub.
- **Some hubs** also have a freewheel.

- **E-gears still use** conventional front and rear mechanisms.
- **Wires are routed** through the frame to the mechanism.
- **A charger is required** for the batteries.

VARIATIONS

- **Hub gears** can have 3–14 gears and are normally run with a single front chainwheel.

- **The latest rear derailleurs** for road bikes work with a wide range of cogs; older types with indexing may work with only a limited number.
- **Front derailleurs** are used with double or triple chainsets.

- **Fixed-wheel systems** for track and road differ in their gearing, with track bikes geared more highly.

- **E-gears work** with both 10- and 11-speed drivetrains.
- **The top-end brands** are made for professional riding, but e-gears are now also supplied for mid-priced road bikes.

ADJUSTMENTS

- **Turn the barrel adjuster** at the hub to alter the cable tension.

- **Turn the rear derailleur** screws to fix the range of movement and the position under the largest cog.
- **Turn the front derailleur** screws to fix the position and the range of movement.

- **Slide the rear wheel** back and forth in the drop-out ends to maintain tension in the chain.

- **After fitting** by a trained mechanic, both derailleurs automatically self-adjust after each change.
- **Batteries need charging** every quarter; cells in wireless systems require more frequent charging.

Manual shifters

Gear-shifters allow you to change gear when pedalling. The right-hand shifter controls the rear derailleur, and the left-hand shifter moves the front derailleur. Road bike shifters are integrated within a unit inside the hood of the brake lever. Mountain bike and hybrid shifters clamp separately around the handlebar. There are two main types: trigger and grip shifters. Trigger shifters, unlike grip ones, can be set to different positions, allowing riders to tailor the handlebar set-up to fit their individual preferences. Shimano also makes an integrated brake and gear-shifter, known as an STI lever.

Cable anchor pin secures brake cable

Brake cable is pulled by brake lever, closing brake callipers

Brake lever pivot pin allows brake lever to pull on brake cable

3

Pivot enables gear lever to move

Shifter lever rotates ratchet wheel, pulling gear cable

Brake lever is pulled to activate brakes

 PARTS FOCUS

Gear-shifters are "indexed" by a ratchet mechanism, which is activated by pressing the trigger or twisting the grip.

① The **ratchet wheel** pulls the gear cable in set increments, causing the derailleur to move and pull the chain into a new position.

② The **cable anchors** secure the end of the gear cable within the shifter mechanism. The cable must be fully seated in the anchor to provide tension.

③ **Pivot pins** inside the lever body provide leverage for the shifter lever, allowing it to pull on the tensioned gear cable.

④ The **lever body and hood** contain the internal mechanism of the shifter, holding it in place and protecting it from wear and damage.

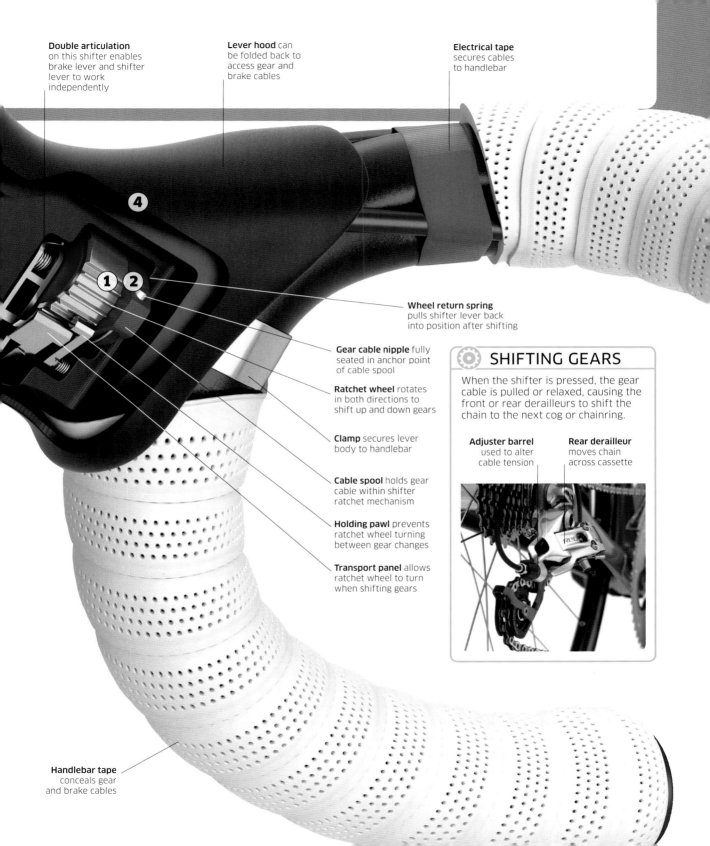

Double articulation on this shifter enables brake lever and shifter lever to work independently

Lever hood can be folded back to access gear and brake cables

Electrical tape secures cables to handlebar

4

1 **2**

Wheel return spring pulls shifter lever back into position after shifting

Gear cable nipple fully seated in anchor point of cable spool

Ratchet wheel rotates in both directions to shift up and down gears

Clamp secures lever body to handlebar

Cable spool holds gear cable within shifter ratchet mechanism

Holding pawl prevents ratchet wheel turning between gear changes

Transport panel allows ratchet wheel to turn when shifting gears

SHIFTING GEARS

When the shifter is pressed, the gear cable is pulled or relaxed, causing the front or rear derailleurs to shift the chain to the next cog or chainring.

Adjuster barrel used to alter cable tension

Rear derailleur moves chain across cassette

Handlebar tape conceals gear and brake cables

External gear cables

Over time cables will stretch through use and affect the tension. Frame-mounted gear cables can develop rust within the cable housing, causing friction that impedes gear-shifting. The solution is to fit new cables and housing.

BEFORE YOU START

- Secure your bike in a frame stand
- Unfold the new cables and cable housing
- Locate the gear-shifter housing the cable you want to change

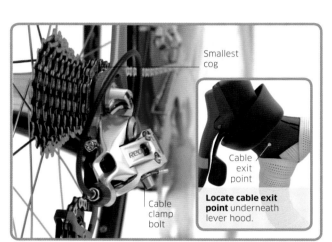

Smallest cog

Cable exit point

Locate cable exit point underneath lever hood.

Cable clamp bolt

1 **To reduce tension** in the chain, set it to the highest gear on the cassette using the gear-shifter. This will ensure that the gear cable engages with the shifter mechanism correctly when installed.

Inner gear cable

Snip off cable end cap cleanly

2 **Using an Allen key**, loosen the cable clamp bolt on the rear derailleur (mech), and cut off the inner cable end cap. Doing this will release the inner cable and allow it to travel back through the housing.

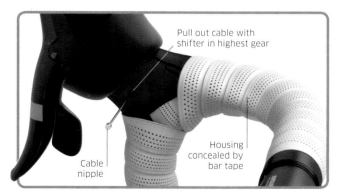

Pull out cable with shifter in highest gear

Housing concealed by bar tape

Cable nipple

3 **Peel back the lever hood** and squeeze the brake lever. Give the cable housing a push where it exits the handlebar, then pull the inner cable from the shifter mechanism at the lever.

4 **Working from the rear** to the front of the bike, remove all of the cable housing from the frame. (Housing concealed by handlebar tape can usually be reused as it is less exposed to the elements.)

Workshop tip: Shimano gear cables have a slightly bigger nipple than the one on a Campagnolo gear cable. The cables are not compatible across systems, so make sure you have sourced the right ones.

Ensure cable cutters are sharp

Fit ferrule to end of cable

Ferrule

Cable

Drip some oil inside housing before threading cable.

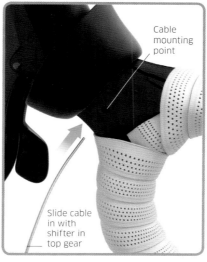

Cable mounting point

Slide cable in with shifter in top gear

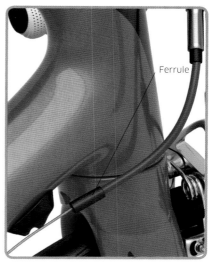

Ferrule

5 **Using the existing housing** as a guide, trim the replacements to length and fit ferrules on the ends. Oil the new inner cable.

6 **Thread the cable** fully into the shifter and housing, locking the cable nipple into the shifter. Test all of the gears fully.

7 **Ease the cable** along the cable housing mounted on the handlebar, then out towards the first external frame mount.

Ferrule

Cable frame mount

8 **Thread the cable** through each piece of housing, fitting ferrules to the end of each length and into the frame mounts. Pass the cable along the bike and through the bottom bracket guide. Fit the remaining cable housing, securing it into the rear frame mounts.

9 **Feed the cable** through the cable clamp, pull it taut, then tighten the bolt. Squeeze the gear shifter to pull the cable into place.

Internal gear cables

If your bike becomes sluggish when shifting gears, or the gear levers are slow to return to position, your gear cables are corroded, and you will need to install new ones. The method shown here is for fitting new cabling for the rear derailleur (mech), but it also applies for the front one.

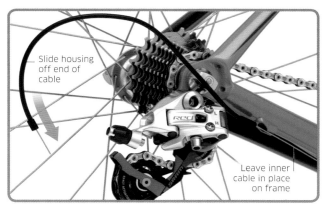

BEFORE YOU START

- Secure your bike in a frame stand
- Unfold the new cables to remove any tension
- Pull back the gear-shifter hood for the cable you wish to change

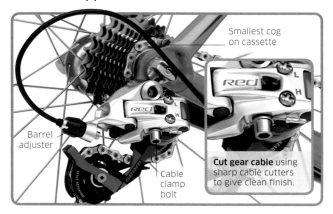

Smallest cog on cassette

Barrel adjuster

Cable clamp bolt

Cut gear cable using sharp cable cutters to give clean finish.

1 **Set the gears** to the smallest cogs on the chainring and the cassette, and cut the existing gear cable cleanly ahead of the cable clamp. Using an Allen key, loosen the cable clamp bolt and free the cable.

Slide housing off end of cable

Leave inner cable in place on frame

2 **Leaving the existing cable** in place, slide the rearmost piece of cable housing off the free end. Detach the housing from the frame mounts, and set aside the ferrules if you plan to reuse them.

3 **To guide the new cable** through the frame, thread a long, thin tube over the free end of the existing cable. Carefully slide it along the length of the cable, through the entry and exit ports of the frame.

Plastic tube

Tape

Secure ends of tube where they enter and exit frame.

4 **Secure the ends** of the tube at both ends of the frame with tape. Pull the old cable through the frame from the front. Once it is free, disconnect the cable from the gear-shifter (see pp.132–133).

TOOLS AND EQUIPMENT

- Frame stand
- Sharp cable cutters
- Set of Allen keys
- Thin plastic tubing
- Tape
- Ferrules
- Pointed tool
- Oil
- Magnet

Workshop tip: The thin tube should be long enough to reach from the entry point to the exit point of the frame. If you still lose the end of a cable within the frame, you can use a magnet to guide the cable to the exit point.

New housing

Clean cut will help inner cable slide through

Old housing

Ferrule | Housing

Fit ferrules to ends of housing. (These secure housing into frame mounts and components.)

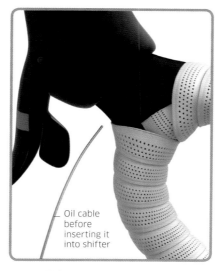

Oil cable before inserting it into shifter

Ease cable into guide tube at frame entry point; push it through.

5 **Using the existing housing** as a guide, cut new pieces to length. Use sharp cable cutters to ensure the cut ends are clear.

6 **Holding the cable** in one hand and the shifter in the other, feed the cable into the shifter until the whole cable is through.

7 **Feed the cable** through the concealed housing on the handlebar. Thread the cable into the tube on the frame (see step 4).

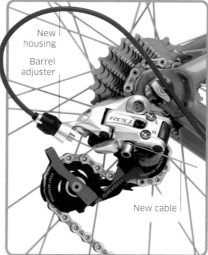

New housing

Barrel adjuster

New cable

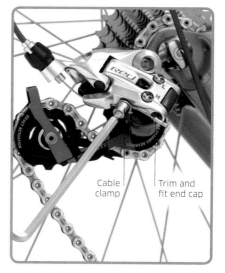

Cable clamp | Trim and fit end cap

8 **Once the new cable is routed** through the frame, pull the guide tube free by sliding it off the end of the cable at the rear.

9 **Fit ferrules** to both ends of a piece of housing, and pass the cable through. Secure the housing in the frame mount and derailleur.

10 **Feed the cable** through the cable clamp, pull it taut, and tighten the bolt. Trim the cable end. To index the gears see pp.148–149.

Electronic shifting

A recent innovation once reserved for professional cyclists, electronic gear-shifting is increasingly found on many road, mountain, and utility bikes. Electronic derailleurs work just like mechanical ones, but are moved by an electric motor on the derailleur rather than a metal cable. The motor is powered by a rechargeable battery, and is activated when the shifter is pressed. Once set up (see pp.138–139), electronic shifting is quick and precise – reducing chain wear – and the lack of cable stretch means that the derailleurs should never need adjusting. While Shimano and Campagnolo use electric cables to connect the shifters and derailleurs, SRAM's system is wireless.

PARTS FOCUS

An electronic rear derailleur is the same as a mechanical derailleur, other than the motor. SRAM units also include a detachable battery.

① A **motor** inside the derailleur precisely shifts the derailleur arm. Unlike manual systems, every shift moves the derailleur exactly the same distance.

② The **derailleur arm** moves the chain across the cassette, inwards or outwards, according to the gear selected. It also retains tension in the chain.

③ The **jockey wheels** perform two essential tasks: the top wheel guides the chain when shifting gear and the lower wheel keeps the chain tensioned.

④ **Pivots** on the derailleur allow the arm to move vertically – keeping the chain under tension – and laterally – across the cassette to change gear.

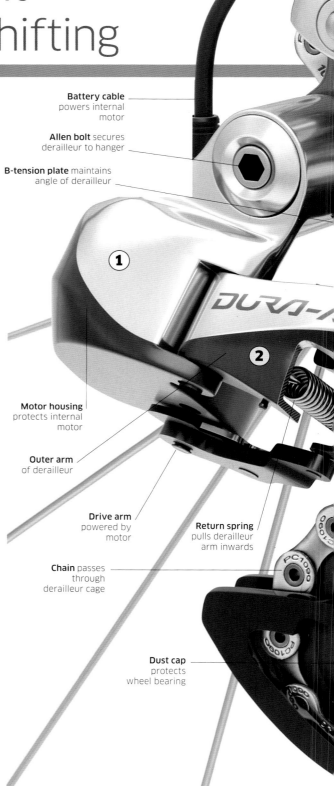

Battery cable powers internal motor

Allen bolt secures derailleur to hanger

B-tension plate maintains angle of derailleur

Motor housing protects internal motor

Outer arm of derailleur

Drive arm powered by motor

Chain passes through derailleur cage

Return spring pulls derailleur arm inwards

Dust cap protects wheel bearing

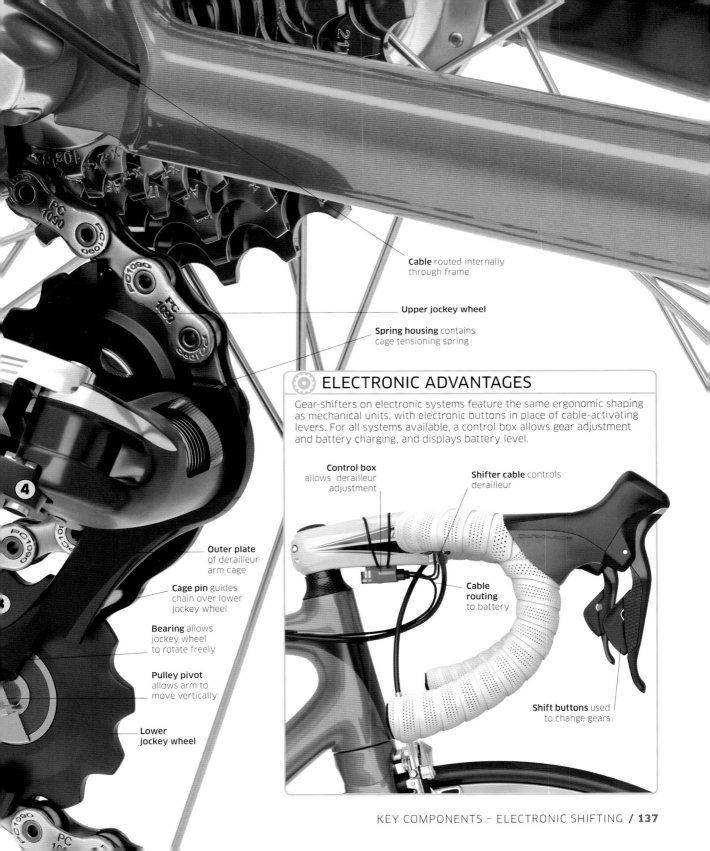

Cable routed internally
through frame

Upper jockey wheel

Spring housing contains
cage tensioning spring

⚙ ELECTRONIC ADVANTAGES

Gear-shifters on electronic systems feature the same ergonomic shaping
as mechanical units, with electronic buttons in place of cable-activating
levers. For all systems available, a control box allows gear adjustment
and battery charging, and displays battery level.

Control box
allows derailleur
adjustment

Shifter cable controls
derailleur

Cable
routing
to battery

Shift buttons used
to change gears

Outer plate
of derailleur
arm cage

Cage pin guides
chain over lower
jockey wheel

Bearing allows
jockey wheel
to rotate freely

Pulley pivot
allows arm to
move vertically

Lower
jockey wheel

Shimano Di2 systems

An electronic drivetrain, such as the Shimano Di2 system, offers precise reliability – a motor shifts the chain at the same speed and distance every time. Electronic wiring means there is no cable stretch to worry about either. If the shifting has become sluggish or you have fitted a new cassette, you may need to fine-tune the system.

 BEFORE YOU START

- Ensure that the battery is fully charged
- Secure your bike in a frame stand
- Check for wear on the cassette and chain

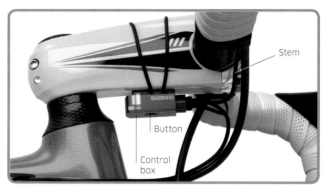

Stem

Button

Control box

2 **Locate the control box**, which can be found on the stem or beneath the saddle, depending on your bike. Press and hold the button until the "adjustment mode" light comes on.

Chain on middle cog of cassette

1 **Use the buttons** on the gear-shifter to move the chain to one of the middle cogs on the rear cassette, such as fourth or fifth gear. The chain can be set on any position on the chainring.

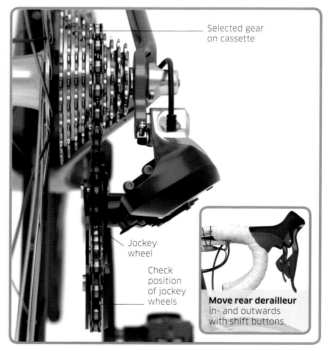

Selected gear on cassette

Jockey wheel

Check position of jockey wheels

Move rear derailleur in- and outwards with shift buttons.

3 **Use the shift buttons** to adjust the position of the rear derailleur (mech) relative to the cassette. The teeth of the jockey wheels should align vertically with the teeth of the cog of the selected gear.

Workshop tip: The Di2 derailleur has a built-in protection feature. If the bike falls over the system will need to be reset. Press and hold the button on the control box until the red light flashes, and pedal through the gears – the derailleur will shift and reset.

Hold button until light goes off

Check chain shifts gear quietly

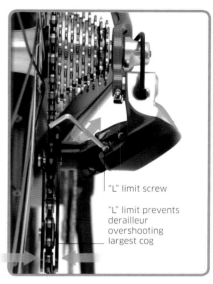

"L" limit screw

"L" limit prevents derailleur overshooting largest cog

4 **Switch the control box** back to "normal mode". The light will turn off. You can use the shifter buttons to change gear again.

5 **Turn the pedals** and shift up and down the gears. If the chain rattles, the derailleur is not in line. Make further adjustments.

6 **Shift to the lowest gear** on the cassette. Turn the "L" (low) limit screw so the teeth of the jockey wheels align with those of the cog.

"H" limit prevents derailleur overshooting smallest cog

Turn "H" limit screw with Allen key

7 **Shift to the highest gear** on the cassette. Turn the "H" (high) limit screw on the derailleur to align the teeth of the jockey wheels vertically with those of the smallest cog. The derailleur will move inwards.

8 **Pedal the bike** to ensure that everything is working correctly. Shift through the gears from highest to lowest, then back, to test for quick, smooth shifting. Readjust the derailleur if required.

The front derailleur moves the top of the chain sideways between the chainrings. When a new gear is selected, the gear cable comes under tension and pulls on the arm of the derailleur to move the cage on the mechanism. The cage pushes the chain sideways; this causes the chain to run at an angle and fall onto the teeth of a smaller chainring or engage with the pick-up ramps of a larger chainring. The front derailleur is attached to the frame either via a clamp around the seat tube or directly ("braze on"). Derailleur parts may be made of aluminium alloy, steel, plastic, or carbon fibre.

⚙ SHIFTING GEARS

When the gear-shifter is pressed, the gear cable is pulled or relaxed, causing the front derailleur to move sideways, guiding the chain across the chainrings.

Chain moves between chainrings

Derailleur controlled by gear cable

Wheel rim

Chain guided by front derailleur

⚙ PARTS FOCUS

A front derailleur has a sprung arm moving on pivots, a cage to shift the chain, and a mount to fix the mechanism to the frame.

① The **cage** consists of two plates between which the chain passes. The inner plate pushes the chain outwards; the outer plate pushes it inwards.

② **Shifting pins** on the inside of the larger chainrings catch the chain and lift it so that the links engage on the larger chainring.

③ The **derailleur mount** may consist of a clamp, as shown, or a "braze on" fitting that is bolted to lugs welded to the frame. Both types are common.

④ **Limit screws** stop the derailleur from moving too far and pushing the chain off the chainrings. They may require adjusting (see pp.142–143).

Spoke

Chainstay

Arm supports and moves cage mechanism

Gear cable may enter derailleur from above or below

Pivots at top and bottom of arm enable it to move

Seat tube is usual location for "braze-on" derailleur

Bolt anchors free end of gear cable

Return spring pulls derailleur inwards

Outer plate of derailleur cage

Inner plate of derailleur cage

Front derailleurs

The front derailleur (mech) moves the chain from one chainring to another. If the chain rattles or slips off when shifted onto the largest gears, then the spring mechanism may have seized, and you will need to adjust or replace the derailleur.

BEFORE YOU START

- Secure your bike in a frame stand
- Remove the chain (see pp.158–159) and the gear cable
- Detach the cable from the derailleur by reversing step 8
- Remove the existing derailleur by reversing step 1

Outer plate of front derailleur

1–3mm gap required

2 **Set the height** of the front derailleur above the chainrings. Check the manufacturer's instructions for the correct height: the derailleur's outer plate usually sits 1–3mm above the largest chainring.

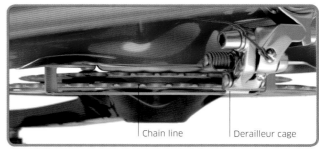

Chain line

Derailleur cage

3 **Look from above** at the chain line. Move the mech towards or away from the frame of your bike by hand. Ensure that the inner and outer plates are sitting parallel to the chainrings.

Mounting bolt

Outer plate

Inner plate

Largest chainring

1 **Position the derailleur** so that the outer plate is just above and parallel to the largest chainring. Use an Allen key to tighten the mounting bolt so that it is held in place but can still be moved by hand.

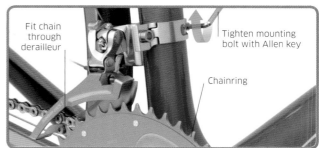

Fit chain through derailleur

Tighten mounting bolt with Allen key

Chainring

4 **When the derailleur is positioned** correctly, tighten the mounting bolt fully to secure it in place. Refer to the manufacturer's instructions for the correct torque setting. Refit the chain (see pp.158–159).

Workshop tip: Gear cables that are rusty, dirty, or frayed will make it harder for you to change gear correctly. It is therefore a good idea for you to replace old cables (see pp.132–135) at the same time as fitting a new front derailleur.

5 **Using the gear-shifter**, set the chain on the smallest chainring, and the rear derailleur to the lowest gear (the largest cog) on the cassette. This is the furthest that the chain will need to travel.

Follow existing cable route

Leave cable end free

6 **If you are fitting** a new gear cable, set the front shifter to the lowest gear, and run the cable from the shifter following the original routing (see pp.132–135). Do not fasten the cable in place.

1-2 mm

Low limit screw

Derailleur cage

7 **Using a cross-head screwdriver**, turn the "low limit" screw (marked "L" on some models) on the front derailleur, so that the inner plate of the mech cage sits about 1-2 mm from the inside of the chain.

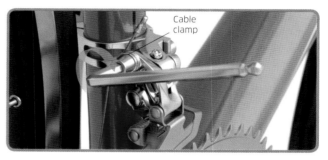

Cable clamp

8 **Close any barrel adjusters** with your fingers. Feed the end of the gear cable through the cable clamp on the derailleur and fasten it in place with an Allen key. Trim the cable and fit an end cap.

1-2 mm

High limit screw

9 **Using the shifters**, set the chain to the largest chainring and onto the smallest cog of the rear cassette. Turn the "high limit" screw until the outer plate of the derailleur is 1-2 mm from the chain.

Barrel adjuster

10 **Use the shifter** to move the chain from one chainring to another. If the chain does not pass smoothly between chainrings, turn the barrel adjusters in small increments to adjust the cable.

Rear derailleurs

The rear derailleur on your bike shifts the chain between the cogs on the rear cassette. It has an arm with a parallelogram mechanism that moves using pivots, and is controlled by the tension in the gear cable. When you press the gear-shifter the derailleur releases slack in the cable. The return spring in the derailleur then forces the parallelogram to move, taking up the slack, and pulls the bottom of the chain sideways. When you are not changing gear, the cable tension keeps the derailleur in position. Rear derailleurs vary in length – longer models are required for cassettes with a larger range of gears.

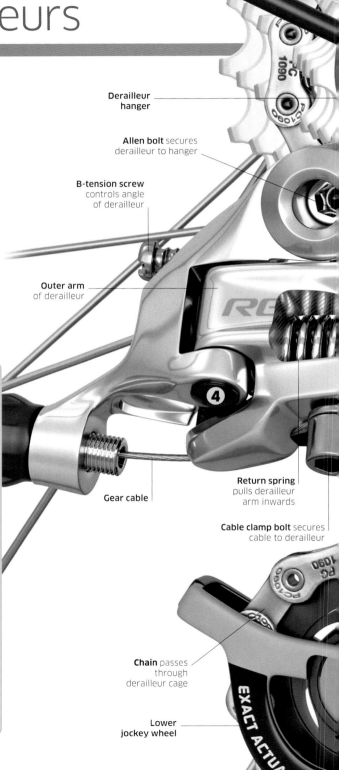

Derailleur hanger

Allen bolt secures derailleur to hanger

B-tension screw controls angle of derailleur

Outer arm of derailleur

Return spring pulls derailleur arm inwards

Gear cable

Cable clamp bolt secures cable to derailleur

Chain passes through derailleur cage

Lower jockey wheel

⚙ PARTS FOCUS

The rear derailleur comprises an arm with pivots, to move the chain, and jockey wheels, to maintain tension on the chain.

① The **jockey wheels** are held within a cage fixed to the derailleur arm. They keep the chain taut as it shifts between cogs on the cassette.

② The **hanger** supports the derailleur on the frame. It is a separate component on some bikes, while on others it can be part of the frame.

③ The **limit screws** on the derailleur adjust the range of movement at either end of its range, and so, prevent the chain from over-shifting. The limit screws should be set correctly (see pp.148–149).

④ The **pivots** allow the derailleur to move inwards and outwards beneath the cassette.

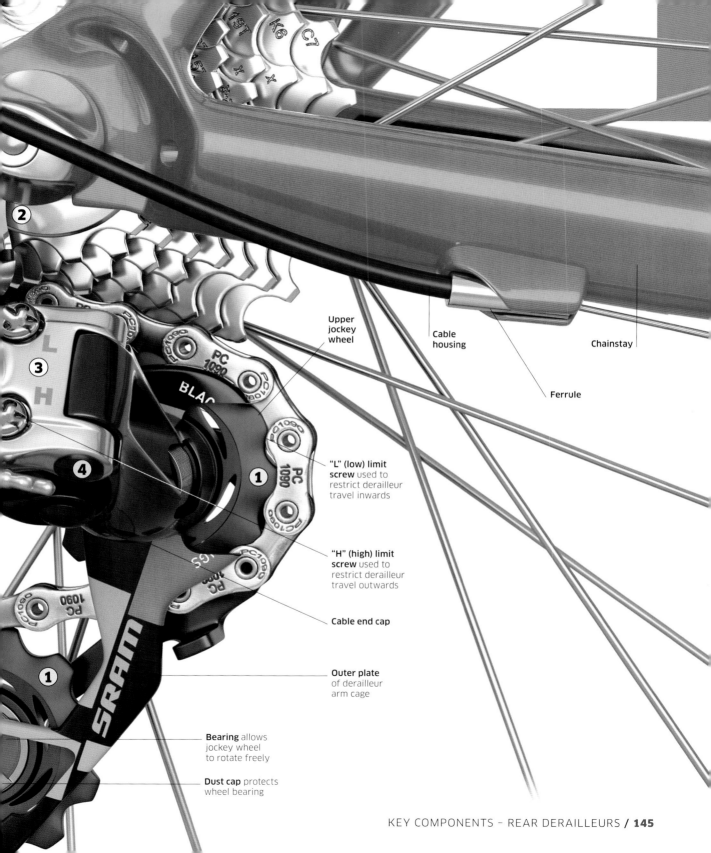

2

3

4

1

1

Upper
jockey
wheel

Cable
housing

Chainstay

Ferrule

"L" (low) limit
screw used to
restrict derailleur
travel inwards

"H" (high) limit
screw used to
restrict derailleur
travel outwards

Cable end cap

Outer plate
of derailleur
arm cage

Bearing allows
jockey wheel
to rotate freely

Dust cap protects
wheel bearing

Rear derailleurs

The rear derailleur (mech) shifts the chain between cogs on the cassette as you change gear. If the spring mechanism becomes worn it may seize, causing the bike to slip between gears, and you will need to replace the derailleur.

BEFORE YOU START

- Secure your bike in a frame stand
- Remove the chain (see pp.158–159)
- Remove the existing derailleur by disconnecting the gear cable, and reversing step 2

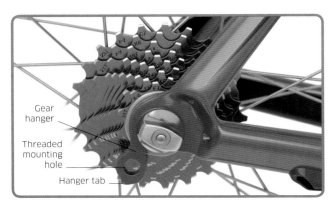

Gear hanger

Threaded mounting hole

Hanger tab

1 **Grease inside the threaded mounting hole** on the gear hanger to ensure that the derailleur will move freely. If your bike has a bolt-on hanger, check that it is sitting straight and fits securely.

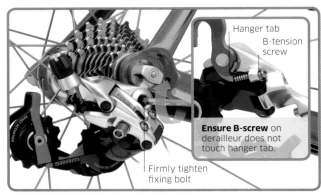

Hanger tab
B-tension screw

Ensure B-screw on derailleur does not touch hanger tab.

Firmly tighten fixing bolt

2 **Angle the rear derailleur** at 90° to its normal position, and fit its fixing bolt into the mounting hole. Tighten it with an Allen key. To check that it is secure, push it to see if it springs back into position.

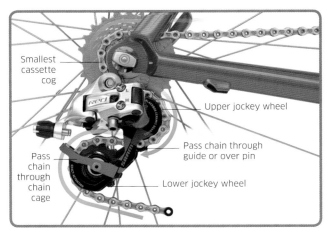

Smallest cassette cog

Upper jockey wheel

Pass chain through guide or over pin

Pass chain through chain cage

Lower jockey wheel

3 **Rest one end** of the chain on the smallest front chainring. Pass the other end over the back of the smallest cassette cog, the front of the upper jockey wheel, and the back of the lower jockey wheel.

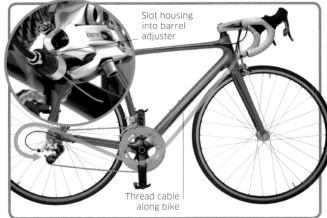

Slot housing into barrel adjuster

Thread cable along bike

4 **Attach the gear cable** (see pp.132–135) and route it along the frame, adding cable housing where required. Feed the cable through the barrel adjuster, and secure the last section of housing.

TOOLS AND EQUIPMENT

- Frame stand
- Grease
- Set of Allen keys
- Chain tool or quick-release link
- Screwdriver
- Oil

Workshop tip: Once you have fitted the rear derailleur onto the gear hanger, lightly spray oil onto the pivot points and the jockey wheels.

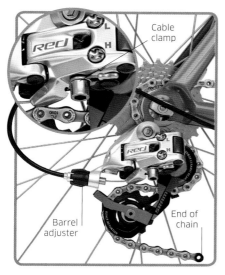

Cable clamp

Barrel adjuster

End of chain

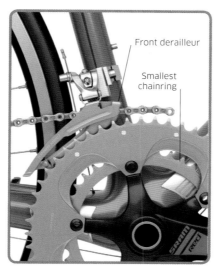

Front derailleur

Smallest chainring

Chainstay

Bring ends of chain together

5 **Thread the cable** into the cable clamp on the derailleur. Pull the cable taut and tighten the clamp bolt using an Allen key.

6 **Feed the other end** of the chain through the front derailleur, and pass it over the front of the smallest chainring.

7 **Bring the two ends** of the chain together below the chainstay. Gravity will help to keep it in position on the bike.

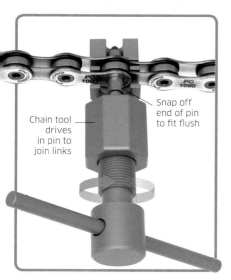

Chain tool drives in pin to join links

Snap off end of pin to fit flush

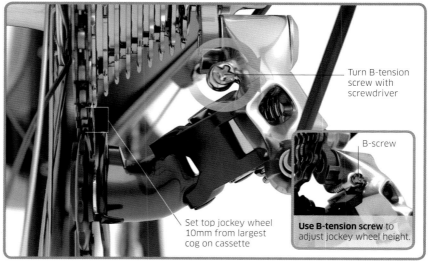

Turn B-tension screw with screwdriver

B-screw

Set top jockey wheel 10mm from largest cog on cassette

Use B-tension screw to adjust jockey wheel height.

8 **Join the ends** of the chain together, according to the type of chain you have. Most use pins (as above) or quick-release links.

9 **Shift the chain** onto the largest cog on the rear cassette. Adjust the B-tension screw on the rear derailleur so that the top jockey wheel is about 10 mm away from the largest cog. This will ensure that the derailleur acts effectively, without interfering with the cogs.

Rear derailleurs

Mechanical bicycle gears are controlled by the tension of the gear cable. When the cable is correctly adjusted, the gears will shift smoothly and easily. If the chain rattles or slips into another gear while you are pedalling, or if the gear does not change at all, this indicates that the tension in the gear cable has changed, and the rear derailleur (mech) needs to be indexed.

 BEFORE YOU START

- Replace the gear cable if worn or damaged (see pp.132–135)
- Clean the rear derailleur and apply oil to the spring
- Secure your bike in a frame stand, rear wheel off the floor
- Shift the chain on to the smallest chainring

Cable clamp bolt

Barrel adjuster

2 **Loosen the cable clamp bolt** with an Allen key to release the cable and pull it free. Wind the barrel adjuster clockwise until it no longer turns, then rotate it anti-clockwise by a one full turn.

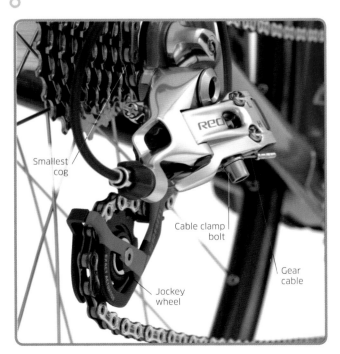

Smallest cog

Cable clamp bolt

Gear cable

Jockey wheel

1 **Use the gear-shifters** to set the chain on the smallest cog on the cassette (the highest gear), and the smallest ring on the chainring. This will reduce tension in the gear cable, and offer you some slack.

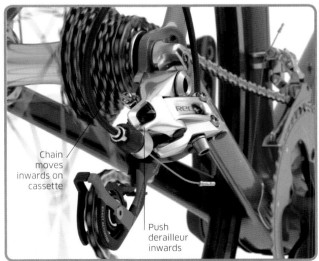

Chain moves inwards on cassette

Push derailleur inwards

3 **Turn the pedals** slowly with one hand. Use your other hand to push the body of the rear derailleur inwards, so that the chain moves to the second smallest cog on the cassette.

Workshop tip: The B-screw controls the angle of the derailleur and its distance between the top jockey wheel and the cogs. It should be close to, but not touching, the cassette. To adjust, shift it to the largest cog. Wind the screw in to move the wheel closer.

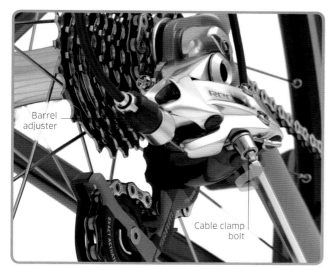

Barrel adjuster

Cable clamp bolt

4 **Insert the gear cable** into the cable clamp, pull it taut, and tighten the cable clamp bolt. Check the top jockey wheel is aligned with the second smallest cog. If not, turn the barrel adjuster anti-clockwise.

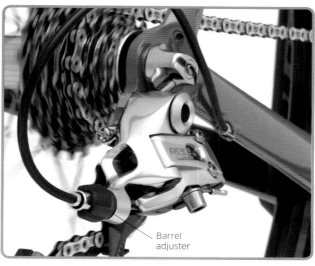

Barrel adjuster

5 **Turn the pedals** and shift through the gears from lowest to highest. If the chain skips two gears, turn the barrel adjuster clockwise. If the chain is slow to move to higher cogs, turn it anti-clockwise.

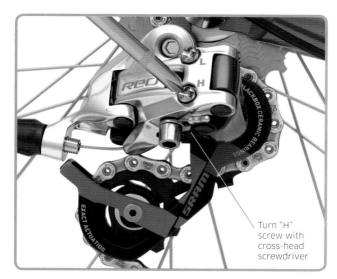

Turn "H" screw with cross-head screwdriver

6 **Set the "H" (high) limit** on the derailleur to stop the chain jumping off the end of the smallest cog. Shift to the highest gear, and turn the "H" screw until the top jockey wheel sits directly under the smallest cog.

Turn "L" screw with cross-head screwdriver

7 **Set the "L" (low) limit** to prevent the chain from overshooting the cassette in the lowest gear. Shift to the lowest gear, and turn the "L" screw until the top jockey wheel sits directly under the largest cog.

Hub gears

A hub gear comprises a set of gears housed within a sealed unit attached to the rear wheel. The number of gears ranges from two or three in a traditional Sturmey-Archer hub, or six to eight in a Shimano hub, to 14 in a Rohloff hub. Gear sets comprise "planet" gears that rotate around a fixed "sun" gear, all held within a ring gear. Hub gears work on most types of bicycle, although they are rather heavy for racing bikes. They are known for reliability and longevity, as the components stay clean and dry inside the hub shell. Hub gears are simple to fit, but need professional servicing owing to their complexity.

Spoke

Hub shell
contains gear
mechanism

 PARTS FOCUS

Hub gears such as a Shimano Alfine 8 (right) have few serviceable parts. Only the cable needs occasional adjustment (see pp.152–155).

① The **yellow bars** visible in the observation window slip out of alignment when the gear cable tension needs to be adjusted.

② The **cable pulley** changes the gear inside the hub gear as the gear cable is pulled or relaxed by the gear-shifter on the handlebar.

③ The **utility hole** on the cable pulley allows you to relax the gear cable and remove the cable fixing bolt in order to take off the wheel (see pp.82–83).

④ The **cable holder** on the cassette joint supports the cable housing, allowing the cable to be set at the correct tension.

Seat stay

Chainstay

Cable
end cap

Alignment
window shows
alignment bars

Cable housing
slots into
ferrule

Cog driven
by chain

1

4

2

Locknut
on hub gear

Non-turn
washer slots
into drop-out

3

Cable fixing bolt
secures cable to
cable pulley

Wheel axle

Drop-out locates
wheel and hub
in frame

Axle nut secures
wheel to frame

Shimano Alfine 8

Hub gears are renowned for their reliability, and require little maintenance once set up. Gear cables can stretch over time, however, causing problems when you shift between gears. This issue is simple to fix, and requires no tools.

1 **Locate the observation window** on the hub gear – it should be on the underside or the top of the hub itself. Two yellow bars should be visible. Clean the window if required.

Shift through gears from first to fourth

2 **Put the hub** into its "adjustment mode" by changing into first gear and then back to fourth using the shifter. Fourth gear is shown as the number 4 on the gear-shifter on some models.

Aligned bars signify that hub gear needs no further adjustment.

3 **Check the two yellow bars** in the window. If they are misaligned (as shown), the hub is out of alignment and you will need to adjust the cable. If they are aligned (inset), no adjustment is needed.

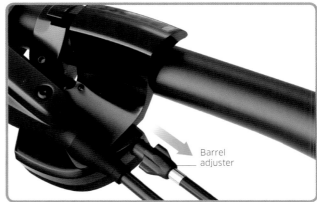

Barrel adjuster

4 **To fix the hub alignment**, locate the cable barrel adjuster, which is usually found on the gear-shifter. Unlock the barrel mechanism by pulling the collar outwards. The barrel will now turn.

Caution! If your hub gear continues to have problems, even though the yellow bars align, take it to a bike repair shop. Hub gears are complex, and are not designed to be taken apart. You may damage the hub permanently if you attempt any repairs yourself.

Turn barrel clockwise or anti-clockwise to align bars

Take shifter out of adjustment mode by changing to first gear

5 **Turning the barrel lock** causes the bar on the right of the window to move. Turn the barrel clockwise or anti-clockwise until the bars in the hub observation window align.

6 **Once you are happy** with the adjustment, take the shifter out of adjustment mode by changing into first gear. Then shift into the highest gear, before finally shifting back into fourth.

Bars aligned

Misaligned bars signify that hub gear is still not correctly aligned.

7 **Check the alignment of the bars** in the observation window again. If they are still misaligned, repeat steps 2–6, turning the barrel and shifting the gears until the bars line up correctly. Once aligned, take the bike for a ride, then check the yellow bars once more.

VARIATIONS

Shimano Alfine hub gears are available with four, seven, eight, or 11 gears, and all models are adjusted in the same way. There are a number of small differences to be aware of, however. You should also refer to the owner's manual.

- Shimano Alfine hubs with four, seven, or eight gears are adjusted with the shifter set in fourth gear. The 11-speed model is adjusted in sixth gear.

- The alignment bars on the Alfine 8 hub are yellow. On other models they are red or green.

Sturmey-Archer three-speed

Sturmey-Archer hub gears have been used for decades on a wide range of bicycles, from utility road bikes to modern folding ones. The hub is very reliable but it cannot be serviced at home. The gear cables can stretch, hindering gear selection, but this is an easy problem to fix.

BEFORE YOU START

- Secure your bike in a frame stand
- Make sure that the rear wheel is centred in the forks
- Wipe away any dirt and grease from the area around the hub gear
- Check the gear cable for any damage

Adjustment gear indicated by circle on gear-shifter

1 **Set the hub gear** into "adjustment mode" by selecting the second gear on the gear-shifter. (This gear is commonly used as the adjustment gear on modern shifters.)

Protective cover

2 **The hub linkage** and fulcrum on modern bikes may be concealed by a protective cover. If so, unclip the cover from the bike to access the linkage, taking care not to snap the retaining clips.

12.5 cm (5 in)

Fulcrum clip

3 **If the bike has** a separate fulcrum clip, check that this is secure and positioned at least 12.5 cm (5 in) from the hub. To adjust it, loosen the screw on its rear, reposition the clip, and retighten the screw.

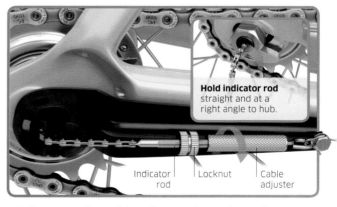

Hold indicator rod straight and at a right angle to hub.

Indicator rod | Locknut | Cable adjuster

4 **Unscrew the cable adjuster** from the indicator rod to disconnect it fully. Hold the indicator rod so that it points straight out of the hub, turn it clockwise to tighten it fully, and loosen it by half a turn.

TOOLS AND EQUIPMENT

- Frame stand
- Degreaser or cleaning fluid
- Cloth
- Small screwdriver
- Grease

Caution! You may damage the hub if you use it with misaligned gears. If you have problems selecting a gear, or the hub slips, check that the tension in the gear cable is correct. If the problems persist take the bike to a bike shop for specialist attention.

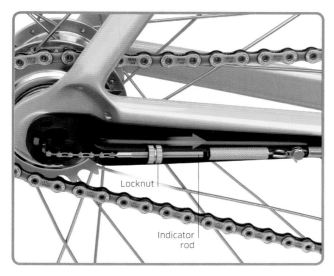

Locknut

Indicator rod

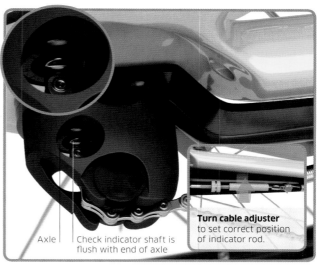

Axle | Check indicator shaft is flush with end of axle

Turn cable adjuster to set correct position of indicator rod.

5 **Check the indicator rod** for any damage. Clean and grease its threads, then screw the rod back into the cable adjuster by hand. Loosen the locknut on the indicator rod by a few turns.

6 **With second gear still selected** on the shifter, turn the cable adjuster until the end of the indicator shaft is exactly level with the end of the axle, when seen through the observation window.

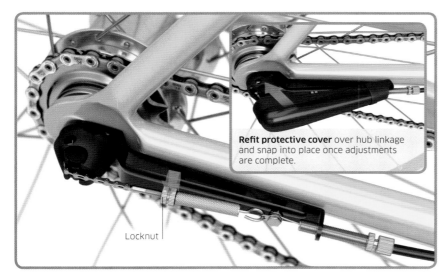

Refit protective cover over hub linkage and snap into place once adjustments are complete.

Locknut

7 **Tighten the locknut** on the cable adjuster to fix the new setting. Shift between the gears to check that they work with no slipping. Refit the cover over the hub linkage. Take the bike for a test ride in a safe area, and make any further adjustments if required.

🔍 FIVE-SPEED HUBS

A Sturmey-Archer five-speed hub gear is adjusted in a similar way to the three-speed model.

- Select the second gear on the shifter and turn the cable adjuster so no more than 2.5mm (1 in) of the indicator shaft protrudes over the axle end.

- Tighten the locknut against the cable adjuster.

- Select fifth gear, turn pedals, then reselect second gear.

- Check the position of the indicator rod, and readjust if required.

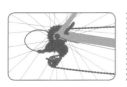

Chains and cassettes

The chain and cassette – the cluster of sprockets on the rear hub – transfer drive from the chainset to the rear wheel, converting your pedalling energy into forward motion. A chain consists of more than a hundred links, each of which is made up of two plates that are joined by pins and rollers, which allow the links to rotate and flex. Chains vary in width depending on the number of sprockets – ranging from 8 to 12 – on the cassette. Each link fits snugly either side of a tooth on the sprocket, which is stamped with "ramps" – grooves that allow the chain to shift more smoothly from one sprocket to the next.

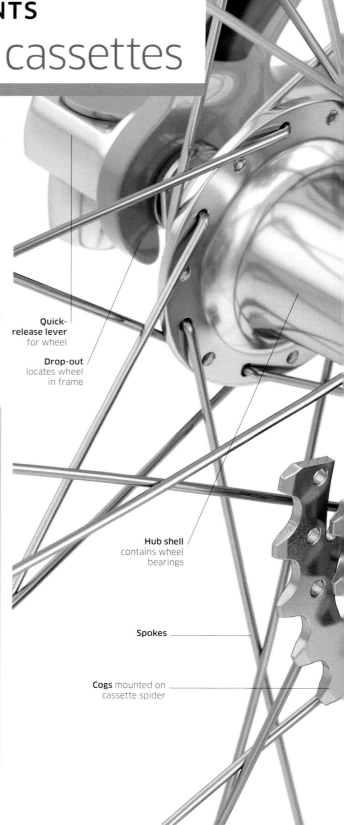

Quick-release lever
for wheel

Drop-out
locates wheel
in frame

Hub shell
contains wheel
bearings

Spokes

Cogs mounted on
cassette spider

PARTS FOCUS

The cassette consists of up to 12 sprockets with a varying number of teeth – from 10 to 50 – offering a multitude of gear ratios.

(**1**) The **lock ring** holds the cassette onto the free hub. You will need a special tool to remove it if you change your cassette (see pp.160–161).

(**2**) A series of **cogs** in different sizes make up the cassette, which each provide a different ratio. The smallest cog gives the highest gear.

(**3**) Cassettes feature **spacers** that ensure the correct distance between cogs. The number of spacers depends on the type of cassette.

(**4**) The **rear derailleur** is not part of the cassette, but performs the vital function of shifting the chain across the cassette, allowing you to change gear.

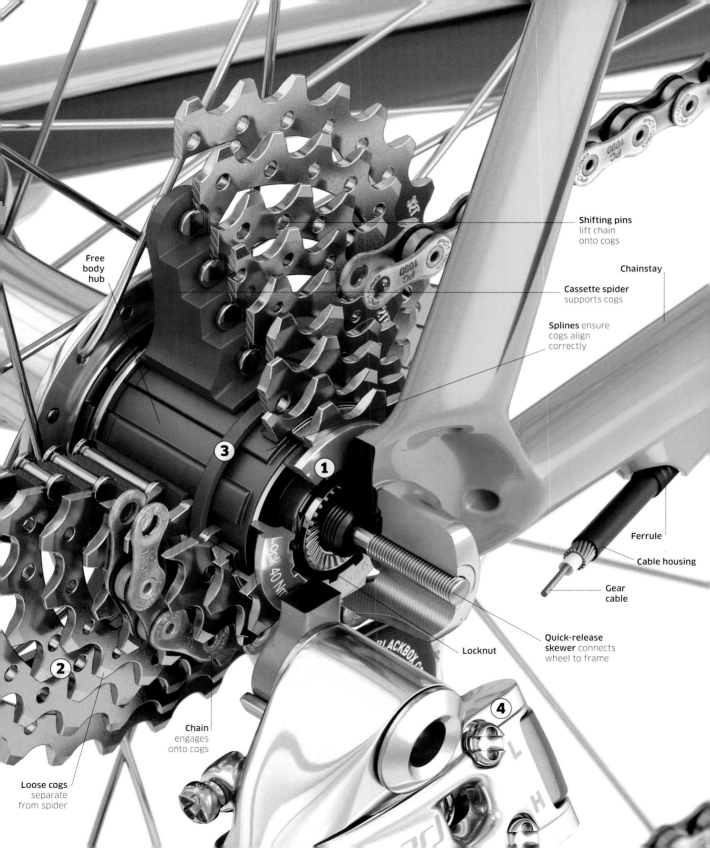

Shifting pins
lift chain
onto cogs

Chainstay

Cassette spider
supports cogs

Splines ensure
cogs align
correctly

**Free
body
hub**

Ferrule

Cable housing

**Gear
cable**

Locknut

**Quick-release
skewer** connects
wheel to frame

Chain
engages
onto cogs

Loose cogs
separate
from spider

Bicycle chains

Your bike chain takes a lot of wear and tear as it is constantly twisted and put under strain. It requires oil to work smoothly, which in itself attracts grit and grime. Slipping gears may be a sign that your chain needs replacing.

BEFORE YOU START

- Ensure that the chain is on the smallest cog at the back and the smallest chainring at the front to provide enough slack
- Place a chain wear indicator onto the chain. The indicator pins should slot into the links; if not, the chain has stretched

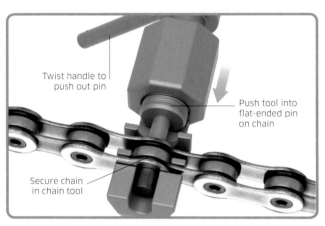

Twist handle to push out pin

Push tool into flat-ended pin on chain

Secure chain in chain tool

1 **Lift the chain** off the chain ring and onto the bottom bracket. Select a link on the lower length of chain, and locate the chain in the chain tool. Wind the handle to push the pin out, and remove the chain.

Derailleur cage

Rotate chainring using pedal

2 **Thread one end** of the new chain through the front derailleur (mech) cage until it catches on the teeth of the chainring. Turn the pedals and draw the chain downwards.

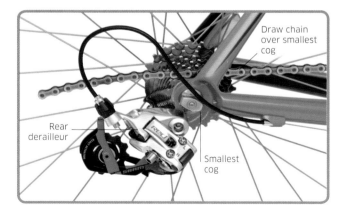

Draw chain over smallest cog

Rear derailleur

Smallest cog

3 **Pull the other end** of the chain towards the rear derailleur so that it rests on the smallest cog of the cassette. It is now ready to be threaded through the rear derailleur.

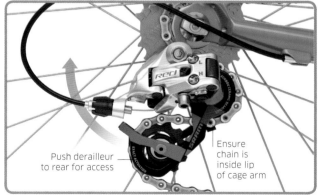

Push derailleur to rear for access

Ensure chain is inside lip of cage arm

4 **Thread the new chain** through the rear derailleur. Feed the chain downwards carefully – clockwise over the top jockey wheel, and anti-clockwise over the bottom jockey wheel.

Workshop tip: A new chain may need to be shortened, as if it is too long, it may jump off the chainring. Chains vary in length. To find the optimum length, wrap the chain around the biggest cog at the back and the biggest front chainring at the front, and add two links.

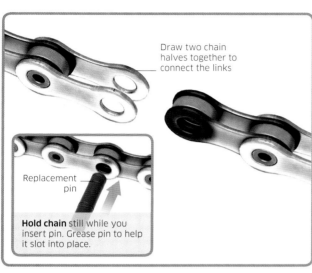

Draw two chain halves together to connect the links

Replacement pin

Hold chain still while you insert pin. Grease pin to help it slot into place.

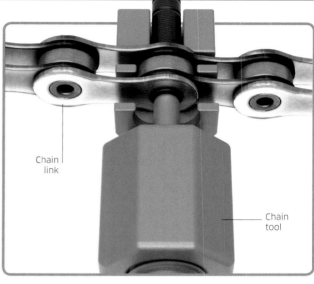

Chain link

Chain tool

5 **Bring the two ends** of the chain together underneath the chainstay. Push the thin end of the replacement pin between the two links to hold the chain together.

6 **Slot the chain** into the guide on the chain tool. Twist the handle of the tool to push the replacement pin into the links, and securely join the lengths of chain together.

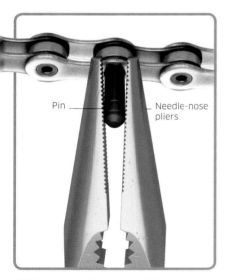

Pin

Needle-nose pliers

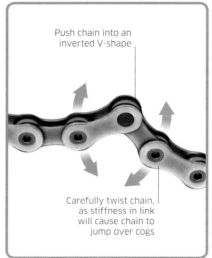

Push chain into an inverted V-shape

Carefully twist chain, as stiffness in link will cause chain to jump over cogs

CHAIN LINKS

Many manufacturers now make special chain connectors that mean you can remove and replace your chain easily – sometimes without tools.

- The SRAM "PowerLink" has two halves with an integrated pin. Snap the link into place and apply tension to secure it. The link can be released manually.

- Shimano chains feature a hardened connecting pin with a flared end for extra strength.

- Campagnolo's Ultralink comes with a chain segment so several links can be replaced at once.

7 **Snap off the end** of the pin using needle-nose pliers. Some chain tools can also be used to shorten the chain pin.

8 **The chain will feel** stiff at the join. Apply oil to the link and manipulate the chain with your hands until the link moves freely.

▶ REMOVING AND SERVICING A CASSETTE
Rear cassettes

Cassettes are susceptible to wear, especially if you allow dirt, grease, and road salt to build up, causing your chain to slip and jump. Although cassettes can be cleaned in situ, they are best removed to do a more thorough job.

🔧 BEFORE YOU START

- Prepare a clear space where you can lay out the parts
- Remove the rear wheel from your bike (see pp.80–81)
- Select the correct lock ring tool for your cassette

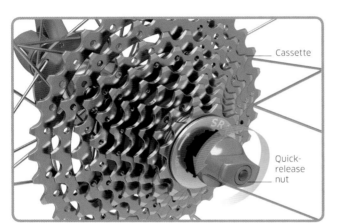

Cassette

Quick-release nut

1 Remove the skewer by fully unscrewing the quick-release nut in order to access the lock ring. Then slide the skewer out of the hub, being careful not to lose the conical springs on each side.

Loosely tighten quick-release nut onto lock ring tool.

Lock ring tool

2 Using the correct lock ring tool, fully insert the serrated edge of the tool into the lock ring on the cassette. Replace the quick-release nut to hold the tool in place, as it is turned.

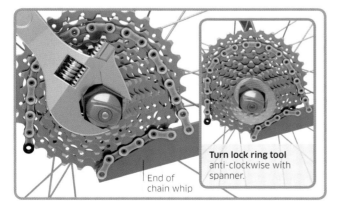

End of chain whip

Turn lock ring tool anti-clockwise with spanner.

3 Fit a chain whip around the third largest gear of the cassette. Holding the chain whip firmly to stop the cassette turning, grip the lock ring tool with an adjustable spanner, and unscrew the lock ring.

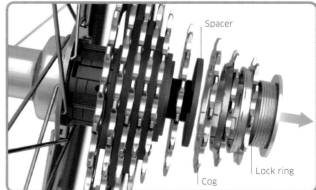

Spacer

Lock ring

Cog

4 Undo the quick-release nut, remove the tool, and unscrew the lock ring. Slide the cassette from the freehub. Some cogs may be loose when removed; make a note of their order and any spacers used.

Workshop tip: Apply a thin layer of grease to the grooves of your freehub body to prevent rust. If any corrosion is already present, use a hard-bristled brush to clean it off gently.

Clean in gaps

Brush cogs firmly

PARTS FOCUS

Many cassettes are only compatible with specific hubs, so check this when buying new components.

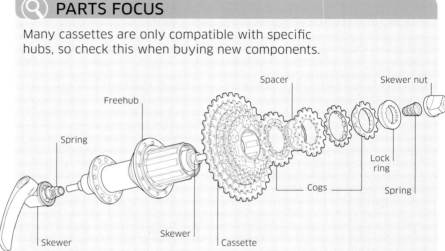

Spacer

Skewer nut

Freehub

Spring

Lock ring

Cogs

Spring

Skewer

Cassette

Skewer

5 **Clean the cassette** and cog teeth with a hard-bristled brush and degreaser. Wash off the dirty fluid with soapy water.

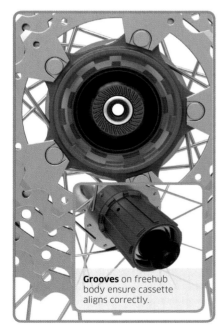

Grooves on freehub body ensure cassette aligns correctly.

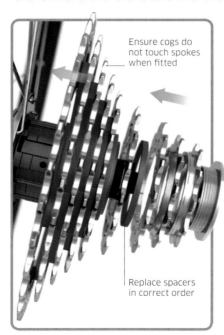

Ensure cogs do not touch spokes when fitted

Replace spacers in correct order

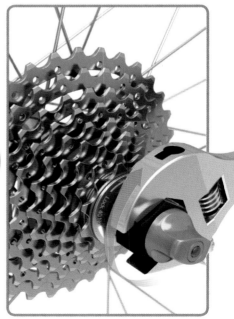

6 **Line up the cassette body**, known as the spider, with the grooves on the freehub. They will only fit in one arrangement.

7 **Push the cassette** and cogs onto the freehub body. Ensure that you return the spacers in the correct order.

8 **Refit the cassette** to the hub using the lock ring tool and a spanner to tighten it. You can now replace the wheel and chain.

Chainsets

The chainset comprises the cranks, chainrings, and bottom bracket. When choosing a chainset, consider the size of the chainrings and the number of teeth, which affects the gearing, and select a crank length to suit your leg length, which will make pedalling easier. You should also choose a chainset to suit the style of riding you are intending to do.

TYPE	SUITABILITY	KEY COMPONENTS
FAST ROAD Fast road chainsets should be light but very stiff. These chainsets are often fitted with bigger chainrings, offering a higher range of gears for race riders.	■ **Racing** and other competitive road events.	■ **The crank and spider** are made as a single piece. ■ **The two chainrings** must work with 10- to 11-speed chains. ■ **The axle** is press-fitted on splines on the right side and secured with a pinch bolt on the left side.
TRAINING/CYCLO-CROSS/SPORTIVE These mid-level chainsets provide similar performance to more expensive versions, so are suitable for more general riding, although they are stiffer and tend to weigh more than premium models.	■ **General road riding**, training, or sportives. ■ **Cyclo-cross racing**. ■ **Gravel riding**.	■ **The crank and spider** are usually made as a single piece. ■ **The two chainrings** must work with 10- to 11-speed chains. ■ **The axle** is press-fitted on splines on the right side and secured with a pinch bolt on the left side.
TRACK/FIXED/SINGLE-SPEED These chainsets have wider teeth and only one chainring. They are very stiff in order to cope with high pedal forces.	■ **Track** cycling and racing. ■ **Single-speed** city riding.	■ **The crank and spider** are usually made as a single piece. ■ **The wider chainring** is usually only compatible with wider 3.18 mm (0.125 in) chain. ■ **The axle** is typically fitted into the frame with the BB.
MOUNTAIN BIKE MTB chainsets vary from triple-ring chainsets, which provide a wide range of gears to double-ring sets, which offer a saving in weight, and single-ring sets, often favoured for simplicity.	■ **Hill climbing**, if the bike has a triple-ring chainset that includes low gears. ■ **Downhill riding** on a single-ring chainset.	■ **The crank and spider** are usually made as a single piece. ■ **The two chainrings** must work with 10- to 11-speed chains. ■ **The axle** is press-fitted on splines on the right side and secured with a pinch bolt on the left side.

Many components are made of lightweight aluminium, but the highest-end road-bike chainsets have components of carbon to save weight. You may need a much tougher chainset if you are intending to do any heavy off-road riding, to reduce the risk of debris from the trail damaging or even breaking the chain mid-ride.

MATERIALS

- **Cranks and spiders** are usually aluminium. Cranks are hollow.
- **High-end chainsets** have carbon-fibre cranks and hardened alloy chainrings.
- **Axles** are hollow and generally lightweight steel.

VARIATIONS

- **Cranks are** 165–175mm to suit different leg lengths. They are typically 172.5mm.
- **Popular chainrings** have 53–39 teeth or mid-compact 52–36 teeth.

MAINTENANCE

- **Breakages** are rare, but after a knock the cranks should be checked for cracks.
- **Hooked chainrings** indicate excessive wear and should be changed.

- **Cranks and spiders** are usually aluminium.
- **Cranks** are often hollow but may be solid on budget chainsets.
- **Axles** are hollow and generally lightweight steel.
- **Entry-level bikes** may be fitted with a square taper BB.

- **Cranks are** 165–175mm long to suit different leg lengths. They are typically 172.5mm.
- **Popular compact chainrings** have 50–34 teeth.
- **Cyclo-cross rings** may use 46–34 teeth.

- **Breakages** are rare, but after a knock the cranks should be checked for cracks.
- **Hooked chainrings** indicate excessive wear and should be changed.

- **Cranks and spiders** are usually aluminium.
- **Axles** are hollow and generally lightweight steel.
- **Chainrings** may be made of aluminium or steel.

- **Cranks are** 165–175mm long.
- **Longer chainsets** may hit the ground when you are pedalling through corners or banking on a track.
- **Popular chainrings** have 48–49 teeth.

- **Off-road riding** accelerates wear on the chainrings, so check chainrings and chain regularly.
- **Check cranks** for damage or cracks.

- **Cranks and spiders** are usually aluminium.
- **Cranks are often** hollow but may be solid on budget chainsets.
- **Axles** are square taper and use a square taper BB.

- **Cranks are** 165–175mm long to suit different leg lengths. They are typically 172.5mm.
- **Popular chainrings** have 40–28 teeth or mid-compact 38–26 teeth.
- **Triple chainsets** have 40-32-22 teeth.

- **Breakages are rare**, but after a knock the cranks should be checked for cracks.
- **Play at the BB** and a slack chain should be checked and changed.

Chainsets

The chainset rotates around the bottom bracket (BB) when you turn the pedals; it consists of the crank arms and chainrings. Square taper units (see pp.168–169) are bolted to the BB axle, while modern chainsets (see pp.166–171) are bonded to a one- or two-piece axle. Touring bikes and some mountain bikes have three chainrings for a wider range of gears. Road bikes have two chainrings to reduce weight, while some cyclo-cross, gravel, and mountain bikes use a "1x" (single) chainring. Chainsets are made of carbon or a solid piece of aluminium, so that they are strong enough to transmit your pedalling forces without flexing.

PARTS FOCUS

The **chainset** consists of the cranks and 1–3 chainrings, which have between 22 and 53 teeth for the chain links to slot onto.

① The two **crank arms** transmit the pedalling action of the rider to the chainring and chain, which in turn rotate the cassette and rear wheel.

② The **spider** is part of the drive (right) side crank arm, and consists of a number of arms onto which the chainrings are bolted.

③ The **axle** joins the crank arms and is bolted to, or integrated with, the BB. A larger diameter axle will improve the stiffness of the chainset.

④ The **BB cups** screw or press into the frame and support the axle, allowing the chainset to rotate smoothly and without loss of torque.

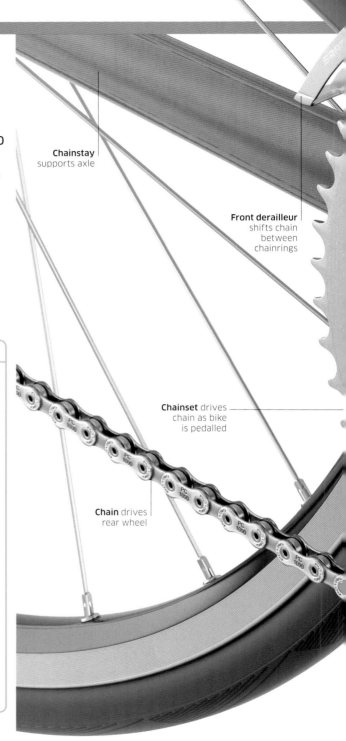

Chainstay supports axle

Front derailleur shifts chain between chainrings

Chainset drives chain as bike is pedalled

Chain drives rear wheel

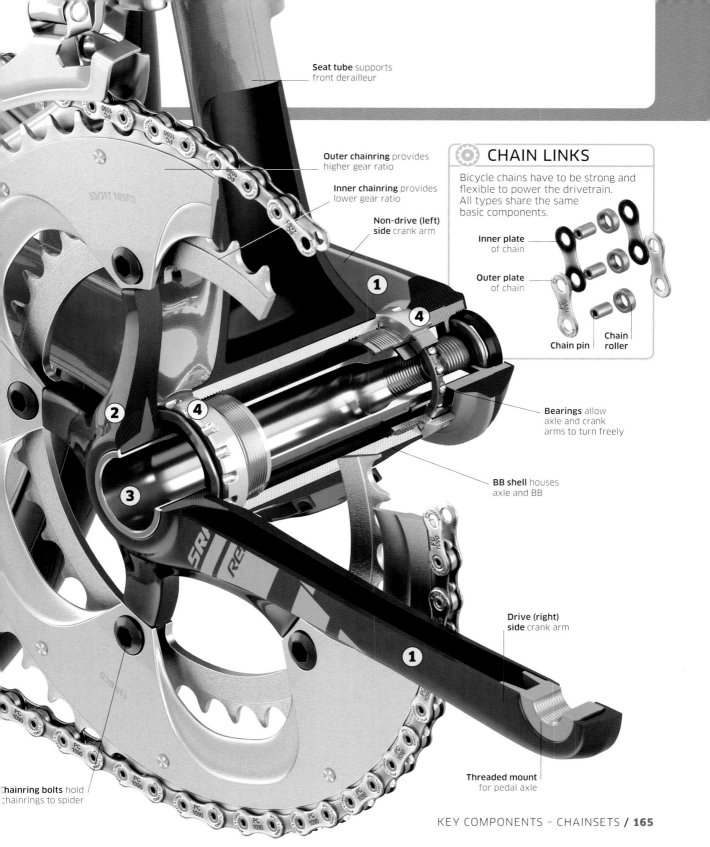

Seat tube supports
front derailleur

Outer chainring provides
higher gear ratio

Inner chainring provides
lower gear ratio

Non-drive (left)
side crank arm

CHAIN LINKS

Bicycle chains have to be strong and
flexible to power the drivetrain.
All types share the same
basic components.

Inner plate
of chain

Outer plate
of chain

Chain pin   Chain
roller

Bearings allow
axle and crank
arms to turn freely

BB shell houses
axle and BB

Drive (right)
side crank arm

Chainring bolts hold
chainrings to spider

Threaded mount
for pedal axle

Shimano HollowTech II

Shimano HollowTech chainsets feature a hollow axle, which is connected permanently to the right-hand crank and which the left-hand crank is also attached to. You will need to remove the chainset if you want to replace or service your bottom bracket (BB).

BEFORE YOU START

- Secure your bike in a frame stand
- Prepare a clear space where you can lay out the parts
- Place a dustsheet down to catch any grease
- Refer to the manufacturer's instructions for the correct pinch bolt torque setting

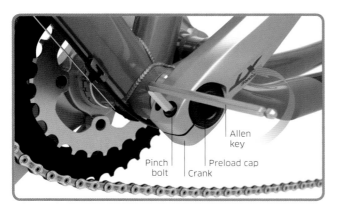

Allen key
Pinch bolt
Crank
Preload cap

1 **Using a 5 mm Allen key,** loosen but do not remove the two pinch bolts on the non-drive (left) side crank. The bolts should be positioned on the left-hand side of the bike frame.

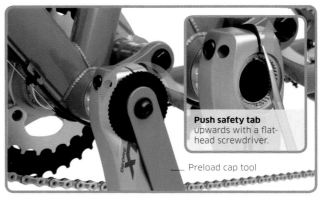

Push safety tab upwards with a flat-head screwdriver.

Preload cap tool

2 **Remove the preload cap** using the specific preload cap tool by unwinding it anti-clockwise. Then, using a small, flat-head screwdriver, disengage the safety tab by pushing it upwards.

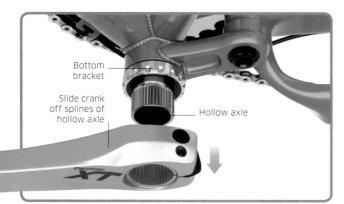

Bottom bracket
Slide crank off splines of hollow axle
Hollow axle

3 **With the safety tab disengaged**, slide the non-drive (left) side crank from the splined axle. If it does not move freely, you may need to wiggle it from side to side in order to dislodge it.

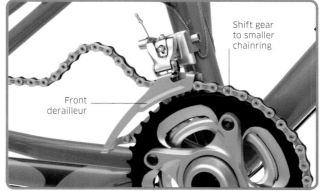

Shift gear to smaller chainring
Front derailleur

4 **Shift the front derailleur** (mech) to the smaller chainring. Lift the chain away from the chainring and allow it to hang freely so that it does not get twisted when you remove the chainset from the frame.

Workshop tip: To make things easier when you are removing the non-drive (left) side crank, fully remove the pinch bolts and the safety tab. This will ensure there is no tension in the clamp.

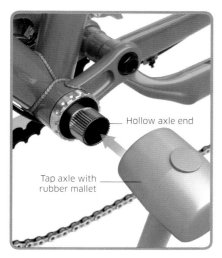

Hollow axle end

Tap axle with rubber mallet

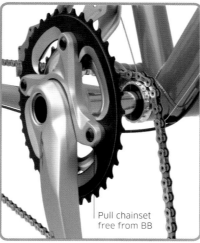

Pull chainset free from BB

SHIMANO TOOLS

Refitting a Shimano HollowTech II chainset requires specific tools and information, which you may not have.

- The preload cap tool is supplied with the chainset, and is vital for fitting and removing it. If yours is lost or damaged, you must buy a replacement.

- If you fit the chainset using a torque spanner, the torque settings required are printed next to the pinch bolts. If they are missing, find them online at Shimano's Tech Resource.

5 **Using a rubber mallet**, firmly but carefully give the hollow axle a few taps until it passes through the BB.

6 **Gently pull the chainset** from the drive (right) side of the BB. Rest the chain on the BB, to avoid it touching the ground.

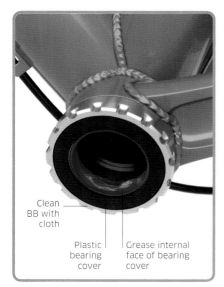

Clean BB with cloth

Plastic bearing cover

Grease internal face of bearing cover

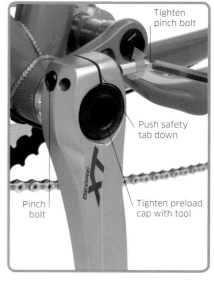

Tighten pinch bolt

Push safety tab down

Pinch bolt

Tighten preload cap with tool

7 **Clean the inner surfaces** of the plastic bearing covers on the BB where the axle sits, and apply fresh grease using your fingers.

8 **Push the chainset** through the BB, doing as much as possible by hand and finishing with the rubber mallet, if necessary.

9 **Refit the non-drive (left) side** crank and replace the preload cap. Push the safety tab into place and tighten the pinch bolts.

Square taper-types

Square taper chainsets are common on older bikes, and those fitted with square taper bottom brackets (see pp.178-79). The chainset and crank arm fit onto the square bottom bracket (BB) spindle; you will need a crank puller tool to remove them. Detach the chainset whenever you are servicing, or replacing, the BB.

BEFORE YOU START

- Secure your bike in a frame stand
- Prepare a clear space where you can lay out the parts
- Clean around the BB
- Spray oil on to the crank bolts to help to loosen them

Clean crank
bolt threads

2 **Clean and lubricate the threads** inside the crank. Use a cloth to clean the thread on the removed bolt. Check that the bolt and any washers are in good condition, and apply fresh grease to the bolt.

Chainring

Turn crank bolt
anti-clockwise

1 **If the crank has plastic bolt** covers, remove these on both sides. Take out the bolt and any washers on the drive (right) side using an Allen key. Hold the arm of the crank still as you work.

Crank puller

3 **Making sure that the end** of the crank puller tool is fully unscrewed, carefully screw the threaded end into the crank by hand. Screw it in tightly – turning clockwise – with your fingers.

TOOLS AND EQUIPMENT

- Frame stand
- Cleaning cloth
- Oil
- Set of Allen keys
- Grease and paintbrush
- Crank puller tool
- Set of spanners

Caution! To avoid damaging the threads of the crank, ensure they are clean before inserting the crank puller tool. Also make sure that the crank puller is positioned straight onto the threads to prevent cross-threading.

Insert Allen key into crank puller

Rest chain on BB

Remove chain

4 **With the crank puller tool** fitted to the crank, use a spanner or an Allen key to turn the end clockwise. The crank puller tool will push the crank off the frame and away from the BB spindle.

5 **Once the crank puller tool has pushed** the chainring off the BB spindle, lift the chainring away from the bike, taking care not to drop it. Lift the chain off the chainring, and rest it on the BB.

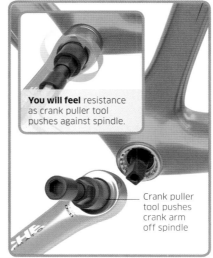

You will feel resistance as crank puller tool pushes against spindle.

Crank puller tool pushes crank arm off spindle

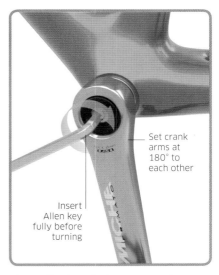

Set crank arms at 180° to each other

Insert Allen key fully before turning

6 **Unscrew the crank puller** tool from the chainset using a spanner or Allen key. Clean the threads of the crank puller tool.

7 **On the non-drive (left) side**, remove the crank bolt, screw in the crank puller and tighten as before to remove the crank arm.

8 **Refit the chainset**, starting with the non-drive (left) side crank arm, reversing the steps 1–7, as shown here.

Campagnolo Ultra-Torque

Campagnolo's drivetrain systems are widely used. Their Ultra-Torque and Power Torque chainsets utilize similar technology, and are fitted in the same way. If there is any creaking or play in the chainset, you should remove it to resolve the issue. You will also need to take off the chainset when replacing a bottom bracket (BB).

BEFORE YOU START

- If the crank bolt is corroded, spray it with penetrating oil
- Put the chain on the inner chainring

Fully remove bolt, then clean and grease it, before reusing later.

Allen key

2 **Insert a long-reach 10 mm Allen key** into the centre of the spindle on the drive (right) side. Ensuring it is fully engaged, turn it anti-clockwise to loosen the crank bolt from the centre.

Safety clip

1 **Temporarily lie your bike** on its side for easier access to the safety clip. Remove the safety clip using needle-nose pliers, and keep it safe. Secure the bike in a frame stand for the remainder of the task.

Remove chain from chainring

Turn chainring as chain is removed

3 **Remove the chain** from the chainring, by lifting the rear derailleur (mech) to release tension from the chain. Rotate the chainring and lift the chain from it. Rest the detached chain on the BB.

Workshop tip: Before refitting, apply grease to the thread of the crank bolt. This will prevent the bolt from rusting or degrading over time, and make future removal easier. Hold the drive (right) side crank arm steady when loosening or retightening the crank bolt.

Chain will hang loose

4 **Ease the drive (right) side** crank out of the BB. Take care not to damage the crank or drop any of the components.

PARTS FOCUS

Several chainset systems exist, and so parts from different manufacturers are often incompatible with one another.

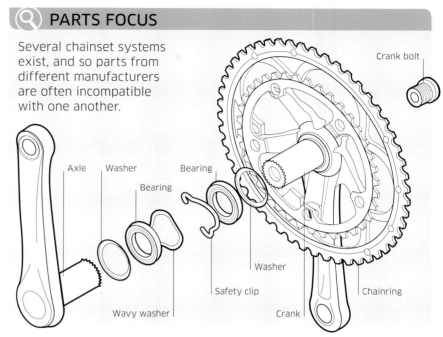

Crank bolt

Axle

Washer

Bearing

Bearing

Wavy washer

Safety clip

Washer

Crank

Chainring

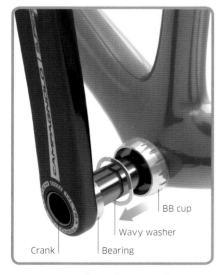

BB cup

Wavy washer

Crank

Bearing

5 **Remove the other crank arm** and the wavy washer (the "brown" washer on Campagnolo Power Torque chainsets).

Ensure chain is fitted properly

Refit and clip in safety clip fully before riding.

6 **To refit the chainset,** first clean the axle and the BB, then re-grease them. Check that the wavy (or brown) washer has not flattened over time, and replace it if necessary. Reinstall the chainset by reversing steps 1–5.

SRAM Red

Made from lightweight carbon fibre, SRAM Red chainsets feature a hollow axle, which is connected permanently to the drive (right) side crank, and which the left-hand crank fits onto. You will need to remove the chainset if the bottom bracket (BB) needs cleaning or replacing. If replacing, make sure the new BB is the correct size for the SRAM chainset.

 BEFORE YOU START

- Secure your bike in a frame stand
- Prepare a clear space where you can lay out the parts

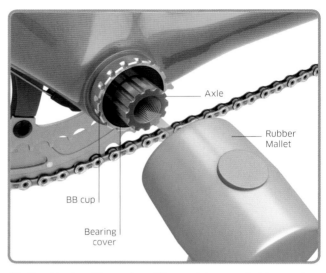

Axle

Rubber Mallet

BB cup

Bearing cover

2 **Gently tap the axle** with a rubber mallet to push the chainset from the BB. The bearing covers may come away from the BB cups as the axle is removed. If this happens, push them back in using your fingers.

8mm Allen key

Crank arm

1 **Insert an 8mm Allen key** into the crank bolt on the non-drive (left) side and turn it anti-clockwise to release the crank from the axle. Remove the crank arm and set aside.

Pedal

Unhook chain to stop it getting tangled

Chainrings

3 **Unhook the chain** from the chainrings and allow it to fall freely away. This is important as you need to avoid the chain twisting when the chainset is pulled through the BB. Rest the chain on the BB.

Workshop tip: If the cranks spin less freely after refitting, it may be due to the fresh grease in the BB seals. This will resolve itself as the BB beds in, so be patient.

Axle

Bearings protected by bearing cover

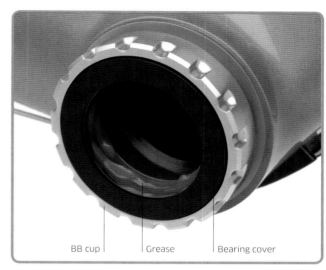

BB cup | Grease | Bearing cover

4 **Pull on the chainring** to slide the axle from the BB. If there is any sign of play or looseness in the crank arms or noise from the bearings you may need to replace the BB (see pp.176–177, 180–181).

5 **Clean the BB** thoroughly with degreaser and a cloth. Apply liberal amounts of fresh grease to the inner surfaces of the BB, including the bearing covers where the axle sits.

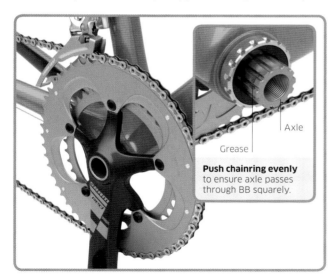

Axle

Grease

Push chainring evenly to ensure axle passes through BB squarely.

Grease

Tighten crank bolt fully by turning Allen key clockwise.

Crank arm

6 **Grease the axle** to help the chainset slide back into place easily and prevent corrosion. Push the chainset back through the BB from the drive (right) side, passing it through the chain first.

7 **Grease the spindle** of the non-drive (left) side crank and slide it onto the axle, ensuring that the splines line up. Tighten the crank bolt with an Allen key. Hook the chain back onto the chainrings.

Bottom brackets

An essential component on every kind of bike, the bottom bracket (BB) fixes the crank arms to the frame via an axle, which is supported by bearings that allow it to rotate freely. Square taper (see pp.178–179) and Shimano Octalink BBs use an axle integrated into a "cartridge" unit, to which the crank arms are fitted. Large-diameter axle systems – such as Campagnolo Power and Ultra-Torque (see pp.176–177), Shimano HollowTech (see pp.180–181), and SRAM GXP – have an axle built onto the cranks that slides inside the bearing cups, which are located on either side of the frame's BB shell. These systems use sealed bearings for durability and ease of maintenance.

 PARTS FOCUS

BBs are screwed or pressed into the BB shell of a frame, and allow the cranks to rotate freely.

(**1**) The **crank bolt** sits inside the axle, fixing the non-drive (left) and drive (right) side cranks together.

(**2**) The **axle** sits inside the BB shell and cups, and rotates when the cranks are turned. It may be integrated into a cartridge BB (see pp.178–179) or the drive (right) side crank (see pp.180–181). Alternatively it may be split into two halves that are bonded to each crank (see pp.176–177).

(**3**) The **BB cups** contain the bearings, and screw or press into either side of the BB shell.

(**4**) The **bearings** sit inside the BB cups and are contained inside sealed units, for added protection.

Drive (right) side crank includes spider for chainring fitting

Outer chainring has more teeth, giving higher gear ratio

Inner chainring has fewer teeth, giving lower gear ratio

Chain transmits propulsion from chainrings to rear wheel

Safety clip
unique to
Campagnolo
BBs

Wavy washer
is unique to
Campagnolo BBs

BB shell houses
axle and BB

**Large-
diameter axle**
for improved
power transfer

**Non-drive
(left) side** crank
connects pedal
to BB axle

▶ REPLACING A BOTTOM BRACKET
Campagnolo Ultra-Torque

Campagnolo Ultra-Torque chainsets have bearing cups that sit on the frame's bottom bracket (BB) shell, with replaceable bearings fitted onto the axle. Vibrations or noise are signs that the bearings are worn and will need to be replaced.

🔧 BEFORE YOU START

- Secure your bike in a frame stand
- Prepare a clear space where you can lay out the parts
- Remove the chainset from the BB (see pp.170–171)
- Source replacement bearings if your bike's are worn

Cloth

Axle

1 **Using a cloth and degreaser**, thoroughly clean the drive (right) side crank arm. Wipe away any grit and dirt from the axle, and clean inside it. Wipe the inside of the BB shell to remove any grease and dirt.

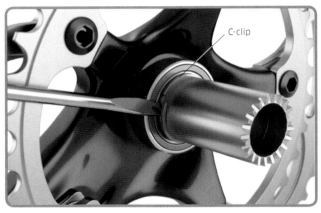

C-clip

2 **The drive (right) side crank** has a "C-clip" to stop the axle from moving laterally in the BB. Prise it from the bearing with a flat-head screwdriver, then pull it off the axle by hand. Take care not to lose it.

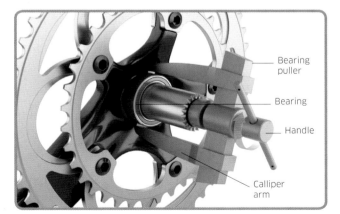

Bearing puller

Bearing

Handle

Calliper arm

3 **Fit the bearing puller** over the axle so that the tips of the calliper arms pinch underneath the bearing. Turn the handle clockwise. As the tool presses on the axle, the calliper arms will pull the bearing free.

Axle

Bearing

Chainset

4 **Once the bearing is loose**, remove the bearing puller and pull the bearing off the axle with your fingers. If there is any damage to the axle surface, you may need to replace the chainset.

Workshop tip: Put a cloth underneath the crank arm before using the bearing puller and bearing installer tools. This will protect the arm from scratches during the removal and refitting process.

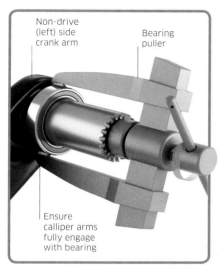

Non-drive (left) side crank arm

Bearing puller

Ensure calliper arms fully engage with bearing

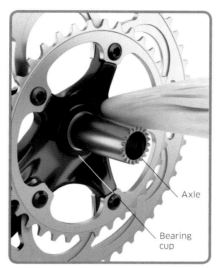

Axle

Bearing cup

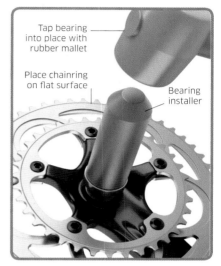

Tap bearing into place with rubber mallet

Place chainring on flat surface

Bearing installer

5 **Fit the bearing puller** onto the non-drive (left) side axle, with the arms engaged with the bearing. Free the bearing as in steps 3–4.

6 **Using a cloth**, thoroughly clean both sides of the axle and the bearing cups with degreaser. Check the parts for signs of wear.

7 **Slide the new bearing** onto the drive (right) side axle. Sit the bearing installer over the axle and lightly tap the bearing into place.

Grease on bearing cup

C-clip

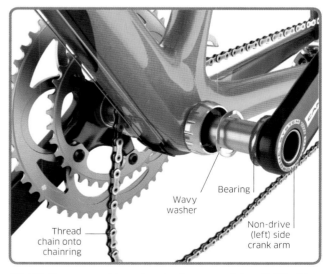

Thread chain onto chainring

Wavy washer

Bearing

Non-drive (left) side crank arm

8 **When the bearing** is fully seated on the axle, apply grease to the bearing cup and the area around it. Put on the C-clip. Slide it onto the axle, up against the bearing, so that it fits snugly.

9 **Fit the second bearing** to the non-drive (left) side crank arm using the bearing installer, as in step 7. Hang the chain on the BB, and refit the chainset and non-drive (left) side crank arm (see pp.170–171).

Cartridge-types

A cartridge bottom bracket (BB) unit has a sealed chamber for the bearings. These bearings can become dry and worn through use, causing the BB to creak when you pedal. A worn cartridge unit cannot be serviced and should be replaced.

⊙ BEFORE YOU START

- Secure your bike in a frame stand
- Remove the chainset (see pp.168–169)
- Secure the chain to the chainstay
- Prepare a clear space where you can lay out the parts

Fit splines on BB remover tool into slots on BB cup

Ensure remover tool is fully engaged before turning with spanner.

Splined BB remover tool

1 **Fit the splined BB remover tool** into the cup on the non-drive (left) side of the BB. Fasten the adjustable spanner over the tool and turn it anti-clockwise to loosen the BB cup.

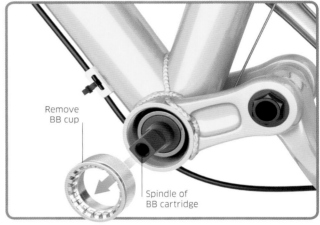

Remove BB cup

Spindle of BB cartridge

2 **Continue to loosen the BB cup** using the spanner, until you can unscrew it the rest of the way by hand. Remove the old cup from the non-drive (left) side of the frame.

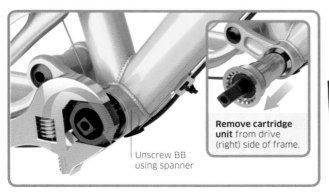

Remove cartridge unit from drive (right) side of frame.

Unscrew BB using spanner

3 **Fit the BB remover tool** to the drive (right) side. BB cups are marked with an arrow to indicate the direction in which to tighten them. To loosen them, turn the spanner the opposite way.

Measurements printed on shell

SHIMANO
BB-UN55
VIA SINGAPORE
68
BC1.37 x 24
L←LL113→R

Shell width (typically 68mm, 70mm, or 73mm)

Spindle width (normally 107–127.5mm)

4 **Check the shell** and spindle width on the old BB unit. If these figures are not on the shell, measure the widths with a measuring calliper. (You must replace the BB unit with one of the same dimensions.)

TOOLS AND EQUIPMENT

- Frame stand
- Splined BB remover tool
- Adjustable spanner
- Measuring calliper
- Cloth or small paintbrush
- Degreaser
- Grease

Caution! BBs may be Italian or English threaded, which means they are tightened in opposite directions. Arrows on the BB cups show direction to tighten them.

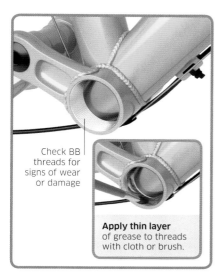

Check BB threads for signs of wear or damage

Apply thin layer of grease to threads with cloth or brush.

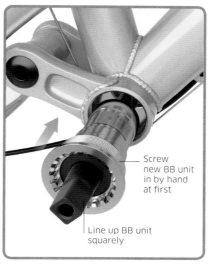

Screw new BB unit in by hand at first

Line up BB unit squarely

Turn tool backwards until you hear a click as threads engage

5 **Check the BB threads** for damage and remove any dirt or debris using some degreaser and a cloth or small paintbrush.

6 **On the new BB unit**, remove the left-hand cup (marked "L"). Insert the unit into the drive (right) side of the bike frame.

7 **Use the remover tool** to screw in the unit. To avoid cross-threading, first turn it the "wrong" way until the threads engage.

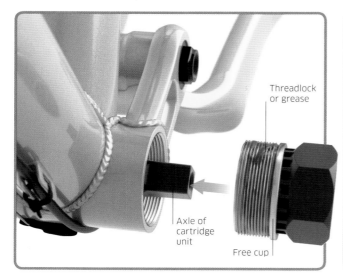

Threadlock or grease

Axle of cartridge unit

Free cup

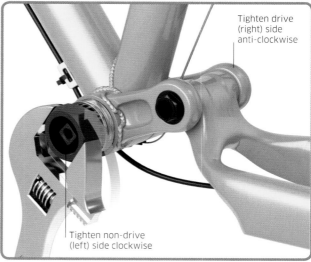

Tighten drive (right) side anti-clockwise

Tighten non-drive (left) side clockwise

8 **Grease the thread** of the free cup. Check that the cartridge unit is centred inside the bike frame – there should be equal space all around the unit. Screw the cup in by hand until it is finger tight.

9 **Once both cups are** finger tight, use the BB remover tool together with the adjustable spanner to tighten each side as firmly as you can. Finish by refitting the chainset (see pp.166–173).

Shimano HollowTech II

The Shimano HollowTech II bottom bracket (BB) is widely fitted to many modern bikes, and works in conjunction with the HollowTech II chainset (see pp.166–167). Noise, roughness, and side movement indicate that your BB is worn.

BEFORE YOU START
- Secure your bike in a frame stand
- Remove the chainset (see pp.166–167)
- Clean the area around the BB
- Lightly grease the thread of the BB cups

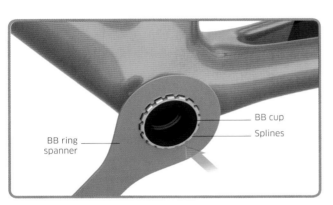

BB cup

Splines

BB ring spanner

1 **Starting on the non-drive (left) side** of the bike, fit the BB ring spanner over the splines of the BB cup. Loosen the cup by turning it in the opposite direction to the "tighten" arrow printed on it.

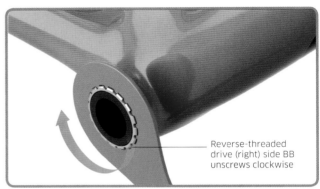

Reverse-threaded drive (right) side BB unscrews clockwise

2 **Repeat on the drive (right) side** of the bike, this time turning the BB ring spanner clockwise. The drive side is reverse threaded, which prevents the cup from unscrewing as it is being ridden.

PARTS FOCUS

A Shimano HollowTech II BB consists of these components.

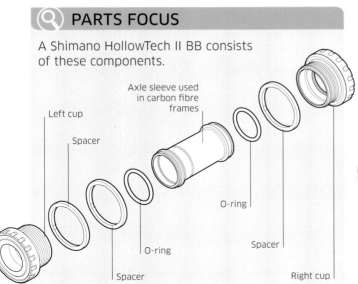

Axle sleeve used in carbon fibre frames

Left cup

Spacer

O-ring

O-ring

Spacer

Spacer

Right cup

Inner cover fitted for use on bikes with carbon frames

3 **Fully unscrew both external cups** until the whole BB unit comes out – once they are loose enough, unscrew them by hand. The drive (right) side cup may be attached to an axle sleeve, if fitted.

TOOLS AND EQUIPMENT

- Frame stand
- Cloth
- Grease
- Bottom bracket ring spanner
- Degreaser

Caution! If you find there is any damage to the threads of the BB shell, or you accidentally cross-thread the BB, you may need to have the frame rethreaded by a professional mechanic.

BB shell

BB shell threads

Degreaser

Grease

Apply fresh grease liberally to threads inside BB shell.

Axle sleeve sits inside BB shell

Line up BB cup to prevent cross-threading

4 **Thoroughly clean out the threads** of the BB shell with degreaser and a cloth, and wipe dry. Check the BB shell for corrosion and remove it, then generously grease the BB shell threads.

5 **Screw the drive (right) side** of the new BB into the shell, turning it anti-clockwise. Do this by hand as far as possible, as too much torque may damage the threads if they are not correctly aligned.

BB cup | Splines

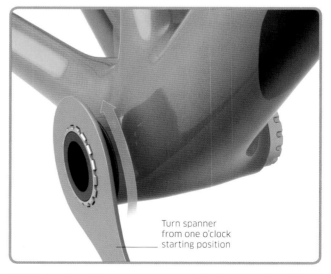

Turn spanner from one o'clock starting position

6 **Screw in the non-drive (left) side cup** in the direction of the "tighten" arrow printed on it. Ensure that the cup is aligned with the thread on the shell. Tighten the cup by hand until it is finger-tight.

7 **Using the BB ring spanner**, fully tighten the BB cups on both sides. Make sure that the spanner is squarely on the splines, as if it slip off under pressure, it may damage the splines.

▶ CHOOSER GUIDE

Pedals

Many new bikes come with basic flat pedals, and some may have toe clips and straps. However, many modern pedals are designed to lock into the bottom of a cycling shoe, allowing you to generate force through the complete revolution of the pedal stroke, vastly improving pedal efficiency. Once your shoe has clicked into place it can also be adjusted for varying

TYPE	SUITABILITY	OPERATION
FLAT PEDALS These basic pedals have no means of holding the foot in place. They are very easy to use and are especially popular on downhill mountain bikes as they allow riders greater control of the bike through the pedals.	■ **Everyday utility cycling** or for commuting short distances. ■ **Mountain biking**, especially rides involving technical downhilling. ■ **Cargo bikes**, as they give riders greater control, allowing them to counterbalance their cargo.	■ **Made from a simple pedal plate** with no option to strap in. ■ **Despite the simplicity** of its design, it is possible to push down just as hard on a flat pedal as any other pedal.
CLIPLESS ROAD The most popular type of clipless pedal, these can only be used with a rigid-soled road shoe and a mounted shoe plate specific to the brand of pedal used.	■ **All types of road racing**, competitive sportive riding, and training.	■ **The clipless system** is fitted on one side of the pedal, usually with a retaining lip at the front and a spring-loaded locking mechanism at the back. ■ **The system** makes it possible to customize the amount of float.
DOUBLE-SIDED CLIPLESS Entry on both sides makes this type of pedal easy to click into. Favoured for off-road riding, they are also popular for general road riding as the shoe used for this pedal has a grippy sole that can be walked in.	■ **General road**, commuting, or off-road riding as the pedal is designed to shed mud and it uses smaller clears that are recessed into the tread of some shoes, making them more suitable for walking in.	■ **The raised clipless mechanism** works with a small, metal cleat that attaches to your cycling shoe with two bolts and pushes back a retaining lip on the pedal. ■ **The clipless style** has varying degrees of float and some quick-release tension options.
TOE CLIPS AND STRAPS New riders often prefer to start with pedals equipped with toe clips and straps because they can be used with non-cycling shoes and do not lock the shoe to the pedal. The straps can be let out for a very loose fit.	■ **New cyclists** who want added power but are unsure about clipless pedals. ■ **For distance riders**, as the toe clips and straps make it possible to ride long distance on the road in stiff-soled shoes.	■ **Toe clips** stop the foot sliding forward and the straps can be tightened to hold the shoe on the pedal. ■ **A shoe plate** can be slotted over the back of the pedal for serious road use.

degrees of "float" – the distance by which your foot can move on a pedal before it detaches and which you can adjust to suit your riding requirements. There are road and off-road versions of clipless pedals to suit every level of rider, and simple strap and cage pedals are available for those who prefer more traditional options too.

KEY COMPONENTS	SHOE TYPE	ADJUSTMENTS
■ **The body** is made from steel alloy or plastic with plates bolted to the front and rear. ■ **Pedals** on mountain bikes typically have a bigger platform with small spikes that are screwed in, to aid grip.	■ **Any flat-soled shoe** are suitable for flat pedals but leather or very hard soles may not grip well and could cause the foot to slip off, unbalancing the rider.	■ **There are no adjustment options** on a flat pedal.
■ **The body is** made from carbon fibre, with an integral quick-release in steel, plastic, or composite. ■ **The clip mechanism** is spring- or tension-operated.	■ **Lightweight road shoes** with smooth, rigid soles made of carbon or composite, and drilled for universal shoe plate, three-bolt, threaded inserts. ■ **Shoes are vented to** keep feet cool.	■ **The level of float** is changed in various ways, depending on the model of pedal but it is usually adjustable via a grub screw on the spring mechanism or a tensioned plate.
■ **The body** is made from alloy with steel or titanium with a spring-operated mechanism. ■ **The minimalist design** prevents mud clogging the pedal.	■ **Road or off-road style** shoes with rigid lugged or grippy soles designed for walking or running in cyclo-cross races. ■ **Sliding two-bolt** shoe-plate mount is recessed in the shoe's sole, allowing a rider to clip-in if they wish to.	■ **Can be customized** to increase or decrease the level of float in various ways, depending on the type of pedal.
■ **The body** is made from steel alloy or plastic with shoe plates bolted to the front and rear. ■ **The toe clip and straps** hold the shoe in place.	■ **Any kind of shoe** can be used on flat pedals, and on pedals with toe clips and straps but no shoe plates. ■ **Traditional,** leather-soled cycling shoes must be used if pedals have shoe plates.	■ **The strap wraps around** the shoe and can be tightened and released using quick-release on the strap.

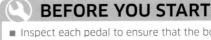

▶ SERVICING PEDALS
Greasing axle bearings

Pedals rotate thousands of times per ride, and when close to the ground they are exposed to water and dirt, causing wear. Worn pedals do not spin freely and make cycling less efficient. Servicing pedals is a quick task, and you should check your pedals for wear every 12–18 months.

BEFORE YOU START

- Inspect each pedal to ensure that the body is not cracked
- Check the pedal axle is not bent; if it is, replace it
- Put the chain onto the largest chainring
- If the pedal is stiff, spray it with penetrating oil
- Prepare a clear space where you can lay out the parts

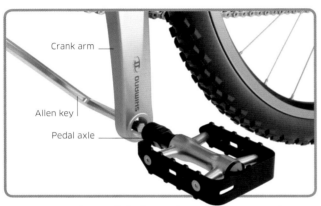

Crank arm

Allen key

Pedal axle

1 **Remove the pedals** from the crank arms, using an Allen key or spanner, according to the pedals you have. The drive (right) side pedal unscrews anti-clockwise, the non-drive (left) side, clockwise.

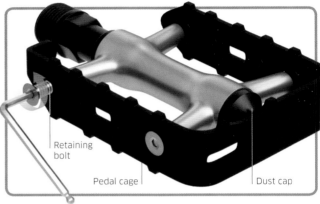

Retaining bolt

Pedal cage

Dust cap

2 **Remove the pedal cages** using an Allen key, unscrewing the retaining bolts anti-clockwise. If the bolts are stiff, spray them with penetrating oil. Clean the bolts and threads, and set them aside.

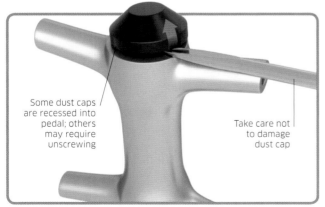

Some dust caps are recessed into pedal; others may require unscrewing

Take care not to damage dust cap

3 **Hold the pedal** vertically with the dust cap up and the axle down. Prise off the dust cap with a flat-head screwdriver to give access to the bearings. Put the dust cap safely to one side.

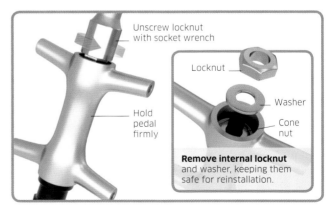

Unscrew locknut with socket wrench

Locknut

Washer

Hold pedal firmly

Cone nut

Remove internal locknut and washer, keeping them safe for reinstallation.

4 **Insert a socket wrench** onto the internal locknut. Hold the pedal firmly and turn the locknut anti-clockwise. Remove the locknut and the metal washer beneath it to reveal the cone nut.

Workshop tip: If you do not have a grease gun, you can use an old spoke to help push grease into tight gaps, such as pedal axles.

Locate socket wrench fully

Turn socket wrench anti-clockwise to undo cone nut

5 **Use a socket wrench** to unscrew the cone nut anti-clockwise from the end of the axle. Hold the axle steady.

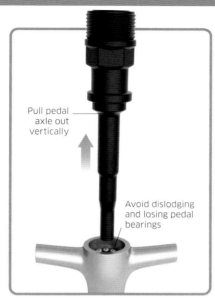

Pull pedal axle out vertically

Avoid dislodging and losing pedal bearings

6 **Turn the pedal** over and pull the axle out of the pedal body. Take care not to dislodge the bearings inside the pedal.

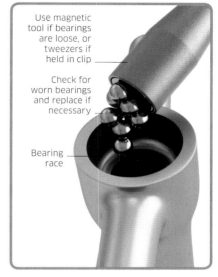

Use magnetic tool if bearings are loose, or tweezers if held in clip

Check for worn bearings and replace if necessary

Bearing race

7 **Remove the bearings** using a magnetic tool or tweezers. Clean the bearings, axle, and the bearing races inside the pedal.

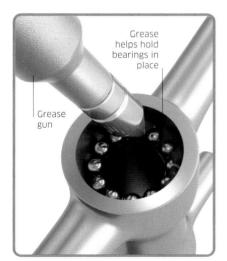

Grease helps hold bearings in place

Grease gun

8 **Grease the inside** of the pedal. Insert the bearings back into the bearing races on both sides of the pedal, and apply more grease.

Locknut

Washer

Cone nut

Ensure cone nut, washer, and locknut are refitted in correct order.

Take care not to dislodge bearings when inserting axle

9 **Slide the pedal axle** back into the pedal body. Fit the cone nut, tightening it loosely. Refit the washer and the locknut.

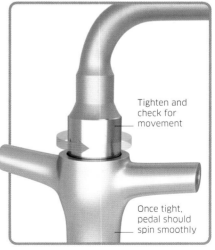

Tighten and check for movement

Once tight, pedal should spin smoothly

10 **Fully tighten the locknut** and refit the pedal cage. Grease the thread on the pedal axle before fitting it to the crank.

▶ FITTING CLEATS
Cycling shoes and cleats

If you use clipless pedals, you will need to fit cleats to your cycling shoes. Cleats are usually supplied together with clipless pedals. Make sure new cleats are compatible with your shoes and your pedals. To ride effectively and avoid knee injury, you will need to set the position and angle of the cleats to work with your feet.

BEFORE YOU START

- Remove any old cleats and clean the cleat bolt holes with a small brush
- Sit down, wearing your normal cycling socks
- Feel along the inside edge of each foot to locate the bony knuckle at the base of your big toe
- Put on your cycling shoes and find that same bony knuckle

Position foot correctly in relation to pedal, by lining up bony knuckle at base of big toe with pedal axle.

Ensure that your foot is straight and that your ankle sits above pedal

Put your foot on pedal at bottom of pedal stroke

1 **Wearing your cycling shoes**, sit on your bike; you may need to lean against a wall or a support. Place your feet on the pedals with the balls of your feet directly over the pedal axle.

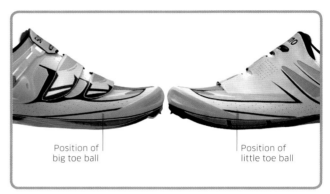

Position of big toe ball

Position of little toe ball

2 **To determine the position** of the cleats, with your shoes on, use a non-permanent pen to mark out the position of the balls of your little toe and big toe on each shoe. Take your shoes off.

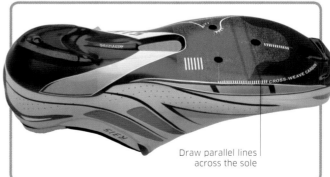

Draw parallel lines across the sole

3 **Turn each shoe** over in turn, and using a rule, draw a line across the sole from the big toe mark and a parallel line from the little toe mark. The centre of the cleat should sit between these lines.

Caution! Ensure that your cleats are compatible with your shoes. There are two main forms: twin-bolt cleats are typically used on mountain bikes, and three-bolt forms on road bikes. Some shoes for twin-bolt forms offer two pairs of bolt holes for precise fitting.

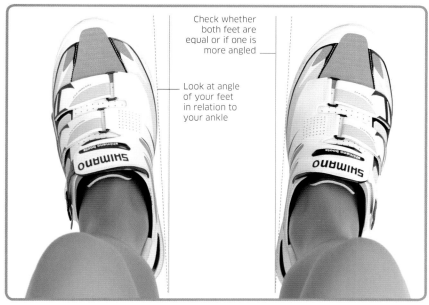

Check whether both feet are equal or if one is more angled

Look at angle of your feet in relation to your ankle

4 **To determine the angle** at which to set the cleats, sit with your feet hanging freely off the ground. Check whether your feet naturally point outwards (duck-footed), inwards (pigeon-footed), or straight ahead (neutral). Note the approximate angle of each foot.

FINE-TUNING

You can make fine adjustments to match your riding style.

- Moving the cleat sideways will affect how close your foot sits to your bike's centreline. If you ride with your knees wide at the top of the pedal stroke, move your cleats inwards so your feet move outwards. If you ride with narrow knees, move the cleat outwards.

- Cleats are colour-coded to show the amount of "float" (movement possible when the cleat is engaged with the pedal). Zero-float or fixed cleats keep the shoe locked in; those with 6° or 9° range allow feet to twist while pedalling.

5 **Grease the cleat bolt threads** and loosely screw the cleats in, aligning the centre of each cleat with the marks on the sole.

6 **Twist each cleat** so that the base sits within the marks you drew in step 3. Angle the front to match the angle of your feet.

7 **Tighten the cleat screws** equally, one by one. Try out the cleats while sitting on the bike as in step 1. Adjust them if required.

SUSPENSION

▶ CHOOSER GUIDE
Suspension

Suspension is designed to absorb shocks and improve traction over bumps and dips on rough terrain. Therefore, it is mainly used on mountain bikes and some hybrid ones. Parts may include telescopic front forks, rear shocks, suspension seat posts or stems, and flexible frames. As always, before purchasing any of these parts, do consider the type of riding you will be doing.

TYPE

SUSPENSION FORKS
Almost all MTBs, and many hybrid bikes, have telescopic forks. Bikes with only front fork suspension are called "hardtail" MTBs. Forks are measured by their travel (the amount they move).

REAR SHOCKS
Many MTBs have both front suspension forks and a rear "shock", this is called "full suspension". They vary in the amount of travel, the springs used, and the pivot system (the most common types being single-pivot and four-bar).

FLOATING DRIVETRAIN
This rear suspension system has multiple pivots and linkages, and a bottom bracket that is fixed to a link between the front and rear triangles so that it can move with the suspension.

SUSPENSION SADDLE/SEAT POST
Suspension seat posts and saddles can be an easy, inexpensive way to improve ride quality for general riding. Even springs under the saddle offer basic shock absorption for utility bikes.

SUITABILITY

- **Off-road riding** on rough or rocky terrain.
- **Downhill and freeride bikes** that use longer-travel suspension (up to 230 mm/9 in of travel).
- **Cross-country bikes** that use short-travel forks (80–100 mm/3–4 in).

- **Off-road riding** on very rough or rocky terrain; especially on technical downhills.

- **A wide range of terrain types;** a floating drivetrain provides sensitive traction and allows highly efficient pedalling.

- **Rough road riding** on cobbles or uneven metalled surfaces.
- **Long rides**.
- **Hardtail mountain bikes**, if a full rear suspension system is not desired.

OPERATION

- **Suspension** is provided by compressed air or metal springs; it is often adjustable and includes a lock-out function.
- **The fork** can usually be set for the rider's weight using a preload adjuster.

- **The rear triangle**, or swingarm, holds the rear wheel and is joined to at least one pivot point on the main triangle of the frame.
- **A shock absorber (shock)** controls movement in the swingarm.
- **Many shocks** can be locked-out for road riding or climbing.

- **The rear triangle**, or swingarm, is joined to pivot points on the main triangle of the frame.
- **A shock absorber (shock)** controls movement in the swingarm.
- **The BB and chainset** sit on a separate link between the front and rear triangles.

- **The most basic form** of shock absorption is given by metal springs under the saddle.
- **Suspension seat posts** have a spring set on a piston to provide shock absorption.

Even if you are intending only occasional riding on rougher roads, adding suspension to your seat post can make cycling easier and more comfortable. For more serious trail riding, or even downhill and cross-country sessions, you should consider upgrading to suspension forks or even to a full-suspension set-up.

KEY COMPONENTS

- **The fork body** comprises a steerer tube, crown, stanchions, sliders, and an axle.
- **The springs utilize** inner chambers of pressurized air or metal coils.

- **The rear shock unit has** pressurized air springs or a metal spring.
- **The pivot system** enables the rear triangle to articulate independently of the rest of the frame.

- **The rear shock unit** utilizes pressurized air springs or metal coils.
- **A pivot system** enables the rear triangle to articulate with the rest of the frame.

- **The body of the seat post** may include an internal spacer, internal spring, piston, and outer casing.
- **On some seat posts**, arms and pivots allow the saddle to move down and back.

VARIATIONS

- **Single-crown forks**, used on most MTBs, have one crown at the base of the steerer tube.
- **Dual-crown forks** have a second crown at the top of the steerer tube. They give extra stiffness for downhill bikes.

- **Single pivots** have a swingarm that connects to the front triangle at one pivot point, usually just above the BB.
- **A four-bar system** has twin pivots with a linkage. A shock is located between the linkage and a fixed bracket on the frame.

- **Various types exist**, including the i-Drive, Freedrive, and Monolink systems.

- **Suspension seat posts** have an integral, damped tube. Posts may be made of aluminium, with stainless steel for pivots.
- **Elastomer dampers** may be fitted to suspension seat posts or used alone.
- **Simple sprung saddles**.

MAINTENANCE

- **The stanchions** should be inspected for scratches, nicks, or leaks, all of which can indicate damaged seals.
- **After a front-end impact,** the fork should be checked for bends or damage.

- **The shock** must be checked to stop oil leaking past the seals.
- **There should** be no wear in the pivot points, linkages, or frame bearings.
- **The swingarm tubes** or spars may take damage and need repairing after a collision.

- **The shock** must be checked to stop oil leaking past the seals.
- **There should** be no wear in the pivot points, linkages, or frame bearings.
- **The swingarm** or linkages may take damage and need repairing after a collision.

- **For suspension seat posts,** the spring should be regularly lubricated to prevent stiffness and squeaking.
- **Elastomer inserts** must be changed if they are worn or start to harden with age, or if a firmer or softer ride is required.

Suspension forks

Suspension forks act by compressing and rebounding to absorb vibration and bumps. They help to keep the front wheel in contact with the ground over rough terrain and ease rider fatigue. The forks contain a steel coil spring or an air spring. The speed of the spring's action is controlled by damping from a piston within an oil reservoir. Both the damping and the spring action can be adjusted according to rider weight, preference, and terrain. You should keep suspension forks clean and service them after every 20 hours of riding (see pp.198–199). Some types also need specialist servicing once a year.

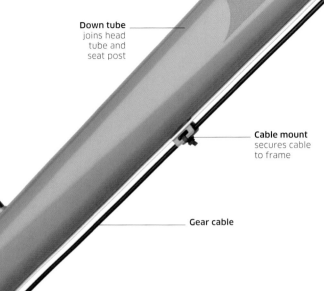

Down tube
joins head tube and seat post

Cable mount
secures cable to frame

Gear cable

PARTS FOCUS

Suspension forks comprise an air spring (shown here) or metal coil, fixed stanchions, and mobile sliders. Many also have a lock-out.

(1) The **stanchions** are fixed to the crown and contain the suspension mechanism, including the damper piston and air chamber or coil spring.

(2) The **sliders** are connected to the front wheel, and move vertically up and down the stanchions as the suspension compresses and decompresses.

(3) The **air chamber** provides pressure within the stanchion. This pressure can be increased or reduced to adjust the suspension (see pp.194–195).

(4) The **lock-out** mechanism locks the suspension so that the forks do not compress. It is used to save pedalling energy when riding on smooth surfaces.

FRONT SAG

Suspension compresses a small amount under a rider's weight. This is shown on the O-ring (see pp.194–195) and can be adjusted if desired.

Head tube

Fork crown

Stanchion

Brace

O-ring

Slider

Headset

Air valve allows air to be added or released from air chamber

Top cap sits at top of air chamber

Air chamber used to pressurize suspension

Fork crown joins stanchions to steerer tube

Lockout dial locks forks

Compression damper controls fork rebound speed

(1)

(2)

(3)

(4)

O-ring used to set suspension sag

Spring seal keeps dirt out

Fork seal protects suspension from dirt

Piston head sits at top of slider

Tyre

Oil chamber contains suspension oil

Damper piston compresses oil in chamber

Flow valve regulates damping

Damper shaft pushes damper piston

Damper head seal at base of piston

Disc brake calliper

Head seal on air chamber

Disc rotor

Drop-out holds wheel axle

Rebound control allows fork rebound to be adjusted

Setting the front sag

Sag is the amount by which the suspension compresses under a rider's weight, which you can alter to suit different riding styles or terrain. The steps shown here are for air-filled forks, which are the most common. Coil sprung forks can be adjusted by changing the preload setting.

BEFORE YOU START

- Add air to the shock absorbers to the pressure that the manufacturer recommends for your weight
- Recreate your normal riding weight: put on your usual riding clothes, shoes, helmet, and backpack, and fit any water bottles, hydration packs, or panniers

O-ring or rubber band

Base of fork stanchion

1 **Slide the O-ring** down to the base of the fork stanchion. If the stanchion does not have an O-ring, tie a rubber band to the base. Never use a cable tie, because it could scratch the stanchion.

Apply bodyweight to handlebar

Fork fully compressed

2 **Hold the front brake** firmly, ensuring that the bike cannot move forwards. Push down on the handlebar with your full weight to compress the suspension fork as far as it will go.

50% 100% 75% 25%

O-ring indicates amount of movement

Using tape measure, note how far O-ring has been moved by stanchion.

3 **Release your weight** from the fork, allowing the suspension to return to its original extended position, then measure the distance from the base of the stanchion to the position of the O-ring.

O-ring at base of stanchion

4 **Push the O-ring** back down to the base of the stanchion. Mount your bike and, standing on the pedals with your weight over the handlebar, travel a short distance. Do not use the brake or pump the fork.

Caution! If the fork has a travel-adjustment dial, ensure that you position it at the "full-travel" setting before performing these steps. If the fork has a "lock-out" switch, set it "open" to allow the fork to compress and decompress fully.

New position of O-ring

25% of full extent of fork travel

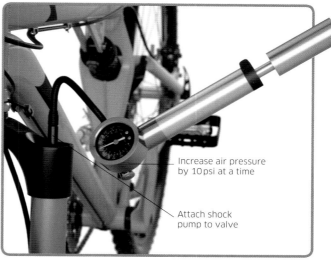

Increase air pressure by 10 psi at a time

Attach shock pump to valve

5 **Dismount carefully** and note the new position of the O-ring. For cross-country or trail riding it should be at 20–25% of the total sag measured in step 2, and at 30% for downhill riding.

6 **If the sag is greater** than your required setting, attach a shock pump to the valve at the top of the stanchion and pump in air at increments of 10 psi. Repeat steps 3–5 to check the new setting.

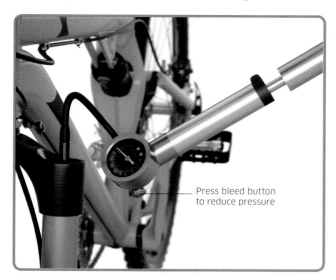

Press bleed button to reduce pressure

Desired amount of sag

Valve at top of fork stanchion

Position of O-ring

7 **If the sag is lower** than your desired setting, release some air from the fork – 10 psi at a time – by pressing the bleed button on the shock pump. Repeat steps 3–5 to check the new setting.

8 **Take the bike for a ride**, then retest the amount of sag by running through steps 3–5 again. If necessary, adjust the amount of air pressure once more, as in steps 6–7.

▶ **ADJUSTING FRONT SUSPENSION**
Tuning suspension forks

Suspension forks can be adjusted to provide comfortable, controlled steering for your weight and the terrain on which you are cycling. One form of adjustment is "damping" to control the rate of the fork's compression (downward travel) and rebound (return to normal). Correct damping ensures that the forks will respond quickly and smoothly on uneven ground.

⊙ BEFORE YOU START

- Refer to the manufacturer's instructions for the recommended suspension settings
- Prepare a clear space where valve caps can be laid out
- Keep a notebook and pen to hand so you can jot down different settings as you try them out

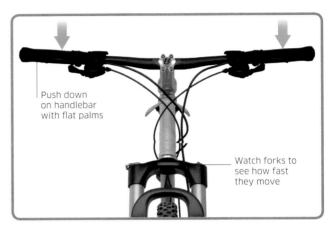

Push down on handlebar with flat palms

Watch forks to see how fast they move

2 **Unwind the rebound dial** and reset it at one-third of its full extent. Then test the rate at which the forks rebound by pushing down on the handlebar, keeping the palms of your hands flat.

Fork leg

Rebound dial

1 **Open the rebound dial** at the base of the fork leg by turning it anti-clockwise as far as it will go. Then screw it clockwise, counting the clicks it makes until it is closed again. Divide this number by three.

Turn rebound dial clockwise to increase damping and slow rebound speed.

Tyre will bounce if there is excessive rebound

3 **Check your front tyre** to see if it stays in contact with the ground. If it skips off the ground, the rebound is too high. Turn the rebound dial clockwise to increase the damping and stop the bouncing.

Workshop tip: Some suspension forks can have the distance they travel vertically increased or decreased by inserting or removing plastic spacers inside the fork legs. Refer to the manufacturer's instructions if this applies to your forks.

Turn rebound dial anti-clockwise to reduce damping and increase rebound speed.

Tyre stays in contact with ground

Feel how smoothly or roughly the fork reacts when braking

Note how fast forks travel – they should not "dive" or "bob" over bumps

Forks should absorb small impacts smoothly

Tyre should have good contact with the ground

4 **If the fork rebounds** too slowly, turn the rebound dial anti-clockwise to reduce the damping and increase the speed at which the fork reacts. The reaction should be smooth and not stiff.

5 **Put on your normal riding gear** and go for a ride over bumpy terrain to check how the suspension feels. Make further adjustments as needed, moving the dial by small amounts until you are happy.

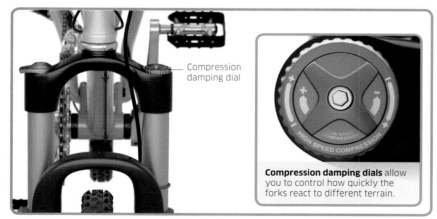

Compression damping dial

Compression damping dials allow you to control how quickly the forks react to different terrain.

6 **If your bike's suspension forks** feature compression damping, you may need to tune it to prevent them from compressing fully or "bottoming out" while riding. Compression damping is adjusted by turning the dial on the top of each fork. Test and correct as necessary.

AIR-SPRUNG FORKS

Some air-sprung forks have an adjustable negative spring to control the fork's sensitivity to small bumps. Initially, the spring should be at the same air pressure as the main spring.

- Inflate air-sprung forks to the correct pressure for your weight.

- There are two types of shock pump: high pressure and low pressure. Use the correct pump for your suspension.

The lower legs

Suspension forks bear the brunt of rough terrain, so need regular maintenance to ensure that they perform properly, and to prolong their lives. You should service the lower legs after every 25 hours of riding time, and you should ideally replace the seals and oil after 200 hours.

BEFORE YOU START

- Remove the stem and forks (see pp.54–57)
- Remove the front wheel (see pp.78–79)
- Remove the rim brake callipers, if fitted (see pp.114–115)
- Ensure that the forks are clean, and free of dirt and grit
- Refer to the fork manufacturer's instructions (see step 8)
- Lay out a dustsheet to catch any excess oil

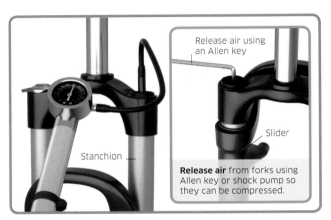

Release air using an Allen key

Slider

Stanchion

Release air from forks using Allen key or shock pump so they can be compressed.

1 **Fasten a shock pump** to the air valve on the fork, and note the pressure. Release the air, using the bleed button on the pump, or by pressing the valve on the fork with an Allen key.

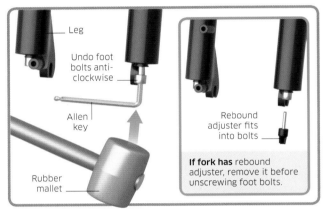

Leg

Undo foot bolts anti-clockwise

Allen key

Rubber mallet

Rebound adjuster fits into bolts

If fork has rebound adjuster, remove it before unscrewing foot bolts.

2 **Insert an Allen key** into the foot bolts at the base of each leg and unscrew by three turns. With the Allen key still in the bolt, tap it using a rubber mallet to loosen the damper shaft within the lower legs.

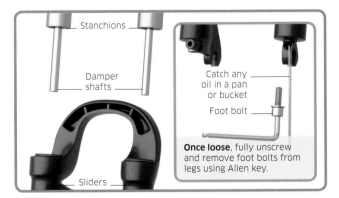

Stanchions

Damper shafts

Catch any oil in a pan or bucket

Foot bolt

Sliders

Once loose, fully unscrew and remove foot bolts from legs using Allen key.

3 **Fully unscrew the foot bolts**, then pull the lower legs to ease the sliders from the stanchions. If stiff, tap them free with a rubber mallet. Clean the stanchions and inspect the surface for scratches.

Spring ring

Foam rings sit inside seals

Wiper seal

Work a cloth around inside wiper seal to remove grease and dirt.

4 **Remove the spring ring** from the top of each wiper seal on the slider, and use a screwdriver to ease out the foam ring inside. Clean the rings and the inside of the seals with an alcohol-based cleaner.

Ensure lint-free towel does not get stuck in slider

Grease wiper seals with suspension grease

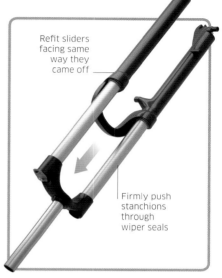

Refit sliders facing same way they came off

Firmly push stanchions through wiper seals

5 **Wrap a lint-free towel** over a long screwdriver. Insert it into the sliders and wipe the inside of them thoroughly.

6 **Refit the foam rings** and spring rings to the wiper seals, then apply suspension grease around the inside of the seals.

7 **Rotate the forks** so that the stanchions are positioned diagonally. Push the sliders halfway onto the stanchions.

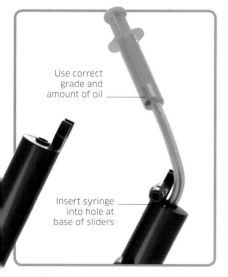

Use correct grade and amount of oil

Insert syringe into hole at base of sliders

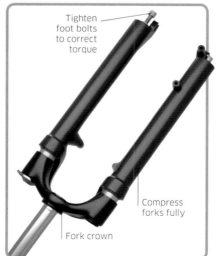

Tighten foot bolts to correct torque

Compress forks fully

Fork crown

Attach shock pump to air valve

Add air to fork to correct pressure

8 **Inject suspension oil** into the sliders using a syringe. Refer to the fork manufacturer's instructions on which oil to use.

9 **Compress the forks** and hold them in place. Replace both foot bolts and the rebound adjuster, if fitted. Clean any spilt oil.

10 **Repressurize the fork** to its original pressure using a shock pump. Refit the forks to the bike (see pp.54–57).

Rear suspension

Rear suspension systems keep the rear wheel in contact with the ground over rough terrain to maximize traction and give a smoother ride. Rear shock units, the central part of the system, contain a steel coil spring or an air spring, which allows the suspension to compress or rebound to absorb bumps and dips. The speed of the spring's action is controlled by damping pistons inside oil- or nitrogen-filled chambers. The spring action and the damping can be adjusted according to your weight, personal preference, and the terrain you are riding on. You need to keep the shock unit clean and service it after every 20 hours of riding. Some types also need specialist servicing annually.

REAR LINKAGE

There are several designs of rear linkage, and the location of the rear shock will vary accordlingly. The shock still performs in the same way, however.

Seat post

Linkage

Rear shock

PARTS FOCUS

Rear suspension systems have a shock unit that acts on pivots and linkages on the frame to allow the rear wheel to move up and down.

① On some systems (such as the one shown here) one or more **linkages** join the rear shock to the rear triangle of the bike frame.

② **Pivots** between the linkages and/or on the frame allow the rear triangle to rotate around them so the rear wheel can move up and down.

③ The **shaft** forms the lower half of the shock unit. It contains the nitrogen and oil chambers, and the pistons that provide damping.

④ The **air chamber** occupies the top half of the shock. Air can be added or released to adjust air pressure when setting the sag (see pp.202–203).

Allen bolts secure linkage to pivots

Linkage allows suspension to move

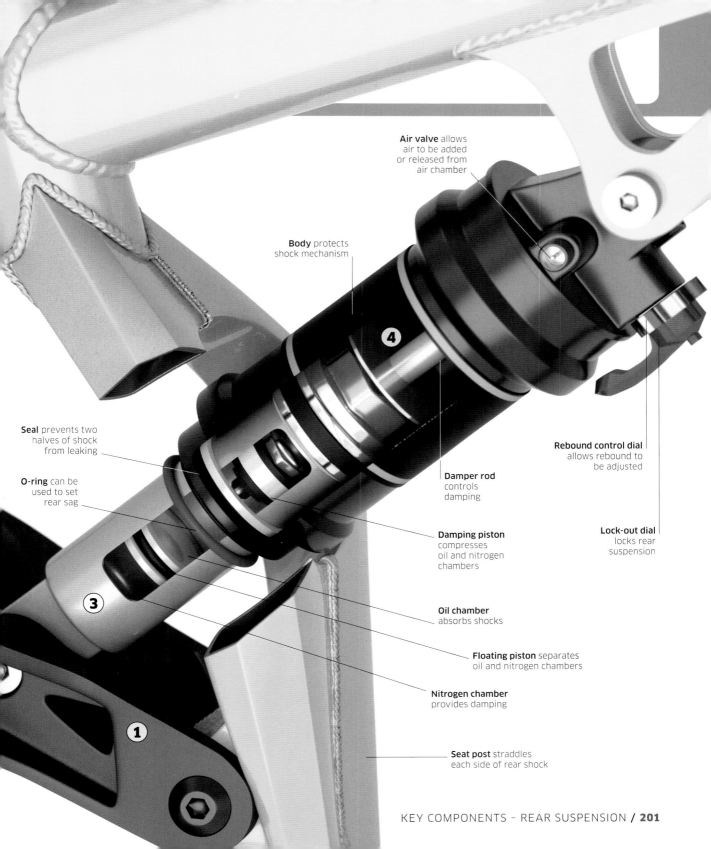

Air valve allows air to be added or released from air chamber

Body protects shock mechanism

④

Seal prevents two halves of shock from leaking

O-ring can be used to set rear sag

③

Damper rod controls damping

Rebound control dial allows rebound to be adjusted

Lock-out dial locks rear suspension

Damping piston compresses oil and nitrogen chambers

Oil chamber absorbs shocks

Floating piston separates oil and nitrogen chambers

Nitrogen chamber provides damping

①

Seat post straddles each side of rear shock

Setting the rear sag

Rear suspension is designed not only to give a comfortable ride but also to keep the back wheel on the ground for maximum grip and pedalling efficiency. To do so, shock absorbers (shocks) need to be able to compress and expand to cope with bumps and and any dips you encounter.

🔧 **BEFORE YOU START**

- Position your bike against a wall
- Add air to the shock absorber to the manufacturer's recommended setting for your weight with a shock pump
- Put on your normal riding gear (see pp.196–197)

Shock body moves along shaft to allow compression and rebound

Main body of rear shock

Shock seal

O-ring

If O-ring is missing, tie a cut rubber band around shaft, ensuring it is tight.

1 **Slide the O-ring** up the shaft until it sits against the rubber shock seal of the shock body. If the bicycle has no O-ring, tie a cut rubber band around the shaft, and push it against the shock seal instead.

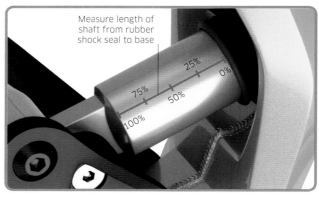

Measure length of shaft from rubber shock seal to base

0%
25%
50%
75%
100%

2 **Measure the shaft**, and divide its length by four. Most shocks require 25% sag, but as a precaution check your shock manufacturer's instructions to determine the recommended amount of sag.

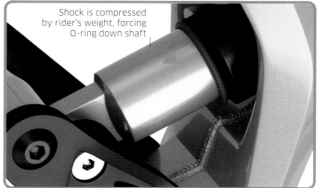

Shock is compressed by rider's weight, forcing O-ring down shaft

3 **Wearing your riding kit**, mount the bike carefully so that the rear suspension is compressed by your full weight as it would be on a normal ride. Avoid bouncing the shock as you get on.

TOOLS AND EQUIPMENT

- Shock pump
- Riding gear
- Cut rubber band
- Ruler

Workshop tip: Before you start to adjust the rear sag, ensure that any lock-out or pro-pedal switch on the shock is turned off so that the shock can move through its full distance of travel.

4 **Dismount carefully**, so that the shock decompresses, and check the position of the O-ring on the shaft. It should have travelled between 20% and 30% along the exposed length of the shaft.

5 **The optimum extent of shock travel** is around 25% along the shaft. If the O-ring or band has moved beyond 25%, then the sag is too much; if it has moved less than 25%, then the sag is too low.

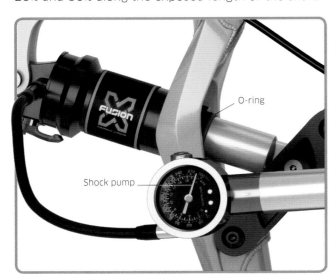

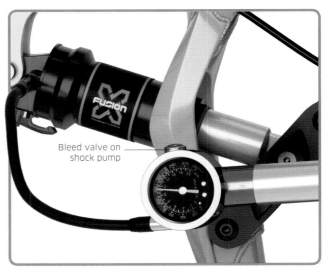

6 **Attach a shock pump** to adjust the air pressure inside the shock. If the sag is too low, increase the air pressure at increments of 10 psi at a time. Retest the sag and add more air as required.

7 **If the sag is** too high, use the bleed button on the shock pump to release air from the shock and reduce the air pressure. Retest the sag (see steps 1–4) and repeat as necessary.

OWNER'S GUIDE

▶ REGULAR MAINTENANCE
Planner

A maintenance timetable can be a useful way to keep on top of any work you need to do on your bike. By scheduling regular sessions for basic fixes, you will reduce the likelihood of wearing out parts prematurely or having an accident on the road.

EVERY WEEK

DRIVETRAIN
As one of the most complex parts of a bike, the drivetrain needs constant maintenance.

- **Check chain** for wear (pp.40–41).
- **Ensure gears** are shifting properly (pp.40–41, 130–138).
- **Inspect cables** for fraying or wear (pp.40–41).
- **Tighten crank arms** and chainring bolts (pp.40–41, 166–173).
- **Oil chain** and jockey wheels if bike was ridden in the rain (pp.44–45).

STEERING AND WHEELS
Wheels and steering may require frequent attention if you are riding more on trails than on roads.

- **Check headset** is correctly adjusted and allows for easy steering (pp.40–41).
- **Check quick-release** levers are functioning (pp.40–41).
- **Ensure wheels** are in true and have no broken spokes (pp.40–41, 88–89).
- **Inspect handlebar** and stem for cracks and ensure stem bolts are tightened (pp.40–41).

BRAKES
Brakes can prevent all manner of accidents so regular maintenance checks and repairs are crucial.

- **Inspect inner cables** for fraying and outer cables for wear, then oil with lube (pp.44–45).
- **Ensure pads** are aligned and not worn (pp.40–41).
- **Tighten disc** and caliper bolts (pp.100–101, 118–119).
- **Check for cracks** in brake parts (pp.40–41).
- **Inspect hydraulic hoses** for wear or leaks (pp.40–41).

SUSPENSION
Regularly checking suspension systems can prevent small problems from developing into larger ones.

- **Check over fork** and shock exterior surfaces for cracks (pp.40–41).
- **Inspect stanchions** under shock boots for cracks (pp.192–193).
- **Tighten top caps**, crown bolts, and shaft bolts (pp.196–199).
- **Lubricate fork stanchions** with wet lube (pp.44–45).

ELECTRONICS
Motor performance will be more efficient if your bike runs smoothly.

- **Ensure battery** is fully charged.
- **Clean bike** so there is less resistance when cycling and battery drains more slowly (pp.142–143).

Safety tip: Bear in mind that regular maintenance work does not replace the safety checks that you should undertake before every ride. You should also check your frame over for cracks and damage and lubricate it every time you give it a clean.

The sample schedule below gives an idea of how often you should check over your bike if you ride often. A heavily used model will need much more attention, while a bike for infrequent, short road journeys will require far less maintenance.

EVERY MONTH

- **Check bottom bracket** runs smoothly (pp.174–181).
- **Oil chain** and jockey wheels (pp.44–45).
- **Tighten pedals** if needed (pp.184–185).
- **Check sprocket teeth** on chain/cassette ring are not worn or missing (pp.156–157).
- **Ensure rear derailleur** pivots are fixed (pp.144–149).
- **Spray derailleur pivots**, cables, and clipless pedal release mechanism with lubricant (pp.44–45).

- **Check hubs** for any roughness, tight spots or play on axles (pp.44–45).
- **Ensure there are no splits** on rubber hub seals (pp.90–91).
- **Inspect headset covers**, if fitted (pp.52–53).
- **Oil hub seals** (pp.90–91).

- **Ensure discs** are aligned and not worn (pp.40–41).
- **Grease inner cables** and oil inside outer cables (pp.44–45).
- **Replace brake pads** of frequently ridden mountain bikes (pp.120–121).

- **Eliminate any play** in forks and shocks (pp.196–199).
- **Check fork stanchions** to see if oil line is visible (pp.192–193).
- **Inspect fork and shock seals** for cracks or slackness (pp.198–199).
- **Ensure there is no fork** or shock sag (pp.194–197).
- **Turn bike upside down** and store overnight so oil can spread through fork.

- **Check electronics cables** outer for wear or splits.

EVERY SIX MONTHS

- **Check for play** in freewheel (pp.78–83), freehub body (pp.90–91), and rear derailleur frame bolt (pp.144–145).
- **Ensure jockey wheels** are not worn (pp.144–145).
- **Oil hub gear** and check pedals do not feel rough or notchy and are not worn (pp.44–45).
- **Replace chain** if used less regularly (pp.158–159).
- **Replace cogs** (pp.160–161) and inner and outer cables (pp.132–135).

- **Inspect bearings** in open-bearing hubs for wear (pp.94–95).
- **Check for wear** in bearings and bearing surfaces in headsets (pp.54–55).
- **Grease open bearing** hubs (pp.94–95) and headsets (pp.54–55).
- **Replace handlebar tapes** and grips (pp.62–63).

- **Grease** brake bosses (pp.44–45).
- **Replace** inner or outer cables (pp.132–135).

- **Remove headset** to check fork steerer for cracks (pp.54–57).
- **Replace fork oil** (pp.44–45).
- **Have suspension** serviced by trained technician.

- **Check working** of electronic gear-shifters (pp.136–137).

▶ TROUBLESHOOTING
Steering, saddle, wheels

The stationary components on your bicycle deserve the same careful maintenance as its moving parts. The handlebar, stem, saddle, and seat post bear your weight and provide comfort, while the wheels and headset must turn smoothly and without play.

⚠ PROBLEM

Steering does not respond as expected when you move the handlebar. Other symptoms might include:

- **Steering feels delayed** or imprecise.
- **Cracked or bubbling paintwork**, cracks in the frame around tube junctions, or soft or springy carbon.

Seatpost wobbles loose or slips down gradually during riding. You might also notice:

- **Saddle** is not straight.
- **Pedalling is harder** when sitting down, due to the lower-than-normal saddle height.

Bicycle handles uncertainly when riding around corners. Other symptoms include:

- **Wheel rattles** on the hub or wobbles in the frame.
- **Brakes rub** against the wheel.

Wheel rim or tyre rubs against the brake, frame, or fork whenever you are riding. Symptoms might include:

- **Loose or broken spokes** rattle in the wheel.
- **Wheel is buckled**, most often following a crash.

Resistance when riding, whether coasting or pedalling. You might also notice:

- **Grinding or squeaking** from either wheel.
- **Tyre rubs** against the frame or brakes.

🔍 POSSIBLE CAUSES

- **Handlebar** may be bent or not aligned correctly.
- **Headset** is too tight, too loose, or worn.
- **The forks** or frame may be bent.

- **Seat post diameter** may be too small for frame.
- **Saddle clamp** might be loose.
- **Seat post clamp** may be loose, or have slipped up the seatpost.

- **Tyres** could be under-inflated.
- **Bearings** of the cup-and-cone hubs may be loose.
- **Wheel** may be out of true.
- **Worn** or incorrectly adjusted headset.

- **Wheel** might be out of true after an impact due to spokes loosening.
- **Wheel** may have been incorrectly inserted in the drop-outs.
- **Tyre bead** could be incorrectly seated inside the rim.
- **Brake** is misaligned.

- **Hub bearings** could be dirty, worn, or too tight.
- **The wheel** might be out of true, or the tyre bead incorrectly seated inside the rim.
- **Brakes** may be misaligned.

Problems with these parts can cause significant discomfort or difficulty when riding. If you are unable to steer properly or feel your wheels are not running smoothly it is essential to identify the cause of the problem and possible remedies as swiftly as possible.

 POSSIBLE SOLUTIONS

Check alignment of the handlebar. The stem should be in line with the wheel, so the bar is at 90 degrees to the wheel. Replace bent handlebar (pp.60–61).

Check the headset moves freely and without play. Adjust it if necessary, and/ or grease or replace the bearings and races (pp.54–57).

Inspect the frame and forks for rippled paint, cracks, or bent tubes. Replace them unless made of steel, which can be fixed by a frame builder.

Swap the seat post for one with the correct diameter. To find the right size, measure the internal diameter of the seat tube (pp.68–69).

Tighten the saddle clamp, ensuring that the jaws of the clamp are in the correct position around the saddle rails (pp.68–69).

Remove the seatpost clamp and clean it, as well as the top of the seat tube. Reassemble clamp, grease and reinsert the seat post, and tighten appropriately (pp.68–69).

Check that the tyre is not flat – patch or replace the inner tube if so. Then inflate to the manufacturer's advised pressure (pp.48–49).

Adjust the cup-and-cone hub's bearings so that they are tight, with no lateral play.

True the wheel so that the rim runs straight, adjusting the tension of the spokes in the out-of-true area with a spoke key (pp.88–89).

Spin the wheel to gauge the severity of the buckled wheel. Replace the broken spokes and true the wheel, or replace the wheel entirely (pp.88–89).

Remove the wheel and reinsert, correctly centred in drop-outs. Tighten the axle nuts evenly on each side, or fully tighten the quick-release (pp.78–81).

Deflate the inner tube, pinch your fingers around the tyre to squeeze the bead inside the rim, then run your hands around the tyre. Reinflate the tube (pp.84–87).

Overhaul the cup-and-cone hubs and check races, cones, and ball bearings for wear. Regrease and tighten if unworn. Replace worn or pitted parts.

True the wheel so that it runs straight. Check that the tyre bead is correctly seated in the rim – if not, deflate the inner tube and reseat the tyre bead (pp.84–89).

Adjust the brake alignment with the rim, ensuring that the pads are parallel to the wheel rim. Check the centring and adjust if necessary (pp.112–117).

▶ TROUBLESHOOTING
Rim brakes

Although mechanically simple, fully functioning brakes are essential for safe cycling – failure can have dramatic and dangerous consequences.

Good, well-maintained brakes should deliver ample braking power to trim your speed quickly and effectively or bring you to a halt.

⚠ PROBLEM

🔍 POSSIBLE CAUSES

Brakes make a noise when you pull the brake levers to slow your bike. Symptoms include:

- **Squealing or scraping** when the brakes are applied.
- **Juddering** when the brake pads hit the wheel rim.
- **Brake pads rubbing** against the rim.

- **Squealing may be** due to the brake pads being angled flat or tail-in to the rim, or dirt and pad residue on the rim.
- **Scraping or grinding** may be caused by the pads being old and hard, or contaminated with dirt and grit.

Bicycle slows down when you pull the brake lever but you cannot lock the wheel to stop the bike. You might also notice:

- **The brake lever hitting** the handlebar when you pull it.
- **Poor braking** in wet weather.

- **Brake pads may be too far** from the rim due to pad wear, cable stretch, or the brake quick-release being open.
- **Poorly aligned brake pads** may be slipping under the rim.
- **Link wire on cantilever brakes** may be badly adjusted.
- **Pads or rims** may be worn, dirty, or contaminated. Steel rims, which provide poor friction in wet, could be to blame.

Brakes gradually or rapidly lose power, with no reduction in speed despite pulling hard on the levers. Other symptoms might include:

- **A sharp crack** from a snapping brake cable.

- **Cable-clamp bolt** may be loose or brake cable may have snapped.
- **Brake pads** might not be not secured tightly on brake arms.
- **Cable housing** end-caps might be missing.

Brakes do not spring back fully when you release the brake lever, and the pad sticks against or near to the rim. You might also experience:

- **A spongy feeling** when the brake levers are pulled.
- **More resistance** than you are used to when pedalling.

- **Pivot bolts are too tight**, preventing brake arms from moving freely.
- **Dry, corroded, or worn** brake cable and/or housing.
- **Brake pads** are out of alignment with rim, and have worn unevenly with a lip of pad trapped under rim.
- **Spring tension** insufficient to push arms away from rim.

Brakes are stiff or difficult to apply when you pull the brake lever. Other symptoms include:

- **A grating sound** coming from the brake lever.
- **Resistance or sticking** from the brake cables when the brake lever is pulled.

- **Brake pivots or bosses are worn**, corroded, or dirty.
- **Cable is corroded** or routed incorrectly.
- **Brake lever** may be clogged with dirt or damaged.

Any problems with brakes pose considerable danger both to yourself and other road users but if you spot the symptoms early and take quick action to identify and then resolve the problem, you drastically reduce the potential risk of a life-threatening crash or accident.

POSSIBLE SOLUTIONS

Toe-in the brake pads so that front of pad is angled towards the rim, touching the rim first during braking. Check the brakes are centred (pp.110–117).

Clean the rim using degreaser and a brush to dislodge any hardened pad residue, then rinse off with water (pp.42–43).

Replace the brake pads if worn past the depth-marker grooves. If not, use a scalpel to level the pad, then sand it gently (pp.110–111).

Reset the brake pads by moving them towards the rim, or adjusting the cable at the clamp or barrel adjuster. Close the brake quick-release (pp.104–105, 112–117).

Check the pads and rims for wear and replace if there is evidence of scoring or wear to the rim. If not, clean the surface of both, and run sandpaper over the pads (pp.42–43, 110–111).

For cantilever brakes, loosen the cable clamp and adjust the link wire to the correct angle for optimum brake power (pp.114–115).

Tighten the cable-clamp bolt, replacing the brake cable in the case of a breakage (pp.104–105).

Replace the cable housing end-caps, and check the housing itself for rust or wear. Apply lubricant and replace the housing if necessary (pp.104–105).

Tighten the brake pads on the brake arm, ensuring they are centred and aligned with the rim (pp.110–117).

Loosen the pivot bolts until the brake arms can move unhindered. Lubricate the pivot points or apply grease to the brake bosses (pp.44–45, 116–117).

Lubricate or replace the brake cable and/or housing. If the pads are worn, replace or cut off the lip with a scalpel, then reset to the rim (pp.44–45, pp.102–105, pp.110–111).

For V- or cantilever brakes, remove the brake arms and place the spring tension pin in the brake boss' uppermost hole (pp.112–115).

Clean and lubricate the brake pivots or bosses. Try wire wool or fine sandpaper to remove or smooth over rust corrosion (pp.42–43).

Clean or replace the brake cable and/or housing, ensuring the cables are correctly routed and seated into the cable stops, and the end-caps are fitted (pp.42–43, 102–105).

Clean the brake lever, lubricate its pivot point, and grease the cable housing where it meets the lever. Replace it if broken (pp.42–43, 102–105).

▶ TROUBLESHOOTING
Disc brakes

The most powerful and reliable form of bicycle brake, disc brakes are also popular because of the "modulation" – fine control over braking power – that they offer the rider. While discs are robust and effective even in poor conditions, look after them to greatly improve their performance.

⚠ PROBLEM

Brakes squeal when you pull the brake lever to reduce your speed or halt the bike. You might also notice:

- **Reduced braking power** when you apply the brakes.
- **Vibrations or juddering** during braking.

Brake pads rub against the rotor when you are riding. Other symptoms might include:

- **Grinding or scraping** sounds when the wheel rotates.
- **Excessive wear** on pads and rotor.

Loss of braking power when you pull the brake lever, meaning you find it impossible to lock the wheel completely. You might also notice:

- **Increase in stopping distance** when braking.
- **Brake lever hits handlebar** without stopping the bike.

Brake pads do not spring back from the disc rotor after you have finished braking. You might also notice:

- **A scraping noise** once the brakes are released.
- **A grinding** from the cable as mechanical disc brakes are applied.

A spongy feeling at the brake lever when you apply the hydraulic disc brake. Other symptoms might include:

- **A different "bite point"** – the position in the brake lever's travel at which the brakes come on – each time you pull the lever.

🔍 CAUSES

- **Contamination from** lubricant, degreaser, brake fluid, or grease may have leaked onto the disc rotor or brakepads.
- **Rotor surface** may be worn or roughened.
- **Calliper bolts** may be loose and vibrate when braking.

- **The rotor may be warped** due to an impact when riding, such as the bike falling on its side, or getting damaged during storage or transit.
- **Brake callipers may be misaligned** with the disc rotor.
- **Brake pads may be too close** to the disc rotor.

- **Contamination from** lubricant, degreaser, brake fluid, or grease may have leaked onto the disc rotor or brake pads.
- **Pads may be** glazed over, worn out, or not "bedded in".
- **Brake lever "reach"** – distance between lever and handlebar – may be badly adjusted.
- **Air may have** entered brake system.

- **Brake cable and/or housing** may be dirty, frayed, or corroded, which inhibits brake-pad movement.
- **Hydraulic pistons may be dirty** sticking within the brake calliper rather than moving freely.
- **Dirt has jammed** the lever arm of the mechanical disc-brake calliper.

- **Air may be in the system** if pumping the brake – repeatedly applying and releasing lever – improves braking power and results in a firmer feel.
- **Fluid may be leaking** from hydraulic hoses.
- **Brake fluid may have boiled** due to prolonged braking or natural ingress of water over time.

As disc brakes are complex, it can be hard to identify which part of the system contains the fault. However, using this chart, it should be possible to narrow down the possible causes behind any difficulties with your disc brakes and identify the potential solution.

 POSSIBLE SOLUTIONS

Clean the rotor with isopropyl alcohol, or replace it if badly worn. Gently sand the pads and rotor with fine-grade sandpaper (pp.42–43).

Check the calliper-fixing bolts and rotor-fixing bolts, and tighten to recommended torque ratings (pp.120–121).

Consider using organic brake pads rather than metallic ones. Ensure that metallic pads are fully "bedded in" (pp.120–121).

True the rotor by bending it back into line with an adjustable spanner. If the rotor is badly warped, replace it (pp.120–121).

Reset the calliper so the disc rotor is centred between the pads. Loosen the calliper-fixing bolts, centre by eye, and retighten.

Adjust mechanical disc pads independently to prevent rubbing. Adjust the outer pad by tweaking cable tension, and the inner pad with the adjustment screw.

Burn contamination off the pad with prolonged braking down a safe slope. Or hold pad over a blowtorch or gas hob on low setting. Clean a contaminated rotor.

Bed in new pads by riding at speed, dragging the brake for 5 seconds, then locking the wheel. Repeat up to a dozen times. Sand off any pad glaze.

Adjust brake-lever travel by turning the reach adjuster or grub screw. For cable discs, tighten the barrel adjuster on the brake lever.

Clean and lubricate the cable and housing, or replace them. For best braking power, secure cable with the calliper arm set at fully open (pp.42–45).

Clean pistons. First, take out the pads and pump lever until pistons protrude from calliper. Clean then reset with a piston-press tool or screwdriver wrapped in a rag.

Strip and clean the lever arm and calliper body of a mechanical disc, removing the wheel and pads first.

Bleed the brake to expel air bubbles from the hydraulic system (pp.108–109).

Inspect hydraulic hoses, especially at joints. Tighten any leaking joints and bleed air from the brakes (pp.108–109).

Replace brake fluid with the same type of fluid – do not mix up mineral and DOT fluids. Then bleed air from the system (pp.108–109).

▶ TROUBLESHOOTING
Transmission

The transmission is the most complex system on your bicycle, with the greatest potential for faults to develop. From gear-shifters to cables, cranks to pedals, derailleurs to bottom brackets, sprockets, chainrings, and chains, there is a lot to go wrong.

⚠ PROBLEM

The chain slips or skips, giving way under pressure when you pedal. You may notice:

- **Chain crunches** when pedalling out of the saddle.

ⓠ POSSIBLE CAUSES

- **Chain links may be stiff**, indexing poorly adjusted, or – if skipping happens only in particular gears – sprockets or chainrings may be worn.
- **The derailleur hanger** or rear derailleur may be bent.
- **The chain may be dirty or worn**, or chain links twisted due to jamming between frame and chainrings or sprockets.

Rear derailleur shifting is sluggish or inaccurate, with several pedal turns before changing gear. Other symptoms include:

- **Chain jumps** multiple sprockets when shifting gears.
- **The chain falls** into the spokes or between the frame and smallest sprocket.

- **The cable or housing** may be dirty, worn, or stretched.
- **You may be** using brake housing instead of gear housing.
- **A worn or broken** shifter might cause poor shifting.
- **The rear derailleur pivots** or jockey wheels may be worn.
- **A dropped chain** may be due to badly adjusted indexing or limit screws, a loose cassette lock ring, or an incorrect chain.

Front derailleur does not change gear correctly. Symptoms might include:

- **The chain falls off** into the BB or crank.
- **The chain will not shift** into smallest or biggest chainring.

- **The front derailleur may be badly adjusted**, cable may have stretched, or be incorrectly inserted in cable clamp.
- **The chain may be dirty**, preventing accurate gear-shifting.
- **The chainring(s) may be bent** or loose.
- **A worn or broken** shifter may cause inaccurate shifts.
- **Cable or housing is dirty**, corroded, frayed, or split.

Resistance when pedalling, which may cause fatigue and potential injury. You might notice:

- **The bicycle coasts freely** when you are not pedalling.
- **Creaking or crunching noise** from the BB, pedals, or chainrings.

- **The BB may too tight**, dirty, or worn, making it difficult to pedal.
- **The pedals may be too tight**, dirty, or worn.
- **Chainrings might rub against the frame**, causing damage to paintwork and compromising strength of frame.

The electronic shift system is not functioning correctly when you change gear. Symptoms include:

- **The gears change intermittently** or not at all.
- **A loss of power** at the derailleurs' electric motors.

- **The electric cable connector may have come out**, or have been compressed at handlebar by bar tape or other clamps.
- **Battery may be flat** due to insufficient charging.
- **Incorrect limit-screw adjustment** will require greater force for derailleur to change gear, draining battery of power.

However if you use this chart to spot the warning signs, you may be able to resolve problems before they become too large.

As with all of these charts, if, after consulting the releveant pages in the book, you still can't fix the problem, ask at a bike shop for help.

 ## POSSIBLE SOLUTIONS

Loosen stiff links by flexing the chain laterally. If the chain, chainrings, or cassette are badly worn, replace all three – worn parts cause new parts to wear faster (pp.158–161).

Adjust indexing by turning the rear derailleur barrel adjuster until the chain stops skipping. Straighten or replace derailleur hanger; replace bent derailleur (pp.148–149).

Remove twisted chain links, ensuring the chain is long enough to reach the largest chainring/ sprocket. Replace chain if worn; clean if dirty (pp.158–159).

Replace broken cables or housing; if in good condition, clean and lubricate. Check all ferrules are present, and gear housings are used (pp.148–149).

Check the gear-shifter is clean and functioning correctly – replace it if is broken. If the pivots are worn, replace the derailleur. Replace jockey wheels if they are worn.

Adjust the rear derailleur limit screws and indexing. Ensure the cassette lock ring is tight. Replace with a chain of the correct width and brand. (pp.148–149, 158–159).

Loosen the cable and move the derailleur by hand to check it reaches all the chainrings. Adjust the limit screws if not. Clean the cable and fasten in clamp (pp.148–149).

Clean the chain, chainrings, sprockets, and derailleurs. If a chainring is bent, use an adjustable spanner to straighten it. Tighten the chainring bolts (pp.42–43).

Check the gear-shifter is clean and functioning correctly – replace if it is broken. Replace a broken cable or housing; clean and lubricate if not (pp.42–45, 132–135).

Overhaul or replace the BB, cleaning and greasing the bearings if possible. Tighten to ensure free movement but no play (pp.176–181).

Overhaul the pedals, cleaning the axle, bearings, and bearing surfaces. If the bearings or surfaces are worn, replace them. Or replace the entire pedal (pp.184–185).

Adjust or replace the bottom bracket and/or the chainset, to increase the clearance of the chainrings and frame (pp.158–159, 176–181).

Check that all cables and connectors are correctly inserted and unimpeded. If detached, reinsert them with the correct tool (pp.138–139).

Check the indicator light to verify the battery level. Remove and fully recharge the battery if necessary.

Adjust the limit screws to ensure that the movement of the derailleurs is not impeded (pp.138–139).

Glossary

Terms in *italic* within an entry are defined under their own headings within the glossary.

Allen bolt A threaded bolt with a hexagonal depression in the centre of its head.

Allen key Hexagonal-shaped tool that fits *Allen bolts*.

Axle The central shaft around which a bike wheel spins.

Barrel adjuster A small cup attached to the end of a cable and used to lengthen cable housing and thus adjust cable tension.

Bead The edge of a tyre that sits on a wheel.

Bearing A mechanism that usually consists of a number of ball bearings and circular channels, or races. It allows two metal surfaces to move freely while in contact.

Binder bolt A bolt integrated into the frame at the top of older style *seat tubes* which clamps the *seat post* into the frame.

Bleeding The method of removing air from brakes.

Block Alternative name for *cassette*.

Boss Threaded metal fixture on a bike frame to which an item, such as a bottle *cage* or a *brake calliper* arm rack, is attached.

Bottom bracket (BB) Rotating unit that connects the *cranks* on either side of the BB shell to each other.

Bottom out A term that describes the point when a *suspension* fork or shock absorber reaches the limit of its *travel*.

Brake lever The metal or plastic lever attached to the end of the brake cable and pulled to engage the brake.

Brake lever hood The body in which the *brake lever* sits, connecting it to the handlebar.

Brake travel The distance a *brake lever* moves before the brake pads engage the braking surface on the rim or *hub* of a wheel.

Cable end cap A small, metal cap, closed at one end, that fits over the cut ends of a cable to prevent fraying.

Cable mount A housing that keeps the cable housing stationary but leaves the inner cable free to move.

Cage A lightweight frame, usually of plastic, in which drinking bottles can be stored and easily accessed. Also a component of front and rear *derailleurs*, and pedals.

Calliper The arms on a *calliper brake* that clamp onto the wheel rim, thereby stopping the wheel's motion.

Calliper brakes Single brake mechanisms which bolt onto the frame and whose arms reach around the tyre from above.

Cantilever brakes Brakes that attach separately to the fork on either side of the tyre.

Cassette A series of *cogs* attached to the *freehub* that range in size to give different *gear* ratios.

Chainring A toothed ring attached to the *cranks*, which drives the chain and, in turn, the *cogs* and the rear wheel of a bike.

Chainset The assembly of *chainrings* and *cranks*.

Chainstay The frame tube joining the *bottom bracket* shell and rear *drop-out*.

Cleat A plastic or metal plate that fits to the sole of a cycling shoe and engages into a *clipless pedal* to hold the foot on the pedal.

Clinchers Tyres that clinch to a wheel rim, fitting over the top of an inner tube.

Derailleurs can be fitted to road and off-road bikes, and move the chain across the cassette and chainring when shifting gear.

Clipless pedal A pedal with a mechanism to engage the *cleat* on the sole of a cycling shoe and hold it securely in place. Called "clipless" because they replaced pedals that had toe clips and straps.

Cog A circular metal object with teeth, sometimes used as an alternative term for *sprocket*. It usually describes the parts within a hub gear that can be combined to give different *gear* ratios.

Compression The action of a *suspension* system when it absorbs an impact from the terrain. The term refers to the compression of the spring.

Cone Part of a cup-and-cone wheel hub that holds the *bearings* against the cup.

Crank The lever that joins the pedals to the *chainrings* and transfers energy from the rider's legs to the *drivetrain* of the bike.

Damping The process that absorbs the energy of an impact transmitted through a *suspension* system. It controls the speed at which any form of suspension responds to uneven terrain.

Derailleur A component that shifts the chain between *cogs* on the cassette (rear derailleur) and between *chainrings* attached to *cranks* (front derailleur); it allows multiple gearing on bikes. See also *Mech*.

Derailleur hanger A metal extension that is fitted to the rear *drop-out* allowing the rear *derailleur* to be mounted on the bike.

Dishing The act of centring a wheel on its *axle*.

Double-butted tubes Bike tubes that are thick at the ends but thin elsewhere.

Down tube The frame tube that joins the *bottom bracket* shell to the *head tube*.

Drivetrain The assembly of pedals, *chainset*, chain, and *cogs* that drives the bike forwards by transmitting leg power into wheel rotation. See also *Transmission*.

Drop out A slotted plate at the end of the *fork* legs and stays, into which the *axle* of a wheel is attached.

Drops The lower straight part of a road handlebar that extends back toward the rider.

Dual pivot brakes offer greater stopping power than traditional single-pull callipers. They are common on modern road bikes.

Dual-pivot brakes A version of a *calliper brake* in which each brake arm moves on a separate pivot.

Expander bolt A bolt that draws up a truncated cone or triangle of metal inside a metal tube in order to wedge the tube in place. Commonly found inside the stem of a threaded *headset*.

Ferrule A cap placed on the end of cable housing to secure it to cable mounts or components.

Forks The part of the bike that holds the front wheel, typically consisting of two blades joined at the crown.

Freehub A mechanism, part of the *hub*, that allows the rear wheel to rotate while the pedals remain stationary.

Freewheel A mechanism that does the same job as a *freehub* but can be screwed on or off the *hub*.

Gear An expression of the *chainring* and *cog* combination, linked by the chain, that propels the bike.

Gear satellite A disc on a hub *gear* that rotates when the gear cable is shifted, moving the *cogs* within the *hub* to change gear.

Gear-shifter The control mechanism, usually on the handlebar, used to initiate gear-shifts.

GPS Global Positioning System, a satellite-based navigational network used in cycling for navigation and to record speed and other ride data, via a handlebar-mounted device.

"Granny ring" The smallest *chainring*, used to engage low-ratio small *cogs* for climbing steep hills.

Groupset A matched set of components from a single manufacturer which are engineered to work together. The groupset features both *derailleurs*, *chainset*, *gear-shifters*, brake *callipers*, a chain, and a *cassette*.

Grub screw A headless, threaded bolt with a single diameter throughout its length.

Headset The *bearing* unit that attaches the *forks* to a frame and allows them to turn. There are two varieties: threaded and threadless.

Headset spacers Circular rings made of alloy or carbon that fit above the *headset* and can be used to raise or lower the *stem* to change a rider's position.

Head tube The frame tube through which the *steerer tube* runs.

Hexagonal bolt or nut A threaded bolt with a hexagonal-shaped head, or a hexagonal-shaped nut that fits onto a threaded bolt.

Hex key An alternative name for an *Allen key*.

Hub The central part of the wheel, through which the *axle* runs and which allows the wheel to spin freely.

Hydraulic A mechanical system that uses compressed fluid to move an object.

Interference kit A fastening that relies on friction to keep parts together.

Jockey wheels The part of the rear *derailleur* that shifts the chain between *gears*.

Link wire A small cable that connects the two arms of a *cantilever brake*.

Lock ring/locknut A ring or nut used to tighten onto a threaded object and secure it in place.

Mech Short for mechanism. Device that pushes the chain onto a larger or smaller *chainring* or *cog*. See also *Derailleur gears*.

Negative spring A device that acts against the main spring in a *suspension* system. In *compression*, for example, a negative spring works to extend the *fork*, helping to overcome the effects of *stiction*.

Nipple The piece of metal attached to the end of a cable that secures the cable in the control lever.

A seat post supports the saddle and is inserted into the seat tube. Set the height of your seat post to suit your riding style.

Pawl The curved bar or lever that engages with the teeth of a ratchet to ensure it can turn only one way.

Play A term used to describe any looseness in mechanical parts.

Presta valve A high-pressure *valve* found on road bike inner tubes.

Presta valve nut A *locknut* found just above the *valve core* thread. The nut must be opened to pump up the inner tube.

Quick-release mechanism A lever connected to a skewer that locks or releases a component from the frame.

Quill A type of *stem* that fits inside the top of a *steerer tube* and is held in place internally.

Rear triangle The rear of a bicycle which includes the *seat stays*, the *chainstays*, and the *seat tube*.

Rebound A term to describe the action of a *suspension* system after it absorbs an impact from the terrain. It refers to the extension of the system's spring.

Rotor A flat metal disc that rotates alongside the bike wheel and provides the braking surface for disc brakes.

Seat post A hollow tube that holds the saddle and is inserted into the *seat tube*.

Seat post clamp A piece of plastic fitted to the frame that holds the *seat post* in position.

Seat stay The frame tube joining the *bottom bracket* shell and rear *drop-out*.

Seat tube The frame tube that holds the *seat post*.

Shifter lever The lever pressed to shift *gears*.

Sidewall Part of the tyre between the *tread* and rim.

Spider A multi-armed part that connects the *chainring* to the axle of the *bottom bracket* or the *cogs* in a *cassette*.

Spindle A part that attaches the *bottom bracket* to the *cranks*.

Spring-tension pin The end of a *cantilever* or *V-brake* return spring that fits into a locating hole on the bike's brake mounting *bosses*.

Sprocket An alternative name for a *cog*.

Stanchions The upper legs of a *suspension fork*.

Steerer tube The tube that connects the *fork* to the *stem* and handlebar.

Stem The component that connects the handlebar to the *steerer tube*.

Stiction A term that combines the words static and friction. It describes the tension between moving and static parts at rest, such as the seals and *stanchions* in a *suspension* fork.

Suspension An air/oil or a coil/oil system that absorbs the bumps from a trail or road. The system is either integrated into the *fork* or connected to the rear wheel via a linkage.

Threads The spiral grooves cut into metal that allow separate parts to be screwed or bolted together.

Top tube The frame tube that joins the *seat tube* to the *head tube*.

Torx key A type of screw head with a six-pointed, star-shaped head sometimes used on *stem* bolts and clamps instead of an *Allen key*.

Transmission A bike's transmission is made up of those parts that transfer the rider's energy into forward motion – the pedals, chain, *chainset* and *cogs*. See also *Drivetrain*.

Travel A term that refers to the total distance a component moves in carrying out its purpose. For example, travel in a *suspension* fork is the total distance the *fork* has available to move in order to absorb a shock.

Tread The central part of a tyre that makes contact with the ground.

Triggershifters *Gear-shifters* that respond to the flick of a trigger-like *shifter lever*.

Twistshifters *Gear-shifters* that respond to the twist of a special grip on the handlebar.

V-brake A type of *cantilever brake* with long arms on which the cable attaches to one side, and the cable housing to the other.

Valve The part of a tyre tube that connects to the pump.

Valve core The inner parts of a tube *valve*.

Viscosity A rating system for oils, which also refers to the weight. A light oil has low viscosity and moves quicker than a heavy oil through a given *damping* mechanism. This results in a faster-acting *suspension* system or reduced *damping*.

Wheel jig A stand that holds a wheel so that its rim runs between two jaws. Used in truing a wheel after replacing a broken spoke.

Wheel-retention tabs Small protrusions on front drop-outs that prevent wheels from falling off frame when *quick-release mechanism* is open.

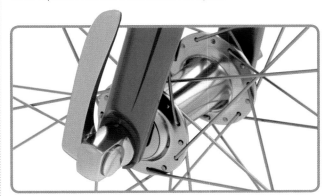

Quick-release levers can be opened without tools, allowing you to remove wheels and release brake cables quickly and easily.

Index

Page numbers in **bold** refer to main entries.

Acknowledgments

The publisher would like to thank the following for their kind permission to reproduce their photographs:

(Key: a-above; b-below/bottom; c-centre; f-far; l-left; r-right; t-top)

14 Koga: (c). **15 Kalkhoff Bikes:** (bl). **17 Genesis Bikes UK genesisbikes.co.uk:** (tr). **Giant Europe B.V.:** (br). **Look Cycle:** (cl). **Ridley Bikes:** (bl). **Tandem Group Cycles:** (tl). **24 Condor Cycles Ltd:** (2/cl, 3/cl). **Extra (UK) Ltd:** (1/cr, 2/cr, 3/cr, 4/cr, 3/b). **Getty Images:** angelsimon (1/t, 2/t). **Tredz Bikes:** (1/cl, 1/b, 2/b, b). **25 Blaze.cc:** (1/bl, 2/bl). **Condor Cycles Ltd:** (2/t, 1/br, 3/br). **Hope Technology:** (bl). **Tredz Bikes:** (1/t, 3/t, 4/t, 2/cl, 3/bl, 2/br). **Wheelbase:** (5/t, 1/cl, 1, 3/cl). **26 Condor Cycles Ltd:** (2/tr, 2/cl, 3/cl, 5/cl, 3/b). **Getty Images:** mooltfilm (1/cl). **Lazer Sport:** (cr). **Tredz Bikes:** (1/tr, 4/cl, 1/cr, 2/cr, 3/cr, 1/b, 2/b). **27 Busch & Muller KG:** (2/cl). **Condor Cycles Ltd:** (1/tl, 1/bl). **Hammerhead:** (1/r). **ICEdot:** (2/bl). **LINKA:** (4/b). **Lumos Helmet lumoshelmet.co:** (4/r). **Scosche Industries Inc:** (2/r). **Tredz Bikes:** (2/tl, 3/tl, 1/cl, 3/b, 3/r). **28 Condor Cycles Ltd:** (1/tr, 3/tr, 1/b, 2/b). **ROSE Bikes GmbH:** (5/b). **Tredz Bikes:** (1/tl, 2/tl, 3/tl, 4/tr, 3/b, 4/b). **Triton Cycles:** (2/tr). **29 Extra (UK) Ltd:** (3/tl, 2/tr). **Radical Design:** (3/b). **Tailfin:** (4/tl, 5/tl). **Tredz Bikes:** (tl, 2/tl, 1/c, 2/c, 3/c, 4/c, 1/b, 2/b, 4/b). Wheelbase: (1/tr). **30 Condor Cycles Ltd:** (1/bc, 2/bc). **31 Condor Cycles Ltd:** (1/tl, 2/tl, 4/tl, 5/tl, 2/tr, 3/tr, 1/c, 2/c, 3/c, 4/c, 1/b, 2/b, 3/b, 4/b, b). **Extra (UK) Ltd:** *(5/c).* Tredz Bikes: *(3/tl, 1/tr).* *32 Tredz Bikes:* (1/b, 2/b). *33 Condor Cycles Ltd:* (3/b). *Tredz Bikes:* (1/t, 2/t, 3/t, t, 1/c, 2/c, 3/c, 4/c, 1/b, 2/b, 4/b, 5/b). **36 Extra (UK) Ltd:** (6/b). **Tredz Bikes:** (3/tr, 1/tr, 2/tr, 1, 2/b, 3/b, 4/b, 5/b, 7/b, 8/b, c). **37 Getty Images:** VolodymyrN (4/bl). **Tredz Bikes:** (1/tl, 2/tl, 3/tl, 1/tr, 2/tr, 3/tr, 4/tr, 5/tr, 1/bl, 2/bl, 3/bl, 5/bl, 6/bl, 7/bl, 8/bl, 1/br, 2/br)

All other images © Dorling Kindersley
For further information see: **www.dkimages.com**

In addition, Dorling Kindersley would like to extend thanks to the following contributors for their help with making the book: DK India for additional line artwork: Assistant animator Alok Kumar Singh, Production Co-ordinator Rohit Rojal, Audio Video Production Manager Nain Singh Rawat, Head of Digital Operations Manjari Hooda. Additional design assistance; Simon Murrell

Claire Beaumont, a former racing cyclist, is now the Marketing Manager and a lead creative at London-based, bespoke bicycle manufacturer, Condor Cycles. A consultant on DK's *The Bicycle Book*, Claire is also co-author of *Le Tour*: *Race Log* and *Cycling Climbs*, and has written about cycling for magazines, including *The Ride Journal*, *Cycling Weekly* and *Cycling Active*.

Ben Spurrier, a passionate cyclist, is the head bike designer for Condor Cycles, London. Awarded by *Wallpaper* magazine in 2011 for a special edition range of bikes, Ben has been a member of the judging panel for the annual D&AD (Design and Art Direction) New Blood awards, and has spoken at The Design Museum, London, about bikes and design. He has also worked with many leading magazines, including *Australian Mountain Bike*, *Bike Etc*, and *Privateer*.

Brendan McCaffrey is an illustrator, designer, cycling enthusiast and amateur bike mechanic based in Las Palmas in Gran Canaria, Spain. An industrial design graduate from NCAD, Dublin he has worked for the past 20 years producing illustrations for clients in the videogame, toy and product industries. **www.bmcaff.com**

Model Credits:
3D Roadbike model by Brendan McCaffrey
3D Mountain Bike model supplied by Gino Marcomini
Additional models supplied by Brendan MCaffrey, Gino Marcomini, Ronnie Olsthoorn & Moises Guerra Armas

USING ESSENTIAL OILS
FOR
HEALTH & BEAUTY

USING ESSENTIAL OILS
——— FOR ———
HEALTH & BEAUTY

DANIELE RYMAN

Windward

This edition published 1986 for Portland House/Windward
by Century Hutchinson Ltd
Brookmount House,
62-65 Chandos Place
London WC2N 4NW

The text of this book is based on material previously
published in The Aromatherapy Handbook by Danièle
Ryman (Century Publishing 1984)

ISBN 0-7126-1105-3

For a catalogue of Danièle Ryman's own essential oils and
essences (these can be purchased by mail order), write to
her at The Marguerite Maury Clinic, Park Lane Hotel,
Piccadilly, London W1

None of the suggestions or information in Using Essential
Oils for Health and Beauty is meant, in any way, to be
prescriptive. Always consult your doctor if in any doubt.

Edited, designed and produced by The Paul Press Ltd,
22 Bruton Street, London W1X 7DA

Project Editor Susanna Rabey
Art Editor Bill Mason
Photography Jon Bouchier
Picture Research Liz Eddison

Art Director Stephen McCurdy
Editorial Director Jeremy Harwood
Publishing Director Nigel Perryman

Typeset by Wordsmiths, Street, Somerset
Origination by London Offset Colour Ltd
Printed and bound in the Netherlands by Royal Smeets
Offset BV, Weert

CONTENTS

INTRODUCTION

Using Essential Oils for Health and Beauty is every reader's introduction to the potential of aromatherapy in the two inter-related fields of beauty and health.

As far as I am concerned, aromatherapy has been a way of life for me since the very first day of my life. The room in which I was born was filled with peach blossom and lilac, and I was later told by my grandmother that it was customary to welcome a baby in this manner, as its first breath of fresh air should be vivified through the scent of flowers Thereafter, throughout my youth, my family and I practised the therapy without ever being conscious of its name. We massaged oils on our bodies when we were tired, took tisanes for insommnia and digestive upsets, inhaled the essential oils of plants when we suffered from bronchitis, colds and flu, and even used aromatic substances in cooking to help digestion. It was not unusual either to go on walks in the pine forests to breathe the pine scent, believed to be a preventative against tuberculosis.

It was Marguerite Maury, the pioneer of aromatherapy, whom I met in Paris when I was twenty, who made me aware that I had been practising it all my life. It was she who convinced me that it should be taken seriously, and that I would be able to express my need to treat and heal people through it. So my life took this direction and I left the Beaux Arts, where I had been studying art, and went to work under her guidance until she died in 1968.

After her death I carried on her work and research. Later I widened its scope to include the sense of smell which I felt had been neglected because of our culture's visual bias. When I began delving into the subject, I discovered that this had not always been the case. In the past, people had been far more aware of the sense of smell and the therapeutic function of smell.

The purpose of this book is to make people realise that this form of alternative medicine is open to all to practise and that it is extremely simple to bring nature back into urban lives through a 'rainbow' of scents. After all, we should not forget what Hippocrates, the father of medicine, said: 'The way to health is to have an aromatic bath and scented massage every day.'

Danièle Ryman, 1985

AROMATHERAPY AND THE SENSES

UNDERSTANDING SMELL

The sense of smell seems sadly neglected today, while the senses of sight and hearing are increasingly relied upon for information about the environment in which we live. Though, in the past, the sense of smell was one of the most potent constituents of behaviour and indeed of survival, nowadays most of us are not even aware that this sense is one of the most subtle means of communication we possess, nor that it is one of the earliest means by which we form a bond with the world. When a baby is born, the first thing it does is to take a deep breath, inhaling the different odours in the air. Indeed, because at this stage, the eyes are closed, it uses its sense of smell to recognise its mother and the security she represents. To primitive men and women, the sense of smell was as important as it still is for many animals; only modern civilisation has made us neglect its influence.

Yet, although most of us are unaware of it, we practise aromatherapy every day. We take flowers or a plant to a friend who is ill. We use bowls of pot pourri to create a harmonious atmosphere in the home. If we have flu or a cold we rub eucalyptus in an oily base on to the chest to help to clear the head. And we add scented essences to the bath to help us unwind at the end of a hectic day or simply to pamper ourselves.

THE MAGICAL PHEROMONES

Humans, like animals, produce odoriferous substances called pheromones (the name comes from the Greek 'Pherein', to carry, and hormone, to excite), which are used to identify, attract, and – in animals – to mark territory. Human pheromones are chemically similar to the hormones secreted by the endocrine glands which circulate in the blood to bring about all kinds of physical changes, but they are actually manufactured by the apocrine glands dotted around the body. We all emit pheromones which radiate into the air around us and are detected by other people who are usually quite unaware of the effect.

Pheromones in animals act as a kind of language whereby they communicate instinctively with one another. All kinds of dogs, cats and many other animals leave scents to pass on messages about territory, destination, sex, and so on. A hunted fox with a pack of hounds following his scent, for instance, will backtrack several times across a river to muffle the aroma of his trail,

Animal instinct Many animals rely on an acute sense of smell to warn them of danger and to help them to locate food. The latter instinct is exploited by man in some blood sports, such as foxhunting (above). Humans, however, have a much poorer sense of smell, though primitive peoples, who still live in close contact with the land, may sniff the ground to pick up the scent of the animals they are hunting.

and will always search for a flock of sheep or other animals to mingle with so as to disguise his identity. Primitive tribesmen smeared their skins with animal scents in an attempt to camouflage their own pheromones and prevent them being detected by enemies, an idea probably suggested by their observations of the animal world.

The habits of ancient or primitive peoples reveal that they used their sense of smell far more than we do today, together with the senses of sight, sound and touch. Primitive man would sniff the ground to find out whether other peoples had passed that way – which makes sense, as several apocrine glands are found on the soles of the feet while pheromone molecules are known to linger on the soil for as long as fifteen days. American Indians did this until comparatively recently; they were also known to be able to smell the odour of a dead man's body up to ten miles away!

BACK TO BASICS

Opposites attract The female Australian Emperor Gum Moth attacts its mate by smell. The pheromones it produces can be detected several miles away.

Perhaps the reason we have moved away from using our sense of smell is because we associate sniffing with animal behaviour, seeing it as a primitive function that civilized man should leave behind him. Standing on two feet probably had something to do with it too. But, whatever the reason, we are now discovering the roles that pheromones play in our lives, and much of the evidence which suggests that smells act as messengers and alter our behaviour patterns comes from studies of animals.

In animals, the other important purpose of pheromones is sexual attraction – most obvious in the Emperor moth, whose mate can be attracted by smell from several miles away. That different animals produce their own variety of pheromones obviously helps to ensure the survival of the species. Research suggests that men and women too are sexually responsive to each other's pheromones. In New Guinea, for instance, a man will unashamedly waft a handkerchief that has been tucked in his armpit under the nostrils of his partner to arouse her to passion after the last dance.

Generally speaking, the pheromones produced by men have a musky aroma whereas women's, although similar, are usually subtler and perhaps rather sweeter. A woman's pheromones vary during her monthly cycle, and a man is most receptive and attracted to her smells at the time of ovulation. A woman's sensitivity to a man's pheromones also fluctuates with her sex hormones, and her sense of smell becomes dulled from about two days after conception until about the third month of pregnancy.

THE SCENT OF FEAR

Fear produces its own distinctive pheromones in humans and animals. When an ants' nest is invaded, for instance, some of the ants secrete a pheromone which induces the rest of the group to rally and ward off the intruder. Animals can detect fear in humans: a horse or a dog senses from your pheromones when you are nervous. And it may be a literary cliché, but it is possible to detect fear in others through the sense of smell.

Your sense of smell can also protect you from all kinds of danger, and in my experience it can even save your life. During sleep, most human senses are dulled, but the olfactory sense retains its acuity around the clock. This was invaluable to the survival of primitive man, for while he rested, exposed to the elements, he could be assured of being able to detect the presence of a threatening stranger or animal. Nowadays, although we can lock doors for safety, the ability to detect unusual obtrusive odour is still a precious asset. Twice my sense of smell has warned me of the presence of fire, waking me during the night in time to allow me to save the lives of my family and myself. During waking hours too, the same sense can warn you of the presence of a gas leak or poisonous fumes, so that you can react in time to escape from danger.

Interestingly, the sense of smell is often deadened during sickness, not only by colds or flu, but even by illnesses which do not necessarily interfere with the nasal passages.

Seasonal fragrances Trees, herbs and plants possess their own natural scents, the individual qualities of which can soon be detected. There are seasonal variations as well – the scent of autumn leaves, for instance, differs considerably from that of the fresh growth of spring.

AROMATHERAPY AND THE SENSES

HOW WE SMELL

What do different aromas consist of, and how do they work to have such profound effects on behaviour, mood and physical functioning?

'Smell' is usually used to refer to something that is rather offensive, whereas 'odour' is neutral, neither particularly pleasant or unpleasant, and 'scent' is applied to perfume or the trail left by an animal. However, they are all caused by odoriferous substances consisting of volatile molecules that can pass through air and water. The study or science of smell is technically called 'osmology' (from the Greek osme, smell), and odoriferous substances or smells are known as osmyls. Unlike with light and sound, scientists have not quantified smell into measurable units, perhaps even today because the mechanism of smell perception remains something of a mystery.

The molecules of an odour are perceived by a bundle of highly sensitive nerve cells located on the membranes lining the nasal passages (nostrils). These nerve cells make up the organ of olfaction, which in humans is no larger in size than a thumb print, but in animals can be ten to thousands of times larger, a fact that helps to explain why their sense of smell is far more developed than ours. Nevertheless, our sense of smell is 10,000 times more sensitive than that of taste, and as each of the nerves in the nose is a tiny branch of the brain, information about a certain smell is relayed incredibly quickly, whereas the detection of taste, sound, and touch is far less direct.

During our lifetime the degree to which we use our sense of smell changes. Babies rely heavily on the olfactory organ to help them seek nourishment, for they can detect the pheromones a mother secretes from her breasts as well as the sweet odour of her milk. In early childhood too, we react spontaneously to different smells; studies suggest that children with a sharp sense of smell are often the most intelligent. But children are unable to discriminate naturally between a good smell and a bad one, and pick up most of their notions as to which smells are acceptable and which are nasty from parents or schoolfriends.

Research has shown, however, that young children are highly attracted to the smell of strawberries and vanilla. Some manufacturers have capitalised on this by scenting the rubber with which children's dolls are made with artificial strawberry essence!

Between the ages of ten and eighteen, chldren develop a liking for the fragrances of orange and musk, as well as stawberries and vanilla, although it is not until adulthood that the sense of smell becomes rather more sophisticated and individual likes and dislikes for different odours are displayed. This individuality plays an important role in determining the people to whom we are attracted, the kind of environment in which we feel happiest, the flowers we would choose for the home and so on. There is a sexual difference in the kinds of smell that attract too. Men tend to be attracted to more complex mixes of spicy and floral fragrances, and women prefer simple, single ones.

MEMORABLE SMELLS

Another intriguing aspect of smells or aromas is their ability to evoke memories – not just visual images of past happenings, but also the emotions felt at that time. I will always remember the smell of my mother's perfume, Rose of Rochas. It still has a calming and comforting influence on me, as I associate it with her coming upstairs to kiss us goodnight. In the same way, the smell of Gitanes tobacco reminds me of my father, for it used to impregnate his hair, skin and clothes, and in its presence I feel secure and protected.

AROMATHERAPY AND THE SENSES

Why don't you experiment yourself with memories by imagining different smells? Shut your eyes and remember the first time you went to the seaside. Concentrate on the smell of the salt and seaweed – this should make you feel excited and happy. Conjure up the smell of the country, of farms, chickens and cows, of fields or corn and wheat, the smell of pine forests. Travel back in time and remember your first day at school, and you will probably sense a feeling of anticipation mixed with fear and excitement as

Stimulating the memory
Characteristic smells can serve as a catalyst to the memory. Because of the link between the nose and the limbic system, the part of the brain that controls emotions smells act as powerful emotional triggers. A whiff of seaweed, the smell of a wheatfield, the scent of apple blossom may instantly recall memories of long-ago holidays, for instance.

you recall the smell of wooden desks and blackboard chalk. Remember your first love and the flowers he may perhaps have given you. Such smells invariably evoke pleasurable sensations. Poets and writers have often gained inspiration from different scents: Proust, when he lived in Paris, would travel 100 kilometres to Normandy to inhale the apple blossom. It is also interesting to note that different fragrances often feature strongly when there is mention of love in novels or poems.

To me a sharp sense of smell is an invaluable possession. When I was young I could recognise my mother's friends by the trail of scent they would leave in the corridors. I felt very wary of one of them and I'm sure she had a hostile smell although I didn't understand this at the time. It was not until several years later that I learned from my mother that she had one day found her friend secretly drinking some of my milk ration (it was wartime) and topping it up with water. There is a saying in French, "Je ne peux pas le sentir", which literally means "I can't smell him", meaning "I don't trust or like him". This is probably a residual memory of when we would have used our sense of smell to determine whether we were attracted or repelled by another person's pheromones.

CHEMICAL SMELLS

It seems a shame that we have become obsessed with washing away the very smells that attract other people to us – the pheromones – keeping them at bay by using deodorants and replacing them with perfumes. I'm sure that it is because we are continually told, via the media, that the secretions we produce smell unpleasant, and we have been instilled with a fear of uncleanliness should we allow them to linger. Of course, this is a terrible distortion of the truth, firstly because within a matter of half an hour they will have been replaced, and secondly because there is nothing unclean or unpleasant about our pheromones. In fact they are very attractive; perfumers use extracts of animal glands such as civet, ambergris and musk in their creations, as they are known to appeal to our sense of smell because of their similarity to our own secretions. The eccentric Salvador Dali is even said to have rubbed male goats' faeces into his moustache before going out for the evening. As he was considered incredibly attractive to and successful with women, this unusual facet of his nocturnal preparations would seem to bear this point out!

The idea perpetrated by perfume manufacturers that we should replace our own natural fragrances with imitations is not only in bad taste, but possibly harmful. Because the raw materials are incredibly expensive, synthetic substitutes have to be used, but they can cause distressing skin rashes and allergies.

Many other odours that are man's creation do us no good at all. The fumes that come from industry and traffic can actually cause illness because they continually stress the body. The harmful effects of smog and of lead in petrol are well known. And, unfortunately, we try and camouflage many unpleasant fumes with synthetic flowery commercial sprays, which only make matters worse. I have been told that manufacturers of such 'air fresheners' use in them chemical compounds with anaesthetic properties, such as glyoxal, which deaden the sense of smell for more than an hour, and also irritate the bronchial tubes, sometimes provoking even asthma. They also add very potent odoriferous molecules which, because they are so overpowering, drown the unpleasant scent. This gives the impression that it has disappeared although it is actually still there, just temporarily submerged in a sea of other, to my mind, equally noxious smells. No wonder they can make us feel so nauseous.

Other harmful chemicals often used in aerosol furniture sprays, window cleansers and so on are chlorine, ammonia and formaldehyde. These also anaesthetise the olfactory organ and, because they are irritant, can cause allergies and rashes as severe as bad sunburn.

As the sense of smell is so basic a part of us, we could benefit from a greater awareness of the role it plays in our everyday lives. I would go so far to say that we ought to re-educate our senses of smell, perhaps learning in school how to tell good smells from bad smells, how to differentiate between those that will do us good and those that may harm us. Aromatherapy – literally therapy through aromas – goes a long way towards this re-education.

TEST YOUR SENSE OF SMELL

You can first improve your sense of smell by introducing a new smell into your life every day. It could be a flower, fruit, vegetable, herb or essential oil. Even a chemical used in the household (these enable you to recognise the presence of dangerous toxic fumes in the home).

The way to approach new smells is to sniff the odours or scents at a distance of 5-10cm (2-4in). Close your eyes and visualise the item and continue the process for as many times as you wish, until you have the smell fixed in your mind. Have a notepad nearby and make some record of your reactions to the smell. For example, whether you liked or disliked it, whether you found it hot or cold, whether it was strong or subtle, musky, floral, minty, putrid, pungent, camphorous, citrus and so on. After all, this is how wine tasters, who smell as well as taste, develop their art; and no serious brandy drinker would taste until he had warmed the snifter and inhaled the rising aroma.

Here is a simple game to play with family or friends. One person at a time should be blindfolded and tested on their ability to recognise ten different smells. These are listed on a notepad and the performance is marked against each item. The person being tested must not touch the source of the smell and the objects must be presented in a different order for each participant. Clues to the items being smelled can be given to beginners, and the winner is the one who scores the highest marks.

Choose your odoriferous substances from anything you have available. Vegetables should be cut into to release their smell as should some fruit; citrus fruits may need their peel scraped to release their pungency, and herbs like rosemary or bay may need a preliminary squeeze.

The following lists give a selection of possible items to use.

Fruit

Apple	Melon	Pineapple	Raspberry
Banana	Orange	Strawberry	Tangerine
Lemon	Peach		

Vegetables

Asparagus	Cauliflower	Garlic	Mushrooms
Broccoli	Celery	Horseradish	Onion
Brussels sprouts	Fennel		

Herbs

Basil	Fennel	Rosemary	Tarragon
Bay	Marjoram	Sage	Thyme
Dill	Mint		

Fluids

Brandy	Lubricating oil	Turpentine	Whiskey
Coca-cola	Methylated spirits	Vinegar	Wine
Gin	Sherry		

Store-cupboard Ingredients

Coffee	Orange (or other) marmalade	Redcurrant (or other) jelly	nutmeg, etc.)
Honey	Peanut butter	Spices (cloves, coriander,	Tea (Indian and China)
Mustard	Raspberry (or other) jam	cumin, curry powder, ginger,	Yeast

Household Staples

Aftershave	Firelighters	Shampoo	Toothpaste
Bleach	Furniture polish	Shaving Cream	Washing-up liquid
Face Cream	Perfume	Soap Powder	

AROMATICS IN HISTORY

Aromatic substances played important roles in the medicinal practises of the Hebrew, Greek, Arab, and Indian civilisations, but the therapeutic use of essential oils was born with the ancient Egyptians, for whom it was a way of life. Records dating back to 4500BC tell of the use of balsamic substances, perfumed oils, scented barks and resins, spices as well as aromatic vinegars, wines and beers in medicine, liturgy, astrology and embalming.

Hieroglyphics on papyri and steles in the temple of Edfu indicate that aromatic substances were blended to formulations by the high priests and alchemists to make perfumes and medicinal potions. The Papyrus of Ebers shows the widespread use of aromatherapy in pharmacology and pathology, for it contains a number of recipes of aromatic mixes designed to treat a variety of illnesss. And on the Papyrus of Edwin Smith, formulations can be found for restoring youthfulness to ageing men. We learn that Egyptians treated hay fever with a mixture of antimony, aloes, myrrh, and honey. They were also surprisingly well versed in methods of contraception: they would blend a concoction of acacia, coloquinte, dates and honey, and insert into the vagina, where it would ferment to form lactic acid, which we now know acts as a spermicide.

Within the magnificent temples, high priests built their own laboratories, where they crushed barks and distilled flowers to obtain the ingredients for their own aromatic potions, the formulations of which were kept a closely guarded secret. Seeds like caraway, roots like angelica, barks like cedarwood, and resins like frankincense were put into wine or oil, and slowly the aromatic substances would permeate the liquids, which were drunk or burned in religious ceremonies. The Egyptian priests also used a sophisticated method of extraction called enfleurage in which the odoriferous molecules are absorbed from the petals or leaves of plants by grains of sesame seeds. This technique is still used today in some parts of India.

One of the favourite perfumes called kyphi, was a mixture of sixteen different essences and was frequently used in religious ceremonies. Plutarch wrote of it: "The smell of this perfume penetrates your body by the nose. It makes you feel well and relaxed, the mind floats and you find yourself in a dreamy state of happiness, as if listening to beautiful music." Unlike mind-expanding drugs or alcohol, kyphi allowed the inhaler to remain alert and responsive, even though he may have felt as if he had been transported to another plane. High priests and pharaohs often inhaled it while meditating, a practice recorded in many inscriptions. Frankincense was also popular and was believed to encourage spiritual awareness and develop psychic faculties.

Gifts for the gods In ancient Egypt, the birthplace of aromatherapy, aromatic substances were so highly prized that they were offered to the gods. Here, Queen Nefertiti is seen making an offering.

RELIGIOUS AROMAS

Priests also acted as spiritual healers, being capable of treating mental disorders such as depression, mania and acute nervousness, which suggests that their knowledge of how different aromas affect the psyche was highly sophisticated.

The lotus was the sacred flower, because, in Egyptian mythology, it was the first living thing to appear on earth; when the petals unfurled, the supreme god, representing intellectual rulership, was revealed to them. The lotus grew in abundance along the banks of the Nile, but many other plants and flowers, such as the blue orchid, which were highly valued for their aromatic properties, had to be imported from Somalia, Malaysia, India and even as far afield as China. And, because some of the flowers were so highly prized, making essences was usually a secretive business.

Such trading flourished under the rule of Queen Hatshepsut (c1490-1468BC), the only woman to become a pharaoh. She adored fine perfumes and encouraged the use of cosmetics and the bold eye make-up that we associate with the ancient Egyptians.

Sacred scents The gods Isis and Osiris (right), two of the most important deities of ancient Egypt, each had a special fragrance – artemisia for Isis, marjoram for Osiris. On special holy days, the statues of the gods were covered with scented oils. Perfumes and oils played a major part in every aspect of Egyptian life. Queen Hatshepsut (far right), here depicted drinking from the udder of the cow-goddess Hathor, encouraged the import of rare flowers for making perfumes and popularised bold eye make-up. Sennufer (left), the keeper of the royal gardens in the reign of Tuthmosis III, is holding a lotus – the sacred flower of Egypt – to his nose.

It was not unusual for hundreds of thousands of kilogrammes of plants to be distilled for the creation of scented oils which were then burnt in the temples. On special days the statues of the gods would be covered with scented oils. Each god and goddess had their own fragrance – artemisia for Isis, marrubium for Horus marjoram for Osiris – and if the pharaohs wished to elicit favours from these supreme beings or thank them for success at war, they would burn these aromatic oils for their pleasure.

AROMATIC HARMONIES

When one considers the sheer magnificence of their jewellery, buildings and paintings, it is not difficult to imagine just how sophisticated was the science of aromatherapy in Egyptian times. They had an extensive vocabulary for plant aromas, which were classified into "notes". The skilled high priests (or perfumers) would mix together a number of harmonising notes to create a perfume in a manner akin to the composition of a melodious piece of music. Each pharaoh and his family had a number of different perfumes especially composed for them, which were designed to be worn at different times of day and on particular occasions, on account of their power to evoke or intensify certain emotions. For example, a perfume for war or battle would stimulate feelings of aggression, whereas another for meditation would promote a state of tranquillity and thoughtfulness.

Different flowers also symbolised different things to the Egyptians. Just as we might send telegrams or cards to one another to wish good health during illness or to show our affection or love, they would send each other the appropriate flower.

The embalmer, an important figure, knew that plants possessed natural antiseptic properties valuable for preserving human bodies. Each embalmer developed his own formulation, which he guarded fiercely. Traces of resins like galbanum and spices such as clove, cinnamon and nutmeg have been isolated from the bandages of mummies. Such preservatives were obviously remarkably effective, since fragments of intestine examined under the microscope have been found to be completely intact after thousands of years.

THE ART OF EMBALMING

The process of embalming is fascinating, if rather stomach-turning. Herodotus wrote that the embalmer would use a fine stick with a hooked end to draw out part of the brain through the nostrils, before injecting a solution of aromatic herbs and solvent into the cavity. He would then open up the abdomen with a sharpened stone from Ethiopia and remove all the viscera, which were washed with aromatic palm wine. The abdomen was subsequently filled with myrrh, galbanum and other spices before being stitched up. The viscera went into four different pots called canopic jars, whilst the body was soaked in natron (sodium carbonate solution), left for seventy days, then washed and wrapped in bandages that had been steeped in aromatic resins.

The whole process could take as long as six months before the body was ready to be encased in a series of elaborately inlaid caskets, which fitted into the sarcophagus. Such an elaborate and lengthy treatment was reserved for high priests and pharaohs; a much simpler method was employed for those of lowlier origins.

Although the high priests, doctors and embalmers were recognised as experts in aromatherapy, even ordinary Egyptians possessed a knowledge of the value of aromatic substances in cooking. They would add caraway, coriander or aniseed to their breads of millet and barley to make them easier to digest. Mint, marjoram and parsley were also widely used, and garlic was valued for its power to stave off the ever-present threat of epidemic.

UNDERSTANDING ESSENTIAL OILS

Essential oils, the substances which give plants their aromas, have many applications. They can be used to beautify the skin and retard ageing, to prevent and treat a host of common illnesses, or to create a particular mood. Aromatherapy is the art of using essential oils to promote health and beauty.

Essential oils are frequently referred to as the 'soul' of the plant or as its hormones, but they could also be likened to the pheromones secreted by humans. If you take a few leaves of lavender or rosemary and rub or squeeze them between your fingers, you will smell the distinctive aroma of the essential oil that has oozed on to your skin.

Most flowers, seeds, barks, grains, roots and resins, as well as leaves, contain essential oils, usually in minute quantities. Sometimes several essential oils can be extracted from the same plant. The orange tree, for instance, contains one essential oil, orange in the rind of the fruit; another called petitgrain, is obtained from the leaves, and yet another, neroli, is responsible for the wonderful scent of the flowers. Each has its own smell and therapeutic properties.

Often the smallest flowers are the most intensely perfumed. At the beginning of this century it was thought that if plants were bred to produce larger flowers, they would have a stronger fragrance than the original smaller ones. But, because the plant uses more energy to grow larger blooms, it actually produces fewer essential oils.

Flowers from the east
Relatively little has changed since this anonymous illustrator depicted the production of Bulgarian rosewater at the turn of the current century. It still takes some two tons of rose petals to produce a single kilo of essential oil.

UNDERSTANDING ESSENTIAL OILS

Essential oils vary in quality and in the intensity of their colour. Some are almost colourless or a pastel shade: camomile is bluish, basil is light green and Bulgarian rose is pale pink. Others are deeply pigmented: patchouli is brown, violet leaves are a very dark green, and rose is an orange-red.

Essential oils are unlike other vegetable oils such as almond and sunflower, because (with the exception of garlic and cinnamon) they are lighter than water and are usually highly fluid (although some are more viscous, of a honey-like consistency). The odoriferous molecules tend to be extremely volatile because of their unusually high number of free electrons, so they evaporate quickly, especially when warmed. A test you can try for yourself involves simply applying a few drops of essential oil of lavender to a piece of ordinary white writing paper. The patch will be slightly coloured and you will see it disappear in a very short time as the aromatic substances vaporise and disperse to scent the air.

THE PROPERTIES OF ESSENTIAL OILS

When Sir Alexander Fleming discovered the antibiotic penicillin in 1928, it too was 'natural', isolated from a culture of mould. Today, of course, penicillin is synthesised in the laboratory, which is perhaps why so many people have allergic reactions to the drug: the artificial variety is considerably stronger than its natural counterpart.

Naturally derived antibiotics, like essential oils, act slowly, and only kill the bacteria or viruses, but also stimulate the body's immune system to strengthen resistance to further attack. Taking strong drugs, on the other hand, is rather like cracking a nut with a sledgehammer, for they not only kill the harmful bacteria, but also destroy the beneficial ones in our intestines, responsible for maintaining a good environment for digestion and for making significant quantities of B complex vitamins.

The trouble is that we have come to expect instant cures and think that the only antibiotics of any value come in pill form. Many people find it hard to believe that essential oils from plants are actually just as effective, if not more so. They may take longer to show results, but as it may have taken a long time for the symptoms of the illness to reveal themselves, so they are unlikely to disappear overnight. There are no miracle cures.

Even up until the last war, essential oils of clove, lemon, thyme and camomile were employed as natural disinfectants and antiseptics to fumigate the maternity wards of

Essence of health In the past, aromatic essences were used as fumigants in times of plague or domestic illness. Oil-makers worked constantly in order to meet the demands of a society beset by unhealthy conditions; this 16th-century woodcut shows one at work.

hospitals and to sterilise instruments used in surgery and dentistry. In fact, all essential oils, whether they come from flowers, fruits, resins, or barks have antibiotic, antiseptic, anti-viral and anti-inflammatory properties to a greater or lesser extent.

All essential oils, whether they come from flowers, fruits, resins or barks, have antibiotic, antiseptic, anti-viral and anti-inflammatory properties to some degree.

The ancient Egyptians used essential oils in embalming because they knew of their ability to prevent flesh from decomposing. Hippocrates, too, was aware of their antibacterial properties, for when an epidemic of plague broke out in Athens, he urged the townspeople to burn aromatic plants at the corners of the streets to protect themselves and to prevent the plague from spreading.

Centuries later, when the plague reared its ugly head in England (in 1665-6), Charles II's doctor also declared that every householder should fumigate his rooms with aromatic essences to fight this scourge. At this time, it was common practice to wear pomanders containing garlic and cloves around the neck for protection.

CHEMICAL PROOF

Scientists working in a number of different fields around the world – doctors, professors of medicine, chemists and biologists – have carried out laboratory tests which increasingly prove – and confirm – that essential oils have the ability to prevent the proliferation of harmful bacteria. Such tests involve adding a few drops of essential oil, such as lavender, to a culture of microbes. The time it takes to destroy the colony of bacilli gives a good indication of how strongly antiseptic or antibiotic that particular essential oil is.

It is certain that constituent molecules lend an essential oil its bacterial properties, and they vary in efficacy. Phenol, for example, is the strongest, and because it makes up 80 per cent of Spanish oregano, this essential oil is consequently a powerful antibiotic and antiseptic, as are eucalyptus, clove, niaouli, thyme, sandalwood, lemon, cinnamon, lavender and mint. Then come the aldehydes, alcohol, esters and finally the acids, in order of diminishing potency. I should point out, however, that the natural essential oil is infinitely superior to pure phenol because, as I mentioned earlier, the presence of the other molecules

Starting from basics The perfumer sorts through his raw materials. From Johannes Baptista della Porta's 'Magia Naturalis', Nuremberg, 1715

in the oil actually serves to reinforce its healing action.

Luckily, we do not have epidemics of plague to cope with as they did in the past, but we do still suffer from frequent colds and flu, especially during the winter months, which can be extremely debilitating, and essential oils can be tremendously helpful for keeping such ills at bay, and for treating the symptoms too.

Another useful property of essential oils is their ability to soothe inflammation and reduce swelling. The Egyptians knew of this property too, classifying essential oils from plants according to their colour tones and heat, as opposed to their constituent molecules. To them they were either hot or cold, dark or clear, damp or dry, and heavy or light. As in the philosophy of Chinese medicine, which divides all things into yin and yang, they believed that balance was absolutely crucial to the harmonious functioning of the body and mind. So, for an affliction such as rheumatism; or a swelling caused by water retention, a hot and dry oil such as rosemary or ginger would be applied to redress the balance. When put into practice, this theory still does work exceptionally well.

WHAT MAKES AN ESSENTIAL OIL

Each essential oil is made up of numerous different organic molecules which dissolve in alcohols, oils, emulsifiers, ether or chloroform. The individual aroma and therapeutic properties of each essential oil depends on the combination and concentration of these constituent molecules, which belong to several different chemical families.

ALCOHOLS
Menthol in mint, linalol in ylang ylang and lavender; geraniol in geranium and rose; nerol in neroli and orange; borneol in lavender and pine.

ALDEHYDES
Citral in lemongrass and mandarin; benzoic in benzoin and laurel; citronellal in lemon, eucalyptus and melissa; vanilline in vanilla and styrax.

ACIDS
Cinnamic acid in styrax; benzoic acid in ylang ylang.

PHENOLS
Eugenol in clove; thymol in thyme.

ESTERS
Benzyl acetate in styrax; linalyl in bergamot and lavender.

UNDERSTANDING ESSENTIAL OILS

ACETONES
Cineol in eucalyptus; jasmone in neroli and jasmine; irone in iris.

TERPENES
Pinene in cypress; camphene in petitgrain and juniper; terpineol in coriander; phellandrene in lemon and sage; limonene in lemon, carrot and mint.

Each essential oil is an incredibly complex substance, for it contains a number of different alcohols, esters, phenols and so on. Eucalyptus, for example, is made up of 250 different constituents, which is why it is almost impossible to reproduce it exactly with synthetic ingredients. The therapeutic value of an essential oil also depends largely on the synergistic reaction between the component molecules, which is why man-made imitations never have the same power to heal as their natural counterparts.

EXTRACTING THE ESSENTIAL OILS

Essential oils can be obtained from plants in a number of ways, and the right method is important for it will influence the ultimate quality and therapeutic properties of the oils.

MACERATION
An example of this technique is enfleurage, often used for flowers like jasmine and tuberose. High quality flowers or petals that have not been damaged in any way are spread out on a tray lined with fat or vegetable oil. The flowers are left for sixteen to seventy two hours, then replaced by fresh ones at regular intervals, until the fat is saturated with their perfume. This is a painstaking process that can last for up to three months before the aromatic substances can be separated – in a process called defleurage – from the fat with a solvent and purified. Essential oils extracted in this way tend to be of a superior quality to those obtained by distillation and, consequently, they are usually more expensive.

DISTILLATION
Distillation has been used as a method of extracting essential oils from plant material for thousands of years. The ancient Egyptians were known to place their raw material and some water in a large clay pot. Heat was applied and the steam that formed had to pass through layers of cotton or linen cloth placed in the neck before escaping. The essential oils became trapped in this material, and all that had to be done to obtain them was

Towards the oil The extraction of essential oils often involved distillation in order to obtain a pure, concentrated essence. Here, an 18th-century version of the process is shown.

to squeeze out the cloth periodically. It is still the most common means of extraction: steam is passed over the leaves or flowers, possibly in a vacuum or under pressure, so that the essential oils within them vaporise. When the steam is cooled, the essential oils condense and, because they are not water soluble, they separate and can be collected quite easily.

DISSOLVING

Sometimes it is preferable to use a volatile solvent such as alcohol for extracting gums and resins like galbanum and myrrh. In the case of fresh flowers and plants, however, ether or benzine may be used instead.

PRESSING

This technique is not commonly employed commercially, but it can be used to squeeze the essential oils from the rinds and peels of fruits like oranges and lemons.

CARING FOR ESSENTIAL OILS

Because essential oils are delicate, volatile substances, they should be kept away from strong light, in dark bottles, at a cool temperature – the bathroom may seem a logical place but is likely to be too hot and humid to preserve essences at their best.

USING AROMATIC PLANTS

BASIL

Basil

The Greek word for basil is okimon, meaning 'quick', because the plant grows so rapidly, but a Byzantine princess who relished its perfume and beauty gave it the name basilikon. In India, the Hindus believed that basil offered protection to the soul in both life and death, so it was frequently used in religious ceremonies. In Egypt basil was mixed with myrrh and incense for use in embalming.

Its therapeutic properties are rather controversial, because there are so many different varieties of basil. Generally, it is a good diuretic, and a nerve and stomach fortifier. It gives relief from difficult periods, dyspepsia, insomnia and migraine. Women suffering from swollen breasts when pregnant may find a compress of rose water and infused basil helpful.

Dr. Jean Valnet, a French expert on aromatherapy, considers it to be a valuable regulator of the menstrual cycle. It is also helpful in relieving depression, anxiety and lack of concentration.

Added to food, it improves digestion, and the dried plant can be smoked instead of tobacco to give relief from asthma.

BENZOIN

This essence has a lovely scent reminiscent of vanilla and is often used as a fixative in perfume. It is extracted from the resin of trees, native to Malaysia, Java and Borneo, that grow to about 20 metres (60 feet) in height, each tree yielding 500-600g (about 1-1¼lb) of resin. It is useful for treating respiratory problems such as asthma, when breathing in is difficult, and skin problems such as melanosis when skin becomes pigmented.

Benzoin is inhaled or used in oil for massage.

Benzoin

BERGAMOT

Bergamot belongs to the orange tree family and was discovered by Christopher Columbus when he went to the Canary Islands. Bergamot now grows further afield as well, in southern Italy, Sicily, and along the Ivory Coast of Africa. The essential oil, distilled from the peel of the fruit, has a lovely emerald green colour, and a spicy lemon scent. It has strong antiseptic and tonic properties and is good for fighting infections, and boosting the body's natural defences to help it fight back the onset of disease.

Care should be taken when applying it externally, however, because one of its constituent molecules, furocoumarine, can provoke abnormal pigmentation of the skin in strong sunlight.

Bergamot

CAJPUT

The name and oil derive from the Malay kayu-puti, literally white tree, which grows abundantly in Malaysia and the Molucca Islands. The essential oils are extracted from the leaves and buds, and have a very aromatic, hot smell. Cajput is a strong antiseptic and benefits the pulmonary, intestinal and urinary tracts.

Added to a bath, cajput is a treatment for cystitis. Massaged into the skin, it relieves rheumatic conditions, while inhalations of the oil helps alleviate colds.

CAMOMILE

The essential oils distilled from freshly dried camomile flowers have a lovely blue colour which later turns greenish yellow. Camomile was a sacred flower in Egypt and was offered to please the sun god Ra and used as a remedy for fever.

It is a good tonic, digestive, antiseptic and sedative, (it reduces and calms fever), and promotes the healing of wounds thanks to one of its constituents, azulene. Camomile helps to treat eczema and acne by soothing the inflammation. It is also good for stings and bites, cystitis, amenorrhoea, dysmenorrhoea, bronchitis, asthma, coughs, migraine and the neuralgia of flu.

For external use on the face, add 2 drops to 2 teaspoons of soya oil. For a body massage oil, mix 2 drops of camomile with 2 drops of rosemary in 4-5 teaspoons of soya oil. This can help to relieve rheumatic aches and pains. As a tonic and stimulant for children and old people who have been ill, add 5-6 drops to a warm bath.

Cajut

Camomile

CARDAMOM

The essential oils come from the distillation of the seeds found in the fruits of various plants belonging to the ginger family. They have a lovely fresh smell which neutralises the odour of garlic. Dr. Leclerc, a famous French naturopath and herbalist, believed that cardamom

was one of the best carminatives (an aid for wind and flatulence), digestives, stimulants, nerve and heart tonics.

It is also an effective diuretic and is even better when used with other essences such as juniper which reinforces its action. When chewed, cardamom seeds provide an excellent remedy for halitosis.

CEDARWOOD

The cedarwood tree comes from North Africa, Morocco and Algeria, and its wood has a lovely fragrance. The essential oil has a syrupy consistency and, like sandalwood, is balsamic. The ancient Egyptians used it frequently in embalming.

It is antiseptic and benefits the urinary system, providing a remedy for cystitis and bladder infections. It is also good for the respiratory system and treats bronchitis. Cedarwood can help skin troubles like eczema, and could be used in hair care to treat falling hair and alopecia. It is a general tonic and possesses aphrodisiac properties as well.

CINNAMON

In ancient Chinese medicine, cinnamon was looked upon as a panacea, and around 2700BC no prescription was considered complete without it. Cinnamon is one of the oldest spices known and was used not only by the Chinese, but also by the Romans, Greeks and ancient Egyptians, who always added it to their wines and meals.

It actually originates from Malaysia and Sri Lanka, and has a distinctive hot, peppery aroma and taste. It is a good remedy for flu and also helps to treat fatigue and depression.

Cinnamon

CLOVE

Cloves were discovered by the Arabs when their travels took them to the Molucca Islands off the east coast of Africa. They then spread to Malaysia, Sri Lanka, and the Seychelles. In China it was considered respectful to chew cloves before meeting the emperor for this purified the breath.

Clove is one of the most effective antiseptics known and is good for treating all kinds of infections such as flu and colds. It benefits people suffering from rheumatism and helps to ease the pains of childbirth, so women in labour should take wine steeped with cloves.

Clove

CYPRESS

Cypress trees come from the East and all the Mediterranean countries. The essences, which are obtained by distillation of the leaves, twigs and cones of the tree, are slightly yellow and their perfume is agreeable and tenacious. In ancient Egypt cypress essential oils were valued for their medicinal properties, and the wood itself was used to make the sarcophagi.

The essences relieve circulatory problems such as varicose veins and piles and benefit the urinary system.

EUCALYPTUS

The eucalyptus tree originated in Australia and was later introduced to North Africa and the Mediterranean coast-line. The essential oils extracted from its silvery leaves are pale yellow in colour, have a fresh, aromatic smell, and are highly medicinal. The essence's principal constituent is eucalyptol which gives it strong antiseptic properties.

It is excellent for respiratory problems, providing an effective remedy for coughs, asthma, bronchitis, catarrhal discharge, and the fever which accompanies flu. It can be used to treat cystitis, skin problems, and to heal cuts and burns. It also acts as a stimulant for the nervous system.

For a natural fumigant when someone is ill at home, boil some eucalyptus leaves in water, and let the vapours disperse through the house. For bronchitis, leave an infusion of leaves (or of the oil) near the bed at night.

Eucalyptus

Fennel

FENNEL

Fennel is a very decorative and aromatic plant which has long been regarded as a potent diuretic, and can be taken for this purpose in wine, liquor or vinegar. It is also good for the stomach, stimulating the secretion of milk after childbirth, and is a mild laxative and stimulant. It also provides a useful remedy for cystitis, a weak bladder and asthma, and can be taken in Bordeaux wine for easing a cough.

An infusion of fennel herb to 500ml (a scant pint) of water can be applied to the eyes to reduce itching and inflamation brought on by an infection.

USING AROMATIC PLANTS

Frankincense

FRANKINCENSE

This essential oil is extracted from the gum resin obtained by making an incision in a tree which grows in Arabia and south-east Africa. The essential oil is yellowish in colour and has a balsamic aroma. Its perfume becomes slightly lemony when mixed with myrrh and aromatic spices, and the sweet-smelling smoke exuded when this mixture is burned was often used in religious ceremonies. It is a good nerve tonic, antiseptic, and pectoral (good for the chest).

Add 5-6 drops to a bath, or place a few drops on a glass slide left by the radiator, if you want to relax or meditate.

GALBANUM

The essence comes from a gum resin obtained from a species of fennel which grows in Persia. It is yellow in colour, and has a lovely hot, pungent, aromatic fragrance.

It can be used to treat skin problems such as abscesses and inflammation, and also encourages the formation of scar tissue. For an oil to rub into affected areas, mix a few drops in a peach kernel or almond oil.

GARLIC

Garlic

Like onion, garlic is strongly antibiotic. It not only keeps colds and viral infections away, but drives them out, speeding recovery from illness. A good source of iodine, garlic is highly recommended for anyone with an underactive thyroid gland, who suffers from poor circulation, or has a weight problem. My grandmother would use garlic cloves as suppositories when we had a cough or cold as children. Garlic also benefits anyone with high blood pressure or a rheumatic condition.

GERANIUM

Geranium originates from Africa and in 1690 was brought to Europe. The essence, often called geranium Bourbon-la-Reunion (from the island near Madagascar), is usually colourless but can be yellowish green, and has a strong but agreeable smell. An imitation of its aroma is frequently made by mixing a few of its constituent molecules with essences of sandalwood and citronella.

Geranium essence is good for skin problems such as frostbite, dermatitis and inflammation. It helps the cicatrisation of wounds and treats haemorrhoids and bad circulation.

For a skin massage oil, mix 2-3 drops in 2 teaspoons of soya oil. For haemorrhoids apply 1 drop mixed with cold cream. For inflammation of the breast when breast-feeding, mix 3 drops into some cold cream.

Geranium

LAVENDER

Lavender originated from Persia, the Canary Islands and the Mediterranean coast, and many different varieties grow throughout Europe today.

Lavender essence is effective in the treatment of skin troubles such as bruises, frostbite, erythema, acne and dermatitis, and also reduces swelling. It brings relief to rheumatic conditions, and is particularly good when mixed with juniper, cypress or ginger. Add 2 drops of each to 2-3 teaspoons of soya oil and massage into the affected area. For skin conditions, add 3 drops to 2 teaspoons of oil.

It was Dr. Gattefossé, one of the founding fathers of aromatherapy, who discovered the marvellous burn-healing powers of lavender. When he severely burned his hand in the laboratory, he plunged it, accidentally, into the nearest bowl - full of essential oil of lavender. The pain ceased and the burn healed very quickly thereafter.

For bad burns, apply pure essence of lavender straight-away, wrap the affected part in gauze or muslin (to let the skin breathe), and repeat two to three times per day, about every four hours. For less severe burns, when cooking for instance, dab on lavender oil immediately, and cover. If you have no essential oil available, get some lavender flowers or leaves from the garden, apply to the burn, and wrap as above.

Lavender

LEMON

The lemon tree (Citrus medica or Citrus limonum) was cultivated in the Middle East and India for the therapeutic properties of the fruit, from which the essential oil is derived. Introduced into Europe by the Arabs, the tree is now well established throughout the Mediterranean. According to an 11th Century French account, Eve is said to have prized the lemon above all other fruits in paradise.

(continued on p.38).

FROM FLOWER TO ESSENTIAL OIL

Tracing the pathway from lavender flowers to pure essential oil makes it clear why the oil is far superior in quality and also more expensive than any artificial copy.

Lavender is a member of the labiate family which, like umbelliferous, myrtacous, rutaceous, lauriferous, terebinthous and coniferous plants, is particularly rich in essential oils. The essential oil should be highly scented and very pleasant, varying in colour from dark yellow to dark greeny yellow. Its principal constituents are esters such as linalyl and geranyle, alcohols such as garaniol, linalol and borneol, and terpenes like limonene and binene.

It takes approximately 200kg (440lb) of fresh flowers to obtain 1kg (just over 2lb) of essential oil and because the flowers do not travel very well, extraction often has to take place on the spot, soon after the flowers have been gathered.

The quality of the oil depends on a number of different interacting factors. The time of picking is vital, and once the flowers are ready, harvesting should be completed in a matter of two weeks, for if there is any delay the odoriferous substances will be lost. As with wine, the quality of essential oils varies from year to year, so there are good, and not so good, vintages. This is not really surprising when you consider that the climate, the composition of the soil, the geographic location – the altitude, whether the lavender is grown in a secluded valley or on an exposed mountain slope –all influence the ultimate quality of the essential oil. For example, flowers picked from plants living in a natural environment, as they do in parts of Persia or 750-1,500 metres up in the Alps of southern France, give a more subtle perfume than their cultivated English counterparts. This is because the French lavender is richer in linolyle acetate, which gives rise to a fruitier and sweeter note, considered more pleasant than the camphoric English lavender with its higher proportion of lineol – and it is, as a result, much more expensive.

Sometimes the colour, as well as the smell, of the oil can make it easy to tell a good from a poor quality one, the best being a dark or greeny yellow shade. Paler and more insipid-smelling oils are not so desirable, so other constituents are sometimes added to alter them, which, of course, has the adverse effect of diminishing their therapeutic properties.

Creating the oil From earliest times to the present day, little has changed when it comes to the first stage of preparing an essential oil – the raw materials still have to be gathered (left). Distilling, too, is carried out along the same lines, though modern technology has improved on traditional methods (below).

USING AROMATIC PLANTS

Lemon essence, which contains the aldehyde citronellal,has strong antiseptic properties. It is good for colds and flu, coughs and sore throats. It purifies the blood and promotes good circulation and minimises rheumatism, skin blemishes, vein problems and cellulite, and alleviates cracked nipples during pregnancy.

Lemon

LEMONGRASS

This sweet-scented grass is cultivated in India, the African Congo, the Seychelles, Indonesia, Sri Lanka and Brazil, principally for seasoning food. The essential oil has a lemony aroma and its main constituents are citral (which is strongly antiseptic) and geraniol.

It is useful as an external antiseptic and makes a good foot bath for sweaty feet and athlete's foot. It soothes fevers and gives relief from migraine and headaches.

MELISSA

This plant is cultivated throughout Europe and grows wild in woods and fields. The essence is more or less colourless, but can have a slight yellow hue, and smells lemony.

It is anti-spasmodic, stimulant (for the nervous system), and tonic for the cardiac system or heart. It helps treat depression, nervous anxiety and palpitations as well as neuralgia and sciatica, so it is particularly beneficial to many elderly people.

Rub into the chest an oil made by adding 5 drops of essence to 2 teaspoons soya oil. This can be used as a general body oil too. Add 6 drops to the bath for nerves, anxiety or palpitations. When depressed, drink an infusion of the plant. Add 2 pinches of the plant to 500ml (a scant pint) of boiling water. Let stand for 10 minutes, and sweeten with honey if liked.

Melissa

MINT

Mint is one of the best known of all the herbs and grows in abundance in Britain as well as in the mountains of Provence and around Paris in France. Its name derives from mente, a Latin word meaning 'thought', because it stimulates the brain.

The Greeks believed it capable of preventing menstruation. It is also thought to be good for the voice, so perhaps singers could benefit from it, and it helps to heal ulcers, excites the appetite, gives relief from insomnia and dyspepsia, fortifies the nerves, and is an excellent expectorant, relieving mucus. A tisane or tea of mint should be taken for coughs and colds; for bad catarrh, it is even better with eucalyptus added.

Mint

MYRRH

Essence of myrrh comes from a yellowy brown gum resin and originates from Arabia and Persia. The essence itself may be any shade of yellow, from very pale through to a deep golden colour, and it has a highly aromatic and camphor-like smell. Myrrh has been used in religious ceremonies since antiquity, and the ancient Egyptians, who called it 'phun', used it for embalming purposes as well.

Its principal constituents are terpenes, pinenes, and phenols. It has good antiseptic properties, reduces inflammation, and treats skin problems such as acne and dermatitis. For external application,make an oil by adding 2-4 drops of essence to 2 teaspoons of soya oil.

NEROLI

Essence of neroli is obtained by distilling the fresh flowers of the bitter orange tree. The most esteemed oil comes from the bitter orange, citrus bigaradia and is known as neroli bigarade, whilst another, called neroli portugal, comes from a sweet orange tree. Neroli is a very expensive essential oil (1 ton of flowers is needed to produce 1 kg or 2 lb of oil), and it has a yellowish colour which can turn brown when exposed to light. It is rich in alcohols like nerol, linalol and graniol.

Neroli is highly beneficial to the nervous system, and effectively treats anxiety and nervous depression. Because it has a slightly hypnotic effect, it induces sleep and acts as a natural tranquilliser. It is also a natural blood cleanser and helps improve bad circulation and menstrual tension.

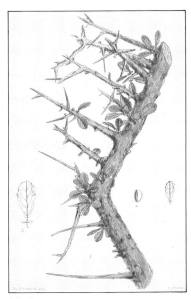

Myrrh

Neroli

NIAOULI

Niaouli is the essence extracted by distillation from the bush Melaluca Verdiflora, a member of the myrrh family which grows in the Pacific and the Far East. It was introduced to Europe in the 17th Century after its

discovery by early Pacific explorers.

Niaouli contains phenol, a powerful antibiotic and antiseptic, and is therefore useful, combined with clove, pine, cinnamon or eucalyptus, for treating and preventing colds and flu.

PATCHOULI

Essence of patchouli comes from the dried branches of a plant which originated in Malaysia and the Seychelles. The essential oil is brown and viscous, and has a strong, persistent smell. It is often used as a fixative in perfumes. It is a good antiseptic and can be applied wherever there is infection. It reduces inflammation, soothes burns, and helps to treat skin problems such as seborrhoea, acne, dermatitis and allergic reactions.

For the skin, make an oil by adding 2 drops of essence to 2 teaspoons of almond oil. Add a few drops to your shampoo if you have excessively oily hair.

PINE

The essential oils come from both the resins and needles of the pine tree, of which there are 150 varieties. I consider the best essences are those extracted from the needles of pines that grow in Scandinavia and Russia. The essence is very pale yellow and has a lovely balsamic smell which it owes to its principal constituents - pinene, sylvestrene, phellandrene and cadinene.

Pine

Pine is an excellent antiseptic which benefits the respiratory system (helping flu, colds and brochitis), and the urinary tract (helping treat cystitis). It has a revitalising action and benefits children and adults alike.

It is also anti-rheumatic and particularly effective when mixed with lemon or juniper. Add 2 drops of each to 2 teaspoons of soya oil, and rub into the affected are.

For inhalation to ease the symptoms of flu and colds, add 2 drops of pine, 2 drops of niaouli and 2 drops of eucalyptus to 500ml (a scant pint) of hot water.

ROSE

The rose initially came from the East, but there are now many hundreds of different varieties which grow nearly everywhere. However, only three reproduce faithfully to give true perfume of rose, and they are rose centifolia, rose damask and rose gallica. Throughout history, rose has been the perfume of kings and pharaohs. It was also used both as an aphrodisiac for women and, ironically, in religious ceremonies.

It usually takes about 2 tons of rose petals to produce just 1kg (2lb) of essential oil, and for this reason it is one of the most expensive of the essences. The best essences to look for are Bulgarian, Moroccan, Oriental rose and Rose de Grasse. It is not surprising that imitations of rose are often made by mixing some of its constituent molecules with essential oils of lemongrass, geranium and citronella.

Rose is a general tonic and fortifier, and has a particularly effective action on the nervous, circulatory and respiratory systems. It is good for all skin problems, from eczema, wrinkles and dryness to puffiness and congestion of the pores.

It is also believed to be a sexual stimulant for women, and may help those who complain of frigidity. It makes a good body oil for special occasions.

Rose

ROSEMARY

This is perhaps the best known and used aromatic herb. The Greeks and Romans,who believed it symbolised love and death, used it in religious ceremonies and feasts. It was also favoured by the ancient Egyptians, and traces of rosemary were found when the tombs of certain pharaohs were excavated.

The term rosemary actually comes from the Latin rosmarinus, meaning 'rose of the sea', for it can be found growing wild along the coast in most Mediterranean countries.

The herb is strongly antiseptic and is also a stimulant, cholagogue (benefiting the liver), and diuretic. It is also an important remedy for rheumatism.

Rosemary

SAGE

Since antiquity sage has been regarded as a sacred herb. Its name derives from the Latin verb salvere, to save, and it appears to benefit any ailment.

The ancient Egyptians gave it to women who were unable to bear children, and also valued it as a remedy for plague. According to the memoirs of Saint-Simon, a writer well acquainted with the goings-on at the French court, Louis XIV took an infusion of sage ever night before going to bed, and it was to this that he attributed his long and fruitful life. The Chinese still value it so highly that they will

USING AROMATIC PLANTS

give 4.5kg (10lb) of their tea for 450g (1lb) of sage leaves.

Sage is renowned for helping to promote and normalise menstruation. It can also be used for treating rheumatic conditions, catarrhal discharge, haemorrhage, and excessive sweating, and is recommended for convalescents. It has a calming effect and also improves the condition of hair.

Sage

SANDALWOOD

Grown in India, Malaysia, Java, Borneo and Australia, the Sandalwood tree (Santalum) has a hard, fragrant wood that has long been burned as incense. The essential oil, as well as being an attractive perfume, is a powerful antibiotic and antiseptic, sandalwood is valuable in treating all infections. Cystitis responds well to this essence, which also helps to reduce puffy skin when used as an oil for the face. Its effect is soothing and healing.

THYME

Thyme grows wild in the South of France and other Mediterranean countries. Its use can be traced back to the ancient Egyptians who incorporated the essential oils of thyme into embalming fluids. The Greeks, who named it thumos, meaning 'smell', were known to drink an infusion of thyme at the end of a banquet. It is a tonic and stimulant, is good for the chest and helps treat asthma, flu, coughs, fever, nervousness, as well as aches and pains.

Applied externally, it reduces the swelling of rheumatism and oedema. It also relieves the discomfort of a swollen stomach.

Sandalwood

Thyme

YLANG YLANG

These trees – known as perfume trees – are native to the Far East, the Philippines and Malaysia, but are also found in Asia, the Seychelles, Tahiti and India. The essential oil, which is distilled from the fresh flowers, is pale yellow and has an exquisite perfume. In the past the flowers were mixed in coconut oil and used to improve the condition of the hair, to soothe insect bites, and to fight infections. The pure essences were also used to treat malaria. Ylang ylang is antiseptic, aphrodisiac and tonic to the nervous system. It also benefits the hair if added to shampoo.

AROMATHERAPY IN ACTION

As you will have read in the preceding pages, aromatherapy, the use of essential oils and essences to treat health and beauty problems, has an extremely long history, going back to the time of the ancient Egyptians if not before. The tenets that held good then still hold good today.

This part of the book shows you how you can put the principles of aromatherapy into action – not just to help you cope with specific health and beauty problems, but also to improve the quality of life for you. You can put aromatherapy to work in hundreds of seemingly minor, yet significant, ways. Something as simple as a bowl of pot-pourri can make all the difference to a room's atmosphere, for instance, while you can use essential oils and essences to alleviate all kinds of illnesses and conditions, from skin problems to PMT. And remember, too, that aromatherapy can help you come to terms with the strains of modern living – try an aromatherapy massage and feel stress literally float away!

PRACTICAL AROMATHERAPY

Essential oils can be applied in several different ways to prevent illness and to treat various ailments. They can be massaged into the skin, added to a warm bath, inhaled as a vapour, or taken internally, for all these methods will help them to reach the inner parts of the body which need to be protected or healed. The olfactory organ and the sense of smell are vital factors, of course, but the most effective way to use essential oils is through the skin.

SKIN: THE BODY'S LARGEST ORGAN

Few people realise that the skin is the largest organ of the body; in a person weighing around 75kg (165lb), the skin will constitute approximately 3kg (6½lb) of this weight, whereas the liver is responsible for a mere 1.5kg (just over 3lb). On the whole, the skin is only about 1-2mm deep (about the thickness of a 1p coin) but on the palms of the hands and soles of the feet it is greater, and can even be as thick as 4mm at the top of the neck, near the skull.

Skin is composed of two distinct layers: the outer epidermis, the only part we see, which is continually renewing itself as new cells are formed and old ones are shed from the surface; and a deeper layer called the dermis which contains the connective tissue that lends skin its remarkable strength, suppleness and pliancy. The skin is endowed with a very good supply of blood which is brought to the surface by tiny capillaries, and is also teeming with nerve endings which are responsible for our perception of touch and pain.

One of the skin's main functions is the elimination of wastes, of sweat, and of excess sebum, the lubricating oil produced by the sebaceous glands (which are most active during puberty, causing greasy skin and spots). These are excreted through tiny pores which cover the entire surface of the skin. Oxygen and carbon dioxide also pass in and out of the skin, in a kind of respiration akin to that which takes place in the lungs.

Exactly how essential oils are taken up by the skin still remains rather a mystery, but it is quite possible that they pass in through the pores which produce sweat and sebum. And because the odoriferous molecules of an essential oil are extremely volatile, it is possible that they diffuse through the skin in the same way as other gases.

Many are sceptical of the ability of the skin to absorb essential oils, or any other substances for that matter, seeing it as an impenetrable barrier. But this is not the case: essential oils have the ability to penetrate right into the deep layers of the skin and from there travel to the various organs, glands and tissues of the body. Once they have passed through the epidermis, they seep into the

Maximum benefit Adding a suitable essential oil to a bath can be extremely beneficial, as this enables your body's skin to absorb the oil itself, while you can inhale the vapour.

small capillaries in the dermis and are carried all around the body in the blood. They are also taken up by the lymph fluid which bathes every cell in the body. Experiments with guinea pigs have shown that if a few drops of lavender oil labelled with a radioactive substance are applied to a patch of shaved skin, when the animal is killed and dissected about an hour and a half later, the essential oil can be detected in the kidneys. A simple test you can carry out yourself which shows just how effectively essential oils are absorbed and transported around the body, is to rub the soles of your feet (or those of a friend) with a clove of garlic. A few hours later you will be able to smell garlic on the breath.

WHAT HELPS WHERE

Different essential oils are picked up and fixed in different parts of the body. Violet leaves, for example, are found concentrated in the kidneys, rosemary in the intestines, and sandalwood in the bladder, whilst neroli and ylang ylang, known for their soothing and relaxing properties, are attracted to the nervous system. It seems that certain organs or glands which are in need of help selectively take up different essential oils and use them in the same way as they would utilise the vitamins and minerals they need to function properly. This is perhaps the reason why essential oils have gained a reputation for being able to boost a sluggish organ into action.

Because it is in continual contact with the external environment, the skin also plays an essential role in forming a first line of defence against the bacteria and viruses in the air around us. Deep beneath the skin there are many protective bacteria, and these find their way into the dermis. Their job is to keep the harmful bacteria such as coli bacteria, staphylococci and streptococci, which land on the surface of the epidermis, at bay. Washing the skin with a mild soap and water helps to flush away these harmful bacteria, together with the excess sebum and sweat that accumulate on the surface of the skin. However, washing with too strong a detergent can also destroy the good bacteria, as can strong peeling treatments, ultraviolet light and skin trauma such as burns.

Thanks to their natural antibacterial and anti-viral properties, daily application of essential oils can build up the skin's natural resistance to the illnesses such germs can bring. When they are applied to the skin, they should first be diluted in a vegetable oil such as almond or soya, for most of them are fairly strong and if rubbed in neat, may cause an irritation. They are also tremendously helpful for treating burns and cuts, and in other instances when the integrity of the skin is damaged. They not only reduce the possibility of infection but also stimulate the regeneration of new skin cells.

Skin also acts like a mirror, reflecting the internal health of the body. In days gone by, a soft, flawless skin of milky paleness was thought of as the height of beauty; nowadays we know that a vital, glowing, healthy – not pale – skin also means a healthy body. Conditions such as cutaneous irritation, eczema and skin lesions all point to the fact that something is amiss.

After the skin has taken up essential oils, the oils are eliminated through the normal channels, in the exhaled air, sweat, urine and faeces, and the organs and glands through which they pass benefit from their presence.

HOW TO USE ESSENTIAL OILS

THROUGH MASSAGE

The best and most effective way to treat with essential oils is by massage. This could be as professional or as perfunctory as you like, but the rubbing action will activate the nerve endings and stimulate the circulation of blood to the surface of the skin – and thereby ease the entry of the oils. And massage is such a relaxant anyway.

Even if correctly applied, essential oils will only be taken up by the skin for a period of about seven to ten minutes, and will not be absorbed well if applied when the body is eliminating – when sweating through anxiety or heat, for instance, or after exercise. And their efficiency in penetrating the skin and reaching the other organs also depends very much on the individual. A large amount of subcutaneous fat will impede their passage, as will water retention and poor circulation.

IN THE BATH

Another effective way of treating with essential oils is to add a few drops to a warm bath. Make sure that the room is warm, and that the door and window are closed to keep in the vapours. Immerse your body completely for at least ten minutes, relax and breathe deeply. A certain quantity of odoriferous molecules will penetrate the skin, whilst others will stimulate the nerve endings of the olfactory organ in the nose in the same way as they do when inhaled as a vapour.

These nerve endings are an extension of the limbic portion of the brain which is responsible for governing our feelings of pleasure, contentment and well-being, as well as our appetite, thirst, and sexual behaviour. They also connect with another part of the brain called the hypothalamus which in turn sends chemical messages to the pituitary gland, often referred to as the master gland, as it controls every other endocrine gland in the body (the thyroid, adrenals and ovaries, etc). So, by this indirect route, the essential oils can also exert a powerful influence over the hormonal secretions from the glands, helping to stimulate an underactive organ or soothe an agitated one, so as to re-establish harmonious functioning. The most familiar example of this is the digestive juices starting to flow when the odour of cooking food is detected. Also, via the brain, odoriferous molecules can influence the autonomic nervous system, having either a stimulatory or a soothing effect on our body and mind.

In the same way as they pass through the skin, these volatile substances are also diffused from the lungs into the bloodstream and are carried around the body. Other compounds such as the lead in petrol fumes find their way into the blood in the same fashion, but in contrast this toxic mineral has a highly deleterious effect on the brain and other tissues, altering behavioural patterns and learning abilities in children, whilst giving rise to headaches, fatigue, irritability and a wealth of other niggling ailments in adults.

AS A VAPOUR

Obviously the vapours of essential oils are inhaled while sitting in a bath with added oils, or when massaging or being massaged with oils. A more direct method of inhalation is to add a few drops to a bowl of hot water. Lean over the bowl, about 22.5cm (9in) from the water, with a towel enclosing both your head and the bowl, and inhale.

IN FOOD OR DRINK

Essential oils can also be taken internally, in the form of tisanes or teas made from flowers or leaves, and as the herbs and spices with which we cook.

The essential oils present in the petals and leaves of herbs and other plants can be absorbed by the cells that line the stomach and intestines and from there they enter the bloodstream and lymph fluid and circulate around the body. At the same time they actually aid the proper digestion of foods. Some essential oils are rich in certain vitamins – rose and neroli, for example, contain vitamin C, whilst most others have a fair proportion of vitamins A, E and D – so they possess nutritive as well as therapeutic properties.

But I must stress that it is exceedingly dangerous to take essential oils undiluted by mouth as they are very concentrated and will have powerful and sometimes disastrous effects. Occasionally I will prescribe them myself, but even then I would only use those that have had the terpenes (which can irritate the stomach lining) removed, and I would never advise anyone to take pure essential oils internally themselves.

BASIC EQUIPMENT

There are a few items which are necessary – or useful –for treating with essential oils. They are:

- a china bowl
- a dropper for measuring out the oils
- a steel or enamel saucepan
- a few small square towels (babies' nappies are ideal)
- some small amber-coloured glass bottles with screw caps in which to keep the prepared oils (capacity about 30ml or 1fl oz)
- a teaspoon, a tablespoon and an eggcup.

FACIAL MASSAGE

1. Having applied the appropriate massage oil to face and neck, use index fingers to apply pressure at several points along the jawline. Work from the chin to the ears.

2. Apply pressure with the thumbs to the hollows at side of the nose, then work at intervals along nose-to-mouth lines to the centre of the chin.

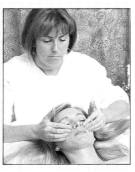

3. Use all your fingers as shown to apply pressure under cheekbones, working from the side of the nose out to the ears.

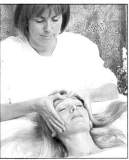

4. Working in parallel lines from the eyebrows upwards to the hairline, use thumbs to apply pressure at several points along the lines. You will find that this is particularly good when it comes to coping with headaches, catarrh and general facial puffiness.

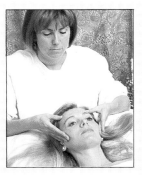

5. Work with your thumbs in smooth, sweeping movements to trace a line from the centre of the forehead to the temples.

6. Use your index fingers to apply pressure to the tearduct at the inner corner of each eye. Disperse the pressure by smoothing outwards under the eyebrows.

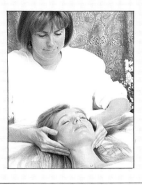

7. Press the fingers of one hand gently against the outer ear. Massage the whole ear from back to front, using a circular motion, but without rubbing the skin. Massage the other ear at the same time in exactly the same way.

8. Use the flat of the hands to apply pressure at points along the collarbone, working from below the throat out towards the shoulders.

AROMATHERAPY MASSAGE

Guidelines Before you embark on a full body massage, read through these guidelines carefully.

*If a massage is intended to treat a particular condition, use the appropriate essential oil or formula given elsewhere in this book. Otherwise use lavender for a relaxing, calming effect, or lemongrass as a stimulating tonic.

*Unless otherwise specified, use three drops of essence in an eggcupful of soya oil.

*If you are giving a full massage, you should follow through this sequence:

    back of head and neck
    spine (avoid in pregnancy)
    legs
    feet
    upper chest area
    abdomen (avoid in pregnancy)
    feet
    face.

*Apply the oil in stages, too, At the start, ask the person you are massaging to lie face down. Apply the oil to the back of the neck, the back, and the back of the legs. After these parts have been massaged, ask him or her to turn over. Apply the remaining oil to the front of the body, the front of the legs and the face.

*For a relaxing massage, press each pressure point for two to three seconds. For a pickmeup, hold each point for a single second.

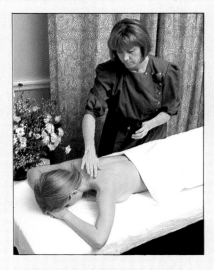

1. Start the massage by applying oil to the back of the neck and the back of legs.

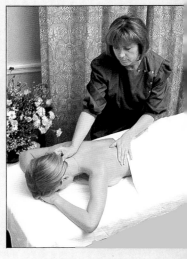

2. Then, using one thumb, work down t neck, one side at a time, applying pressu at equal intervals.

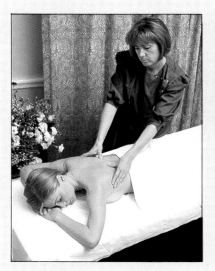

6. With thumbs on either side of the spine, work up the back using small upward and outward movements to disperse energy from the pressure points. Start at the base of the spine.

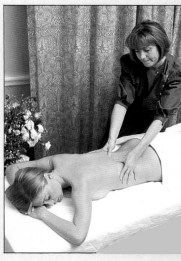

7. Finish this stage at the base of the nec The idea is to slowly disperse energy fro the pressure points. Take care to keep th in parallel.

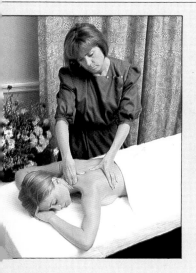

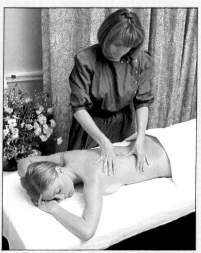

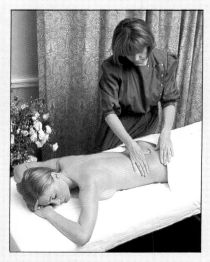

Using both thumbs together on the same side of the spine, work down the spine from the base of the neck.

4. As you work down the back, you apply the pressure about 1cm (½in) from the spine. This stage of massage can be either relaxing or stimulating, but omit this stage if you are pregnant.

5. Finish the first stage of spinal massage at the coccyx (tailbone). Then work down the other side of the spine as you did before, trying to keep the pressure points parallel.

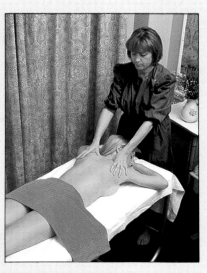

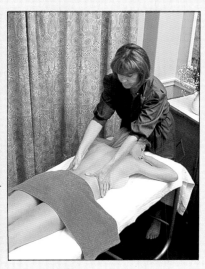

Massage the shoulders with a kneading motion. Your aim is to relieve the knots of tension that build up there.

9. With thumbs on either side of the spine, work down the back with gentle downward movements about 1cm from spine.

10. Start at the base of the neck and finish at the tailbone as before. Then switch to the other parts of the body, as detailed in the massage guidelines.

AROMATHERAPY AND BEAUTY

True beauty is an expression of inner health, youthfulness and sexuality, as nothing is more attractive than a fresh, flawless complexion that literally glows with vitality. Barefaced is best and no-one should have to rely on cosmetic coverage, as women did even a decade ago, to disguise a less than perfect skin.

Women have been attempting to beautify their skin from the outside since antiquity, by applying various weird and wonderful concoctions. And within the last fifty years, there has been a phenomenal growth in the number of skin-care products on the market, with women spending more and more money on such treatments for the face. The problem is that the changes such creams can bring about are minimal, for they only work superficially. The real nature of skin is determined by inner health, and many women have less than perfect skins because of the battle their bodies wage continually with the hectic twentieth-century lifestyle: fast convenience foods, stress, lack of exercise, and industrial pollutants, all these, and more, work to undermine the conditions of the skin.

Queen Hatshepsut, the first woman pharaoh of Egypt, knew more about beauty than most, and was years ahead of her time in realising that aromatherapy skin treatments are unlike any others. Because essential oils can penetrate the skin and help to restore proper functioning to any ailing part of the body, they actually beautify it from within.

In this chapter, I shall look at the ways essential oils, when applied daily, can bring out the best in your skin, correct minor imbalances such as oiliness and dryness, treat troubling skin disorders such as acne, psoriasis and eczema, and prevent the formation of wrinkles by holding back the ageing process.

THE SKIN

To understand how essential oils can work in this way, it is important to know in more detail than defined before, about the structure and functions of the skin.

The outer epidermis consists of many layers of skin cells. New, round, plump ones are produced at the basal layer and travel up towards the surface of the skin, losing their moisture and becoming flatter all the while, until they are shed as dead skin cells. By the time they are ready to be shed, in a process known as exfoliation, these cells are rich in a protein called keratin, the same stuff of which fingernails are composed, so they are quite brittle and scaly. On average, it takes about 120 days for newly formed cells to move up to the skin surface and die. The time, however, varies according to the individual, the

Youthful radiance Heredity's legacy can be enhanced by healthy living and the use of aromatic essences to give you healthy, attractive skin whatever your age.

individual's age, and several other factors.

The epidermis rests on the inner dermis, which acts rather like a cushion, giving strength and support as well as contour to the skin. Within the dermis we find an ordered network of tough collagen fibres, made from proteinaceous material, which lie in a ground substance forming what is known as connective tissue. Also present are elastin fibres which give skin pliancy and stretchability rather than strength. A young, healthy skin has the capacity to increase its size by 50 per cent due to these elastic properties, but this function diminishes with age.

The dermis is richly supplied by many small capillaries which bring oxygen and other vital nutrients to the skin cells and carry away the toxic waste products. It is also well endowed with nerve endings which surround the hair follicles and form a kind of sensory apparatus, transmitting messages from the skin surface concerning temperature, touch and pain, so as to invoke the appropriate response.

Sebaceous glands are also present in the dermis, but they open to the surface at pores located in the epidermis. These glands produce the oily substance called sebum, whose function is to lubricate the skin and to seal moisture in the cells. Their activity determines whether your skin is normal, oily or dry.

In turn, your skin type is influenced genetically, and if you have fair hair, you are more likely to have pale, and perhaps rather delicate, skin than someone who is dark.

So it is quite obvious, if you want your skin to look its best, you should always care for it appropriately.

NORMAL SKIN

People with normal skin are lucky as they tend to have few problems. At the same time, it still needs to be well looked after to keep it supple and ensure that the sebaceous secretions maintain their equilibrium: many things, such as tiredness, illness, rapid weight loss, smoking and drinking, can disrupt this fine balance. To test whether your skin is normal or not, close your eyes and place your index finger on your forehead. If it feels slightly damp, not oily, then it is normal.

To care for your skin, wash with an acid or pH balanced soap in warm water, finishing with a tonic of rose tea, and use a facial oil every day. Make your own by adding 1 drop of rose and 1 drop of camomile essential oil to 3-4 teaspoons of almond oil. Apply this oil every morning and evening.

A good massage will not only help the absorption of the essential oils, but will also stimulate the circulation, encouraging the delivery of fresh blood to the skin cells. Make circular movements with your fingers around the sinus area, over the cheeks and chin, scissor across the forehead and stroke up the neck, back and front.

Use a face mask once a week to help refine the pores. To make your own rose and oatmeal mask, place a cup of oatmeal into a mixing bowl and add boiling water little by little. Mix to a thick paste. Add 1 drop of rose essence and a little almond or soya oil to stop it drying out. You could also make two poultices, one for the forehead and cheeks, and another for the chin and neck. Make two 'sandwiches' with four squares of gauze and some of the oatmeal mix. Apply the poultices to the face, at the same time covering the eyes with cotton wool pads soaked in rose water. Relax and leave for 10 minutes.

Even a normal skin can look dull and lifeless at times, so to improve its colour, work to stimulate the circulation by massage, washing firstly with warm-hot water and then with cold, and by taking plenty of exercise. Eat plenty of foods rich in vitamins C, A and the entire B complex, for they are excellent skin nourishers.

OILY SKIN

During adolescence, when the hormones are undergoing dramatic changes, it is very common for the sebaceous glands to become overactive, and cause a condition known as seborrhoea. The skin looks shiny, the pores are often enlarged, and the skin is more likely to suffer from

MAKING A POULTICE

Making a poultice

Poultices are an age-old way of drawing impurities out through the skin to soothe irritation and to relieve congestion or pain. Their history goes back many thousands of years – they were among the first forms of medicine developed by man. What they consist of is a raw or mashed herb, which sometimes is applied directly to the body as it stands, or moistened first

before its application. Sometimes, too, the contents of the poultice are left exposed to the air; otherwise, the ingredients are wrapped in a cloth and then applied.

Traditionally, the poultices in most frequent use were made of mustard, linseed or fennel; they were particularly popular when it came to dealing with chest complaints and skin ailments. Distilled witch hazel, for instance, is an

excellent remedy for sunburn, bruises, shaving cuts and swelling when used in poultice form. You can also use an essential oils poultice for a concentrated facial treatment, though you should not use this type of treatment if your skin is at all delicate or sensitive, as it may react adversely to the intense application of oils the treatment involves.

The pictures show the various stages. After measuring out the essential

oils and dry ingredients; they are mixed with water and the resulting mixture is then sandwiched between square of cloth to form a poultice. Before applying the poultice, the skin is examined for imperfections and a thin layer of protective cream is smoothed into it. The delicate skin around the eyes is shielded with cotton wool pads, soaked in rosewater, before the poultice is applied to the face.

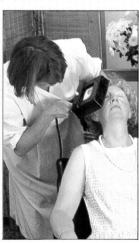  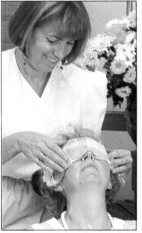 

blackheads and spots. Both are worrying and unsightly.

It is fairly easy to recognise an oily skin: place a piece of blotting paper or fine greaseproof paper on different areas of the skin, and the stains left will give an indication as to just how severe the condition is. Normally, it is only people who live in hot countries and eat spicy foods that have a very bad problem, as both these things provoke the already overactive glands into producing even more oil.

Indeed, if your skin has a tendency towards oiliness, it is worth knowing that it can be made worse by stimulants such as tea, coffee, and the nicotine in cigarettes, by a diet rich in fatty foods (especially meats like pork and lamb), by sugar and foods containing it such as cakes, sweets and biscuits and, on the other hand, by emotional upsets like worry, anxiety, fear and anger.

People who suffer from constipation often have oily skin, so it is important to eat plenty of natural fibre or roughage which is found in raw fruits and vegetables, pulses, legumes, and whole grains.

Certain essential oils can be extremely helpful in treating oily skin, as they have a balancing influence and reduce the activity of the sebaceous glands, so helping the skin to behave as if it were normal.

TREATMENT
Wash the face with a mild, acid balanced soap and cool water. Never use a milky cleanser or cream which will

The importance of diet
No matter how much you spend on cosmetics, they can do no more than camouflage an unhealthy skin, and their ingredients may well contribute to the problem. Aromatherapists believe that a balanced diet is the foundation stone of beautiful skin. Your skin mirrors the condition of your body, so ensure health and beauty by eating plenty of fresh fruits and vegetables, high-fibre foods, lean meats and fish.

leave an unwanted film of grease on the skin. Rinse with warm and then cold water, and finally dampen the skin with cotton wool soaked in a diluted solution of witch-hazel.

Make a facial oil by adding 1 drop of juniper and 1 drop of geranium to 2 teaspoons of soya or jojoba oil. Pour some of this into the palm of your hand and gently massage it into your skin. Once the first application has been absorbed, add another. To aid the penetration of the essences soak a small towel in boiling water, and when it has cooled to hand-hot temperature, wring it out and cover the face as if it were a compress.

Once a week give your face a sauna, by adding 1 drop of juniper and 1 drop of geranium to a bowl of hot water and steaming your face with the vapours.

DRY SKIN

Dry skin results from an inability of the sebaceous glands to produce the quantity of oil needed to prevent the skin from losing moisture. As a consequence it feels taut, as if tightly stretched across the face, and tends to suffer from flakiness. A dry skin is less supple than a normal one, which makes it more prone to fine surface lines, and so it is likely to age prematurely. It is also highly sensitive, and easily irritated by harsh detergents and cosmetics, becoming red and blotchy.

Many things can exacerbate the dry skin condition and even make an otherwise normal skin become dehydrated. Internal causes are illness, a diet deficient in vital nutrients (especially vitamin F, the essential fatty acids), sudden and rapid weight loss, taking drugs such as antibiotics and tranquillisers, and drinking too much alcohol. External environmental hazards take the form of direct sunlight (and sunbeds), central heating, and icy wintry winds.

TREATMENT

A skin that feels tight should never be washed more than once a week, and even then only with a very mild soap. For everyday cleansing make a tonic by steeping camomile flowers in boiling water (or you can use a camomile tea bag instead). When this infusion has cooled, add a few drops of jojoba oil, and wash your face with it.

A marvellously effective facial oil can be made for dry skin by mixing 4-5 teaspoons of almond oil with 2-2½ teaspoons of castor oil (or 2 parts almond to 1 part castor), adding 1 capsule (or ¼ teaspoon) of cod-liver oil, 1 drop of geranium, 1 drop of sandalwood and 1 teaspoon of wheatgerm oil. Massage into the skin with very light

AROMATHERAPY AND BEAUTY

stroking movements only, for dry skin tends to be very delicate and may become irritated with rough handling. Leave the oil on for 10 minutes, applying a warm compress which has been soaked in either rose water or linden tea.

When the skin improves you can use an oil made from almond oil and essences alone.

COMBINATION SKIN

This is a skin that has oily and dry patches, and may be slightly affected by the change of seasons. Most of the time you can treat it as if it were normal, but if the sebaceous glands of the so-called centre panel – the nose, forehead, and chin – flare up, which they may do in periods of stress or just before a period, it is advisable to treat the area with the facial oil prescribed for an oily skin.

SKIN PROBLEMS

The skin is a mirror of body health, and the nature of skin is greatly influenced by changes that take place from within, far more so than by any cream applied to the surface. For this reason any skin problem should be regarded as an indication that your health is not what it could be, and if treatment is to be successful, you have to consider the body as a whole, not just from a superficial angle. A skin problem may be the result of many years of bad eating habits, of acute emotional anxiety, of a biochemical disorder such as hyperglycaemia or diabetes, or of a reaction to aerosol sprays, antibiotics or other drugs – even to skin-care products themselves.

The skin is an organ with many different functions. It helps to maintain constant body temperature by shedding excess heat in the form of water, as sweat that cools as it evaporates on the surface of the skin. In this way it also eliminates toxins or unwanted waste products from the body. By blocking up these natural eliminating channels with the use of anti-perspirants and heavy face make-up the toxins can actually build up in layers within the skin, which, eventually, may be expelled in the form of spots and pimples. Their appearance is often a clear sign that the cleansing organs of the body, the liver and kidneys primarily, are not working properly to eliminate the wastes; the skin is thus called upon to act as a sort of dumping ground to relieve the body of these unwanted substances. Invariably once the liver and kidneys are back to normal, the condition of the skin rapidly improves.

Conditions such as eczema are often a symptom of an internal illness or disorder, and act as a means through which the body can discharge its affliction. Sometimes by curing the eczema with drugs you remove this eliminative pathway, so the problem builds up inside and may erupt, perhaps years later. You can treat the symptoms gently and safely with essential oils, knowing that you will not be causing any damage.

ACNE

Acne is a disorder of the sebaceous or oil-secreting glands of the skin, which gives rise to enlarged pores, blackheads, pimples and pustules. It tends to afflict areas of the skin where these glands are found in abundance — the face and back, for instance. The condition is initiated by an over-production of oil which is too copious for the skin to handle, so it ends up looking greasy. At the same time it blocks up the pores making them appear larger than they actually are, and results in the formation of blackheads. If the sebum in these clogged pores becomes infected by a bacterium such as staphylococcus, which is ever-present on the surface of the skin, spots form that may ultimately turn into unsightly boils. The skin and spots are usually inflamed, and often quite painful to touch.

Sebum secretion actually begins within the uterus, which is why some babies can be born with an oily skin, but this usually disappears within two months, and is no indication that the child will develop acne in later life. Acne flares up most during the pubescent years, afflicting many adolescents and young adults. Sometimes it corrects itself after the mid-twenties and sometimes it does not subside again until after middle age. One of the underlying causes of this over-production of sebum is thought to be a glandular disorder which gives rise to hormonal imbalance, usually characterised by a predominance of male hormones or androgens. The fact that the severity of this condition changes throughout the menstrual cycle reinforces the idea that the sex hormones are involved, for acne tends to flare up about a week before a woman is due to begin her period. Indeed, even women with good skins may find they develop a few pimples around this time.

THE ROLE OF STRESS
Stress and anxiety, both of which interfere with the levels of hormones in the body, also spell trouble for acne sufferers, and a vicious circle can often be set into motion with worry giving rise to more spots and these causing further worry.

Acne sufferers can invariably be helped by exercise, especially outdoors, and by paying careful attention to their diet. Well-balanced meals concentrating on foods rich in vitamins A, B1, B2 and B6, plus plenty of fresh fruit and vegetables, are vital. Fatty foods such as pork and lamb should be avoided, as should stimulants like tea, coffee, alcohol and cigarettes which only aggravate the acne condition: they should be replaced by mineral water, tisanes and, in small quantities, fresh fruit juices diluted with water.

Essential oils can go a long way towards helping an acne skin become healthy again. They can banish the spots, heal up the scars and reduce the inflammation that make this condition so unpleasant. Most of the young people who come and see me at my practice with this problem have tried antibiotics and all the other drugs on the market but to no avail.

One such client, very typical of acne sufferers, is a young girl who had been on strong antibiotics for six years, so long that her skin was no longer responding; the boils were still appearing, whilst the scars were red and inflamed. She had recently lost her job and felt that her acne had been responsible, because it was so unattractive.She was very depressed, her self-confidence and self-esteem were low, and she desperately needed help.

NATURE'S CURE

I explained that a natural cure would be a lengthy process and she could not expect overnight results. In fact it might be a year before substantial improvements could be seen. She accepted this and had some treatments. I discovered that the antibiotics had not helped, in addition to which she admitted to drinking alcohol and coffee freely, and replacing her meals with nutritionally inadequate snacks.

She carried on using the oils at home and I kept a check on her diet. It was three months before there was any improvement, but small patches of her facial skin began to clear and the scars healed. One and a half years later she has a beautiful skin, and it is difficult to tell that she ever suffered from such a problem.

Another success story, and luckily there have been many, is that of a seventeen-year-old boy who had been suffering from acne for four years. The antibiotics he had been taking had worked for about three months before becoming ineffectual, which led to even stronger ones being prescribed. When I saw him the acne was so advanced that his face was swollen and marred by abscesses. He only came to see me once because he lived so far away, but I gave him a cleanser, oil and cream to use together with pure essences which could be applied undiluted to the infected spots. After a few months patches of healthy skin started to appear, and nine months following his visit he sent me a photograph, and I found it difficult to believe it was the same person. His skin was healthy-looking and clear except for the odd pimple from which all teenagers occasionally suffer, and the treatment has stood the test of time.

TREATMENT
All too often people with acne resort to using powerful detergents and alcoholic astringents to remove every trace of oil. The skin needs a certain amount of oil for lubrication and protection, however, so it is not long before the sebaceous glands resond by producing even more oil, so exacerbating the problem. Although people are wary of using oils on an already oily skin, it should be remembered that essential oils are actually made up of molecules such as alcohols, phenols, and terpenes and because they are quickly absorbed, little trace of oil is actually left on the skin. They not only help to restore equilibrium to the sebaceous glands but they also keep the bacteria in check because of their natural antibiotic properties. But perhaps most interestingly of all, they act at a much deeper level on the glands to correct the hormonal imbalances, although they do take time to work, and you have to persevere.

Treatment involves cleansing, steaming, applying a facial oil to improve the general condition of the skin, and applying pure essences to treat the spots themselves.

CLEANSING
Wash the skin with an unscented pH balanced or acid soap, in hot water, and rinse thoroughly in cold. You can always use mineral or distilled water if you are concerned about dehydrating effects.

Make an astringent by boiling a sprig of fresh, or a pinch of dried thyme in 2 cups of water for 2 minutes, then leave to infuse for 5 minutes. Add the juice of half a lemon and rinse the skin with this solution, two to three times a day. Because it is not strongly perfumed, this lotion is also suitable for men, who should apply it after shaving.

You can make a compress by soaking a piece of gauze in this solution, wringing out the excess and covering the face with it for 5 minutes. This is a good treatment before going out in the evening.

FACIAL SAUNA
This should be done three or four times a week when the acne is severe, and reduced to once a week when it begins to improve. Boil a kettle of water and wait until it has cooled to hand-hot temperature (about 38°C/100°F), not scalding.

Pour into a bowl and add:
1 drop of lavender
1 drop of camomile
1 drop of lemon
If the condition is very acute you could mix together any two of the following essences instead: neroli, juniper, lavender or clove. Whichever essences you choose, the technique is the same: hold your face over the bowl with a towel enclosing the bowl and your head, and let the vapours work on your skin.

FACIAL OILS
To be used morning and evening after cleansing.
2 tablespoons of soya oil
2 drops of lavender ‹
1 drop of camomile
1 drop of lemon
Mix together and keep in an amber bottle. Make two applications, the second once the oil of the first has been absorbed. To aid absorption apply hot compresses to the face 5 minutes after the second application. Also effective are the essences of myrrh and patchouli. Myrrh should be mixed in soya oil (3 drops of essence to 2 teaspoons of oil) and patchouli in almond oil (2 drops in 2 teaspoons of oil).

PURE ESSENCES
Because of their strong antibacterial properties, undiluted essential oils – any of the ones recomended – are useful for applying straight to the pimples and pustules on a cottonwool bud every day.

BROKEN CAPILLARIES

This is the Anglo-Saxon woman's complaint, for it afflicts fair, delicate skins which also tend to burn in the sun. It is characterised by the appearance of fine, red spider veins on the cheeks which make them look ruddy. Often the capillaries are not actually broken, just weak and transparent, so that the blood shows through them. It is important to avoid drinking stimulants such as tea, coffee and chocolate as well alcohol which cause the capillaries to dilate; the skin must also be protected from direct sunlight and icy winds. It is advisable not to take over-strenuous exercise. Never wash your face with hot water or use a facial sauna if you suffer from broken capillaries,and avoid taking hot baths.

Use a cool compress of parsley tea on the face daily: boil 3 sprigs of fresh parsley in 500ml (a scant pint) of water for 2 minutes, and leave to steep for 5 minutes; add

In depth cleansing When aromatic essences are used in a facial sauna, the therapeutic effect is twofold. As your skin is exposed to the essences in vapour form, they are absorbed through the delicate membranes of the nasal passages as well as through the skin, as they would be in a simple facial massage. Their action is thus internal as well as external. The technique is particularly valuable for treating acne, a skin condition which needs scrupulously deep cleansing in order to cure it. The essential oils of juniper, lavender, camomile, lemon, neroli or clove should be used to treat this problem. You need not rely on the specialised equipment shown here to give yourself an effective sauna. By covering your head with a towel and leaning over a bowl of hand-hot to boiling water containing the oil of your choice, you can reap the same benefits.

two drops of rose and leave to cool.

Massage the face very gently with a facial oil made from a mixture of 1 drop of parsley, 1 drop of camomile, 2 teaspoons of soya oil and 1 teaspoon of wheatgerm oil. If you use this oil every day, within a few months you will notice that the high colouring has faded, for the essential oils have the ability not only to drain the capillaries, but also to strengthen them. Eating foods rich in bioflavonoids and vitamin C, both vital to capillary health –such as oranges, grapefruit and lemons – is also advisable if you are prone to this problem.

CELLULITE

Although cellulite is invariably referred to as a physiological disorder, it may be some comfort to know that most women suffer from it some time or another. To my knowledge, women have always had cellulite, but it only became a problem when they started wearing bikinis and scantily clad young models with waif-like figures began adorning the pages of glossy magazines.

Cellulite is brought on by a hormonal change which encourages the body tissues to retain water, invariably characterised by high levels of oestrogen. When the fat cells become interspersed with this water, the skin takes on an orange peel appearance when squeezed between the fingers, and often feels uneven and bumpy too. Cellulite usually appears on the thighs, buttocks, hips, sometimes the stomach and the upper arms, and even the back of the neck too.

Because cellulite is hormonally related, mild forms of it can come and go, so women may find they have it before periods and that it disappears when their period begins. Pregnant women also seem to have cellulite as this is another time of hormonal upheaval, as do women going through their menopause.

The severity of the condition and whether it becomes a permanent fixture or not depends a good deal on lifestyle. Because stress affects the hormonal balance, nervousness, tension, frustration, shock, anger and so forth can all bring on a cellulite condition, and it is important to relax if you don't want it to stay around. Bad circulation also predisposes women to cellulite, so if your hands and feet feel cold and your skin bruises easily, you will have to take extra care. Hormonal imbalances are often responsible for circulation problems, but so is bad posture, in particular flat feet. It can also go hand in hand with an underactive thyroid gland. A sluggish circulation can be speeded up by taking regular exercise (swimming and walking are perfect), and by following a warm bath (never hot) with a

Changing perceptions
The Three Graces by Rubens.
Once the embodiment of
feminine beauty, these
figures have little appeal for
the modern eye, which
focuses on their unfirm flesh
and puckering skin –
evidence of the condition
known as cellulite. Cellulite
occurs when the fat cells in
the body become
interspersed with
waterlogged tissue, with the
skin in the affected area
taking on an uneven and
lumpy appearance as a
result. Aromatherapy can
play a key part in helping
you to cope with this age-
old problem. Combine
treatment with essential oils
with careful control of diet
and a sensibly planned
exercise routine to improve
your skin texture.

cold shower. Friction mitts or loofahs are also effective in promoting good circulation.

Certain foods also encourage a cellulite condition for they provoke fluid retention. These are salty and smoked foods (cured hams, etc.), sugar, refined carbohydrates such as white flour, and things made from it. Women with allergies to certain foods such as milk, which causes the tissues to swell, will also be prone to cellulite, as will women who have a poorly functioning liver.

Strangely enough, diuretic drinks such as tea, coffee, and alcohol – especially spirits – actually worsen the condition, so it is wise to stay away from them.

TREATMENT
Before a bath, rub your body with a loofah to activate the circulation. Add the following essences to the bath water (which should never be too hot).

DERMATITIS

Dermatitis is an inflammatory skin condition often associated with hereditary allergic tendencies – such as

HOW TO TREAT CELLULITE

Guidelines

This sequence is for the treatment of cellulite. It can be carried out on its own, with an essence such as cypress which is particularly good for cellulite, or it can form part of a full-body massage, in which case the same oil should be used as for the rest of the body. It improves circulation and helps to drain toxic wastes from the tissues.
*Where instructions specify 'apply pressure', maintain the pressure at any one point for 2-3 seconds.

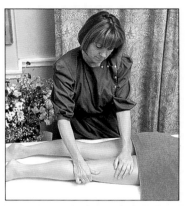

1. Use your thumb to apply pressure to a point 2 inches out from the centre of the back of the knee. Hold for 23 seconds. Repeat. Use same procedure on the other leg.

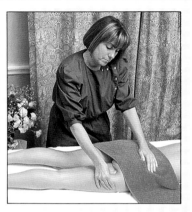

2. Apply pressure to the back of the thigh below the buttock. Repeat. Follow same procedure on the other leg.

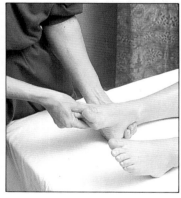

3. Ask the subject to turn on to her back. Apply pressure to the area between the big toe and the first toe. Repeat on the other foot.

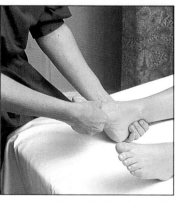

4. Massage the top of the foot, using circular movements. Repeat on the other foot.

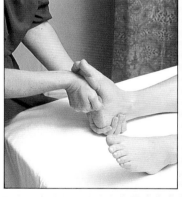

5. Using the knuckles of one hand, rub the arch of the foot, pressing firmly towards the heel. Do this 10 times on each foot to improve circulation.

food allergies to dairy products and gluten, which is a component of almost all grains, particularly wheat. It invariably worsens or appears for the first time when a person has suffered a severe emotional upset or is very fatigued and run-down.

The symptoms are those of eczema, which is often characterized by blister-like eruptions that weep and form crusts. The skin then thickens and flakes, and the eczema patches are often pigmented differently from the rest of the skin.

Certain foods, pollutants, a deficiency of the B complex vitamins, especially vitamin B6, can precipitate dermatitis or exacerbate it when the condition already exists. Supplement your diet with 2-4 capsules of evening primrose oil daily and a capsule of wheatgerm oil (rich in vitamin E). Use cold-pressed soya, corn and safflower oil in your cooking and for salad dressings, as they are all rich in essential fatty acids (more commonly known as vitamin F), and people suffering from eczema are often deficient in this.

Cut down on saturated fats such as those found in meats and dairy products, substituting fish, nuts and seeds instead.

Every day, rub into your skin an oil made from 3-4 teaspoons of soya oil,.plus 2 drops of camomile and 2 drops of geranium.

For very dry eczema, mix about 3 teaspoons of almond oil with the same quantity of castor oil, then add one drop of geranium and one drop of lavender. For very oily eczema, add drops of juniper berry essential oil to the almond and castor oil mixture. Also add to your bath 1 teaspoon of soya oil and a total of 2 drops of the appropriate essences.

ECZEMA

As a treatment for massaging into the skin, add 3 drops of Cedarwood to 2 teaspoons of carrier oil. Alternatively, 2-3 drops of rose essence in 2 teaspoons of almond oil helps to sooth and heal eczematous skin.

MELANOSIS (Abnormal pigmentation)

Add 1 drop of benzoin to two teaspoons of almond oil. Massage into affected area. Avoid exposure to sun.

PSORIASIS

Psoriasis is an unslightly condition, characterised by circular patches of dry scaly skin which are either pale pink or dark wine red in colour. It appears predominantly on the knees and elbows, and sometimes on the scalp and top of the forehead. Fortunately, it rarely appears on the face, except when it is very severe.

The reason for its sudden appearance still remains a mystery, but we do know that if someone in the family has suffered from it, there is a likelihood that you may too.It afflicts both sexes alike, and will appear at any age, but most frequently after twenty. People with fair skins such as Europeans and North Americans seem to be particularly susceptible to psoriasis, and it is rare amongst Japanese and Negro populations.

Once it strikes, psoriasis is likely to linger for a long time, and is notoriously difficult to cure. There are several different types, some of which can actually be brought on by treatment of the psoriasis with corticosteroids. Sometimes it can become so dry that the skin cracks, whichis extremely uncomfortable and painful. In the case of pustular psoriasis the skin can actually become infected, which complicates its treatment even further.

Surprisingly perhaps, psoriasis is not infectious and there is no possibility of catching it by touching someone suffering from it.

Although psoriasis is difficult to cure, it is treatable, and essential oils are tremendously effective. I have helped many psoriasis suffers who have come to the practice.

One lady, a musician, had very bad psoriasis on her hands which were cracked and sore, making it difficult for her to pursue her career. Interestingly, it did not appear until she was thirty, but her mother had been a sufferer too. I asked her never to use detergents – she should use instead a solution of soapwort, one of nature's most effective cleansers – and to rub oils into her hands and keep them on for few hours by wearing cotton gloves. She altered her diet, including plenty of foods rich in vitamin A, took more exercise than before, and two years later she has the occasional rash on her knees, but nothing worse. Her skin has returned to normal.

Another case, a man who had psoriasis on his scalp had been given a black, sticky concoction to smear onto his affected skin by a dermatologist. This treatment helped a little, but he wasn't at all happy with it. I made him a shampoo and a special oil, which have alleviated his problem to the extent that he now absolutely swears by them.

As with skin disorders, psoriasis points to some deep-rooted ailment, and so anything which encourages the health to deteriorate such as smoking and drinking alcohol are best avoided. The condition is also irritated by wearing polyester or nylon next to skin, which prevents it from breathing properly, and people with psoriasis on their scalp should not wear tight-fitting hats or nylon scarves. Extremes of temperature will also aggravate it, so you should avoid sitting next to open fires and, whenever possible, stay in when it's very cold outside.

INTERNAL TREATMENT
Look for foods rich in vitamin A and lecithin. Take 2

capsules of cod liver oil a day, or a teaspoon, and try taking 1-2 capsules of evening primrose oil which can also be very helpful. It is also a good idea to make some sage tea and drink two or more cups a day in place of coffee and tea.

EXTERNAL TREATMENT
Add an infusion of birch leaves or marigold flowers to the bath, if you can obtain these, 2 drops of cajput together with 1 drop of thyme, and use in the bath.

FOR THE SCALP
Before shampooing, massage the scalp with an infusion of marigold flowers. Boil 4 flower heads in 500ml (a scant pint) of water for 2 minutes, let it steep for 5 minutes, and then add the juice of half a lemon.

Alternatively you could rub in a solution of boiled birch leaves mixed with a teaspoon of cider vinegar.

Dilute your shampoo with either birch-leaf or camomile tea and rinse with a tablespoon of either lemon juice or cider vinegar.

Avoid using a hairdryer if possible, letting your hair dry naturally instead, as direct heat will only irritate the condition.

PUFFINESS

When the tissues of the body become laden with water, the face often takes on a puffy or swollen appearance, especially just under the eyes. This often happens just before menstruation, when women are particularly prone to water retention, or it can come after an illness, if you are taking drugs, or if you have an allergic reaction which irritates the sinuses like hayfever. Sometimes it is a sign that the kidneys are not working as well as they might.

To reduce the oedema, wash the skin with a gentle soap, then rinse in cold water. Make up some camomile tea by boiling a pinch of dried flowers in 500ml (a scant pint) of water, and soak a compress of gauze in it. Apply this to the skin – or you could use a camomile tea bag.

Make a face oil by adding 1 drop of sandalwood and 1 drop of geranium to 1 drop of cold pressed almond oil. Massage into the face, applying deep pressure around the sinus area and the mouth. Then reapply a camomile compress and leave for 5–10 minutes.

Never apply a thick cream at night, for this will make the affected area even puffier. As far as food is concerned, stay away from salt and sugar, especially if prone to pre-menstrual water retention. Both, particularly salt, encourage skin puffiness, if you are prone to the problem.

AROMATHERAPY AND HEALTH

AGEING SKIN

Ageing skin Aromatherapy helps maintain the characteristic glow of healthy skin even into maturity. It combats the natural ageing process when skin loses its elasticity and its cells no longer regenerate themselves efficiently. The daily application of essential oils helps to restore nature's balance and eliminates some of the problems arising as the body ages.

Every woman dreads the insidious appearance of wrinkles, which serve as a constant reminder of the years that are passing her by. It would be wonderful to discover an elixir which could ward off the ageing process or, even better, bring about total rejuvenation. But, unfortunately, this will never be possible, because the ageing process is biologically predetermined and no potion in the world is ever going to take wrinkles away. Essential oils, however, can do more than most to slow down their appearance.

One of the fundmental causes of ageing is the slowing down of cell division. Up until the time of birth there is a rapid multiplication of cells following the fertilisation of the female ovum by the male spermatozoa. After birth, this process gradually slows down and continues to diminish until we die. Very little can be done to halt or decelerate this process.

This slowing-down process takes place at a different pace in each person, and certain things slow the natural biological processes down even further: these should be minimised or avoided completely if we are to stay youthful longer. The main culprits are illness, smoking, taking drugs, drinking alcohol, tea and coffee in excess, being subjected to too much stress, not taking enough exercise, and being exposed to radiation.

The quality of food you eat is also very important, for

the organs should be supplied with sufficient quantities of nutrients if they are to function properly. I have seen women who have had anorexia with skins that reflect their internal malnutrition by looking twenty years older than they should.

I have also noticed that a person's attitude to life and their behaviour also affects the rate at which they age, so someone who has gathered a good deal of unhappiness in their lifetime, or who is always dissatisfied, will age far faster than a person who is enthusiastic and in love with life.

As far as the skin is concerned, dermatologists and cosmetic scientists now know that several changes take place as it ages.

SKIN'S ENEMY — SUNLIGHT

Within the dermis the network of collagen and elastin fibres which lend skin its suppleness and firmness begins to alter and as a result deep wrinkles form which can never be removed. Certain things actually encourage these changes to take place, such as the UV rays of sunlight, and for this reason people who live in hot countries and do not shade their skin from the sun tend to have more wrinkles than those who protect their skin from the direct rays, or who live in more temperate climates. Other forms of radiation also accelerate the formation of these wrinkles, but the sun has the added disadvantage of making the skin feel leathery as well.

Changes also take place in the epidermis with the passage of time. As the rate of cell division slows down, the epidermis becomes thinner, and because the newly-formed cells take longer to reach the surface, there is a larger proportion of flat, dehydrated, dead cells which gives the skin a dull, lifeless appearance instead of a fresh, translucent one.

Because the cells of the epidermis do not regenerate themselves as readily as they did when they were younger, it also means that the skin takes longer to heal itself after damage (a burn or cut, for example) than it did before.

All kinds of external factors, such as the climate, and the way you cleanse, protect and nourish your skin,will affect the condition of the epidermis, and looking after it properly from an early age certainly pays off in the long run.

To my mind the daily application of essential oils can go a long way towards helping the skin stay young, for they encourage the cells to regenerate themselves more efficiently. They also act on the sebaceous glands which

Sunlight Nothing ages the skin faster than overexposure to the sun. Tan slowly and carefully, avoiding the harsh noonday sun. The protective and regenerative powers of essential oils can help to compensate for skin dehydration.

often become underactive as we get older, making them produce sufficient oil to keep the skin lubricated, keeping it supple and less prone to wrinkling. Because essential oils penetrate the skin, they are far more active than most cosmetic products on the market. By helping to restore proper functioning to a tired or ailing organ or gland, they can actually eliminate some of the fundamental causes of age acceleration.

This facial oil will help keep a maturing skin young and supple.

3-4teaspoons of almond oil
1 tablespoon of soya oil
1 teaspoon of wheatgerm oil
4 drops of galbanum
1 drop of Moroccan rose

Mix the oils together first, then add the essences. Massage gently into the face and neck and apply a hot compress soaked in an infusion of rose petals. Apply every evening.

Cleanse the skin with a gentle soap, never more than twice a week; the rest of the time use a rose-petal infusion which will not dry the skin in any way (whereas tap water may).

The massaging of the skin that goes hand in hand with applying the facial oils can help to improve the delivery of nutrients to and removal of waste products from the skin cells. It can also improve the muscle tone. We often tend to forget that it is the muscles underlying the skin that give our bodies shape and contour. When they contract, they cause the skin to wrinkle, and this is what gives rise to expression lines, which are fine providing the muscles relax again. However, due to tension, they often enter a steady state of contraction,and if they remain like this for a long time, they cause the formation of permanent wrinkles, usually furrows on the forehead.

Massaging helps to relax these muscles as well as tone up those that are under-exercised and have shrivelled up as a result, and which cause the skin to sag, usually around the jawline. In fact, the reason why face lifts are often so disappointing is because they gather up the sagging skin and stretch out the wrinkles, but actually do nothing to improve the underlying muscle tone which gives the skin its youthful contour.

There are many clients who came to my practice to be treated when their skin started to age eighteen years or more ago, and since then, amazingly, it has not deteriorated any further, for the essential oils have preserved their skin, keeping it as smooth and supple as ever. Some have found that their skin actually looks several years younger than it did before treatment and many who were planning to have plastic surgery found that, to their astonishment, it was no longer necessary.

AROMATHERAPY FOR YOUTHFULNESS

My advice to anyone wishing to preserve the youthful look of their skin is, not only to use essential oils every day, but also to avoid sunbathing or staying out in the sun for any length of time: this applies particularly to those with varicose veins. Always protect your skin during the first week in strong sunlight, and build up a colour gradually, for once your skin has burned, it will become tremendously sensitive. Avoid sunlamps and sunbeds: they give out predominately UV radiation, which may be the rays that give you a suntan but are also the ones that penetrate the dermis to disrupt the stucture of the collagen and elastin fibres, resulting in the formation of deep and permanent wrinkles.

Remember that the skin on the neck is incredibly fragile, and ages more rapidly than the face, so it needs attention too. Bear in mind that it is under a good deal of strain, as it has to lend support to the weight of the head. Poor posture will affect the muscles and cause the skin to wrinkle. When applying your facial oil never forget to massage it into the back, as well as the front, of your neck, if you wish to reap the maximum benefits from it.

Hands may also help to give away your age, as they are continually exposed to the damaging elements. Protect

FACE MASK

Skin deep Face masks help to draw out impurities and firm the texture of the skin. A gentle cucumber gel mask, as shown, is suitable for all skin types. Starting at the neck and taking care not to stretch the skin, apply the mask to the face and neck. Avoid the delicate skin around the eyes by placing pads of cotton wool soaked in soothing rosewater over the area. Leave for 15 to 20 minutes. Remove pads and rinse off the mask with plenty of tepid water

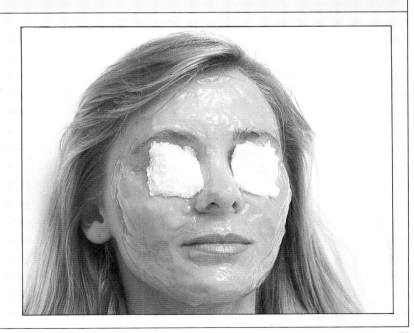

them whenever possible and once a week apply one of the following mixtures.

1. 1 teaspoon castor oil
3-4 teaspoons almond oil
2 drops galbanum

2. 4-5 teaspoons of wheatgerm oil
1 drop of galbanum
1 drop of rose
1 drop of lemon

Mix together and decant into a small bottle. After rubbing into the skin, put on a pair of cotton gloves and leave on for an hour or more. If inconvenient during the day, wear them at night. This oil is also an excellent treatment for dry or sun-parched feet.

HAIR CARE

Most of us tend to think of hair in terms of colour, condition and style, and forget that it also serves a useful purpose in protecting the scalp from extremes of temperature and in regulating the loss of body heat from the head. Approximately 100,000 individual hairs grow from hair follicles in the scalp and they do so at a rate of about 2cm (just under an inch) a month, although this varies from person to person.

In many respects, hair is similar to skin because it reflects inner health. Each hair is made of the tough, stretchable protein called keratin, manufactured by the hair follicle – the same material of which fingernails are made and which is contained in dead skin cells. The condition of the developing hair is largely dependent upon a good supply of blood carrying adequate quantities of amino acids (the building blocks of proteins), vitamins E, C and the B complex, as well as minerals like calcium, zinc, iron and copper, to the hair follicle. Poor health, whatever its cause, can be responsible for hair that lacks lustre and life, and that probably grows unusually slowly into the bargain.

While the hair is being formed, different pigment molecules are laid down which determine its colour. Hair can turn grey early, following illness or a period of intense emotional distress, because such things interfere with the production of the pigment. A nutritionally inadequate diet may do the same thing.

Hair is formed from living material, but the actual hair itself, the hair that you brush, is dead, and after a period each hair is shed and replaced by another. Its condition depends on good health and nutrition but also on how it

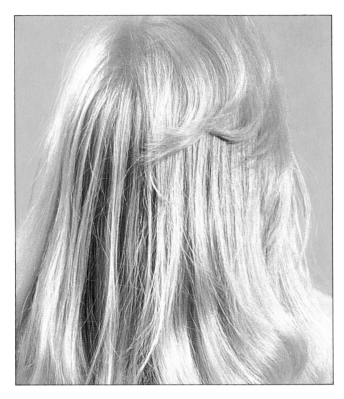

Crowning glory A head of gleaming hair is one of the greatest beauty assets. Hair reflects general health in the same way as skin, so a sensible diet is equally important in this context. Using essential oils as supplements to your hair-care routine promotes excellent hair and scalp condition.

is treated. Many problems such as unmanageability and split ends are caused by actually abusing the hair, using the wrong shampoos or overdoing the styling.

It is important to know your hair, to recognize whether it is normal, or whether it has a tendendcy to oiliness or dryness. Alongside each hair lies a sebaceous gland which secretes sebum to lubricate and protect the hair. If the glands are overactive, and produce more sebum than is needed, the hair becomes oily and will need more frequent washing to take away the excess. Do not resort to a concentrated, oil-stripping shampoo, as this will only stimulate the glands into producing even more oil to compensate. If, on the other hand, the glands are sluggish, the hair will become dehydrated and dry, so you should avoid moisture-robbing hair dryers, heated curlers and exposure to sunlight, wind and sea water.

THE BASICS

Essential oils are extremely helpful in hair care as they have the ability to influence the sebaceous glands and normalise their functions. They are beneficial to all hair types, and leave hair smelling good too.

If you use a mild shampoo, you can wash your hair as frequently as you want – which might be every day for city dwellers and people with oily hair.

Make an infusion of one of the following herbs – camomile, rosemary, sage or nettle – and a cupful to your shampoo to dilute it. Wash it in warm water and for the final rinse use cold distilled or purified water.

Every month treat your hair to a massage with the following oil-

2 teaspoons of soya oil
1 teaspoon of rum
1 capsule of cod-liver oil
1 capsule of lecithin
2 drops of thyme
2 drops of sage

Mix together, and massage into your hair for a few minutes. Then wrap your head in a warm towel to aid the penetration of the oils and leave on for an hour. When washing out the oil use a gentle shampoo, undiluted this time, and aferwards rinse through with fresh lemon if you have fair hair or cider vinegar if it is dark to help restore its manageability and shine. This treatment is particularly good for dull hair and split ends.

GREASY HAIR

If your hair is oily it is perfectly all right to wash it every day so long as the shampoo you use is a mild one and that you dilute it with water. Apply the shampoo once only and rinse the hair well, preferably with filtered water, adding a tablespoon of lemon juice in the last rinse.

Oily hair benefits from being massaged with a few drops of sage or patchouli essence. Rub the essence into the scalp directly with the fingertips. Leave it overnight if possible and wash it off in the morning. If the seborrea is severe, this treatment can be applied two or three times a week.

An alternative treatment is a tablespoon of fresh lemon juice mixed with a teaspoon of rum and massaged into the scalp at night.

DRY HAIR

After washing your hair, use a drop of ylang ylang spread on the palms as a brilliantine. This will give the hair a good shine and make it smell delicious and has the added advantage of being an aphrodisiac!

Once a week massage the scalp with some of the following mixture-

3 drops of sandalwood or ylang ylang
Half an eggcup of almond oil
Half eggcup of soya oil

Brush the mixture through the hair after massaging. Leave it on for a couple of days, the way Indonesian women do, or if you prefer, apply it overnight and wash it off in the morning, shampooing twice.

HAIR PROBLEMS

Most hair problems that are not directly caused by illness, poor diet, excessive smoking, alcohol drinking and so on, can be traced back to excessive use of heated appliances, misuse of chemical treatments such as perming and colouring, and washing with over-strong detergent shampoos.

DANDRUFF

This is a very common problem, caused by the shedding of mature, unwanted skin cells and wastes from the scalp. Like alopecia it is often linked to emotional upsets, hormonal imbalance, poor eating habits, excessive use of chemicals on the hair, and by not rinsing the hair properly. An effective natural way of combatting dandruff is to apply a lotion to the scalp before shampooing. Here are two such lotions:

50g (2oz) sage
500ml (scant pint) boiling water
2 drops oil of sage
2 drops oil of thyme

Boil the sage leaves in the water for 2 minutes, then infuse for 5 minutes. Add the essential oils.

3 nasturtium heads
500ml (scant pint) boiling water
250ml (scant ½ pint) rum
4 drops oil of rosemary

Boil the nasturtium heads in the water for 2 minutes, then infuse for 5 minutes. Add 1 cup to the rum, then add the rosemary oil.

Rub a lotion into the scalp four times a week before shampooing. Then wash the hair with a mixture of 1 part shampoo to 2 parts of sage infusion plus one drop of sage oil. Or use 1 part shampoo to 2 parts of nasturtium tea plus 1 drop of thyme.

PERFUMES

Mention the word 'perfume' and the image that springs to mind is that of a small exquisite glass bottle filled with luxuriously expensive liquid. The word 'perfume' derives from the Latin for 'through smoke', which refers to the time when barks such as cinnamon and woods such as sandalwood were burned to scent the air – a far cry from the bottled varieties with which we spray ourselves today.

In England the idea of perfumery did not really catch on until the time of Elizabeth I. So delighted was this monarch by the perfumed gloves and other scented fineries brought to her by Edward de Vere that she instructed the ladies at court to learn the art of making aromatic water to wear and pot-pourri to scent the rooms. Special gardens were cultivated for the purpose, and ladies at court began sewing sachets of flower petals such as rose and lavender into the seams of their voluminous skirts so that as they swirled the air was filled with scent. The perfume industry began to flourish under the Queen's sympathetic eye. Shakespeare is said to have loved aromatic waters and to have believed that if a man

Tudor scents During the reign of Elizabeth I, the perfume industry began to flourish. The ladies of the court took to making their own aromatic waters and the practice of using pot-pourri to scent rooms came into vogue. At the queen's command, special scented gardens were cultivated so that she could enjoy her new-found interest in perfumes.

wanted to seduce a woman he should wear a perfume of civet, the acrid secretion of the wild cat.

Today the making of perfumes for pleasure has reached a peak of sophistication. The perfumer – known as the 'nose' – has at his disposal 2,000 aromatic substances which he can mix together in an infinite number of ways. These substances may be the essential oils extracted from the leaves and flowers of plants – the resins and barks of trees, the glandular secretions of animals such as the Abyssinian civet, the Canadian beaver or the Tibetan musk deer, or, more commonly nowadays, chemically synthes-ised imitations of these aromatics. So highly trained is the nose's sense of smell that he can recognise and identify about half of all the known aromatic ingredients. (To gauge the acuity of your own sense of smell try the test on page 17).

The perfumer's art is in a number of ways very similar to that of a painter or composer of music. The perfumer Guerlain, in love with a Japanese girl, created for her the well known Mitsouko: in it he brought together all the elements which represented that love to him, thus creating an individual 'picture' in perfume. And, just as a painter or composer can conjure up memorable scenes or events in colours or chords, the 'nose' attempts to recapture an atmosphere by recreating its smell.

When I went to Malaysia for the first time, I was struck by the perfume that hung in the air, an exotic mix of spicy essences such as cinnamon, nutmeg, and clove and other notes contributed by the durians, mangosteens, papayas and bananas sold in the open-air markets. The humid air of the tropics, being particularly suitable for the dispersal of odiferous molecules, is always referred to in novels as heavy with scents. A perfume made by mixing together those different ingredients would always conjure up an image of that visit in my mind.

Coming back to England through London Airport was a strong contrast, for I was met by the smell of commercial antiseptic. As first visual impressions are vital, so are first smell impressions: it would be so much more relaxing if hospital cleaners used less strident antiseptics.

When a perfumer creates a fragrance, he will use aromatic substances to form the top notes, modifiers and base notes of the perfume. The top notes are light, volatile essences, usually of a citrus or floral nature, and are responsible for the first impression a perfume makes. After a while the modifiers or middle notes, which form the heart of the perfume, will come through; these are often essences like rose and jasmine. They are supported by the rich, lingering base notes, such as sandalwood, oakmoss, musk or civet.

In this way the personality of a perfume, created by the interplay between the various different essences, slowly reveals itself. For a perfume does have its own personality. It may be fresh and mischievous, rich and provocative, or heady and seductive – the possibilities are endless.

HOW TO BUY A PERFUME

A perfume will never smell exactly the same on any two individuals, because each person has their own body fragrance, created by their pheromones, which interacts with the notes in the perfume to modify or alter its aroma. For this reason it is never a good idea to choose a perfume on the grounds that it smelled wonderful on your friend; it will smell different on you. You may also find that because the quality of pheromones is affected by physical and emotional changes in the body, a perfume may smell heavenly one day for example and very disappointing the next.

When buying a perfume for the first time, go alone, to avoid being influenced by a friend, and in good mental and physical health, as the different pheromones you produce when you are, say, depressed or unwell, can change the smell of the perfume on your skin. Try a drop or two on your wrist, and don't smell it from too near or your nose will be 'blinded'; hold your wrist at a reasonable distance, and waft it about to allow the odoriferous molecules to rise naturally. Leave it for at least two hours, then see how the perfume has changed or matured. If you still like it, go back and buy the perfume, but not until the next day, just to make sure!

You don't have to stick to one perfume either. As your

Eastern bouquets Since time immemorial, people of every culture have enjoyed perfumes. The Japanese, like the ancient Egyptians, traditionally burned a different aromatic substance for every hour of the day. Japanese women bathed in scented waters (above). Customs of this kind led to the emergence of apothecaries skilled in the distillation of perfume, like this 12th century Arab chemist (above right).

moods change, as your social personality changes in different settings, you may want to wear a different perfume. Women often like to use a number of different perfumes, presumably to suit the different facets of their personality, while men will usually remain loyal to just one aftershave.

Perfume is much more than mere decorative frivolity. It can and should be an extension of your personality, for together with the way you dress it reinforces the image you have of yourself, and provides another outlet for communicating it to others. Perfume can also be a master of illusions, for it can lend a hint of flamboyance which may only be detected through the nose. Carnation, for instance, is known for its ability to banish shyness and induce courage, and I always dab a little essential oil on my chest before I have to speak in front of an audience (in fact, French criminals are said to wear a carnation in their buttonholes for a day before a big job, in order to build up their aggression and nerve!)

But beware of wearing too much perfume, which is not only vulgar, but also makes one seem rather aggressive. Apply it discreetly unless you want to intimidate. For perfumes, like all smells, leave strong impressions on the subconscious mind, and the impression made by a person, or indeed a place, is almost always influenced by the aromatic vapours present at the time.

THE POWER OF PERFUME

A rather charming story tells how a special perfume was made for Queen Elizabeth of Hungary from the essence of rosemary. Although she was 81 at the time, when the King of Poland met her, he was so entranced by her beautiful fragrance that he asked her to marry him. It is also said that, after suffering for years from rheumatism, she became quite fit again when she began using the perfume.

George III was less favourably impressed by the power of perfume. When he came to the throne of England in 1760, he forbad the use of scents and many other cosmetic fineries, because they were used so lavishly by whores, and went so far as to proclaim that women who attempted to seduce men by such means would be condemned to jail for practising sorcery. This perhaps explains why English women since then have traditionally chosen to wear discreet perfumes, usually single florals such as rose and lavender.

The age of discretion In the 18th century George III believed that the use of perfumes with whoring and witchcraft and banned their use on pain of imprisonment. As a result, perfumes were used very discreetly, if at all.

USING ESSENTIAL OILS AS PERFUMES

Rather than buying commercially produced perfumes you might prefer to use essential oils as scents. You may find one that you like using on its own – for instance rose, jasmine or patchouli – or you may want to combine tham for a more complex effect. Either way, essential oils should be diluted in a carrier oil or bought ready diluted specifically for use as scents.

THE FEMALE CYCLE

Changing moods
At every stage of life, a woman's health and well being depend on maintaining the optimum hormonal balance in her body. This balance is affected by the many changes occurring as her body matures. A woman's moods fluctuate, often dramatically, at times of increased hormonal activity – such as during menstruation, pregnancy, childbirth and menopause. Aromatherapy can help to restore any such temporary imbalance, and soothe the sufferer.

Have you ever wondered why women tend to be so capricious? One moment they are assertive and outgoing, the next submissive and introspective. These moods and fancies are largely a consequence of continual fluctuations in the hormones as a result of the menstrual cycle.

It is only in recent years that we have begun to understand properly the relationship between hormones and emotions. We know that the moodiness and uncertainty of the pubescent years are largely the result of hormonal upheavals which take place before the menstrual cycle is properly established. But, even after the hormones have apparently settled down, a woman goes on experiencing emotional highs and lows, because the different reproductive hormones constantly rise and fall in a rhythmic fashion with each cycle.

You will find there are times when you seem to brim with energy and vitality, others when you just want to take things easy and stay at home. If you start making a note in your diary every day for two or three months about how you feel and your attitude to work and the people around you, a pattern is likely to emerge. Being aware of such changes can be a tremendous asset, for it allows you to let your hormones work for you rather than against you.

This chapter looks at the ways in which aromatherapy relates to the menstrual cycle, pregnancy, childbirth and the menopause, and how essential oils can help to treat the problems that arise when the female hormones fail to harmonize.

THE FEMALE CYCLE

THE MENSTRUAL CYCLE

The menstrual cycle begins at puberty and continues until menopause, unless it is interrupted by pregnancy and lactation. The cycle involves several different hormones, which interact in a complex fashion to bring about the maturation of eggs within the ovaries. Presiding over this is a region of the brain called the hypothalamus.

At puberty the hypothalamus starts to send signals to its second-in-command, the pituitary gland, often referred to as the master gland, because it appears to orchestrate the activities of all the other hormone-producing glands in the body. The pituitary responds by releasing what are known as gonadotrophic hormones into the bloodstream. The first of these is a follicle-stimulating hormone. It travels to the ovaries, where it instigates the maturation of an ovum (egg) within it own little capsule or follicle. As the ovum develops, the follicle starts to produce the ovarian hormone oestrogen. By the time the ovum is fully matured, the pituitary has released another of its secretions, called luteinizing hormone. When this hormone reaches the ovaries it triggers the release of the ovum from the follicle: this is ovulation.

The empty follicle, now referred to as the corpus luteum, starts to produce the hormone progesterone. Meanwhile, the mature ovum, which is now highly receptive to the presence of any male sperm, begins its journey, along the channel known as the fallopian tube, towards the uterus (or endometrium), which has been proliferating since ovulation, begins to break down and is shed as blood during menstruation.

The whole cycle usually takes about twenty-eight days, although it is not abnormal for it to be up to seven days longer or shorter. If the beginning of menstruation is counted as the first day, ovulation takes place around the fourteenth day.

AROMA AND THE MENSES

The notion that different odiferous molecules can affect the menstrual cycle is a fascinating one, and is also highly plausible, for the nerve cells of the nose and olfactory system are directly linked to the limbic region of the brain. In a manner similar to that of the hypothalamus, the limbic region influences the secretions of the pituitary gland, which in turn can affect the quantities of oestrogen and progesterone produced by the ovaries.

Evidence that a woman's menstrual cycle can be

Fragrances to attract The constituents of perfumes relating to the natural smells of female pheromones attract the opposite sex. Ritual cleansing and perfuming was indulged in by Japanese courtesans with this fact in mind (above).

affected by the pheromones of people around her comes from studies carried out on women living in institutions who have little contact with men. For examples girls in boarding schools develop a similarity in their menstrual cycles which is disrupted when a member of the opposite sex appears on the scene. And in the presence of men, women appear to have shorter menstrual cycles (less than 28 days) than if they are apart from men, which suggests that the woman's body is trying to make the most of the opportunity by stepping up the frequency of ovulation so as to increase the likelihood of conception.

A woman's pheromones found on skin, in hair and in her bodily secretions (urine, sweat, faeces and vaginal secretions), also change throughout her menstrual cycle. They become progressively sweeter from the first day of her period, reaching a peak at ovulation. At this time, they can cause men to become quite aroused.

This natural attractant wears off as menstruation approaches, and during the menstrual flow women secrete yet another pheromone called trimethylamine. Similar in its chemistry to musk, it is also produced by bitches on heat, which explains why dogs, rather embarrassingly, often become excited by the smell of menstruating women.

SEXUALITY AND SMELL

The acuity of a woman's sense of smell fluctuates too. Women's sensitivity to certain odours used to be attributed to their smoking and drinking less than men. As far back as 1890, a German scientist. Dr Wilhelm Fliess, noted a possible link between the sense of smell and the menstrual cycle. He observed that during menstruation the capillaries in the nose became dilated and sometimes even bled a little. But it was not until 1952 that a French scientist, Dr Le Magnen, established a definite link betwen sexuality and olfaction. One of his studies involved experiments with a substance called exaltolide, extracted from angelica. He tested the reaction of men, women and children to this musky-smelling substance, which is akin in its chemical structure to the pheromones present in the glandular secretions of male civet, wild deer and beavers. Le Magnen found that adult women at the ovulation stage of their menstrual cycle were the only ones responsive to its odour.

Le Magnen's work was revolutionary in its suggestion that women's responsiveness to musky odours – chemically very similar in nature to the male hormone testosterone – was related to their menstrual cycles. It is also interesting to discover that women are a hundred times more receptive to such smells around the time of ovulation than they are at any other stage of their menstrual cycle.

I have often found that the essential oil of angelica is very effective for treating women who have lost the sharpness of their sense of smell. This may happen following a bout of illness such as a cold or flu, or around menopause, when women often complain of tiredness. I also discovered that in Malaysia women frequently take angelica as a fertility remedy, while the men use ginseng.

Since Le Magnen's pioneering work much more evidence has emerged which suggests that the sense of smell is influenced by the reproductive hormones. We know that women on the contraceptive pill do not respond to the musky odours so similar to those of male pheromones, presumably because the hormones within the pill prevent ovulation from taking place. Neither do women who are going through the first few months of pregnancy, possibly because there is no need to attract the opposite sex. Women who have had their ovaries surgically removed or who are going through the menopause and have very low levels of oestrogen and progesterone in their bodies seem to lose the acuity of their olfactory sense too.

CHECK YOUR AROMA RESPONSE

Being aware of the alterations in your sense of smell can be very useful to you. I discovered that my own sense of smell was at its peak twelve to sixteen days after the first day of menstruation, and I liked to work in the laboratory at this time, for I was inspired to make new preparations and perfumes. Work was harder around the time of my periods, and often proved fruitless as the products were not up to scratch. Making such observations helped me to economise on my time, and spared me the frustration of wasted effort.

Why not make a note in your diary every day of the way you respond to the smells of food, perfumes and so forth and see if you notice any pattern relating to your menstrual cycle?

Other changes that take place throughout the menstrual cycle can act as useful guides too. For example, women will find their moods and attitudes are affected by their hormones. They may discover they are most extrovert and confident at the time of ovulation. They feel attractive, find it easier to make decisions, and generally have great energy and drive at this time. Such feelings usually start to wear off as their period approaches.

Before menstruation, women tend to become muddle-headed and clumsier. They are unlikely to be able to deal with stress as well as they normally do, and may feel rather irritable and desperate as a consequence. They will also be inclined to spend time on their own. Primitive tribeswomen actually hide away so they can be by themselves when menstruating. In the West, many women are so difficult to live with around this time that their male companions might well wish they would hide themselves away too!

Most women are unlikely to notice the changes in the quality of their own pheromones during the menstrual cycle, although their male partners might. However, they can be aware of the changes in their vaginal secretions, which tend to be more copious around ovulation and to dry up almost completely just before menstruation. All these things could be used to establish the time when it is unlikely for conception to take place following intercourse. On a twenty-eight-day cycle, we know that ovulation will occur sometime between the twelfth and sixteenth day after the first day of the last period. Bearing in mind that sperm can live for up to three days, the unsafe period spans days nine to nineteen. This leaves about a fortnight when it would be safe to have intercourse, namely the four to five days following the end of menstruation and the nine days before the next period is due.

Naturally the desire to have intercourse will be strongest around the time of ovulation when all the body systems are geared towards it, and this is when a reliable but temporary form of contraception such as the diaphragm with spermicide should be used if you do not wish to become pregnant.

Of course, not everyone's periods are regular and you have to use the knowledge of your own body to work out a timing system which will be effective for you. Women who have been taking the contraceptive pill will have to wait a few months before their natural menstrual cycles are re-established.

I have mentioned natural contraception because I feel that the contraceptive pill falls very short of offering the perfect method. Once hailed as the women's sexual liberator, the pill is now considered a health hazard. Apart from causing unpleasant side-effects such as migraine headaches, depression, irritability, weight gain and oedema, studies now show that pill-taking can be linked to cancer of the breast and cervix. Many women suffer circulatory disturbances when taking the pill and it is thought that these might increase their chances of suffering a heart attack. Indeed, it is also hypothesised that the high levels of hormones circulating in the blood as a consequence of being on the pill may affect the sexual tendencies of a child born to a mother taking it from a very early age.

There is plenty of scope, and a great demand, for a more sophisticated means of contraception based on observations of natural bodily functions. It is time for the scientists to put their heads together and come up with the perfect – that is, a much more natural – form of contraception.

THE FEMALE CYCLE

FEMININE PROBLEMS

Most women suffer upsets in their menstrual cycles at some time during their life, and these can usually be traced back to some kind of hormonal imbalance. The sort of symptoms that accompany such upsets are diverse and are likely to be of an emotional as well as physical nature. Sometimes women are given prescriptions for drugs such as diuretics or tranquillisers to relieve the symptoms, and perhaps even hormones in the form of the contraceptive pill or implants in an attempt to redress the imbalance.

The trouble with such remedies is that they fail to get to the heart of the problem. Because the hypothalamus, pituitary gland and ovaries are all involved in the menstrual cycle, it is likely that the imbalance comes from one of them being either under or overactive. And one of the reasons why stress is such a problem for women today is because it affects the hypothalamus, which in turn transmits its disturbances to the ovaries and other glands, so disrupting the finely tuned balance. The sex glands not only play a role as organs of reproduction, but also relate to feelings of general well-being in the body: when they are not functioning properly, feelings of tiredness and listlessness set in.

Essential oils provide a safe and effective means of treating menstrual disturbances because they appear to stimulate the endocrine glands and work towards

Natural balance The essential oil distilled from the leaves, twigs and cones of the cypress tree (left), has a chemical structure akin to one of the ovarian hormones. It is therefore ideal for use in the treatment of hormonal disturbances related to the menstrual cycle.

normalising the hormone secretions. Dr Jean Valnet, a French expert on aromatherapy, referred to certain essential oils as being menagogues, acting to normalise and promote the menstrual cycle; these are valerian, artemisa, basil, cinnamon, cumin, lavender, melissa, mint, clary sage and thyme. A possible explanation for their influence is that their influence is that certain essences closely resemble the female hormones. Cypress, for example, is believed to have a chemical structure akin to one of ovarian hormones, while hops also contain a substance very similar to oestrogen.

The section below outlines some of the most common problems associated with the menstrual cycle, and how to treat them gently and safely with essential oils.

AMENORRHOEA

This is the absence of menstruation. During puberty, it is not abnormal for a girl to experience one or two periods, and then miss them for the next six or even twelve months. In later life, however, amenorrhoea is often a sign that something is amiss as far as health is concerned.

Women suffering from anorexia nervosa often stop menstruating. This is because the body requires many nutrients, such as vitamins A, E, F, and the B complex, together with minerals (in particular zinc), plus sufficient calories before it can synthesise the hormones involved in the menstrual cycle. A shock or severe emotional stress can also interfere with the cycle, as it affects the hypothalamus, which in turn may stop the production of female hormones. It is also likely that illnesses such as tuberculosis and diabetes will disrupt the normal pattern of menstruation. Insufficient thyroid levels – the condition known as myxoedema – may have a similar effect. Sometimes taking the contraceptive pill may suppress a woman's periods altogether. They usually return to normal when she comes off it.

Women who frequently miss periods or who have only brief, very scanty ones can benefit by drinking tisanes made from sage (which is highly oestrogenic) mixed with camomile as often as possible, as well as using sage in their cooking.

Another treatment is to make the following oil to add to the bath, or to rub into the skin on the tummy and back.

1 eggcup of soya oil
2 drops of sage
2 drops of juniper
2 drops of camomile

Mix these together and use in which ever way you prefer.

THE FEMALE CYCLE

DYSMENORRHOEA

Many women expereience a degree of discomfort when their menstrual flow begins. This takes the form of headaches, backache and abdominal cramps that can sometimes be so painful that it is best to lie down in a darkened room and rest.

It is often a good idea to seek out foods rich in calcium and magnesium before a period is due to begin, as they are needed for muscle relaxtion. Foods rich in the B complex vitamins, especially B6, are also helpful. Liver provides this, as well as the mineral iron lost during menstruation, so it is a good natural way of replenishing the body's supply. Some vegetables – spinach for example – also contain worthwhile quantities of iron.

To ease the pains, drink plenty of herbal teas such as caraway and the same ones prescribed below for premenstrual tension. Avoid taking baths that are too hot.

Make an oil to massage into the skin on your tummy and lower back whenever you feel the need.

2 drops of camomile essence
5 drops of parsley
1 drop of tarragon
1 eggcup of soya oil

PRE-MENSTRUAL TENSION

Around half the women who come to my clinic complain that, a week before their period is due to begin, they suffer from a number of diverse physical and emotional upsets. Many of their symptoms stem from excessive water retention which makes the tissues of the hands, ankles and face swell, cause the stomach to become distended, the breasts to feel very tender, and the legs to feel exceptionally heavy. Sometimes women gain seven or more pounds in weight in the form of fluid around this time, become constipated, and complain of migraine-like headaches, which can be the result of excess fluid creating pressure on the capillaries in the head.

Many women also find that their skin erupts in blemishes and that it generally becomes oilier, as does their hair before their period. Some complain that their circulation becomes sluggish around this time, and others find they develop the symptoms of a mild cold.

Invariably these physical disturbances are accompanied by mood swings. Many find they feel irritable, frustrated, anxious, miserable and prone to fits of temper and tears.

They also talk of being foggy-headed and clumsier than usual. Many of these emotional upsets are linked to a low sugar level in the blood, a problem that seems to be hormonally related and leaves women with strong cravings for something sweet and satisfying in between meals.

Insomnia is another premenstrual symptom, for women who are tense or depressed often find it very difficult to drop off, and invariably just as difficult to wake up.

The precise hormonal disturbances that bring about such symptoms still remain rather a mystery, but scientists now believe the problem lies in an imbalance between the hormones oestrogen and progesterone. It is possible that during the week before a period, oestrogen levels in the blood remain unusually high, whilst progesterone falls too low, creating an imbalance between the two. These hormones seem to work antagonistically, so whereas oestrogen encourages fluid retention, progesterone combats it.

The secretion of both these ovarian hormones is under the control of the pituitary gland, so a deficiency here could certainly upset the balance. The pituitary in turn is greatly influenced by the hypothalamus, in the brain, and this controlling centre also responds to stress and other psychological disturbances. This helps to explain why premenstrual tension can vary in severity from month to month, and why sufficient relaxation is very important around this time if you wish to keep the symptoms under control.

ALLEVIATION

There are a number of different steps to take which can lessen and sometimes totally alleviate the symptoms of premenstrual tension. Sufferers should eat small regular meals, choosing foods rich in the B complex vitamins, particularly vitamin B6 (Found in whole grains, nuts, meats such as liver, and fish like cod, tuna and sardines, sprouting seeds, avocados and soya beans), whilst avoiding refined carbohydrates such as white flour, sugar and things made with them like biscuits, cakes and pastries, as well as fried fatty foods.

Some women who come to see me eat very little for fear of putting on extra weight at this time, and live off coffee to flush out the excess water, and tranquillisers to soothe their nerves, which are in a state of agitation from the coffee. As a consequence their symptoms often become even worse. Eating regularly is essential, for it keeps the blood sugar at a constant level and staves off cravings.

The mineral magnesium is also very useful, as it has a tranquillising action, and foods rich in this nutrient such as almonds, walnuts, raisins, oatmeal and fish should be

How to relax Meditation and relaxationtechniques can help to alleviate pre-menstrual tension. Stimulants such as alcohol, tea and coffee should be avoided; aromatherapy treatment replaces these with soothing herb infusions which act as aids to relaxation.

included in your premenstrual diet. Women should not resort to diuretics to banish the excess fluid retained as they bring about the loss of potassium and other important minerals in the urine, and this results in feelings of even greater depression and fatigue.

Taking plenty of not-too-strenuous exercise such as walking, swimming and yoga is also helpful as it releases tension which otherwise builds up inside, and so are periods of quiet relaxtion.

Aromatherapy treatment includes drinking plenty of herb teas instead of alcohol or stimulants such as tea or coffee. Useful infusion can be made from parsley, mint, calendula (Marigold) flowers, and camomile mixed with orange flowers. Camomile has a soporific action and is very good for those suffering from insomnia. Always boil the teas for 2 minutes and infuse for 5 minutes.

When cooking season your food with sage, basil and thyme, as they make food easier to digest. Indigestion is often a problem before menstruation and sufferers should always try to eat early in the evening to prevent this phenomenon, which is yet another cause of insomnia.

Take two warm baths a day adding 3 drops of neroli or 4 drops of pine. Afterwards lie down on the bed for 10 minutes in a darkened room, placing a pillow under your knees.

For massage make an oil by adding 4 drops of neroli to 1 eggcup of soya oil. Massage into your abdomen, lower back and the back of your neck.

CYSTITIS

Cystitis is a condition characerised by an inflammation of the bladder and it can be extremely painful and debilitating. Bacteria co-exist in large numbers in a healthy bladder, but if something disrupts the balance, an infection can occur which gives rise to this inflammation.

Women on the pill are more prone to cystitis than most, because the hormones in it can alter the bacterial flora in the urethra as well as the vagina. Illness such as bronchitis, a bad cold accompanied by sinusitis, and even a severe chill may provoke a urinary infection. On the other hand, the cystitis may be initiated by irritants such as kidney stones.

Frequent sex stimulates the proliferation of bacteria in the urethra of some women. A simple remedy is to drink plenty of tepid water after intercourse, as this cleans out the bladder. It is also worth remembering that women who take little exercise are also more prone to cystitis, for their weak muscles encourage the retention of urine within the bladder.

A good treatment for cystitis is to keep warm and to drink frequent infusions made by boiling cherries, cherry stalks, or the wispy hairs of corn on the cob. Cherries and fresh sweetcorn are not always available however. Aromatic essences can be used all the year round.

To a warm bath, add 5 drops of sandalwood, pine or juniper oils.

You could also make a massage oil by adding 6 drops of any of the essences above to 1 eggcup of soya oil. Massage into the tummy, lower back and sacral region, then apply hot and cold compresses alternately.

THRUSH

This is a whitish discharge from the vagina caused by the proliferation of unwanted fungus. In bad cases there is severe itching and soreness. It is often brought on by a course of antibiotics. Women who are most susceptible are those using the contraceptive pill, those who are pregnant and those suffering from diabetes.

Avoid wearing underwear made from synthetic fibres such as nylon or polyester, as well as tightly fitting jeans.

TREATMENT
Add to your bath 2 drops of juniper or 2 drops of lavender. You can also use just 1 drop of either of these essences when using a bidet or douching.

PREGNANCY AND CHILDBIRTH

The nine months of pregnancy can be the happiest of your whole life. This is partly because, from the time of puberty, a woman's body has been awaiting the occurrence of this very phenomenon. You will be carrying something born of love, and it is a wonderful feeling to experience it growing within you. Although I know that not every woman is so fortunate, for me, every day of my pregnancy was exciting, and I felt exceedingly contented the whole time.

During pregnancy it is very important that you are healthy and fit, for your physical and emotional state will have great bearing on your child's development. It is particularly essential that you take special care of yourself during early pregnancy for, from the time of conception through the first eight weeks, the foetus is developing at a phenomenal rate.

The foetal cells need a plentiful supply of all the essential vitamins, minerals, amino acids, fatty acids, and so on if they are to grow and reproduce, so it is very important to eat well at this time. Pollen is an excellent supplement to take, for it contains all the nutrients essential to health, so try taking $\frac{1}{4}$ – $\frac{1}{2}$ a teaspoon every day. Also give up tea, coffee and alcohol, replacing them with camomile, sage and rosehip tea, with honey if you wish. Drugs should be avoided in pregnancy if at all possible. Even drugs that can be bought over the counter – for example, aspirin or anti-nausea pills – could possibly be harmful. You should be extremely cautious about all medicines therefore.

Breathing in noxious fumes that contain chemicals or toxic minerals such as lead can be highly damaging to the developing child and may even cause miscarriage. Remember, poisonous things pass from the mother to the foetus, so it is important to protect your baby from anything that could be dangerous at this vulnerable stage.

Pregnancy is characterized by an upsurge in the production of oestrogen and progesterone. Such hormonal changes can bring about certain other changes. You may experience cravings for certain foods and smells and find others make you feel nauseous. Other discomforts may include oedema (swelling), circulation problems, sleeplessness and nervousness.

Essential oils provide an excellent means of treating such things and will generally enhance your feelings of well-being. Because they reach the bloodstream, the essences will also pass to the baby, who benefits from them as well. However, certain odoriferous substances can induce a miscarriage, so it is never a good idea to play around with them. The ones I have prescribed have been shown to be safe, and the recipes have been specially devised so that the constituents are present in balanced proportions.

ESSENTIAL OIL MASSAGE

Guidelines Before attempting this massage routine, study these guidelines carefully.

* Use only very gentle movements on the back and abdomen. Do not apply concentrated pressure in these areas.

* Avoid the abdominal area altogether after the 10th week of pregnancy. Concentrate instead on the foot area.

* Use just I drop of a mild (not strong-smelling) essence, such as neroli, if a calming effect is desired, or orange for a more tonic effect. Dilute in an eggcupful of soya oil.

* Where instructions specify 'apply pressure', maintain the pressure at any one point for 2-3 seconds.

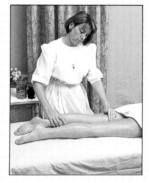

I. Ask the subject to lie face down, or on her side if this is uncomfortable. Apply the oil to the legs, working up from the feet and squeezing gently .

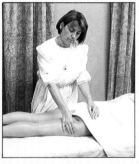

2. Apply pressure with your thumb to back of the thigh. This will improve circulatiion.

3. Using your thumb, apply pressure to the inside back of the ankle. This relieves poor circulation, fluid retention and bladder problems.

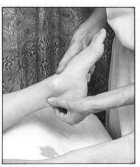

4. Using the fingers of both hands, massage the back of the ankles on the inside and outside of the leg simultaneously. This relieves strain in the back and regulates the ovarian hormones.

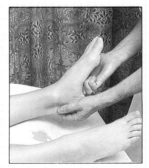

5. Using the knuckles of one hand, press firmly in one even movement from the arch of the foot to the heel. Again, this promotes good circulation.

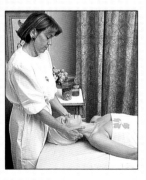

6. Ask the subject to lie on her back. Massage the neck with the fingers, working upwards in small circular movements on both sides of the spine simultaneously. Then work from top of neck outwards along base of skull towards the ears.

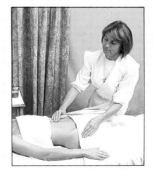

7. Apply oil to the abdomen and massage lightly with a circular motion, taking care to use only the gentlest pressure. Do not do this after the 10th week of pregnancy.

FLUID RETENTION (OEDEMA)

During pregnanacy most women find their tissues retain extra fluid as a normal physiological adjustment which provides extra protection for the foetus. You should never try to combat it with strong diuretic tablets, as these not only flush out the water but take away essential minerals such as potassium and magnesium and this could be damaging to the baby.

If your tissues swell excessively you should step up your intake of vitamin C, which has a mild diuretic action. Some essential oils contain substantial amounts of vitamin C – the citrus ones, orange, and lemon, for instance. Make a massage oil by adding 1 drop of petigrain, orange and rose to 4-5 teaspoons of almond oil. You can also add the pure essences to your bath.

CIRCULATORY PROBLEMS

Varicose veins may develop if you do not take care. This is because the expanding womb constricts the blood flow to the limbs, and the extra weight you are carrying makes it harder for the blood to return from the extremities to the heart.

Look for foods rich in vitamim E to help the circulation, as well as those containing vitamim C. Bioflavonoids are also important, because they strengthen the blood vessels. They are present in the skins of citrus fruits as well as in pollen granules. Gentle exercise is needed to maintain a healthy flow of blood through the system. Flexing the knees and ankles at regular intervals will help to prevent congestion in the legs.

Another good way of helping the blood flow is to place a pillow under your mattress at the end of the bed, so you are lying at a slight angle. Alternatively, place a couple of blocks of wood under the bottom of the bed to raise it slightly off the ground.

Make a massage oil by adding 3 drops of cypress, 2 drops each of lavender and lemon to 1 eggcup of soya oil. Massage into the legs especially. You could also add the pure essences to your bath.

Single essences can also be used for massage. Three drops of cypress or geranium or 4 drops of neroli can be added to 2 teaspoons of soya oil.

Women may also suffer from piles (haemorrhoids) as a result of bad circulation, in which case they should try to sit in a basin of very cold water and massage with the oil recommended for piles in the alphabetical guide.

PREPARING FOR CHILDBIRTH

When your baby is ready to be born, the hypothalamus tells the pituitary gland to release the contraction of the uterus. When I was in Malaysia, I discovered that the women use a lot of nutmeg in their cooking during pregnancy because it strengthens and tones the muscles and primes them for contractions.

Two to three weeks before the baby is due, massage your tummy with the following.

3 drops of nutmeg
2 drops of sage
1 drop of neroli
4-5 teaspoons of almond oil

During the early part of pregnancy, a gentle back massage using the oil you have chosen will help you to relax, and aid the circulation, as well as reducing oedema. But it is not advisable to massage the back after the third month. In advanced pregnancy, a leg massage is very beneficial, and it is also a good idea to get someone to rub the oils into the soles of your feet.

Also sprinkle grated nutmeg on your vegetables, as this will help you to digest them, and add it to any milk you are drinking.

DURING CHILDBIRTH

Essential oils can be very helpful during labour, as they can ease breathing difficulties and promote relaxation.

For breathing, rub an oil made from 1 drop of pine, eucalyptus, and neroli, and 3 teaspoons of almond oil into your chest. For relaxation, add 1 drop of lavender to a bowl of warm water and leave it beside your bed, so that the vapours disperse in the air.

BREAST FEEDING

After childbirth a substance called prolactin is produced by the pituitary gland, which stimulates the glands in the breasts to produce milk. The constituents of this milk are derived from the blood flowing through the glands, so the baby continues to receive all the nutrients he needs in a well balanced form from its mother.

A very special kind of milk is produced during the first few days after childbirth, called colostrum, and it is very

Comfortable suckling
Aromatherapy can benefit both mother and child in the early months of breast-feeding. Many women are discouraged from suckling their baby through fear of losing the shape of their bust, or suffering from cracked nipples. Suckling in fact promotes good muscle tone. The use of essential oils can supplement this action, and soothe any discomfort a nursing mother may experience.

important that the baby receive this milk if it is to be stong and healthy, for colostrum contains antibodies which protect against foreign substances until the baby is capable of making its own. This early protection fills what is called the 'immunity gap', and this is why babies fed on breast milk are far more resistant to infections than those fed by bottle. Another reason why breast milk is best is that babies often have allergies to cow's milk, which manifest as colic, eczema, vomiting, diarrhoea and anaemia.

Breast-feeding should be a joy to the mother, helping to intensify the bond between her and her baby. But many women are put off by the thought that their breasts may sag. On the contrary, breast-feeding helps them regain their shape. During the last nine weeks of pregnancy the hormones oestrogen and progesterone have been priming the glands for milk production, and when a mother breast-feeds, the suckling action tones up the muscles that support the breast as well as those of the uterus. So it is only when breast-feeding is neglected that the breasts suffer.

Some women complain of sore, cracked nipples which make breast-feeding a painful experience. To prevent this happening, massage a mixture of almond oil and lemon juice into the nipples all through pregnancy.

After childbirth, massage the whole breast with an oil made from 4 drops of rose, 2 drops of lemon, and 2 teaspoons of almond oil, which will encourage them to regain their firmness.

If the breasts are inflamed during lactation, rub them

with a mixture of 3 drops of geranium in cold cream.

To stimulate a good flow of milk, add fennel, carrots and lentils to your food as often as you can, and also eat plenty of parsley – chopped in salads, with steamed vegetables or as a juice (if you have an extractor) to mix with fruit juices. Drink a herb tea made by boiling a few hops in water for 2 minutes. Leave to infuse for about 5 minutes and drink a few cups as required.

AROMATHERAPY FOR THE BABY

It is quite a shock for a baby to leave its secure little world inside the womb and to arrive in a strange new one, so it will need comfort and reassurance through touch and pleasant aromas. To its first bath add just 1 drop of lavender or neroli. Because its sense of smell is quite sophisticated even at this early age, it will probably be surprisingly responsive.

Never wash a baby with a harsh detergent soap. If its face is a little greasy, some witch-hazel mixed with purified or distilled water will do nicely instead.

After drying give your baby a gentle massage using light stroking movements with an oil made with 1 drop of neroli and 1 drop of lavender in 1 eggcup of almond oil.

INSOMNIA

If a baby of older than 3 months has difficulty sleeping, prepare an infusion of orange flowers by adding 1 pinch to 500ml (a scant pint) of water, boil for 2 minutes and leave to infuse for 5 minutes. Sweeten with honey and give this drink in-between feeds.

COLIC

Sometimes the reason a baby cries and cries and seems uncomfortable is because of colic. For a baby of 3 months and over, a good remedy is to boil some sliced carrots with a piece of fennel for 45 minutes. Strain, add a teaspoon of honey to the juice and give this when it cries. Or give it camomile tea sweetened with honey.

Fill the baby's room with soothing aromatic vapours by soaking a piece of cotton wool in water containing a few drops of pine and orange essential oils, or lavender and orange. Squeeze out the excess water and leave the pad on or near the radiator.

AROMAS AND THE PSYCHE

As the Egyptians discovered so many years ago, perfumes can profoundly affect a person's emotional and mental state. The Greek physician Hippocrates, 'the father of medicine', said; "The way to health is to have an aromatic bath and scented massage every day." He knew that good health involves both a healthy body and healthy mind and that the two are inseparable. He was aware that essential oils could influence the psyche and benefit the state of mind.

UNLOCKING THE NERVOUS SYSTEM

How essential oils work in this way has only emerged in recent years. As said before, the nerves of the olfactory organ are linked to the limbic portion of the brain, which is responsible, among other things, for controlling emotional well-being. This is why pleasant smells make us feel happy while noxious smells make us depressed and irritable.

Certain essential oils also have a beneficial action on the nervous system. In times of stress the sympathetic branch of the nervous system becomes dominant, and if such a situation is prolonged, you become tired, concentration is impaired and everyday problems grow out of all

Egyptian secrets
Cleopatra depicted by the Victorian artist Alma-Tadema. When the Egyptian queen met Antony, she is said to have had her bedroom carpeted with rose petals, which acted as a powerful aphrodisiac. The essential oils distilled from rose, cedarwood and ylang-ylang have lovely fragrances of great sensual appeal.

proportion. Essential oils work to re-establish the equilibrium between the sympathetic and the para-sympathetic branches of the nervous system and in doing so not only relax the body, but also restore clarity to the mind, stimulate the thought processes, and bring back lost feelings of awareness and control.

Most essences are stimulants. They galvanise the adrenal cortex into action, which leaves you better able to cope with stress than might have been possible before. Stress, as is well known, is a major cause of anxiety, depression, irritability, insomnia and even lack of interest in sex.

Indeed certain essential oils have long been praised for their aphrodisiac properties. One of the reasons why they work so fast and effectively is that again they act directly on the limbic portion of the brain, which is also responsible for sexual behaviour. When Cleopatra first met Antony, the romantic carpet of fresh rose petals in her bedroom was chosen for its aphrodisiac effect.

In a rather less direct way, other essences possess the ability to dynamise fatigued reproductive glands into action, and so work to revive a waning interest in sex.

Certain essential oils have important mood-altering properties, which makes them valuable in maintaining emotional health. They can be added to the bath, or to some oil and massaged into the skin. You could also place a few drops on a glass slide and leave it near a radiator or light so the vapour fills the air.

ANXIETY

Many essential oils have a sedative action on the nervous system and are valuable for massaging and inhaling. Make a nerve tonic by adding 2 drops of neroli and 2 drops of melissa to 4 teaspoons of soya oil. Rub into the chest and tummy, and add the pure essences (2 drops of each) to the bath.

The mineral magnesium is essential for good nerves, which is why it is often referred to as nature's tranquilliser. A dozen almonds a day will provide a plentiful supply.

Rosemary, mint, patchouli and basil can also be used to obtain relief from anxiety.

CONCENTRATION, POOR

Carnation is the essence of choice. It can be used in the bath; rubbed, diluted, into the skin; or added to a pan of steaming water so that the vapour can be inhaled.

MENOPAUSE

Most Western women view the menopause with great apprehension, for they see it as marking the beginning of old age and the end of their good looks. The idea that beauty lies only in possessing an elegant silhouette and a youthful complexion perpetuated by glossy magazines only serves to heighten the fear of menopause.

But the truth is that menopause is simply the end of the menstrual cycle, just as puberty is its onset. It happens because the ovaries gradually cease to respond to the stimulation of the gonadotrophic hormones produced by the pituitary gland. This usually starts to occur between the ages of forty-two and fifty, although it can happen much earlier if a person is suffering from malnutrition, emotional stress, or poor health brought on by illness. As a consequence, the menstrual cycle becomes irregular and eventually stops altogether.

Several different physical and emotional upheavals are linked to the diminished production of oestrogen and progesterone. Many women suffer from hot flushes, excessive sweating, spells of dizziness, weakness and sometimes a reduced interest in sex. These only take place, however, while the body is acclimatising to the changes, and later on they disappear. In this respect, menopause is similar to puberty, when the upheavals in hormone levels give rise to moodiness, water retention or swelling and occasional dizziness. Women will also find that when they are tired or emotionally distressed these hormone-related symptoms can be exaggerated.

One lady who came to me for treatment was very distressed for she was only thirty-five years old and already beginning her menopause. Her frequent trips to the gynaecologist had proved fruitless, and no wonder, for the hormonal changes were being brought on by her exceptionally erratic way of life. She was a career woman, and during the last ten years, had been travelling consistently between England, California and Asia. On top of this, she had adopted highly irregular eating habits, which contributed to the development of peptic ulcers as well as insomnia.

I suggested that she have a course of relaxing treatments at the practice, and that she alter her diet. I also formulated some oils for her to use containing cypress, verbena and rose, along with other essences. They were to be used in the bath, massaged into the skin and taken internally.

Now, she has actually passed through her early menopause, and although she still leads a very active life, the treatments have shown her the importance of relaxing and looking after herself. She no longer suffers from the health problems of a few years ago.

Another woman who had been coming to me for a long time had begun her menopause quite normally when she was fifty. However, she was intensely anxious about getting old, especially as she was married to a man ten years her junior, who was very active. Because she felt she was losing her looks, she shied away from sex, and this problem was intensified by the fact that her husband told her he would soon have to start looking for a younger woman. At the time she was also suffering from indigestion, constipation, cystitis, insomnia and cellulite, which she felt were linked to her menopause.

Searching for clues as to why this should be, I discovered that she ate nothing all day, drinking tea and coffee to keep her going, because she waited to have dinner with her husband. Because they usually ate between nine and ten o'clock at night, she was not digesting her food properly, and this was the main cause of her gastric problems and insomnia, not her hormones at all.

I prescribed eucalyptus for her cystitis, sage to correct the hormonal imbalance and ease her nervous tension and thyme to improve her bad circulation and combat her insomnia.

TREATMENT

For anyone going through the menopause, I would recommend sage and nettle teas, for they are rich in substances akin to the female hormones, while sage is also good for hot flushes. Thyme is very beneficial for nervous problems and can take the place of tea and coffee as a stimulant without creating the difficulties they do.

For those suffering from insomnia, an infusion of passiflora (passion fruit flowers) should produce a good night's sleep.

Make a massage oil to rub into the skin on the tummy and into the back of the neck. This consists of:

3 drops of thyme
2 drops of rosemary
3 drops of basil
3 drops of cypress
1 eggcup of soya oil

In addition, add 3 drops of basil and 3 drops of cypress to your bath; 3 drops of rosemary on their own; or 3 drops of rosemary and 3 drops of basil.

AROMAS AND THE PSYCHE

DEPRESSION

A mixture of equal parts of basil, neroli and lavender makes a good remedy for depression. Use 6 drops in the bath, and rub some on the skin of the tummy afterwards.

Other anti-depressant essences are cinnamon, rose, lemon. eucalyptus, mint and ylang-ylang.

EXHAUSTION

As a pick-me-up, a bath containing 4 drops of ylang-ylang or 6 drops of cinnamon will usually do the trick. Or rub one of these essences, diluted, into the skin.

If you are suffering from more than transient exhaustion, take two baths a day, a stimulating one in the morning (6 drops of lemon oil in warm water) and a calming one at night (3-6 drops of neroli in a hotter bath).

INSOMNIA

One hour before going to bed, take a warm bath to which has been added 3 drops of thyme essence. Or, use 1 drop each of lavender and neroli, or 2 drops of either essence.

If a bath is impracticable, rub one or more of these remedies diluted in soya oil into the solar plexus, the sacrum (at the base of the spine), on the soles of the feet and on the back of the neck.

For a sleep-enhancing atmosphere, place a cup of water with 1 drop of lavender and 1 drop of neroli near a radiator or spray the air with the mixture.

Lettuce, oranges and mandarins have a soporific effect. Do not take a bath directly after eating.

AROMA AND THE ENVIRONMENT

Today both men and women tend to look upon perfume purely as a form of adornment, rather like jewellery or clothes, which perhaps ought to be reserved for special occasions. But this has not always been the case. In the past there were numerous other reasons why perfumes were used and held in high esteem. Looking through history, it is clear that many of the great civilisations also used different perfumes as an invisible form of communication.

AROMAS FOR INCREASED SPIRITUALITY

In Japan a different aromatic substance was burned at each hour of the day. It might have been citrus fruit first thing in the morning or jasmine in the afternoon, which meant that it was almost literally possible to tell the time of day by its perfume. Similarly, in ancient Egypt, different perfumes filled the air throughout the day, but they were specifically used in order to please the sun god, Ra. At sunrise sweet resins rose to the sky to greet him from the temples where they were burned; at midday they were replaced by myrrh. Then at sunset a mixture of about sixteen different aromatic essences including frankincense expressed gratitude for his benevolence. I like the idea of Egyptians recognising the smell of sunset and knowing that as the day was closing, it was time to stop work and join together to pray and share a meal.

The Egyptian high priests were also master perfumers, whose skill in blending together different aromatic

Scented worshipping A Chinese priest makes an offering in a temple (right). Throughout the centuries aromatic essences have been burned as part of religious ritual – from the myrrh of the ancient Egyptians to the incense of the Roman Catholic church.

AROMA AND THE ENVIRONMENT

Aromatic incense A priest burns incense at an altar. Incense is burned in many places of worship, to create an atmosphere which is conducive to spirituality.

substances was highly developed. The perfumes they created were gifts to please the pharaohs, and were also burned in the temples during religious ceremonies. This was not done simply to create a pleasant aroma for the worshippers; they knew that certain aromatic substances possessed the power to influence the psyche and state of mind. They used the same skills in spiritual healing, treating people suffering from depression, anxiety and other emotional disturbances with specially prepared perfumes.

They discovered for themselves that different blends of aromatic essences could help them attain a meditative state characterised by the shifting from one plane of consciousness to another. They also believed that certain essences would cleanse the soul and bring to them a greater sense of spiritual awareness. For the worshippers, such aromas must have instilled in them feelings of blissful peace, tranquillity and detachment from reality, a state exceedingly conducive to prayer.

The Egyptians passed on their knowledge of perfumery to the Hebrew slaves. In the Book of Exodus, when God told Moses to flee from Egypt, He reminded him to take myrrh, cinnamon, olive oil and bullrushes with him. This was so that when Moses reached his destination, and had set up God's tabernacle, he could scent it with substances that would create a spiritual atmosphere reminiscent of Egypt.

Throughout history, perfumes have played a significant role in many forms of religion. In India many old temples are built of sandalwood, and its soothing fragrance is always present in the air. In some temples the practice persists of covering the body with pure essences of rose, sandalwood, jasmine and narcissus in preparation for prayer. And in the western world, even today, incense is burned during services in churches, although most worshippers are probably ignorant of its significance.

AROMAS FOR PLEASURE

Apart from religious and spiritual uses, however, perfumes were also used and enjoyed for the pleasure they gave to the nose. Whether the secret of a single flower or a complex mix of different aromatic essences, perfumes were used by lovers to heighten the forces of attraction between them. Cleopatra's rose petals, for instance, were an effective and delicious concept.

In ancient Greece there came a time when the use of aromatics as perfumes in public places and in homes was so widespread that the Athenian statesman Solon banned their sale on the grounds that the heavily scented air acted as a distraction and provoked allergies.

By the time Europeans eventually started taking an interest in perfume, it was probably as a means of suppressing the odours that filled the air. Although the Romans had undoubtedly brought aromatic substances with them on their extensive conquests, the first mention of the use of perfume in France does not appear until the year 1190. The king at that time, Philip Augustus, bestowed upon the perfumers the privilege of exercising their skills. However, before they could do so, would-be perfumers had to practise blending aromatic essences and learn their properties for four years then appear in front of a jury who would test their skill and knowledge.

Later when Charles II was on the throne, a well-known perfumer called Charles Lily wrote a book in which he spelled out the delights of fragrance. In 1665, it was recommended that aromatic substances should be burned in every house to fight the epidemic of plague, but perfumes also began to be used at this time for the pleasure they could give as well as their therapeutic effects.

CREATE AN AROMATIC ENVIRONMENT

You can extend the use of beautiful aromas to your environment without going to Cleopatra's extreme of carpeting your bedroom with rose petals. Here are a few simple ways to scent the air around you so as to create a pleasing and harmonious atmosphere.

Add a few drops of your favourite essential oil, or a mixture of several, to water and spray the air with atomiser or plant spray.

Place a few drops of essential oil on a glass slide and leave it near a radiator or light so that the vapour fills the air.

Put a few drops into a pan of steaming water just taken off the heat.

Add a few to the water in a humidifier near a fire or a radiator.

Soak a piece of cotton wool in water containing a few drops of essence. Squeeze out the excess and place the cotton on or near a radiator.

Have bunches of aromatic flowers around the house.

Make or buy a pot-pourri. When the scent has faded, simply refresh it by adding some essential oils to the mixture.

Burn incense.

Use scented pillows. For the bedroom you can buy pillows specially designed to help you breathe easily and sleep well.

Plant a scented garden.

PLANT YOUR OWN SCENTED GARDEN

Elizabethan England was renowned for its beautifully fragrant and romantic gardens – tended on the whole by women, while the men saw to the vegetables. The poet Francis Bacon wrote of such gardens: "Those which perfume the air most delightfully not passed by as the rest but trodden upon and crushed are three, that is burnet, wild thyme and watermints. Therefore, you are to set whole alleys of them to have the pleasure when you walk or tread."

The fragrance of the different flowers, trees, shrubs and herbs and their curative properties are, for me, far more valuable than their colours and shapes. I think it important that the notes of each aromatic plant harmonise as they do in a perfume; and that they should be mentally uplifting, so that walking in the garden will always be a pleasurable experience to the nose.

Once you have a knowledge of the properties of the various aromatic essences, you will be able to choose the plants for your garden to suit your desires and needs. I am merely going to give a few tips on which plants are companionable, which are not, and where each one belongs in your perfumed gardens.

Medicinal plants like camomile, basil, calendula, hyssop, hops, mint, sage, fennel and lemon verbena should form the heart of your fragrant garden. They may be surrounded by shrubs of rosemary, thyme and the evergreen sweet bay, for these plants seal in the perfume which radiates from the medicinals. Lavender is perfect for planting along either side of a path, and behind this sweet-smelling shrub, damask roses and centifolia roses smell good.

Scented gardens Since the early 16th century, scented gardens have been planted, making a walk through a garden a totally pleasurable and often curative experience.

Roses also go well with the citrus-like bergamont plant, and with the cooler camomile. French folklore has it that roses benefit from being interspersed with garlic, for its potent aroma keeps the greenfly and other destructive insects at bay.

Never grow carnations in the same beds as roses for they do not go well together, and produce a highly aggressive atmosphere. This applies especially to selecting flowers for perfuming your living room. When you do plant carnations, choose the old-fashioned varieties for they have a sweet spicy smell which is a good nerve tonic and also gives courage to shy people. For this reason, an arrangement of carnations might be a good idea in the home or office of someone wishing to be less shy.

FRAGRANT HERBS

For lining smaller, meandering paths, choose herbs such as mint, parsley and chives, and if you have a garden seat, surround it with aromatic rosemary.

Angelica and artemisa also go well in a perfumed garden because they are quite fragrant, and can be planted as and where you wish. And you might bed some pelargonium in a corner of your garden,for both the leaves and flowers are scented and you can detect their perfume from a distance. Camomile, lemon verbena and mint also grow well in proximity to this flower.

If you have a shady or wooded area in your garden, plant pine and cypress trees at the back as they form a barrier which prevents the odiferous molecules from escaping. They also have a beneficial action on the respiratory system, as does lilac, although, unfortunately, it only flowers for a short period of time.

A eucalyptus would be useful at the bottom of your garden, firstly because of its stunning silvery foliage, and secondly because it keeps the flies away during the summer months.

Train honeysuckle and jasmine to climb around your house, so that when you open the windows their fragrance seeps into the rooms. Do not have them around your bedroom, however, or if you do always close the window at night; their scents are very stimulating and will prevent you from falling asleep. A lime tree would be lovely near a bedroom window, or perhaps a few orange trees (not too common in Great Britain), because of their calming and tranquillising influence.

If you like growing your own vegetables, it might be worth considering planting marigolds with them, for their scent helps to keep the insects away. In a similar manner, mint and sage protect cabbages.

Of course, different flowers bloom at different times of the year, and some careful thought will need to go into selecting your plants so that their fragrances will mingle together at the same time.

For spring, it will be a good idea to plant daffodils, bluebells and narcissi as their perfumes all harmonise with each other. And, for the winter months, make sure you have planted plenty of hyacinths near your windows, or indoors, for their fragrance will bring untold pleasure to a grey and cloudy day.

Precious pines The rich and pungent smell of pine trees forms a natural barrier to contain the herbal scents of your garden. Pine cones freshen the air with their pleasing fragrance. They are especially powerful when burned in a stove or on a fire.

AROMATHERAPY AND ILLNESS

A medicinal guarantee The Greek physician Hippocrates (460-377 BC), the father of modern medicine, was an advocate of essential oils. He believed in the healing properties of many plants and encouraged their use.

According to Hippocrates, 'there is a remedy for every illness to be found in nature'. The plant kingdom, as well as appealing to our sense of smell, provides us with the means to heal ourselves. Although we know that plants and plant essences featured strongly in all ancient forms of medicine, it was not until the end of the last century that a French scientist, Professor Gattefossé, coined the word 'aromatherapy', by which he meant the therapeutic use of odiferous substances, obtained from flowers, plants and aromatic shrubs, through inhalation and application to the skin. Marguerite Maury, a biochemist and one of the pioneers of aromatherapy, described the aromatic extracts of plants as the 'purest form of living energy that we can transfer to man'.

TREATING ILLNESS

Aromatherapy can be used not only to treat and cure illness effectively but, perhaps more importantly, to prevent us from losing our good health in the first place.

Today we fight a constant battle to stay well. Many of us live and work in large cities or towns where we are, in a sense, trapped in confined spaces which constrict our freedom of movement and diminish the exercise we should be getting to keep us fit. Cars, automatic washing machines, desk jobs, all encourage this sedentary existence. We are under constant bombardment from radiation, which has a damaging effect on the chemistry of all the cells in our bodies. Even the television which we spend so much time watching emits a significant degree of radioactive waves.

Nowadays people experience a good deal of psychological stress which comes from the anxiety of a demanding job, and the even greater fear that that job might be lost. More and more women pursue careers, often on top of running a home and looking after a family, which puts demands on them that were unknown even fifty years ago.

In addition, there is the ever-escalating quantity of traffic with its noise and pollution. All these things act as stressors which diminish the energy reserves needed to fight off illness and stay healthy. Of course, it is impossible to turn back the clock, and it would be foolish to refuse to accept these technological advances. Instead, we have to adapt ourselves to cope with the ever-changing environment, and this is where aromatherapy is so helpful. For by inhaling the essences and massaging plant oils into the skin, we can build up natural resistance to stress and illness.

In a way, aromatherapy is giving back the environment which we miss by living in towns and cities, as it recreates the fragrances of the trees and flowers which would naturally surround us in the country.

We are more aware today than ever before of the potential side-effects of some drugs, especially the anti-depressant and tranquillising pills that are frequently resorted to when pressures of job or life in general become too great to bear. Anyone reluctant to turn to tranquillisers, antibiotics or other pills to help them alleviate seemingly minor problems as diverse as nervousness, insomnia, headaches, influenza and swollen joints, will find aromatherapy invaluable. It provides the means to treat such ailments before they turn into much more serious kinds of illness. It is also an ideal means of curing young children's ills and injuries, and a daily application of plant oils will even help alleviate the pains of rheumatism and arthritis from which so many older people suffer.

Before you start, you will need the following items when using aromatherapy to treat illnesses:

- a china bowl
- a dropper for measuring out the oils
- a steel or enamel saucepan
- a few small square towels or babies' cloth nappies
- some small amber glass

bottles with screw tops in which to keep the prepared oils (they should hold about 30ml or 1fl oz)
- a teaspoon, a tablespoon and an eggcup
- a dropper for measuring the essential oils

MEASURING THE OILS

Essential oils are measured in drops (hence the dropper), but measurements of the carrier oil are less critical, so I have given them in teaspoons, tablespoons and the less usual eggcup. Most eggcups measure about 30ml or 1 fl oz.

A TO Z OF AROMATHERAPY TREATMENTS

Below is a list in alphabetical order of the principal conditions for which essential oils have been shown to be effective treatments.

ABSCESSES
Galbanum makes an effective remedy. Add 2-3 drops to almond or peach kernel oil. Apply to affected area.

ACNE
See section on Skin Problems.

AMENORRHEA (Scanty or Absent Periods)
See section on The Female Cycle

ANXIETY
See section on Aromas and the Psyche

ARTHRITIS
Arthritis is an inflammation which afflicts the joints and gives rise to a good deal of pain and stiffness. Sometimes the quantity of synovial fluid, the fluid which lubricates the joints, increases, causing swelling and restricting movement. There are two different kinds of arthritis – osteoarthritis and rheumatoid arthritis – and they often appear after injury, physical over-exertion or intense emotional stress.

Care should be taken to include enough calcium and magnesium in the diet, as these minerals are needed for the production of synovial fluid, too little of which is as painful as too much.

1 drop of thyme
1 drop of rosemary
1 drop of juniper
1 eggcup of almond oil

Mix together and bottle. Rub into the affected areas, which should be wrapped in a hot, damp towel. Try to do this four times a day.

ASTHMA
Asthma is a respiratory problem which often goes hand in hand with bronchitis, nervous disorders and hayfever, and also tends to afflict people of a nervous disposition. During an attack sufferers have great difficulty in breathing and often feel a sense of suffocation, the chest feels tight and heavy, and he or she has to cough to get rid of the mucus.

Sufferers should avoid stimulants such as tea, chocolate

and coffee whenever possible and replace them with herbal tisanes. Take eucalyptus and thyme together, or others like passiflora (passion flower), camomile, valerian and aniseed. It is not generally wise to inhale the vapours of essential oils as asthma sufferers are allergy-prone people and may react to odiferous substances, perhaps actually worsening an attack.

However, inhalation of benzoin can be very beneficial. Three drops should be added to 500ml (a scant pint) of water. Alternatively, benzoin can be used to make a massage oil by adding 1 drop to 2 tsp of a carrier such as almond oil.

ATHLETE'S FOOT
See under feet, sweaty

BAD BREATH
See Halitosis

BITES, INSECT
To soothe the irritation of insect bites, add 4-6 drops of ylang ylang to a bath, or add 4 drops of the essence to 2 tsp of soya oil and rub into the affected areas.

BRONCHITIS
Bronchitis is often triggered off by a bacterial or viral infection, and is the inflammation of the air passages in the lungs. It can be either acute or chronic. Bad posture, lack of exercise and nervous tension can all make you more susceptible to suffering from bronchitis because they reduce the ability of your lungs to work to their full capacity. A poor diet which fails to supply your body with sufficient quantities of nutrients needed to help you fight off the infection can also be a contributory factor, as can tobacco smoke.

The mucus produced by the body to lubricate the respiratory passages contains a natural antiobiotic, and it is also rich in lactic acid, which promotes the growth of beneficial bacteria which keeps harmful ones in check. Tobacco smoke and other pollutants in the air, like sulphur dioxide, can upset the balance of these bacteria, thus making you more susceptible to bronchial infections; they can also irritate the condition once it has taken a hold, so avoid them whenever possible.

In an attempt to expel the mucus manufactured by the inflamed bronchial tubes, we cough, and for this reason bronchitis is often a chesty complaint. Fever and chest pains may accompany bronchitis. Cold, damp air acts as an irritant, as does direct heat from a radiator or open fire.

For long-term prevention of bronchitis add garlic and onions (raw whenever possible) to your food. For added protection and for treatment, take 2-4 garlic pearls daily especially during the winter months. For children, it is a good idea to add 3 drops of tincture of iodine to a mixture of milk and honey which should be taken every day for three months.

During a bout of bronchitis mix together the following:

1 drop of eucalyptus
1 drop of pine
1 eggcup of almond or other oil

Add 10 drops of this to your bath, or inhale every day by adding 4 drops to a bowl of hand-hot water. Breathe in the fumes with your head covered by a towel.

Also rub the mixture into your chest every morning and in the evening before going to bed.

In the case of acute bronchitis, make a tea by boiling 5 cloves and 6 eucalyptus leaves in water for 2 minutes. Leave to steep for at least 5 minutes and then strain and add the juice of half a freshly squeezed lemon.

Drink plenty of fresh pineapple and lemon juice, rose-petal and rosehip tea, sweetened with honey if desired, as often as you can.

Cedarwood can be used as a simple single remedy. Add 6 drops of the essence to the bath, or use 4 drops in 500ml (a scant pint) of hot water for use as an inhalation.

BURNS
Lavender is a simple and very effective treatment for burns, as Dr Gattefossé, the originator of modern aromatherapy, discovered. Lavender oil should be dabbed neat on to the burned skin and covered. If a burn is severe, the lavender should be applied carefully, and the affected area wrapped in gauze or muslin; this should be repeated every four hours.

Patchouli is an alternative to lavender. Use 2 drops in 2tsp of almond oil and dab gently on to affected skin.

These remedies are also effective for sunburn.

CATARRH
See inhalation recipe under Colds and Flu.

CIRCULATION, POOR
See section on Pregnancy and Childbirth

COLDS AND FLU
Many of the symptoms of colds and flu are the same – sneezing, feverishness, aching limbs, sore throat, catarrh and sinusitis. Although flu is invariably initiated by a filtrant virus, just what brings on a cold still remains rather a mystery.

As you lose your sense of smell with either a cold or flu, it is important to shake them off as quickly as possible. My advice is to rest, stay away from work for a few days until you have recovered, and to take the following steps.

When the first symptoms appear, rub your chest, sinus areas (around the eyes and nose) and inside your nostrils with either of the following mixtures.

1 drop of eucalyptus
1 drop of clove
1 drop of pine
1 eggcup of almond or any other cold-pressed vegetable oil

Mix all together, and decant into a glass bottle.

1 drop of cinnamon
1 drop of niaouli
1 drop of lemon
1 eggcup of vegetable oil

Mix all together and bottle.

If you have a fever, which is usually a good sign because it is the body's way of fighting off the virus, your body will be using a good deal of energy. Eating foods which are difficult to digest saps the available energy and you would be wisest to eat very little for the first two days; thereafter eat fresh fruit which helps the cleansing process, and natural yoghurt sprinkled with wheatgerm and sweetened with honey.

Your body will also lose water through sweating and will shed the minerals sodium and potassium, which need to be replaced. Make this tisane, which is rich in these nutrients.

1 stick of cinnamon
2 cloves
2 sprigs of fresh thyme (3 pinches of dried)
1 litre (2 pints) water

Mix everything in a saucepan and boil for 2 minutes, then leave to infuse, covered with a clean cloth, for 5 minutes. Strain and drink throughout the day interspersed with fresh lemon juice mixed with mineral water and honey or fructose (fruit sugar). Keep the tisane in a jug in the fridge for no more than two days.

For inhaling, which will help to relieve the congestion and dispel catarrh, add to a bowl of hot water (not boiling, just hand hot), 4 drops of the following mixture.

1 drop of eucalyptus
1 drop of niaouli
1 drop of pine
1 eggcup of almond or other oil

Inhale for at least 5-10 minutes with a towel over your head, to seal in the vapours, four or five times a day at regular intervals. Alternatively, take two or more warm/hot baths (morning and evening), adding 2 drops of eucalyptus and 2 drops of niaouli while it is running. Soak for 10 minutes, then dry yourself vigorously, wrap up in a warm dressing gown, go back to bed and drink some of the tisane. Whilst you are bathing keep the bathroom door closed to seal in the vapours and make sure that the room is pre-heated.

You could also sprinkle a few drops of the inhaling oil on a cotton handkerchief and inhale throughout the day.

Once the symptoms have cleared, keep using the essences for another ten days, adding them to your bath, rubbing them into your chest, drinking the tisane once a day, taking plenty of lemon and other freshly squeezed juices to build up your resistance; otherwise you will only fall ill again.

For protection against colds and flu, especially if working in an office with other people who are suffering, mix up the following ingredients and decant.

1 drop of eucalyptus
1 drop of clove
1 drop of pine
1 drop of cinnamon
1 drop of niaouli
2 eggcups of almond or other oil

To fumigate your room sprinkle a few drops of this mixture on a ball of lightly dampened cotton wool and place this on the radiator, or mix a few drops of the essences pine, clove, eucalyptus and cinnamon minus the oil, in water and decant into an atomiser to spray your room.

You can also rub some of the essences in oil into your chest and around your nose for added protection.

CYSTITIS
See section on The Female Cycle

DEPRESSION
See section on Aromas and the Psyche

DERMATITIS
See section on Skin Problems

DYSMENORRHEA (Painful Periods)
See section on the Female Cycle

EARACHE
When associated with flu or a cold, earache is frequently brought on by the infection spreading from the nose and

throat. Symptoms may include not only sore ears, but diminished hearing and feverishness as well.

To help fight infection, warm some almond oil in a cup near the radiator and add either a crushed clove of garlic or a teaspoon of finely chopped onion and allow to steep for a couple of hours. Before going to bed, put a few drops into your eardrum using the dropper, sealing in the oil with a small ball of cotton wool and leave it in overnight.

Clean around the outside of the ear with 2 drops of clove mixed with an eggcup of soya oil to help prevent infection – and also to counteract the smell of the garlic or onion!

ECZEMA
See section on Skin Problems

EXHAUSTION
See section on Aromas and the Psyche

FEET, SWEATY
Bathe the feet in a bowl of hot water containing a few drops of lemongrass essence. After bathing, rub in an oil made from 3 drops of lemongrass to 1 teaspoon of soya oil. This is also good for Athlete's Foot.

FIBROSITIS
See under Rheumatism

FLU
See under Colds and Flu

FLUID RETENTION (Oedema)
See under Fluid Retention in section on Pregnancy. (See also under Puffiness in section on Skin Problems.)

FROZEN SHOULDER
See under Rheumatism

GUM INFECTIONS
See under Mouth and Gum Infections

HALITOSIS (Bad breath)
Halitosis can be caused by a good number of conditions, including tooth decay, poor digestion, liver trouble or catarrh. However, this mouthwash will reduce the symptom, making your mouth taste sweeter and your breath smell fresher. To a cup or glass of cooled, boiled water add 1 drop of myrrh essence. Use it for gargling.

HAYFEVER
Hayfever afflicts many people during spring and summer.

Herbs for healing
Throughout recorded history,
herbs have been deliberately
cultivated for purposes of
healing – used on their own
or as part of essences and
infusions. Before the advent
of modern medicine, they
were the main staple of
doctors and apothecaries –
London's Chelsea Physic
Garden, for instance,
provided herbs for the
nearby Royal Hospital. It was
founded in the 17th century.

Sufferers usually have allergic tendencies and react to many pollens, but most commonly grass. Hayfever is characterised by an irritation of the membranes of the eyes and nasal passages which results in a runny nose similar to that brought on by a cold, an itchy nose, eyes and throat, and is often accompanied by violent sneezing and/or a cough. Often the body tissues swell slightly because the histamine released during an allergic reaction causes them to retain water, and the skin tends to feel itchy as well.

Other airborne allergens such as dust, moulds and chemical pollutants can induce similar symptoms. Bad breathing habits can make you more susceptible to hayfever, because the body is deprived of oxygen, which allows the level of carbon dioxide in the blood to rise.

Poor posture, smoking and constipation prevent the body from eliminating the toxic wastes produced during metabolic processes, so they are thrown off in the form of catarrh and a heavy mucus in the alimentary tract. Milk and cheese encourage their formation and should be avoided by hayfever sufferers.

TREATMENT

Take a quarter teaspoon of pollen granules a day, as a very small quantity seems to be highly beneficial. Garlic is also good for hayfever and other respiratory disorders, so add it to your food or take garlic capsules daily.

Make a tisane to drink during an attack by boiling pine needles and eucalyptus leaves, a pinch of each in 500ml (a scant pint) of water. Drink plenty of rosehip tea, rich in vitamin C, a nutrient that is used up during an attack.

For sore, itchy eyes, apply compresses soaked in either cornflower, camomile or marigold infusions.

HAEMORRHOIDS

See Piles

INSOMNIA

See section on Aromas and the Psyche

LEUCORRHEA (Vaginal Discharge)

See section on the Female Cycle

LUMBAGO

See Rheumatism

MELANOSIS (Abnormal Pigmentation)

See section on Skin Problems

MOUTH AND GUM INFECTIONS

This recipe is for pyorrhea, a common infection of the gums, for mouth sores, for an ulcerated throat or after tooth extraction.

Boil a handful of sage leaves in 1 litre (2 pints) of water for 2 minutes, then infuse for 5 minutes. Add 1 drop of oil of myrrh and gargle, swill around the mouth or brush the gums gently with a very soft brush, depending on the area affected.

NEURITIS

See Rheumatism

NEURITIS

See under Rheumatism

PERIODS, PAINFUL (Dysmenorrhea)

See section on The Female Cycle

PERIODS, SCANTY OR ABSENT (Amenorrhea)

See section on The Female Cycle

PILES (Haemorrhoids)

Bathe the affected area with very cold water, then apply a mixture of 1 drop of myrrh and 1 drop of cypress in 3 teaspoonfuls of soya oil. If possible, sit in very cold water before applying the oil.

To soothe the itching of piles and prevent cracking of the skin, mix 1 drop of geranium essence into a small quantity of cold cream and apply to the affected part.

PRE-MENSTRUAL TENSION
See section on The Female Cycle

PSORIASIS
See section on Skin Problems

PYORRHEA
See Mouth and Gum Infections

RHEUMATISM
Rheumatism, like arthritis, is an inflammatory condition affecting the soft tissues, ligaments, tendons and muscles that surround, and are attached to, the joints. Not so long ago the disease was blamed on a virus, but no infective organism has been isolated and the theory has now lost favour.

Rheumatic conditions take a number of forms. These include fibrositis, a form of muscular rheumatism; neuritis, which affects the nerves and the myelin sheath surrounding them; sciatica, a form of neuritis involving the sciatic nerve, which runs from the buttock, down the back of the thigh to the ankle; lumbago, an incapacitating pain in the lumber region of the spine; and frozen shoulder and tennis elbow, which are also rheumatic in nature. This is a good all-purpose remedy for rheumatic complaints:

2 drops of oregano
1 drop of juniper
2 drops of rosemary
1 eggcup of almond oil

Mix together and bottle. Rub into the affected area four times a day if possible.

Lavender is another essence with a specific anti-rheumatic action:

2 drops of lavender
2 drops of juniper, cypress or ginger
2-3 tsps soya oil

This makes a good mixture for rubbing into the skin or adding to the bath.

The beneficial action of pine is best enjoyed in combination with lemon or juniper:

Lavenders blue Lavender yields an essential oil – highly scented and very pleasant to use, varying in colour from dark yellow to a dark topaz – which is invaluable for treating burns, swelling and rheumatic conditions.

2 drops of pine
2 drops of lemon or juniper
2 tsps soya oil

As with arthritis, take care to include sufficient calcium and magnesium in the diet.

SCIATICA
See under Rheumatism

SINUSITIS
This condition is caused by the inflammation of the sinus passages, and the symptoms include nasal congestion, mucus discharge, fatigue headaches, and earache, pain around the eyes, a mild fever and cough. Sinusitis often makes an appearance after you have had a cold or tonsillitus, but can also be triggered off by a deficiency of vitamin A and heavy smoking. Poor mouth hygiene and cold, damp weather do not help either. The best safeguard is to take 2-4 capsules of cod-liver or halibut oil a day for a period of three months. Whilst suffering, inhale 3 drops of the following mixture in a bowl of hot water.

1 drop of niaouli
1 drop of eucalyptus
1 drop of pine
1 eggcup of almond oil

You can also add about 10 drops of this oil to your bath and rub it into your chest and sinus area, keeping this treatment up for two months if you really want your sinusitis to clear for good.

SUNBURN
See under Burns

TENNIS ELBOW
See under Rheumatism

TENSION
See section on Aromas and the Psyche

THROAT, SORE
This often accompanies flu or a cold and can be very uncomfortable. To ease the pain, gargle with either of the following (about 6 times a day).
1. To a glass of cooled, boiled water add honey and the freshly squeezed juice of half a lemon.
2. Boil a handful of dried rose petals in 1 litre (2 pints) of water for 2 minutes and then leave to infuse for 5 minutes. When just warm add 1 drop of lemon essential oil or the juice of one lemon.

You could also drink either of these mixtures six times a day for a couple of days and thereafter twice a day.

THRUSH
See under Vaginal Discharge

TONSILLITIS
See Throat, Sore.

In addition, drink plenty of cool fresh pineapple juice which helps to make the mucus fluid, as well as vitamin C-rich rosehip tea and/or fresh lemon juice mixed with mineral water, sweetened with honey if desired.

A marvellous way of soothing the discomfort is to suck ice cubes made with boiled water mixed with fresh lemon and pineapple juice – as many as you like throughout the day.

VAGINAL DISCHARGE (Leucorrhea)
See section on The Female Cycle

VARICOSE VEINS
Make a massage oil of 3 drops of cypress, 2 drops of lavender and 2 drops of lemon to 1 egg cup of soya oil. Massage into the legs or add a few drops to your bath.

INDEX

Page numbers in **bold** refer to the illustrations and captions

jasmine, 28, 80, 82, 105, 106, 110
jasmone, 28
Java, 30, 42
juniper, 28, 32, 93, 113, 121-2

K

keratine, 52, 74
kidneys, 58, 69
kyphi, 18

L

lactation, 84, 97-9
laurel, 27
lavender, 23, 26, 27, 35, **35**, 78, **79**, 82, 89, 93, 96, 97, 99, 104, 108, 115, 121, 123
Le Magnen, Dr, 86
leaves, essential oils, 23-5
lecithin, 68
Leclerc, Dr, 31-2
legs:
    blood circulation, 96
    varicose veins, 96, 123
lemon, 24-5, 26, 27, 28, 29, 35-8, **38**, 96, 104, 116, 117, 121-2, 123
lemon verbena, 108, 110
lemongrass, 27, 38, 118
lettuce, 104
lilac, 110
Lily, Charles, 107
limbic region, brain, 47, 84, 100, 101
lime trees, 110
limonene, 28
linalol, 27
linalyl, 27
linseed, 55
literature, 15
liver, 58, 90
loofahs, 65
lotus, 20, **20**
Louis XIV, King of France, 41
lumbago, 121
lungs, inhalation of essential oils, 47-8
luteinizing hormone, 84

M

maceration, essential oils, 28
magnesium, 90, 91-2, 96, 101, 113, 122
Malaysia, 20, 30, 31, 32, 40, 42, 79-80, 86, 97
mandarin, 27
marigold, 69, 92, 110, 120
marjoram, 21, **21**, 22
marrubium, 21
massage, 47, 54
    babies, 99
    back, **50-1**
    breasts, 98
    ears, **49**
    face, **49**, 54
    full body, **50-1**
    hair, 76
    head, **49**
    neck, **49-51**
    pregnancy and, **95**
    scalp, 77
    shoulders, **51**
Maury, Marguerite, 111
medicines:
    essential oils as, 18, 24-7, 111-23
    see also drugs
meditation, 106
Mediterranean, 33, 35, 41, 42
melanosis, 67
melissa, 27, 38, **38**, 89, 101
memory, smells and, 13-15, **14**
menopause, 64, 84, 86, 102-3
menstrual cycle, 10, 59, 64, 69, 83-92, 102
menstruation, 84, 85, 86, 87, 89-90
menthol, 27
Middle East, 35
minerals, 74, 89, 91-2, 94, 96, 101, 113, 116
mint, 22, 26, 27, 28, 38-9, **39**, 89, 92, 101, 104, 108, 109, 110
miscarriage, 94
Mitsouko perfume, 79
Molucca Islands, 31, 32
Moroccan rose, 41
Morocco, 32
Moses, 106
moths, sense of smell, 10, **10**
mouth infections, 120
mouthwashes, 118
mummies, embalming, 22
muscles, massaging, 72
musk, 16, 79, 80, 85
mustard, 55

myrrh, 22, 29, 30, 39, **39**, 105, 118, 120-1
myxoedema, 89

N

narcissus, 106, 110
nasturtium, 77
natron, 22
neck:
    ageing skin, 73
    massage, **49-51**
Nefertiti, Queen of Eygpt, **19**
Negroes, 68
nerol, 27
neroli, 23, 27, 28, 39, **39**, 46, 48, 92, **95**, 96, 97, 99, 101, 104
nerve tonics, 101
nervous system, 12-13, 47, 53, 100-1
nettle tea, 103
neuritis, 121
New Guinea, 10
niaouli, 26, 39-40, 116, 117, 122
Nile, river, 20
nipples, cracked, 98
normal skin, 54
Normandy, 15
North Africa, 32, 33
nose, olfactory organ, 12-13, 47, 84
novels, 15
nutmeg, 22, 97

O

oakmoss, 80
oatmeal and rose face mask, 54
oedema, 69, 94, 96, 97
oestrogen, 64, 84, 86, 89, 91, 94, 98, 102
oils, **see** essential oils
oily hair, 75, 76
oily skin, 52, 54-7
olfactory organ, 12-13, 47, 84, 100
onions, 114, 118
orange, 27, 29, 39, 92, **95**, 96, 99, 104, 110
orange trees, essential oils, 23
orchid, blue, 20
oregano, 26, 121
oriental rose, 41

Osiris, 21, **21**
osmology, 12
osteoarthritis, 113
ovaries, 84, 86, 88, 102
ovulation, 10, 84, 85, 86, 87

P

Pacific Islands, 39-40
painful periods, 90
Papyrus of Ebers, 18
Papyrus of Edwin Smith, 18
Paris, 38
parsley, 22, 62-4, 92, 99, 109
passifloria, 103, 114
patchouli, 24, 40, 76, 82, 101, 115
pelargonium, 109-10
penicillin, 24
perfumers, **26**
perfumes, 15-16, 78-82, **78**, **79**, 107
periods, **see** menstruation
Persia, 34, 35, 36, 39
petitgrain, 23, 28, 96
phellandrene, 28
phenols, 26-7, 28
pheromones, 8-16, 80, 85, 86, 87
Philip Augustus, King of France, 107
Philippines, 42
physiology, 12-13
pigmentation:
    hair, 74
    melanosis, 67
piles, 96, 120-1
pillows, scented, 108
pimples, 58, 59
pine, 27, 40, **40**, 92, 93, 97, 110, **110**, 115, 116, 117, 120, 121-2
pineapple, 123
pinene, 28
pituitary gland, 47, 84, 88, 91, 97, 102
plague, 25, **25**, 107
plants, essential oils, 23-5, 30-42 **see also** individual plant entries
plastic surgery, 72
Plutarch, 18
poetry, 15
pollen, 94, 96, 119-20
pollution, 16, 112, 119
pomanders, 25
pot pourri, 8, 78, 108
potassium, 92, 96, 116
poultices, 54, **55**
pre-menstrual tension, 90-2